Leadership Failure *in* Police

Attention Authors

'We Convert Fighters into Writers.' That's the motto of **Manas Publications** since more than four decades. Our message to the world is that India can win the battle not only by the bullet but also by the pen. There is no dearth of intellectuals in our country, but their knowledge is confined to them only. No sincere effort has been made by any other publisher to channelise their knowledge in national interest. That is why the talent of a large number of intellectuals remains latent. An author transforms his knowledge into a manuscript, and it is our job to spread his/her knowledge by converting it into a beautiful book. For over four decades, Manas has been motivating the intellectuals by publishing their manuscripts and would like to publish your manuscript too. So if you or your colleagues have any manuscript ready for publication or are working on it, kindly contact us with detailed synopsis and list of contents. We will transform your work into a valuable publication. If you wish, we can also suggest you the suitable subjects for writing the books related to your area of expertise. Manas is known for its publishing quality and commitments. We take utmost care in production and give wide publicity to the book as well as its author through our National and International distribution network.

Leadership Failure *in* Police

Dr NC Asthana, IPS

Dr Anjali Nirmal

Manas Publications

(We Convert Fighters into Writers)

New Delhi - 110002 (INDIA)

MANAS PUBLICATIONS
(We Convert Fighters into Writers)
(Publishers, Distributors, Importers & Exporters)
4402/5-A, Ansari Road (Opp. HDFC Bank)
Darya Ganj, New Delhi-110 002 (INDIA)
Off. ☏ 23260783, 23265523, Res. 23842660
Fax: 011-23272766
E-mail: manaspublications@gmail.com
manaspublications@yahoo.com

ISBN 978-81-7049-464-5
₹ 995/-

Designed at
Manas Publications

Printed in India at
RK Offsets, Delhi
and published by Mrs Suman Lata for
Manas Publications, 4402/5-A, Ansari Road,
(Opp. HDFC Bank),
Darya Ganj, New Delhi-110 002 (INDIA)

Contents

DECLARATION

In terms of Rule 6 of the All India Service (Conduct) Rules, 1968, we hereby declare that the views and opinions expressed in the book are our own, and not those of the Government. That the views and opinions expressed are our own means that they are our personal intellectual creations and are not endorsed in any way by the Government of India or the cfficial position held by one of us, namely, Dr. N. C. Asthana, IPS. It is further certified that, in terms of Rule 7 of the All India Service (Conduct) Rules, 1968, there is nothing in the book which has the effect of an adverse criticism of any current or recent policy or action of the Central Government or a State Government; or which is capable of embarrassing the relations between the Central Government and any State Government; or which is capable of embarrassing the relations between the Cental Government and the Government of any Foreign State.

Preface

Police is a department to which people go only when they are in acute distress of some kind, and they do expect succour from the police. Unfortunately, the reality of India is that they seldom get it. Not only that the police do not do anything to help the people, they are often the biggest tormentors of the common man. The inaction of the police, their apathy, or their abuse of power is all the more reprehensible because people in distress are in no position to argue with them. If they argue, they invite more trouble. This is an incontrovertible fact. One who has any doubt about it, has either not had enough experience with the police in India or is an outright liar. Anyone can check it for himself anytime.

You can randomly pick millions of people over 40 (so that they are likely to have encountered the police some time in their lives in a substantial manner and their interaction with the police is not limited to that of young students with traffic cops whom they call 'uncle') anywhere in the country and ask them whether the police have had ever helped them without taking bribe or without some recommendation from some quarter; politician, senior officer or whatever—the answer is resoundingly in the negative. The police need one of these two things to do anything that they are supposed to do by law as their duty. A major part of the blame for this sorry state of affairs lies principally and squarely on the shoulders of the police leadership, mainly the IPS (Indian Police Service). The thesis developed and proven in this book is that the IPS officers have failed the nation and the people of this country because they are intellectually bankrupt in the first place; and secondly, because, far from taking action against the errant subordinates, they have all along been colluding with them in their horrible misdeeds so as to get their share of the booty. We know some people may start screaming that the IAS and IPS are what Sardar Patel had described as the 'steel frame' of

India's government machinery and here we are criticizing that. Well, well, one man's fond wishes do not undo a historical wrong! The so-called 'steel frame' never existed in the first place and even if it did, it got rusted a long time back—in any case, it has comprehensively failed to do what it was so pompously expected to do for the common man and the nation. It does not make any difference as to what might have been the original purpose of those at the helm of powers in continuing with the civil services as such after independence. Leave such platitudinous discussions for the civil service aspirants and the IAS, IPS probationers. Whatever might have been the purpose, lofty or foolish, the experiment has gone utterly sour. In the first place, there was no reason to hope that the 'brown sahibs' of the civil services and the armed forces who, in body, mind and soul had been such faithful servants of the colonial regime for so long would overnight acquire 'service to the people' as their leitmotif and swear by it in all times to come. We wonder, one who hoped so, must have been naive beyond imagination. The civil servants and the officers of the armed forces had been loyal dogs of the rulers not because they were disciplined; they were so because they enjoyed being a part of the power and identifying themselves with the rulers.

One who claims that they were disciplined, must admit that they had no mind! Secondly, it was utterly amateurish if not outright foolish to even expect that the mere act of passing an exam which was essentially just another type of university exam with a slightly different syllabus, and two years of ceremonial training with little of substance therein would enable a kid to become a pillar of the nation that we sought to build. Come on, dears, stop daydreaming. Intellect, even if it were to be found in abundance in somebody at some point of time, has nothing to do with integrity, strength of character, or the desire to do one's duty honestly and efficiently. Moreover, the fact is that the selection process itself is farcical. It has never tested the capacity of the man to think independently or creatively. This is proved by the very track record of the IAS and the IPS. Throughout the history of the civil services, at an intellectual level, they have never done anything original; never created anything. Much to their discomfiture and to their utter consternation, we will force them to face the harsh reality right here, right now. Since 1948 till 2011, a whopping 4108 direct recruit IPS officers have been trained in the National Police Academy.

To this, you may, if you wish, add the number of those IP (Imperial Police) officers also who were recruited from 1907 till 1947 and the total number would swell further. The basic idea of recruiting officers directly at a very high level was that, by virtue of being intellectually superior, they would contribute to the service much better than what street cops and subordinate officers with high school education or less could do even after putting in a number of years in service. There could be no other logic for this practice. No other nation of the world does it. Had the nation not believed in this, the system should have been abolished a long time back! Unfortunately, the civil services have utterly belied such fond hopes.

Let us face it. What has been the intellectual contribution of these over four thousand IPS officers to the field of policing (or, for that matter, any other field) in these 63 years? None! Have they done anything for which it could be claimed that only an IPS officer could do that? None! Have they ever thought and created anything? None! The only thing they have done all these years is to put their initials on the files agreeing with their subordinates—disagreeing would demand an application of mind, something they are unable to do. How many professional research papers in peer-reviewed journals or how many serious books on professional subjects (or other academic subjects) have been published by the IAS and IPS officers? Anyone who wishes to find out can do a survey (or a Google search for the lazy) and can confirm that the intellectual contribution of this so-called crème de la crème has been pathetically insignificant. Have they ever created anything original? None! Have they brought about any change in the system for better? None! In essence, police still functions very much the same way it functioned 150 years ago. Its resources have changed; its mind and spirit remains the same. Has the police leadership even analyzed what ails the police? Never! It was left to the Honourable Supreme Court to issue directions in 2006 about systemic changes. The police leadership, by itself, had never said a word that they had any problem with the 150 years old Indian Police Act of 1861—on the contrary, most of them were quite happy with it! It would be extremely generous to say that once selected, the IAS and IPS officers stop growing intellectually.

No, sir, they have never had intellect in the first place! As the very erudite Dr. Samuel Johnson had said, such stupidity is not to be found in nature; they must have taken extraordinary pains to become what we see of them. Intellect grows by constant intellectual effort; the best swords in the world also need regular honing. Unfortunately, civil servants in India presume that selection into the civil services confers them with such magical qualities that they never need to learn anything. We have exposed their intellectual bankruptcy thoroughly in the book—you will see it for yourself.

We will give you an example. All of us are aware of the methods of the police, and the things that they do as a matter of routine. We also know how they torment the people through them. Have the honourable Courts been oblivious to that? No! We have cited hundreds of judgments of the Supreme Court and the High Courts in the book. These judgments show that practically all the methods adopted by the police are at variance with the orders of the honourable Courts, if not utterly illegal. How is it that the police do not obey the Court orders? Three things are possible. They are so lawless that they don't bother about the judgments; they are so utterly ignorant of the law that they have not heard of the judgments; or both. In any eventuality, it makes them outright violators of law, absolute duffers, or both. It has been fashionable in academic and journalistic circles to talk of the image of the police. Only those morons can afford to speak of 'image' who have never been on the wrong side of the police '*danda*'. Gentlemen, forget about the image—image is a matter of perception—the police are indeed bad; actually, much worse than what you can imagine in your worst nightmares. Even if you are middle-aged, you have probably not seen the worst of them. As you go through the pages of this book, you will read real accounts of police atrocities so horrific that you will thank your stars that you or your dear ones have not been victims yourself.

Police brutality and police abuse of power are not aberrations attributed to some deviant individuals; they are the rule and this is very much a systemic failure. The system has failed because the leadership has failed. The leadership suffers both from a lack of moral authority and the sensitivity needed to address the real issue of abuse of power by their subordinates. This emboldens them and they commit more atrocities, thereby creating a vicious circle. This treatise is a ruthless, almost brutal exposé of all that is ugly, beastly, and ghastly in the police in India. It will wake you up from your complacent slumber of decades and jolt your conscience to its very core. You will be shocked and outraged by what these monsters have been doing to our fellow Indians all these years. May be you have had the good fortune of not being one of the direct sufferers so far. But remember, tomorrow it could well be your turn.

If something has not happened to you by sheer statistical chance, it does not mean that it is not happening either. The 'not me' syndrome has never helped anybody; if chance has saved you so far, chance can very well have you in trouble also. If you do not empathize with those hapless people now, no one would empathize with you later. Tomorrow it could be your daughter who is raped at the police station, or your son who is brought dead after an interrogation. Be a responsible citizen; be aware of the truth.This book, we can confidently claim, is the hitherto most comprehensive analysis of police atrocities of all kinds. You will be eternally grateful to us for opening your eyes. Next time you chance upon a senior police officer, you will know that the man is dumb, insensitive and corrupt; financially, morally and intellectually, in every way. It is only because the police leadership has failed that we have reached a situation where the lowliest thug in khaki can maim the lives of innocent people. It is your duty to use your democratic rights to force them to introduce mechanisms that would save you from the depredations of the cops and their bosses.

Some readers might be tempted to think that perhaps the criticism of the police leadership in this book reflects, in some way, our own biases. No, it is not so—we have been most objective. Perhaps, there could have been a remote chance of such an allegation had we been outsiders or 'jealous' of the civil services in some way. One of us is a distinguished senior IPS officer himself with 27 years of service, and the other has been associated with the police fraternity since decades. Where else would you get a better insider view? With the benefit of direct knowledge, we do not suffer from the problem of imaginary notions and 'ivory tower' views which characterize academicians and journalists.

Moreover, the book is based entirely on real facts for which adequate and convincing proof has been given. Backed by a formidable array of the judgments of the honourable Courts, this book is actually an open challenge. As scholars and professionals, we challenge all those who may have the audacity to question our contentions to come forward and give battle to us. In Srimad Bhagavatam (10.72.28), Bhagwan Shree Krishna Himself challenges Jarasandha thus: "*Yuddham no dehi rajendra; dvandvaso yadi manyase; yuddharthino vayam prapta; rajanya nanyakankshinah.*" That is, "Give us battle in the form of a duel, if you think it fitting. We are princes and have come to beg a fight. We have no other request to make of you." Even for lesser beings, a challenge really meant staking one's honour and reputation. In Garg Samhita (Canto Two, Volume Three, Chapter 23, Text 10) we find the Yaksha king Shankhchuda challenging Kansa for a duel with clubs (*gada-yuddham dehi*) and says: "*Aham daso bhaveyam vai; bhavams ca vijayi yadi; aham jayi codbhavantam; dasam sighram karomy aham.*" That is, "If you are victorious, I will become your servant. If I am victorious, I will make you my servant for a very long time." We challenge all the imbecile police leaders—come and give us battle—we promise, we will bury you ten thousand feet deep under the sea. The other option, of course, is to use this book to open your eyes. To all such police officers; young and old; junior and senior; who are not beyond redemption, this treasure trove of knowledge will be of invaluable help to introspect and reform.

We decided that this book had to be written because we are pained by the existing state of affairs. Policing is one of the most important functions of the state. We want the police to improve so that they may serve the society better. But a patient can never be got treated unless he is diagnosed first for what ails him. This book does precisely that. We have divested the police leadership of the veneer of social respectability of the civil services behind which they have been concealing their dark deeds so far; exposed all their sins and paraded them before all to see. The book hits where it really hurts—it is so hard hitting that reading it is like watching the barrage of punches unleashed by Mike Tyson in the ring for full 15 rounds. We have stripped the cops naked and whipped their ass raw—so fiercely that their seven generations would not forget this whipping.

Any change, whether by legislation or by some sort of social oversight, can be made only if the people and the policy-makers first know the problem in its intimate details. The people must become 'involved' if we are to change the monstrosity that the police have become. Now it is for you, our fellow citizens, to do something that would help you get a better police. And hence this book. This book is both a scholarly work and a sensational expose'—the very first vehement assault on the tyranny of the conceited and the ignorant. This is the 'voice of conscience' speaking in a country blinded by terrible ignorance, frightening greed and collective stupidity. Once we have public consensus on the need to change the system, the logical sequel of the book would address that. The sentiments expressed in this book are not those of the authors alone; they are also an articulate expression of the feelings of those millions upon millions who have been suffering in silence since ages but have been unable to express their sufferance in so many emphatic words.

We wrote this book for two reasons—first, because nobody has ever written such an exhaustive, authoritative, informative, bold and hard-hitting book; and second, because it just had to be written. The most despicable way in which the police in general and the police leadership in particular have failed the society cannot be left unexposed.

'Brutes are our theme: are we to blame if minds are brutish, men the same?'

Dr. N. C. Asthana, IPS
Dr. Anjali Nirmal

Chapter 1

How a Fond Dream Turned into a Nightmare?

1.1 Where They Failed?

Everybody knows that the police in India and their leadership have not been able to deliver the goods. What went wrong? How exactly did the concept of the so-called 'steel frame' falter? How did the *rakshak* become the *bhakshak?* How come those who were supposed to be protectors of the people, turned into oppressors and tormentors? Who allowed them to become the beasts that they are now? None but the police leadership. The senior leadership of the civil services could have, at the best, and we mean the very best, served any useful purpose for the nation if they had appreciated two things. First, that while elected government are temporary or transient, they constitute what is permanent in the system and hence their responsibility as the guardian of peoples' interests and public resources is onerous. Second, that they were supposed to discharge the duties of what the *'mantri'* in ancient Hindu polity was supposed to do. In modern Hindi, the word *'mantri'* means an elected minister. Earlier, when the word came into existence, it was not so as there were no elected ministers. Most of the civil servants would not know the cultural origins of the word *mantri*. This would require some intimate knowledge of ancient Hindu polity—you do not learn such things from the Internet. For their information, a *mantri* was one whose job was to give *'mantrana'*, that is, advice to the king. In modern parlance, you can equate them to the so-called secretaries who are employees—the modern *mantri* is a part of the ruling dispensation. The ancient Hindu king was called *raja.*

Now who was entitled to be called a *raja*? A *raja* was not one who merely ruled over his subjects and kingdom (*rajya*). A *raja* was one who did '*ranjan*' for his *praja* or subjects. That is, the primary task and responsibility of a *raja* was the welfare of his people. As employees of the *raja*, the primary task and responsibility of his *mantris* was also the same, that is, the welfare of the people. In other words, all the advice that they tendered or had to tender, should have had only one prime objective—the greater good of the people. The advice had to be given in a purely professional manner without any fear or favour. Goswami Tulsidas also has commented beautifully on this in the Ramcharitmanas. The context was the moment when news was brought to Ravan in his court that Bhagwan Shree Ram had crossed the sea with his army.

All the sycophants in the court laughed at it and said that Ravan who had conquered the *devatas* and the *rakshasas*, need not bother about humans and *vanaras*. Only Vibhishan and another *mantri* Malyawan advised Ravan that a war with Shree Ram would neither be proper nor fruitful. Ravan was very angry with this and exiled Vibhishan from his kingdom. Commenting on this, Tulsidas ji says that if there is a kingdom in which three categories of persons, namely, the *mantri*, the *vaidya* (physician) and the *guru*, out of a fear of displeasing the king, or in the hope of gaining some favours from him, advise him things which he wants to hear and not those which are really good for him, that king stands to quickly lose his kingdom, his dharma and his life, everything.

Sachiv, vaid, guru teeni jaun priy bolahin bhay aas,
Raj, dharma, tan teenikar hoi begihi naas.

(Sundarkand, Doha 37)

Incidentally, Tulsidas ji uses the word '*sachiv*' (which in modern parlance means a secretary) for a '*mantri*'—Hanuman Prasad Poddar ji, in the Gita Press rendering of the Ramcharitmanas, also translates it that way. Ravan exiled Vibhishan but eventually ended up losing everything. The aforesaid three categories of persons are the foremost advisors of a king—they should speak nothing but the truth and in doing so, they should have the welfare of kingdom in mind, not the likes or dislikes of the king. The Romans had said the same thing but in a slightly different way: "*Salus populi suprema lex est*", that is, "The welfare of the people shall be the supreme law." With the civil servants in India, the exact opposite of this lofty ideal has taken place. Instead of advising the rulers for the benefit of the people; instead of cautioning them against immoral deeds; and instead of taking a principled stand, they cater to the vanities, the capriciousness, and the insatiable greed of the rulers. *The Indian civil servants have all along actively colluded with the rulers in all their misdeeds and have thus failed the people whom they were supposed to serve.*

1.2 Why They Failed?

Unfortunately, in spite of such lofty ideals expressed so eloquently and beautifully in ancient Hindu polity, scriptures and the '*shaastra*', the welfare of the people was the last thing on the minds of most Indian rulers—never mind what they write in history textbooks about kings getting ponds dug up, roads built up and so on. Most Indian rulers happened to be essentially exploiters of the people; the basic purpose of their life was to indulge in luxuries of the most weird and abominable kind. We have all heard the stories of kings and queens in our childhood but we never heard stories of the people—because people never mattered. Having a strong tradition of rulers who had, irrespective of how they had got the kingdoms, maintained them simply by using coercive force on the hapless, poor people, the people have had always been relegated to an insignificant, inconsequential position in the scheme of things.

The kings maintained their kingdoms for their luxuries and enjoyment, fleeced people for that and fought wars for nothing but their vanities—the people were fooled into believing that the king was protecting them from external aggression! For those who might have read Edward Hunter's 'Brainwashing in Red China', we call it 'Brainwashing in Ancient India'. Leaving aside a few benevolent kings and thinkers, for most of the kingdoms in India, the state came first and the people at the very last. The state existed for the ruler, not for the ruled. Precisely for this reason, the state often perished with the ruler—a phenomenon we euphemistically call the fall of empires in history. All the agencies of the state existed essentially to exploit the people as much as they could and the armed components of the state machinery in particular served more to oppress their own people than to protect them from some external threat.

This bred a very characteristic behavioural pattern in the armed component—uncontrolled, impertinent, aggressive, rude, abusive, arrogant, barbaric—all those traits that characterize the behaviour of the police of even today; a perfect example of historical continuity. There is a simple Hindi word '*uddanda*' meaning roughly the same. Ever wondered how this came about? In Sanskrit, the literal meaning of the word is *'ud-danda'*, that is, 'one who has his stick (*danda*) raised above'. Now who carries his *'danda'* raised above? Well, none other than the cops! Why? The cops carried the stick (*danda*) alright. But the problem was that in ancient India, most people habitually carried some sort of stick—to drive away aggressive dogs, to fight with each other, to kill snakes, to ford rivers and rivulets, to pluck fruits from trees, and a thousand other reasons. How to distinguish them from the policemen? In that era the cops did not wear uniform. The solution was to make the policemen carry their sticks raised above so that they could be recognized from a distance. Now, since the cops were uncontrolled, impertinent, aggressive, rude, abusive, arrogant, barbarous, and brutish, and continued to remain so for centuries, gradually the word *'uddanda'* itself came to acquire the meaning of such behavioural traits!

We have had a strong tradition of the state machinery wielding enormous powers over the people. The same system continued in the modern era as well—the rulers changed, the implements changed but the spirit of the rulers remained the same. Few nations, not to speak of democratic nations in the world, would even think of granting the kind of excessive legal powers, especially pre-emptive powers, that the police in India continue to enjoy till date. Our present statutes allow great latitude to the police in regulating public behaviour ranging from preventive arrests to shooting them down. Such powers have actually increased over the years as the police leadership has very cleverly kept on raising the bogey of what they describe as 'worsening internal security scenario' for the consumption of the gullible masses, an ignorant media and self-serving academicians.

The motive of the colonial masters in giving the police these powers was obvious. They had to control a people whom they did not trust at all; especially after 1857. What is most irritating and actually a proof of the imbecility of the police leadership is that all these 150 years they never made any attempt to 'modernise' the police in this regard. Why? Why did they not ever demand that the powers of the police in India be on a par with those in other nations of the world? Why did they quietly, almost surreptitiously allow a decadent colonial legacy to continue? Can they afford to argue that their duty was just to obey the law and not question it? Certainly not! The cop on the street can perhaps argue that and expect to be pardoned—not those who claim themselves to be the so-called 'steel frame' and recruited at the very highest level in the whole world. A more credible answer could perhaps be that they are so dumb that they were not able to understand the nuances of the law and its ramifications. Why did they leave it for the Honourable Supreme Court to comment on it as late as 2006? Did they not have a mind of their own? If everything is to be done by the courts; if all the mind is to be applied by the courts; why do we need a police leadership in the first place; street cops alone would do. The pseudos among the police leadership do not tire of speaking of the lack of political will—very cleverly, they never speak of a bureaucratic will which they should have had.

The real reason is that they purposefully allowed this colonial legacy to continue because it suits them and they enjoy it. A system which was devised to keep a potentially untrustworthy population under control enables the servants of the system to wield enormous powers. Well, that makes them happy. Isn't it? The powers vested in the servants of the system have been used by them for their own benefit, not for the benefit of the people. Geoffrey Ashe, the famous British cultural historian, in his book 'Gandhi: A Biography' (Heinemann, 1968, p. 288) narrates a horrible incident that took place in Patna in 1930 in the wake of the Dandi March. Dr. Rajendra Prasad had led a huge crowd towards one of the new salt depots. The police, as usual, blocked the road. The protesters staged a sit-in satyagraha and stayed right there for full forty hours ignoring police orders to disperse.

Eventually, the police leadership decided to trample them under the hooves of the mounted police! In Ashe's own words, "the mounted police galloped furiously, the crowd lay flat, the horses shied and pulled up, and the demonstrators had to be physically lifted into trucks." The point to be noted is that the police leadership could take such an inhuman, such an abominable decision. *The horses flinched, the riders did not – the beast turned out to be more human than the human beasts in khaki*! Sadly, even now, the police leadership can be equally dumb, equally insensitive because little has changed over the decades.

1.3 Servility, Thy Motto, Thy Creed

Those who could not learn from the examples of five thousand years of history deserve to be pitied. In fact, it was utterly juvenile to even dream that the Indian police would be able to change its character merely because the system of governance got changed one fine morning. In any case, the IAS and IPS have betrayed the expectations of the nation in every respect. We are quite amused when senior officers with the mind-set of probationers speak of their role in the process of nation-building. Omigosh! Do they even know what nation building is? They merely pass their time as any other government servant does. Those who are enterprising amongst them, go on to systematically loot the wealth of the nation in connivance with corrupt politicians, criminals, businessmen and anyone who by virtue of anything wields power and influence. *Their motto is servility and they cultivate it so skilfully, so assiduously that it is raised to the level of a fine art.* They have actually reduced themselves to servants of whoever wields power so that they may also reap the riches.

In the following, we quote excerpts from an article 'Showing the Way' written by Abhinav Kumar, an IPS officer, in the *Outlook* magazine of February 10, 2011 following an incident on February 6 when a TV grab showed a personal security officer Padam Singh, cleaning the shoes of a chief minister in UP. Sometimes satire conveys things more poignantly than cold, hard facts which dunderheads find difficult it to process in their shrivelled brains and hence the decision to quote from the article. The article was in the form of a letter:

Dear Shri Padam Singh,

I have never had the privilege of serving with you, but if I ever get the opportunity to meet you I would like to kneel and kiss your hand. You represent the pinnacle of 64 years of evolution of policing in modern India. Your one act of wiping the shoes of Chief Minister of Uttar Pradesh, shown on national TV, will go down as the one moment when all the confusion cleared and all the policemen wearing khaki realized the path to their tryst with destiny...Thank you for showing us the truth...

From 1861 to 1947, the British Raj gave us such an efficient model of professional policing. The percept was so simple. Know thy master, protect your master's interests, attack his enemies, and prey on the poor and the powerless with liberal doses of brutality and corruption and you will be valued and trusted and thrown the occasional bone to make you feel special...Despite 60 odd years of Independence, some things have not changed, or ever will. After all, even today, there are only two types of citizens in our country. Those whom the police need to fear and obey, who aren't that many in number, and then the vast multitudes who need to fear and obey the police to lead a life with even a modicum of dignity.

Frankly, I don't see why there is such an outcry at your gesture. Not only have you proclaimed the loyalty and utility of the police force in this country, you have also given us the most effective demonstration in the dignity of labour and social justice that no slogans or political posturing, even from the lady you so visibly served, could ever achieve. In any case what you have done is simply lift the veil on

reimbursements for security-related expenditure on a variety of schemes, including police modernisation, sophisticated weaponry and communications systems, additional armed battalions and high-grade training. Seven of the 14 states, including in the northeast, and Jammu & Kashmir, West Bengal, Maharashtra and Bihar, did not spend even a paisa on the schemes during 2010-11. Another media report in late February 2013 had shown that according to statistics from the Bureau of Police Research and Development, only 58 percent of police modernisation funds had been used during 2011-12. The centre and respective state governments provided Rs. 1,150.1 crore for modernisation but only Rs. 671.19 crore were spent. There is more to the sordid business of modernisation.

The funds that are spent supposedly on modernisation are actually consumed mostly in construction of buildings, police housing and increasing the fleet size of their vehicles—ordinary things which neither 'modernise' the police in the true sense of the word nor require much application of mind in spending on. *The truth is that most of the police leadership is so intellectually bankrupt that they do not even know what they should purchase in modernisation and where really a modern product would be useful.* Quite often they are tempted to purchase certain branded products because smart vendors fool them with Power Point presentations replete with photos or videos of impressive-looking white soldiers and some glib sales talk. *A white soldier or cop using a gizmo is the ultimate proof of its being most useful for the bloody Indians—you do not require any other information.*

Thousands of vendors across the country are making a very decent living by making a fool of the police leadership. None of them has anything other than a one-room office from where they import useless stuff and dump it on the police. Most of them keep track of the modernisation funds allotted to the police and persuade the police leadership to purchase their stuff. Some of them have also learnt the 'fine art' of bringing smart chics with them. No, no, please don't get us wrong; these chics are perfectly good. The vendors take advantage of the fact that an average senior police officer is completely floored by a 'modern-looking' girl who is fair, slim, wears jeans pants, and speaks fluent English—deadly combination. She can sell anything to these duffers for the police—even sanitary napkins for an all-male unit! Unfortunately, purchasing branded products under normal conditions is a violation of purchase rules and sometimes they run into troubles. But there is one more reason why they fall for branded products. If they have to purchase things through open tender, they have to advertise the specifications of the things they require. Now that is a difficult task. They simply lack the brains to frame QRs (Qualitative Requirements or Technical Specifications) which must be generic in character and should not favour a certain brand. This demands technical knowledge even for ordinary things. Flummoxed by the problem, they merely copy the specifications of some brand. It could be the brand of a company which might have bribed them or they could have randomly picked up some brand. The QRs become brand specific and may invite trouble. Therefore, those in the police leadership who want to avoid a vigilance case, avoid purchases altogether and that's how the funds remain unspent.

That's why they are not able to purchase real technical gadgets which would be useful and end up wasting the money on conventional items like photocopiers, desktop computers, LaserJet printers, etc. There is not a single police force in the country that has not purchased all sorts of cheap tools in the name of Bomb Detection & Disposal kit—the list of such tools goes upto 58 and includes such wonderful items as regular pliers, wire cutters, and screwdrivers! We have tried each one of them and they are singularly useless in any real life situation involving a real bomb. We are absolutely sure, they have never been used anywhere in the country successfully for the intended purpose. They sell a telescoping pole for remotely grabbing a bomb for about Rs. 4 lakh or so. It cannot lift even a packet of sweets! It is not to say that things like photocopiers are not required but it needs no imagination that they are not the sort of things which would actually help the police take a step towards modernisation of the professional capability of the police, such as, mobile data retrieval systems that could help collect data from seized mobile phones; computer data retrieval systems that could retrieve all information from the hard disc of a computer; and face and fingerprint recognition search management system that could help police profile criminals and cross-check data on repeat offenders.

In essence, the entire exercise in modernisation has been reduced to only a buzzword to make a fool of the people, the academicians and the journalists. Indians are like adolescents who are fascinated by gadgets. Academicians and journalists think that if the police forces of the country acquire modern gadgets, policing would improve. Nobody knows whether the gadget is really of any use or not. Above all, nobody understands the necessity of improving the policeman. You may load him with the latest Samsung Galaxy Note; a micro-tape recorder; a bug sweep; a Glock pistol; a Taser gun; a high-power motorbike with flashing lights; a high-acceleration car that would be envy of James Bond; a glamorous policewoman as buddy; the whole enchilada—all the stuff that you see in Hollywood cop films and more. The Indian cop would still remain a scoundrel of the highest order—a more efficient scoundrel rather. The police leadership is shrewd enough to exploit this ignorance of the academicians and journalists. They have been too happy purchasing all sorts of unnecessary implements in the name of modernising, but never thought of modernising the very soul of the police.

1.6 Failure at the Intellectual Level

We made a reference to intellectual bankruptcy above. We will elaborate on that in a separate chapter but we will puncture the balloon of the self-proclaimed intellectual 'superiority' of the civil servants over their 'masters' and the people right here.

Why do you think India has gone to the dogs? Is it only because of some crooked politicians? Is it only because of corruption? No, sir! The utter ineptitude of the civil servants is one of the main reasons of this country's present situation. *The civil services are like the digestive system. Irrespective of what you take, eventually it all becomes shit.* That's why the system is stinking like hell. The entire system suffers from what we call a 'universal assault of ignorance'. This is a terrible and shameful secret which the clever civil servants try extremely hard to conceal from us. But we are insiders and know the truth. The officers do little more than licking above and kicking below. In reality, the clerks run the system.

The clerks regurgitate from the rulebooks created by another set of clerks in the past and all those sitting above them merely initial the clerks' lack of wisdom—there has never been any occasion when anybody has ever overruled the mighty clerk or made any original contribution of his own. To disagree with the clerk would require them to have some knowledge and they don't have it. The East India Company had allegedly sought to create a nation of clerks—the buggers did succeed eminently in that. Nearly 178 years after poor Lord Macaulay was wrongly blamed to have expressed that 'desire' of making a 'nation of clerks', India does remain a nation of clerks; people who cannot think independently. If senior police officers ever happen to apply mind of their own, you can take it for granted that it must be to derive some undue advantage or to commit some mischief.

As we make this statement, some fools might be tempted to speak about the progress which India has supposedly made. How do we reconcile that with the observations made above? Ladies and gentlemen, forget about the fabled Indian growth story—the growth, if any, has been there only for some very few. The fact is that paradoxes have nowhere been as stark as they are in modern India. Millions upon millions still sleep hungry; live in conditions worse than hovels; die untreated because they cannot afford the private hospitals; or simply commit suicide in sheer desperation. A frightening disparity exists in every walk of life; and there is great oppression all around—as far as the poor common man (the *aam aadami*, lovingly called 'the mango man' by modern-day Indian avatars of Marie Antoinette) is concerned, there is no justice to be had for him because he cannot afford to spend millions on the exorbitant layers required for getting justice. The so-called growth could perhaps be measured in terms of some economic parameters; but even in that most Indians are excluded. The growth is not reflected in any other sphere.

We would be digressing from the real issue but those who are interested in the subject may read a voluminous amount of literature available on the subject—if they want to read just one book, they may read the book 'An Uncertain Glory: India and Its Contradictions' written by Amartya Sen and Jean Dreze or, if they do not have the brains to read a full book, at least try an incisive piece, 'Putting Growth in its Place' written by the same authors. On an intellectual plane, for example, the fact is that, Indians have practically no original contribution to boast of. Yes, we have an extremely large pool of technically qualified manpower, but that's only a bunch of people who are technically qualified—that's all; nothing more.

They are just not capable of thinking anything original by themselves. In the context of the famous IT industry, we call them 'software coolies'. Somebody else in the world invents and develops technologies—these guys merely use them and we call them professionals! Our so-called centres of excellence in technical education have eventually been reduced to factories producing graduate engineer managers for the private sector. Not only that, they have not been able to create, invent or innovate anything even with the help of those who remain there to do their M.Techs. and Ph.Ds. Let us face it. What is the contribution of the IITs and other top Indian universities to world science or to anything that concerns our lives? What innovation or invention owes its origin to the intellect of the Indians working in India? Nothing.

We depend on medicines to save our lives. We have more than 17,000 drug formulations (and over 75,000 brands) being sold in India. How many of them have been invented in India? Not one, except a solitary Lipaglyn invented in 2013! We use TV sets, mobile phones, air conditioners, music systems, motorcycles, calculators, computers, and cars by the millions upon millions in India—how many of them have been designed in India? Not one—TATA Indica/Indigo and Nano are the only Indian cars designed in India in 66 years!

The rest is manufactured on somebody else's design or creative intellectual effort. Kawasaki, Honda, Suzuki, Samsung, Motorola, Huawei; you name it—they are all foreign designs. The real difficulty lies in creating, inventing or innovating something and that's where we have failed summarily as a nation. We still remain a nation of coolies. Not only that the designs are made by someone else from tiny countries a fraction of the size of India, even the manufacturing of the products in India, if at all it takes place, is on imported machines—the Indians only work on the machines. All over the India Metro rails are projected as growth stories. By God, what is the Indian contribution to the Metro rails except its labour?

The tunnel boring machines are imported; the heavy earth moving machines and cranes are imported; even the Metro coaches are imported. Other nations of the world strove hard to develop creative intellect; we took pride in being able to purchase things invented and made by others. Talk of the defence industry and you would faint. We spend a mind-boggling sum on defence imports because our own research has not been able to make anything worthwhile—the only thing they made was the INSAS rifle which the army now intends to abandon in favour of the imported MCAR (multi-calibre assault rifle). Almost all our weapon systems in the armed forces are imported; the air force has even all the screws imported. The DRDO, the IITs, the private sector—they have all failed us. The prototype of our light combat aircraft Tejas flew on a General Electric (USA) engine; their own Kaveri engine failed. The Arjun tank has only the armour made in India—the power plant, the transmission, the gear box, the gun, the sighting systems are all imported from various German firms. The so-called Air Defence Ship being manufactured in India got its design made by an Italian firm, the turbines from General Electric and the bus bar steel from Russia. According to a BBC report in March 2011, India is looking to spend more than a staggering Rs. 2,70,000 crore ($ 50 billion) over the next five years to modernise its armed forces, including a $10 billion deal to buy 126 new fighter jets.

A puny nation like Israel sells mostly secondary weapon systems to us and even for that we have already spent over Rs. 54,000 crore in the past decade! We are forced to spend such obscene sums on imports because our own R&D has miserably failed us. The fact is, Indians still do not manufacture anything of consequence on their own intellectual input—and when they manufacture, the design, the creative intellect and the machinery are of someone else's. India may be an excellent market for foreign investors—it lost out on the grey matter a long ago. When this is the situation with the so-called best brains in the country employed in R&D, where do the civil servants count?

Let no one boast of the Indian intellect any more and certainly not in the civil services. Since 1948 till 2011, a whopping 4,108 direct recruit IPS officers have been trained in the National Police Academy. You may, if you wish, add the number of IP (Imperial Police) officers also to this who were recruited from 1907 till 1947. What has been the intellectual contribution of these over four thousand IPS officers to the field of policing (or in any other field) in these 63 years? None! How many professional research papers in peer-reviewed journals or how many serious books on professional subjects (or other academic subjects) have been authored by them? Anyone who wishes to find out can do a survey (or a Google search for the lazy) and can confirm that the intellectual contribution of this so-called crème de la crème has been pathetically insignificant.. Have they ever created anything original? Have they brought about any change in the system for better? None!

1.7 Increasing Criminalization of the Police Leadership

The self-proclaimed intellectual superiority of the civil servants having been punctured, only one thing is left for them. They could excel in their deeds to redeem themselves. But, what a terrible disappointment is found even there! The civil servants in general and the IPS in particular forget that respect is earned, not demanded. From whatever we have seen of the Indian police and, we must proudly claim, we have seen a great deal; the Indian police do not deserve any respect at all.

A police force that has no sense of justice; that has no respect for the human rights and dignities of the common man; that only licks the boots of those who are rich and powerful; that has seldom done a right thing; that will dare not speak the truth to powers-that-be, and that has seldom upheld the rule of law deserves no public respect. The police leadership is squarely responsible for this sordid state of affairs. They, in their insatiable lust for plum posts while in service and cushy post-retirement jobs thereafter and, of course, in their legendary stupidity, have allowed the police to slide into a nadir beyond comparison in the world. Since the past 21 years, the police have come to face more serious crime and internal security challenges—terrorism, violent political protests and insurgencies—than before.

And they have no answer for it because they are professionally incompetent. The nature, intensity and profile of crime and criminals have been changing, but the police have not kept pace. The only thing that has increased is the criminalization of the police. Anyone can Google and dig up many frightening stories of the black deeds of the Indian police. The nature of crimes committed by the police is becoming graver every day. It is not merely the cops at the police station level who are responsible for the horrible misdeeds. We have a long list of IPS officers arrested on court orders for fake encounters—several of them in Gujarat alone. Some of them, even at the rank of ADG, have been absconding like common criminals since months. In the infamous Ishrat Jahan fake encounter case, a very senior IB officer of the rank of Special Director has also been questioned by the CBI—the first time in the history of this country when an IB officer has been questioned for his role in a suspected fake encounter. In other words, even they are suspected to have gone the ways of the street cops! A recent case in Rajasthan involved an ADG rank officer for a fake encounter and he had the temerity to remain absconding for nearly nine months in spite of a reward of Rs. 10 lakh on him.

Many other IPS officers are in jail for graft, taking bribe, and possession of drugs. Some have managed to be on the run since years and are yet to be arrested. One DIG rank officer of the Rajasthan cadre who has been accused of raping the wife of his orderly was suspended in 2002, five years after the FIR was lodged against him. A Dausa magisterial Court had ordered all his property, including his house in Noida, seized, but no action was taken by the Noida police. When reporters visited his Noida plot, the residents said they bought the house in 2005. In 1998 itself it was announced that the property belonging to him would be forfeited but nothing could be done.

He reportedly visited Jaipur later and even sold his property. This included a 1,500 square feet plot in Hanuman Nagar, a 10 bigha farmhouse on Ajmer Road and a plot in Vaishali Nagar. Sources claim that while the land transactions were being finalized, he stayed at an IPS officer's bungalow. Obviously, all such masterly 'inaction' has taken place with the connivance of the police leadership. The crookedness of the police leadership and their compulsive habit of covering up their ineptitude becomes most evident following terrorist attacks. Following every so-called terrorist attack, the police and the intelligence agencies go into overdrive. Within a few days if not hours, they claim to arrest the perpetrators of the crime—usually the accused fall in a standard category; generally ranging from the SIMI, the Indian Mujahideen to HuJI. A round of applause in the media follows and the Special Cell, ATS, STF or intelligence officers proceed to nominate themselves for medals. Those who happen to get arrested a little later are called masterminds and ideologues of the attacks; if they sport a beard, all the better to fit in the description.

The media survives on a day-to-day basis. Their interest wanes quickly after the arrests. It is only a few scholars like us who pursue what happened to the criminal cases charged in the courts. It turns out that most of them end in acquittals. What can or what one should one infer from such acquittals? Well, supposing the courts are fair as they are supposed to be, the only logical inference could be that the police had falsely implicated the accused. Remember, implicating someone in absolutely false cases is one of the most powerful tools of oppression which the police possess. The oft-quoted excuse of the police officers is that the job of the police is merely to investigate; it is for the courts to arrive at the truth. Fine, but that's where the catch lies. It does mean that the police have been given a licence to charge anybody with anything and leave it for the courts to decide. The law never stipulated that. Investigation has always to be within the bounds of reason.

Freedom of investigation did not mean an unbridled, arbitrary exercise of power and that too with ulterior motives. The courts will arrive at the truth no doubt but in the process, the poor people will spend years in jail and will have their careers, businesses, lives, families, everything destroyed. Can the police ever compensate for that? ***Friends, Indians, countrymen, lend us your ears. Are you prepared to accept an argument that the atrocities of the police could be dismissed as errors of judgement? Would you allow the police to spoil your entire life, the lives of your near and dear ones and walk away saying 'galati ho gayi'?***

In their rapacity to placate public outrage; to pamper to a sensation-seeking media; and to score brownie points in their own careers, police and intelligence officers have been playing havoc with the lives of hundreds of innocent people. No crime could be more reprehensible than this. Mostly such victims have been found to be poor Muslims. In the process, the policemen not only committed untold atrocities on them but ruined their lives. This has alienated a large section of the people and damaged the very foundations of this secular nation. In the following we will present a glimpse of this saga of falsehood, atrocities and a blatant abuse of power vested in them.

1.8 Misdeeds, Horrible Indeed

1.8.1 *Mecca Masjid Blast Case*

Nine persons were killed in the Mecca Masjid blast on May 18, 2007 and five more died later in the subsequent flare up of violence and police firing. Initially, Islamic fundamentalist groups were suspected to have planned and executed the blasts. Right from paan shop owners, watch repairers, auto drivers to a student pursuing Unani medicine, the police picked up Muslim youth and implicated them in the case overriding objections from community elders and rights groups. However, the very basis of the police argument that fundamentalist Muslim had engineered the blast turned out to be false when subsequent investigations revealed that it was a Hindu fundamentalist organisation, Abhinav Bharat that was responsible for the blast in the mosque. In all, 21 Muslim youth from Hyderabad were wrongly implicated in the Mecca Masjid blast.

They were subjected to third degree torture to force them to admit a crime which they had not committed. The police failed to find any evidence against them and said sheepishly that they were arrested on wrong grounds. Eventually, they were acquitted by the court. This is an excellent example of how the police pick up Muslim youth whenever there is a blast. We will also show how an irresponsible media colludes with them. A journalist Praveen Swami and editorials of *The Hindu,* had consistently declared the arrested Muslim youths as "*Harkat-ul-Jihad-e-Islami* (HuJI)" activists. As early as May 23, 2007 (the Mecca Masjid bombing took place on May 18) Praveen Swami decided who the culprits were.

In his analysis titled "Behind the Mecca Masjid bombing" Swami stated with absolute certainty: "What the Mecca Masjid bombings make clear is that the Islamist threat to India's cities remains in place, notwithstanding the decline in violence since the Mumbai serial bombings..." *The Hindu* editorial of October 15, 2007, titled "Challenge of Islamic terror", begins as follows: "Investigative leads point to the *Harkat ul Jihad-e-Islami* (HuJI), the Islamist organisation behind the Mecca Masjid attack in Hyderabad, as being behind the terrorist strike at the Dargah of Khwaja Moinuddin Chishti in Ajmer....Investigators have been able to establish that many of these attacks were carried out by Islamist terror groups such as the *Lashkar-e-Toiba,* the *Jaish-e-Mohammad,* and the HuJI..." So much so for journalists and editors who claim to be self-styled experts! We do not know whether the police had fed him that theory or he invented it on his own. What we know is that the police appeared to agree with it. Whether the police popularized a theory concocted by them through a journalist or they appeared agreeing with a theory concocted by a journalist, both situations are equally reprehensible. The first shows how crooked they are; the second shows how dumb they are. It is common knowledge, however, that many of the self-styled experts in the media are creations of senior police officers only—in effect, they become mouthpieces of the those officers so as to accord cheap publicity to the officers. Many such journalists have made their careers in journalism only on the strength of the information given to them by their friends in the police leadership. It is a symbiotic relationship—the officers get the publicity they crave for; the journos get supposedly 'authentic material' to publish.

Readers must learn how the police destroyed innocent lives in the process. One example would suffice. One of the arrested youth was Abdul Kaleem, all of 18-years-old. He used to eke out a living selling cell phones and SIM cards while pursuing a course for a medical lab technician. His crime? None. Evidence against him? None! How the police went to him? Since a mobile and a SIM card were also found in the unexploded device, the police, in their 'wisdom' argued that Kaleem was behind the blast—as if, of all the thousands of people who could be selling SIM cards in Hyderabad, it was he who gave them the SIM cards from his shop. As Ashish Khetan pointed out in *Tehelka*, the facts did not matter, the association was enough—and what a contrived one!

So shocking was this abuse of power that the National Commission for Minorities (NCM) recommended a compensation of Rs. 3 lakh each for the youth by deducting the amount from the salaries of policemen responsible for implicating them in criminal cases. Accordingly, in December 2011, the Minorities Welfare Department of the AP government issued an order for a sum of Rs. 70 lakh "towards expenditure to be incurred in connection with confidence building measures and compensation" for 20 cases affected in Mecca Masjid bomb blasts in 2007. Of the 70, 20 were given Rs. 3 lakh each and the remaining Rs. 20,000 each. Even if the compensation of a few lakhs of rupees cannot make up for the sufferings they underwent because of their religion, the decision was historic. For the first time in the history of India, the government admitted that the police had abused its powers and destroyed the lives of innocent people. *The Hindu* too later admitted that the payment of compensation to the acquitted persons was tantamount to admission that they were falsely implicated in the terror case. Even if the blame is eventually thrown on the investigating officers, the police leadership cannot afford to mention even in passing that their subordinates had done all that without their express knowledge or approval.

1.8.2 *Jaipur Bomb Blasts*

A fast track court of Additional District Judge-I in Jaipur acquitted 14 people who had been put behind bars after the May 2008 Jaipur serial blasts on charges of being SIMI activists and giving shelter to some terrorists. The Court's orders once again brought to the fore the malicious detentions made by the Special Investigation Team (SIT) formed to probe the blasts. The court observed that the prosecution failed to establish the links of the accused with the banned organisation SIMI. The Court also found that prosecution had not submitted any substantial documentary evidence proving the direct involvement of the accused in any terror act. The Court observed that the testimony submitted by the eyewitness did not hold enough substance to convict the accused in the charges levelled against them and the allegation of arranging funds, hatching terrorist conspiracy and harbouring accused of Jaipur and Ahmedabad serial blast case were found to be baseless.

The SIT had cooked up a long, convoluted story. This shows the length to which the police can go in harassing innocent people. It had claimed that Sajid Mansoori, who was considered one of the key accused in the Jaipur serial blasts at that time, was in Kota between 2002 and 2006 after giving Gujarat police the slip in 2001. During this period, Sajid, the SIT claimed, had been to Jaipur, Baran, Bundi and Sawai Madhopur several times, to develop his network. He had also gone back to Bharuch in Gujarat in 2006, said the SIT. The SIT claimed that Sajid prepared a core group and Rajasthan's command was given to Munnavar.

He used to work there as a tailor. Ateeq @ Atiq-ur-Rahman was given the post of secretary and Raja @ Imran was made treasurer. "The group was to carry out destructive activities and collect funds," the SIT had said. The SIT had also claimed that Dr. Ishaque Qureshi, his son Toufique Qureshi and another relative, Nazaqat Hussain, were the main agents of the Jaipur blasts. All of them, residents of Waqf area, were detained in Kota. "Dr. Ishaque Qureshi provided shelter to Sajid and he knew about his real identity. His son Toufique Qureshi, who was studying at a Jaipur-based Unani medicine institute, also knew Sajid's real identity," the SIT had claimed. The story fell apart in the court. Can any senior officer claim that the SIT had cooked up the story without their knowledge? If they do so, it would amount to a more serious indictment—that they are so incompetent and their supervision so poor that their subordinates could do anything and they would not bat an eyelid?

1.8.3 *Malegaon Bomb Blasts*

This is a more painful story—an incident where even the CBI committed the same atrocities which the notorious state ATS (Anti-Terrorism Squad) had committed. In November 2011, seven persons walked out of two Mumbai jails after having spent five years in the dark, dingy cells. The seven, accused of planning and executing the 2006 Malegaon serial bomb blasts, were granted bail by a Maharashtra Control of Organised Crime Act (MCOCA) court. Their crime? None! They were absolutely innocent and falsely implicated in the case.

The truth of the atrocities could come to light as late as May 2013 when the National Investigation Agency (NIA) filed its chargesheet in the case against four accused Lokesh Sharma, Dhan Singh, Manohar Singh and Rajendra Choudhary, former members of Rashtriya Swayamsevak Sangh (RSS). Ramji Kalsangra has been shown as absconding accused in the chargesheet. The NIA clearly contradicted the findings of the ATS and the CBI in its chargesheet. In fact, the findings are so diametrically opposite that the ATS and the CBI just do not have any face to say a word in their defence.

The filing of NIA chargesheet confirming the Hindu terror link to the 2006 attacks has paved the way for the nine Muslim youth charged earlier to move court for their discharge in the case. The case was first investigated by the ATS and then by the CBI. The ATS and the CBI had maintained that the blasts were triggered by nine Muslims and that it was an act of Islamic terror. The NIA attributed it to right wing Hindu extremists. There is obviously nothing common between the two. The inescapable conclusion is that the ATS and the CBI had falsely implicated them. "The earlier investigation by ATS and CBI focused on a fake bomb recovered on September 13, 2006," reads the chargesheet filed by the NIA. The NIA said that the ATS and CBI linked the fake bomb incident with the Malegaon blast of 2006. Further, the NIA chargesheet said that the CBI could not find any additional evidence against the accused charged by the ATS.

The NIA has further alleged that the ATS and the CBI had recorded the statements of key witnesses under duress and created bogus witnesses. The NIA has mentioned instances where key witnesses listed by the ATS had retracted their statements. The chargesheet states that a star witness of the ATS, who was an eyewitness to the preparation of bombs, had retracted his statement. The witness has told NIA that his statement was recorded under duress. The chargesheet states that the witness had on November 23, 2006 given the statement before the magistrate court that he was a witness to the making of bombs at the godown of Shabir Batterywala. Soon after, he went missing. It further states that the CBI, which took over the probe later, said it could not trace the said witness. The NIA chargesheet states that the said witness had filed an affidavit in Allahabad court on January 16, 2007 retracting his statement of November 2006. Then the ATS had claimed that it had lifted soil sample from Batterywala's godown where the bombs were allegedly prepared to match it with the soil from the spot where the blast took place. The samples were collected in front of independent 'panch' witnesses. NIA found that they were bogus witnesses created by the ATS, who were never present when the soil was collected.

Wake up, dear readers. If you do not wake up now, you will never wake up. This is what is being done to our countrymen in our country which swears by its democratic ideals. Tomorrow it could happen to you also. And never forget, how easy it is for the police to implicate you—no one is safe from the depredations of the monsters in khaki. All they have to say that they suspect you—and mind it, not every case is lucky enough to get an impartial investigation like this. The mistakes which the ATS and the CBI committed are not errors of judgement or mistakes of fact. They could be nothing but malicious. These Muslim youth had been arbitrarily arrested and imprisoned for a long period with the tag of being 'terrorist' and their families bullied to live with great insult. How can it ever be compensated? The brutes, the crooks in khaki cannot be given a licence to mess up someone's life and then say sorry.

1.8.4 *The Tragic Saga of Mohummed Amir Khan and People Like Him*

Indranil Basu of the *Times of India* has rendered yeoman service to the cause of the hapless people tormented by the police. The following harrowing account is excerpted from his exposé 'Dubbed Terror Mastermind Without Any Proof': "At the age of 18, he had allegedly planted as many as 28 bombs in Delhi and NCR, that too single-handedly in all but one instance. Mohammad Amir Khan had, therefore, been implicated in 19 cases, charged with serious offences such as murder and waging war against the government. Yet, after spending 14 years in jail, he was released last month (January 2012) after being acquitted in all but two cases. Though the courts have been acquitting him since 2001, the prosecution has so far not filed an appeal in any of them. Police officials told ToI they had no plans to appeal even against the last of the acquittals, tacitly admitting that they have no real evidence against Amir in any of those 17 cases. And yet they had no hesitation in projecting Amir as the mastermind of the serial blasts of 1996-97. Amir and his counsel, human rights lawyer N. D. Pancholi, are optimistic about the appeals before the Delhi High Court against the two convictions. All the 19 cases are critically based on the testimonies of two witnesses, both of whom have completely contradicted the prosecution version. Chander Bhan, who was then a tea stall owner in Chandni Chowk, denied the police claim that he had accompanied them, along with Amir, to an alleged bomb factory in Pilakhua run by co-accused Mohammad Shakeel. Worse, Bhan deposed in the court that he had never even seen either of the two accused. The other crucial witness cited by the police, Abdul Sattar, who is the owner of the factory premises, denied that he had ever seen Amir visiting Shakeel in Pilakhua. Much to the police's embarrassment, Sattar also denied that any explosive ingredients had been recovered in his presence from a textile printing unit run by Shakeel.

Thus, by "turning hostile", Bhan and Sattar left a gaping hole in the prosecution story on how the bombs had been sourced by Amir. As if that were not bad enough, the scores of other witnesses cited by the police for the blast sites did not help sustain the prosecution version. While admitting their presence on the blast spot, most of the witnesses claimed to have not seen the person who had placed the bomb. As a corollary, they denied having seen Amir anywhere near any of the blast sites. Even the few who claimed to have seen the person planting the bomb either asserted that Amir was not the same person or their identification of Amir was found doubtful by the court.

Not surprisingly, the Delhi High Court, while overturning his conviction in a Karol Bagh blast, observed that "the prosecution has miserably failed to adduce any evidence to connect the accused appellant with the charges framed, much less prove them." The judgements also point to loose ends left by the police in the multitude of cases they had brought against Amir. In a blast inside a bus near Amba Cinema in February 1997, a witness claimed to have seen Amir plant the bomb. However, not only was his statement recorded a year and a half after the incident, it was found that he gave no description of that person and identified the person as Amir only after he was shown Amir in custody...In the same case, the witness also contradicted himself by saying that the person who had planted the bomb also alighted from the bus still holding the packet he believed to be the bomb. The Court observed, "No reliance can be placed on the sole testimony of this witness."...While he was patrolling a Hindu procession on Qutab Road, a sub-inspector of police saw a suspicious a practice that has been going on in our police forces across the country for some time now. Even serving DGPs are known to prostrate themselves before Chief Ministers and Home Ministers, and you are merely a retired Dy. SP. In fact I think you have only performed the duty expected of you. Imagine if the dust you had cleaned from the shoe had ended up clogging the respiratory system of the power you serve. For people with the wrong allergies, dust can be lethal at times. One shudders to think of the possibility that perhaps her enemies might have planted radioactive dust on her shoes. You acted with an alert mind and abundant precaution sir and for this you should be saluted...

The Indian Police are, thanks to you, the shining example of devotion to duty and the torchbearer of dignity of labour in our country now. Let no one say we don't embrace this idea with heart and soul. No task is too menial or beneath our dignity, as long as the task is commissioned by someone who is truly powerful...The rich and the powerful have the position and the disposition to appreciate our services...

So what if we can't successfully prosecute a few sensational murder cases? So what if we seldom ever get convictions in cases involving high level corruption? So what if victims of religious riots and terror attacks have to wait forever for justice? These are rituals and routines for public consumption. Those in the know, simply ask us to kneel and put out their shoe...Our shoeshine duties leave so little time for uncovering billions of rupees of misappropriated public money. In any case it is so much more fun beating up rickshaw-wallahs and coolies to hear their helpless screams and to grab their hard earned meagre daily wages. Helps us shine a better shoe.

What does the public know? We know which part of the shoe is to be polished and which part is to be licked. Let a lap dog disappear from one of the well-manicured bungalows of Lutyens' Delhi. In no time at all the best sleuths in the country will be on the case and it will be solved. Our masters know what we are good for. And so do we. Protecting their person and their favoured cronies and kith and kin from the petty inconveniences of everyday life, safeguarding their ill-gotten gains from the public gaze. This is our God given mission and we do it well, all this while somehow finding the time to keep their shoes dust free.

Now that we know what is publicly expected of us, perhaps we should formally incorporate it into our training and standard operating procedures. Police academies across the country needlessly place emphasis on tactics, arm-drill, horse riding, baton drill, sword drill, and similar such outdated skills when they should really be teaching us the shoeshine drill. Perhaps the day is not far when along with the cap, the lanyard and the whistle, the shoeshine brush is made an integral part of the police uniform. Like the Sam Browne Belt, the Padam Singh Brush would inspire generations of policemen to perform their duty to shining perfection.

Warm regards,
Abhinav Kumar

1.4 The Bogey of Political Interference

We have attended numerous seminars and otherwise also have had occasion to interact with hundreds of IPS officers both formally and informally in the past decades. The police leadership is very quick to blame the entire political class for their much-hyped, much-maligned interference; the IAS and other services for their jealousy and obstructionism; the people for being deprave and inherently unlawful; the media for not towing the police line all the time; and the judiciary for its lack of appreciation of 'practical constraints'. This is pure bullshit. The simple fact is that the police leadership itself is corrupt—financially, intellectually and morally, in every way.

They have no right to even point fingers at others, not to speak of casting a stone. Statistically, in a very significant number of cases, if not in all the cases, the officers themselves seek out political patronage in order to curry favours with the politicians and wield 'extra' power. In seminars with the academicians or informal talks with the journalists they cry wolf for 'political interference'. That's hypocrisy of the most despicable kind. The relationship of the bureaucracy in general and the police leadership in particular with the politicians is symbiotic.

We will take on their contrived defences one by one. Let us first take the bogey of the so-called 'political interference'. We strongly disagree with the very use of the words 'political interference' which has become so popular in the carefully articulated fulminations of the civil servants. It amounts to being unjustifiably pejorative. The very use of these words shows that the bureaucracy lacks the moral courage and intellectual honesty to admit some of the fundamental weaknesses that have consumed most of the individuals who comprise the system. *The bureaucracy tries extremely hard to project itself as something inherently 'superior' which condescends to 'serve' the hoi polloi but is repeatedly thwarted in its 'noble' attempts by those (read politicians) who are inherently 'inferior' and who, but for the proverbial 'steel frame' coming in their way, would have* packet being exchanged minutes prior to a bomb blast, but could not depose whether Amir was the same person though he "looked like him." The Court said, "It is really strange that being a police officer, he does not try to apprehend the culprit. The testimony of this witness does not inspire any confidence."

After a bomb blast inside a bus in Burari claimed one person's life, witnesses claimed to have seen two boys in mid-twenties alight from bus minutes before the blast took place. The father of the deceased, appearing as a prosecution witness, claimed that though he had seen two boys occupy the seat under which the bomb had been placed and then alight the bus before the blast, he denied that accused Amir and Shakeel were the same boys and said that he had never seen them earlier...Though an eyewitness to a blast in Rohtak claimed to have seen the bomber, the police failed to take follow-up action. As the Court put it, "This witness was material witness and due to non-examination of this witness, the whole prosecution story becomes doubtful...It is also pertinent to mention here that the complainant and other injured witnesses have not been examined by the prosecution despite numerous opportunities."

1.9 Pointers, Potent Pointers

One expected reaction of the police leadership to this expose' would be that we have not included every case in our analysis or there is some cherry picking. By God, unless they are illiterates, they must know that there is a limitation to number of pages in a book. No one can cite all the cases in the country. There are hundreds of cases like these across the country. We can narrate only illustrative cases and intelligent readers can then draw their own conclusions. And the cases cited are enough to indicate the general trend—they prove the point, exceptions notwithstanding. The people must know. Then only they would become more aware and perhaps mount pressure for meaningful reforms rather than cosmetic reforms. That's where a book scores over newspapers or TV.

However, poignant a story may be, people read and forget it the next day. Generally, the newspaper is not available when they need it next. The TV is even more volatile. The TV channels survive on a day-to-day basis. Today, they might air a thought-provoking story. The next day, some kid might fall in a bore well and their attention is entirely taken up by that. A comprehensive analysis at one place in a book makes it a reference of everlasting value which can be referred to any time. We must mention that we are very much aware of the pitfalls of sweeping generalizations. There are no generalizations or undue inferences drawn in this book. We have cited only those cases of police atrocities which were commented upon by the honourable Courts—as such they are very much real—we have cited all the required sources exhaustively in the bibliography and anybody can verify them any time. The information has been taken, as it has to be necessarily done, from public domain—mostly reputed media houses or previously published material of other researchers. The standard practice in research is that one who quotes from a reference and cites it, is not supposed to vouch for the veracity of its contents or be responsible for it.

No researcher can ever claim any personal knowledge of all the reports that he cites or relies upon. If he had to claim personal knowledge, there would have been no need to cite the references in the first place—then they would have become his own averments. In this book, we have cited many media reports or other publications in the public domain where they had adversely commented upon some officers. Since we have cited the references, we are not obliged to check their veracity. We are also not aware whether the officers about whom the media had reported, had ever sued them for publishing wrong reports, and if they had, what was the outcome of that. We have not been able to find any apology tendered by these agencies in the public domain and hence we infer that the reports must have been correct. But if the officers had sued them and had won from the courts before the correction of proofs of this book, those particular parts may please be considered as withdrawn with deep regrets and they would be deleted in the next edition.

Extensive as the data presented in the book are, we have reasons to maintain that the incidents narrated are an excellent representative sample and readers can draw their own conclusion thereafter. The failure of the police leadership was indeed responsible for all those atrocities. Of course, we do not blame anyone in particular by name unless he stands already indicted by a court of law. On December 8, 2012, at a seminar organised by the South Asia Media Commission in Delhi, Justice Markandey Katju had said that 90 percent of Indians were "idiots" who could easily be misled by mischievous elements in the name of religion. Two youths promptly sent a legal notice to him and argued that the statement would bring down the reputation of the country and its citizens. For their information, Justice Katju clarified: "The figure of 90 percent is not a mathematical figure, it simply means that in my opinion a large proportion of Indians (and again I repeat, not all) are fools. I never named you, any community, caste, or sect, and I never said that you are in the category of 90 percent. Hence I do not see how you are defamed."

Those in the police leadership who feel particularly mauled by this book may please take note of this for their edification. Precisely for this reason, we decided not to quote the famous observations of Justice Mulla of the Allahabad High Court (in re **State vs. Mohammad Naim**, Criminal Misc. Case. No. 87 of 1961 and **State vs. Mohammad Naim** on 23 October, 1961, 1962 CriLJ 125) on Indian police in this book because, having been adjudged sweeping generalizations, they later stood expunged by the Honourable Supreme Court (in re **The State of Uttar Pradesh vs. Mohammad Naim** on 15 March, 1963, 1964 AIR 703). Justice Mulla had observed: *"...there is not a single lawless group in the whole of the country whose record of crime comes anywhere near the record of that organised unit which is known as the Indian Police Force."* We must, however, also quote what the Apex Court had concluded: "Having said all this, we must add, lest we be misunderstood, that the conduct of Mohammad Naim and officers like him deserves the severest condemnation, and the *learned judge rightly observed that such conduct required very serious notice by superior officers of the Police. It is difficult to avoid the reflection that unless an example is made of such officers by taking the most stringent action against them, no improvement in police administration is possible."* Our analysis has to be taken in the same spirit.

Chapter 2

Fake Encounters and Foisted Cases: Courts Bash up the Monster

2.1 Murder Most Foul

2.1.1 *The Falsehood of It All*

Fake encounters and foisting of false case are some of the most reprehensible crimes the police commit. No abuse of legal powers vested in the police could be so stark, so sinful, so immoral and so condemnable. Fake encounters are a phenomenon which is almost unique to the monsters in Indian police. In other countries of the world it is, at worst, an exception; in India it is the rule. In other countries, if at all fake encounters take place, it is largely an aberration attributed to the deviant personalities of the individuals concerned. *In India, the police leadership has accorded an informal approval to this ghastly practice.* Of course, in public forums everybody condemns it but one has to be a fool to not admit that fake encounters take place with the tacit approval and blessings of the police leadership. They are the first to jump in front of the TV cameras, claim it to be a great success of the department and garner a fair share of the glory; they are the ones to recommend the 'murderers' for gallantry medals and, if possible, seek one for themselves too. By the same logic, they should also be held responsible for murder when it is proved to be a fake encounter. The police officers have also been found guilty of acting as contract killers for rival criminal gangs or anyone who could pay their fee. Thanks to the honourable courts, many such senior officers now find themselves behind bars. The pattern of fake encounters remains ridiculously the same throughout the country. Why? Because police officers are uniformly dumb across the country. They cannot tell even a lie convincingly! Those killed in encounters are found to be carrying all the necessary identification papers, replete with all their details, such as name, rank in the terrorist or criminal organisation, etc., in their pockets when they face the murderers in khaki. Usually, the cops who, in the normal course of events cannot shoot an elephant at 50 yards are found to shoot in the fake encounters with such fantastic accuracy that the victims die even without firing a single shot. If at all they are shown to have fired, the bullets either go waste or one of them very conveniently lodges itself in some such part of the police vehicle where it could do no harm to anybody. Police personnel seldom get even injured in such encounters.

Isn't it wonderful? Have you ever wondered why? Just compare such fake encounters with real engagements with terrorists in Jammu & Kashmir, the north-east or with the Naxals. Anybody can analyze the history of such fights with real terrorists—practically all of the significant engagements in the history of terrorism in India have been analyzed in our books '**The Ultimate Handbook of Urban Warfare**' and '**Jungle Warfare: An Ultimate Handbook**'. In all of them, the forces (including the Indian army) have never got out cheap. Often they suffer heavy casualties in killed as well as injured. The Naxals manage to inflict casualties on the forces even when they are firing with muzzle loaders. What does it mean? Does it mean that all those who engage terrorists elsewhere do not know how to fight? Or does it mean that the cops who commit fake encounters are Indian incarnations of John Rambo? Well, if they are so good, may be the nation could think of deploying the likes of the Delhi Police Special Cell or the Maharashtra ATS to J&K, north-east and in the Naxal areas. May be they could start a very special training school also. Gentlemen, the fact is that in fake encounters everything is fake. It is outright murder. Send the very same cops in actual combat in J&K, the North-East or Naxal areas and they would either shit in their pants or return draped in the tricolour.

Foisting of false cases may not spill blood as in fake encounters but is equally wicked an act because it is a most slimy way of spoiling someone's life. Every adult Indian knows how much it costs to get out of any criminal case—if it is a false case, the charges would indeed be serious and the evidence assiduously built up. You can rest assured that you will be poorer by several lakhs of rupees. False cases are foisted for various reasons. Sometimes the cops might be interested in teaching a lesson to someone who could be perceived as an irritant (such as activists or some fearless witness to some police crime); sometimes they want to extort money; sometimes, particularly when the foisted cases have charges related to terrorism, they are interested in rewards, medals and out-of-turn promotions; the list is limited only by their ingenuity.

2.1.2 *Revelling in the Sub-Culture of Unjust Violence and Overt Machismo*

Just go through the pages of local papers in vernacular and you will find numerous reports of young IPS officers, particularly after taking charge of districts or ranges, boasting to the dumb journalists that they enjoy the reputation of being 'encounter specialists', and that '*apradhiyon ka safaya kar diya jayega*', etc. The journos utter the words 'encounter specialist' in hushed tones and with great reverence making the officer's chest swell up. Most officers suffer from a hidden desire of trying to appear both macho and violent. We have actual photographs of officers ranging from the rank of SP to ADG (the photo which we have pertains to a Commissioner of Police in a major Metro) where they had posed with revolvers held close to their faces, in the fashion of some third-rate gunslinger from a Western movie (cowboy movies for the uninitiated). Incidentally, at least two such photos were published in reputed magazines also. Fascination with weaponry is understandable; trying to project a macho image by getting photographed with a revolver held close to the face is downright cheap. Looks like these guys had taken the film '*Quick Gun Murugan*' a bit too seriously. Incidentally, the same complex seems to consume them when many of them go on to sport moustaches like those of the dacoits of Chambal Valley in the years gone by.

We wonder how their wives must be suffering them—pity finding a dacoit-looking man in the bed every night! Their ignorance that such a crudity often stems from a deep-rooted unconscious feeling of insecurity regarding their masculinity, could perhaps be pardoned; their ignorance that they look utterly comical in weird moustaches is unpardonable. The police leadership is so intellectually bankrupt that they could never apply any mind to such simple issues in their Uniform Rules either. How short is short hair? How short must be the so-called short sideburns? Had they been well-informed (and which they are certainly not), they would have known that in many countries such as the USA, the Uniform Rules make sketches and prescribe the length of the moustache that can be worn. But these morons could never think of anything like this.

2.2 The Courts Hammer with a Heavy Hand

In May 2011, the Honourable Supreme Court of India expressed its anguish on fake encounters and came down heavily on this inhuman practice. While deciding Criminal Appeal Nos. 1174-1178 of 2011 [in re **Prakash Kadam and etc. vs. Ramprasad Vishwanath Gupta and Anr.**, 13 May, 2011], a Division Bench consisting of Justices Markandey Katju and Gyan Sudha Misra opined that, in cases where a fake encounter is proved against policemen in a trial, they must be given death sentence, treating it as the rarest of rare cases. Fake 'encounters' are nothing but cold blooded, brutal murders by persons who are supposed to uphold the law. The honourable Court further observed, ***"If crimes are committed by ordinary people, ordinary punishment should be given, but if the offence is committed by policemen much harsher punishment should be given to them because they do an act totally contrary to their duties."*** In the following, we reproduce excerpts from the glowing words of the Supreme Court.

"In our opinion this is a very serious case wherein prima facie some police officers and staff were engaged by some private persons to kill their opponent i.e., Ramnarayan Gupta and the police officers and the staff acted as contract killers for them. Thus, the protectors have become the predators. We are of the view that in cases where a fake encounter is proved against policemen in a trial, they must be given death sentence, treating it as the rarest of rare cases. We warn policemen that they will not be excused for committing murder in the name of 'encounter' on the pretext that they were carrying out the orders of their superior officers or politicians, however high. In the Nuremberg trials the Nazi war criminals took the plea that 'orders are orders', nevertheless they were hanged. ***If a policeman is given an illegal order by any superior to do a fake 'encounter', it is his duty to refuse to carry out such illegal order, otherwise he will be charged for murder, and if found guilty sentenced to death.*** The 'encounter' philosophy is a criminal philosophy, and all policemen must know this. ***Trigger happy policemen who think they can kill people in the name of 'encounter' and get away with it should know that the gallows await them."***

The **Apex Court reiterated the same sentiments in August 2011 also.** Police personnel involved in fake encounter killings should be awarded death sentence and hanged, the Supreme Court said. A Division Bench said that police personnel as custodians of law were expected to protect people and not eliminate them as contract killers. The court observed this while directing the surrender of two senior Rajasthan IPS officers (Additional DGP Arvind Jain and SP Arshad) allegedly involved in the fake encounter killing of an alleged gangster

(Dara Singh) by the Special Operations Group of Rajasthan Police on October 23, 2006. The Bench said the accused police officers, if they failed to surrender, would be arrested by the CBI, which was investigating the case.

Earlier, in re **CBI vs. Kishore Singh and Ors.** on 25 October, 2010 [Criminal Appeal No. 2047-2049 of 2010], the Honourable Supreme Court was faced with a case where police officers had chopped off the penis of a man in custody with a barber's razor. The Apex Court observed: "This case reveals how some policemen in our country have not got over their old colonial mentality and are still persisting in barbaric acts in a free country which claims to be run by a democratic Constitution and the rule of law. It also reveals a grisly state of affairs prevailing in our police set up even today." The Court held that it was a pre-meditated act. *In reference to the usual plea of there being no witnesses to the crime, the Court commented: "As regards the argument that there were no witnesses other than Jugta Ram, in our opinion in a police station it is hardly possible for there to be any witness there except the policemen and the victim. A police station is not a public road or public place where people can see what is going on."* Convicting the accused police officials, the court observed: "It was a barbaric act on the part of the accused who deserve no leniency. ***If the protector becomes the predator civilised society will cease to exist***. *As the Bible says, 'If the salt has lost its flavour, wherewith shall it be salted? (Matthew 5, Mark 9.50 and Luke 14.34-35)'; or as the ancient Romans used to say, 'Who will guard the Praetorian guards?'*

In July 2013, 21 persons including 13 cops were sentenced for life for the fake encounter killing of Ram Narayan Gupta @ Lakhan Bhaiya in 2006 in Mumbai. The CBI chargesheet in the fake encounter of Tulsiram Prajapati, through a reconstruction of the incident shows that he was killed while still in handcuffs!

2.3 Cry You Must, for the Truth will Rend Your Heart

2.3.1 *Label Him a Terrorist, and That's the End of It*

A large number of innocent people were accused of being operatives and agents of various terrorist organisations (Al-Badr, Harkat-ul-Jihad-e-Islami, and Lashkar-e-Taiyyiba, etc.) and arrested with great fanfare by the Delhi police amidst much back-slapping. They were charged with the most heinous of crimes: sedition; waging war against the state; criminal conspiracy, planning and causing bomb blasts; training of terrorists; collection of arms, ammunition and explosives and the transfer of funds for terrorist activities. However, perseverance paid and between 1992 and 2012 most of them were acquitted by the courts of all these trumped-up charges. The arrests and subsequent charges were nothing but mala fide. To say that these were unjust acts would amount to a shameful euphemism—it was outright criminal. All these men suffered the most harrowing of experiences for varying lengths of time: illegal detention and torture (both physical and psychological), incarceration and, of course, the trial. And they were not 'liberated' by the acquittals. They returned home to find businesses destroyed; 'broken' family members having suffered the humiliation and trauma of being associated with "terrorists"; children who had to abandon their studies; and parents who had passed away in grief and despair, waiting for them to return.

Yes, we are all aware that it is presumed that the State can do no wrong and the actions of the State cannot be imbued with any ulterior motive. By an extension of the argument, it implied that the officers of the State too, acting on behalf of the State, could not be imbued with any ulterior motive in their acts of commission or omission that turned out to be wrong. Fine. But this is true only to a limited extent. *This does not mean that the police have a licence to commit atrocities and later claim that they were genuine mistakes or errors of judgement. The courts do distinguish between genuine mistakes or shortcomings on one hand, and malicious mistakes on the other.* We are therefore commenting only on those cases where the courts had specifically pointed out that the agencies of the State had abused the powers vested in them. There are reasons to suspect, and we will show at length, that this important agency of the State has indeed abused this privilege. In the cases that we discuss, almost everything was found to be foul—from the intelligence information supposedly made available, to the arrests, recoveries and the investigation itself.

In many countries of the world the State has come to make compensation for many of its wrongs. Why, in our own country, the Andhra Pradesh Government compensated those who were falsely implicated in the Mecca Masjid blast case? That was an excellent gesture, albeit a token one. It marked a new beginning. However, for most of other cases, the sufferers have been offered no apology, no rehabilitation. Worse still, practically none of the officers guilty of framing them have been acted against. This is despite the fact that in the Dhaula Kuan fake encounter case, the Court was of the opinion that, "there cannot be any more serious or grave crime than a police officer framing an innocent citizen in a false criminal case. Such tendency in the police officers should not be viewed or dealt with lightly but needs to be curbed with a stern hand." In May 2013, faulting Delhi Police's Special Cell for investigation done "defying logic, prudence and reason", the Delhi High Court acquitted two J&K businessmen accused of conspiring to bomb New Delhi railway station in 2006. A **Division Bench of Justices S. Ravindra Bhat and S. P. Garg** acquitted Mohammad Iqbal Jan and Mushtaq Ahmad Kaloo noting that there were "significant discrepancies" in the prosecution claim and it suffered from "contradictions and omissions". The Court said police could only show they picked up the two men based on a tip-off, and the statement of the officer leading the raiding party (Inspector M. C. Sharma) was not even recorded. The Court also cited "complete lack of support by public witnesses; dubiousness of the public witnesses themselves (their addresses are vague); suspicious omissions in not investigating the alleged receivers of the explosive, or the omission to take the accused to Deoband to arrest suppliers of the explosives; the complete lack of any explanation why the identity of Mohammad Iqbal, as Faisal, a terrorist, was not probed; no proof that he was part of any Pakistan based terrorist outfit". It put on record its suspicion that police "deliberately" ignored evidence showing the two accused were not terrorists but genuine businessman.

In the following we will quote extensively from a report of the Jamia Teachers' Solidarity Association (JTSA) called 'Framed, Damned, Acquitted: Dossiers of a 'Very' Special Cell', a meticulously prepared study that has rendered yeoman service to the cause of the victims of police atrocities. The JTSA report forcefully brings out that the acquittals discussed were not simply for want of evidence. What judgement after judgement comments on is the manner in which the so-called evidence provided by the police and the prosecution was tampered with and fabricated, how story after story as presented by the prosecution was unreliable, incredulous, and concocted.

In case after case, the pattern of stupidity was found to be the same: The police claim to receive "secret information" from an unnamed informer about a meeting or a suspicious character at a certain location. They reach the spot, search the premises, find "unlawful material" such as pamphlets and CDs, some easily available weapon, or some powder or liquid that is described as a powerful explosive on the person or persons present there, and arrest them. All sorts of mistakes are committed in the process of making up this string of lies. The fact of having received the 'secret information' is never recorded anywhere. No search warrant is ever obtained. The fact of their leaving the police station is never recorded in the General Diary. Search witnesses are always stock witnesses of the police, in spite of the courts having commented adversely on the practice. Seized material is hardly ever secured in a foolproof, tamperproof manner.

Why? All this is done to provide scope for manipulation at a later stage. And to cap the lot, once the arrested person is in police custody, he is miraculously struck by remorse a few days later and volunteers "confessions"—never mind that they withdraw them later. The only inference that can be drawn from all this is that the cops are not only crooked, they are dumb to boot.

Who is responsible for this state of affairs?—both for crookedness as well as dumbness—none but the police leadership! Nothing of this sort is done without the approval of the senior officers. If they try to save their skin by throwing the blame on their subordinates, it is all the more unethical. Experts like us do not find anything surprising in it. Lay men are, however, at times, surprised. When human rights activists, or families of those arrested on charges of terrorism, allege foul play on part of the investigating agencies, many people respond with, 'Surely, there must have been some involvement, or else why would the police arrest him, and not me?' Unfortunately, they are mistaken and partly it is due to this attitude that the police have been emboldened into committing their diabolical deeds. The main reason is that critical questions are seldom asked in any quarter. As far as the Indian public is concerned, they have traditionally had a great deal of respect for authority—whoever it may be, it does not matter. Hence most Indians readily tend to accept the police version with regard to any claim made by them. Journalists, of course, as we have repeatedly discussed in the book, are devoid of any critical faculty and, in any case, are often in league with the police, merely regurgitating the police version. The truth comes out only when the authorities fail to prove the charges and by that time, the people would have lost any interest in the case. The findings of the JTSA report counter and contest the complacence of such all-too-familiar nonsense.

2.3.2 *The Perils of Creating and Exploiting Paranoia for Ulterior Motives*

Like the military-defence industry nexus in the USA, there has come to be a strong nexus of media, police and intelligence agencies in India, whereby the mass media unquestioningly regurgitates the agencies' perspective. Sometimes it is pure ignorance; sometimes it is sheer malfeasance. Over the last decade—particularly between the years 2004 and 2009 for example, as the country was struck by frequent bomb blasts, hundreds of innocent Muslims found themselves automatically and falsely accused of terrorism. At least at the moment of arrest, almost everybody believed that the police had caught the real McCoy. The charges could eventually be proved against very few of them. As we have shown at length in the book, most of them got acquitted from the courts, thereby *gobbled up the nation a long time back. This is a self-serving, self-congratulatory attitude and there is no reason to believe in it.*

This attitude is based on an unstated presumption that the bureaucrats in general and the police officers in particular are inherently 'good' whereas the politicians are inherently 'bad' – that, left to themselves, the bureaucrats would usher in the Utopia but the politicians make them do all the bad things. Dear sirs, this is real life and we know what you are—perhaps you are humming the song '*Duniya re duniya very good very good, duniya wale very bad very bad; upar wala very good very good, neeche wale, very bad very bad*" [from the hit Hindi film Trimurti (1995)]; we are not. This amounts to taking an utterly simplistic view of life and actually sophistry. For God's sake, stop cribbing about transfers—you have played this CD so often that it has lost all its appeal. *You are not so helpless that someone could force you to do 'bad' things. You do bad things because you expect rewards in a million ways—power which you can wield by virtue of being 'close' to the powerful; lucrative posts; the works.*

We do not find any reason to even remotely suspect that the bureaucrats are innocent like the quintessential Victorian maidens who claimed that they did not even know that there was a 'bad thing' called sex until they got deflowered, and that the politicians are Big Bad Wily Wolves hell bent on corrupting the morals of the maidens. Our personal experience in the IPS and other government departments put together for nearly 34 years; observation of the Indian society for a much longer period and interaction with a host of officers over decades has left no doubt that a notion like this is an outrageous lie intended to befool the gullible people, ignoramuses in the media and the blissfully unrealistic academicians. There cannot be any reason to believe that officers who are products of the same society are in any way morally superior to the politicians. It was never so, and it can never be so. There is no reason to believe that two years of training in an academy could erase the value systems which are so very deeply ingrained in the collective Indian psyche since centuries—if training academies think so, they are dumb and have been deluding themselves.

The mechanisms of snuggling and cuddling with the politicians are many—to list them all would involve some gory details and faint-hearted readers might feel scandalized. Still, a few examples would be illustrative as they compete well with the accomplishments of some of the most wretched lackeys in the history of the world. We are personally aware of not one but several top police officers who have stood guard outside (in a figurative sense) guest houses/rest houses (quite suitably rather remotely located) even as some influential politician spent 'quality time' with some woman (certainly not his wife) inside. We personally know the case of at least one woman IPS officer who had herself spent such 'quality time' with a politician even as another sucker from the IPS stood guard outside.

Not that she was a beauty even in the very prime of her youth but Indians greatly relish whatever that comes free. In the legendary work 'Raag Durbari', a village kid asks another, '*Daroga ji kis cheez ke shauqeen hain*'. The other kid enlightens him, '*Jo bhi phokat mein mil jaaye, usee ke shauqeen hain*'. Politicians are no exceptions and appreciate whatever they get free. We have seen top police officers sharing cigarettes with the personal staff of politicians in order to be chummy with them—in one instance, the guy was actually a head constable; though working as a PSO but in reality a very close confidante of the politician. We have seen very senior IPS officers brushing dust off the kurtas of politicians if as much as a little dust blew at the airport. The body language was worth watching; Desmond Morris should have learnt a great deal from it for his research in ethology. Stand at attention at a certain distance. Knees locked; bend from the waist only; extend the right arm forward and brush off some specks of real or imaginary dust ever so softly and delicately. One of us watching it was instantly reminded of the exquisite manner in which the ethereal beauty that was Beena Roy (playing the role of Mumtaz Mahal) steps over the flower petals strewn in her path as Pradeep Kumar (playing the role of Shahjahan) serenades her with those beautiful words '*Paanv chhuu lene do phuulon ko inaayat hogii, inaayat hogii; varanaa hamako nahiin, inako bhii shikaayat hogii, shikaayat hogii*' [film Taj Mahal, 1963].

We have seen senior officers feeding not only the (now famous) birthday cakes but also a more traditional jalebi-dahi to the politicians in the manner of bearers in army/police messes with one hand placed on the bottom of the elbow of the other as the other hand was extended fully. In fact, the SSP and DM in a district used to compete with each other for this blessed task—they might have never fed their own children or dying parents with such devotion. We have seen them taking away the laundry of politicians for proper cleaning from circuit houses. We have seen them getting tea, snacks and lunch not only for politicians but their 'other women' (actually whores, if we drop the pretence of euphemism) as well from their homes delivered at the circuit house so that they were spared the horrible tea, snacks and lunch of the circuit house. We have seen them riding precariously in the trolley of a tractor when the 'other woman' of a chief minister wanted to visit her flood-affected village—by God, if proving that they were indeed falsely implicated. What happens then to our pretensions of a fair and just society? Who is primarily responsible for it? It has to be the police leadership because they created the hoaxes in the first place; others only propagated it.

A large section of the society has often been falling a prey to the overblown and false psychoses created by the nexus of the media, police and intelligence agencies—to such an extent that the people completely close their mind to all reason. The moment a bomb blast took place, the immediate, almost instinctive presumption was that it must have been done by the Muslims in general and the Students' Islamic Movement of India (SIMI) or the Indian Mujahideen in particular, in pursuance of their cross-border, anti-India agenda at the behest of the ISI or the *Lashkar-e-Taiyyiba* in Pakistan—namely, to fight a global jihad and to establish Islamic rule in India once again. To most people, what matters is that someone should be blamed and blamed quickly; if he can be arrested or shot quickly, all the better.

Any voice in protest is sought to be silenced—an ordinary man is likely to be dubbed anti-national for questioning the police and the media. In other words, the unholy nexus of media, police and intelligence agencies has been trying hard to 'manufacture consent' all the time. This is dangerous for the future of democracy because in the process we are alienating millions of people further. As Tarun Tejpal, the editor-in-chief of the *Tehelka* magazine also points out in his piece 'The Thin Red Line' in 2008: "The Indian state must tread carefully for the last many years—abetted by global trends—the state's actions and utterances seem to be deepening a prejudice against Muslims. Catching the mood, Bollywood's arch villains are now mostly Islamic. India has 160 million Muslims—more than Pakistan, more than any other country save Indonesia. Even if 10,000 are radicalised it's barely a tree in a forest. To create an atmosphere that blights the entire forest is a mistake. To foster a psychology of siege in an entire community is a disaster. Before it seeks further bans, the state ought to vigorously introspect."

The very perceptive Herman Goering had said that it is always a simple matter to drag the people along, whether it is a democracy, a fascist dictatorship, a parliament, a communist dictatorship. All you have to do is to tell them they are being attacked, and denounce the pacifists for lack of patriotism and exposing the country to danger. *Similarly, you have only to tell the people that the Indian society (read the great Indian middle class, the rich, the powerful, and the beautiful) is under attack by the Naxals, by the Islamic terrorists, by the insurgents in the North-Eastern states, by the Kashmiri terrorists, and you have the ground ready.*

Anywhere in the world, once you have sensation, you can generate fear and paranoia, and you can do whatever you want – you can expand the security apparatus, you can enact more oppressive laws, you can gain more police powers, you can spend frightening sums on security and weapons, you can peep into the private lives of the citizens, tap their phones, read their mail, and in general come as close to being Orwell's Big Brother as possible. As far as the police leadership is concerned, the desire of getting more and more unbridled power is actually the most important reason of generating paranoia in the minds!

As you read through the book, you will be shocked at the injustice that has taken place in this country which takes pride in calling itself democratic, governed by the rule of law and a rather overly-elaborate Constitution. Mistakes happen everywhere, in every nation. What is horrifying in India that there is no reason to believe that they would not happen again. The system has shown itself to be remarkably retrogressive and capable of committing the same atrocities again and again. God forbid, if there is a series of bomb blasts again, you will once again have the same allegations flying thick and the same people getting arrested, tortured and made to confess – the same witch-hunt all over again.

2.4 The Devil's Fangs are Exposed

In the following we will look at some of the cases pertaining to people who were falsely implicated in terrorism-related cases and in which the honourable Courts summarily exposed the crookedness and the dumbness of the police.

1. **State vs. Tanveer Ahmad, Shakil Ahmad, Ishtiaq Akhtar Dar, Md. Akhtar Dar, Md. Yusuf Lone, Abdul Rauf and Ghulam Md.**

   [FIR No.: 169/92, Police Station: Lajpat Nagar, Under Sections: 4 and 5 TADA (P) Act 4 and 5 Explosive Substances Act read with Section 120-B IPC, 25/54/59 Arms Act, Sessions Case No.: 50/ 2001, Date of Judgement: August 1, 2002]

The prosecution story was that the Special Cell of Delhi Police received information that some Kashmiri terrorists had sneaked into the capital with the intention to commit high profile terrorist acts. Further, that they had made their base somewhere in South Delhi in the house of an exports dealer who possessed one white Maruti Gypsy and one red Maruti van, both bearing J&K numbers and both being used in the service of the terrorists' nefarious designs. On April 29, 1992, information was received that Kashmiri terrorists had been spotted driving around in the red Maruti van. A raiding party was immediately formed and dispatched.

They signalled it to stop. The driver initially slowed down but then raced and sped away. After a chase, during which Inspector Lal Ram fired a shot in the air, the occupants, five in number, were overpowered and apprehended. The five were Tanveer Ahmad, Shakil Ahmad, Ishtiaq Akhtar Dar, Md. Akhtar Dar (the driver) and Md. Yusuf Lone. From the van, the following items were claimed to have been recovered: six photographs of places like Red Fort, Delhi Gate, India Gate and other such places; six blue coloured plastic explosive sticks wrapped in newspaper; one green coloured cloth with 'Islamic writing'; Rs. 20,000 in cash and a diary. (*By God, did you not know that you should have photographs of famous places like the Red Fort, Delhi Gate, and India Gate before you can plan an attack on them? What plastic explosives were they? How did they know they were explosives, even before it was chemically analyzed? For the sake of argument, even if we assume that they were plastic explosive, where in the world you get blue coloured plastic explosives? We have written the world's most comprehensive book on the subject of explosives [**The Ultimate Book of Explosives, Bombs and IEDs**] and we never came across a blue plastic explosive. If you tried hard, you might get non-explosive simulants for plastic explosives in olive green, red or blue. You read that right – non-explosive simulant! And green coloured cloth with Islamic writing? Quite the archetypical filmi image of a terrorist! Isn't it? By the way, since when has it become an offence to keep Islamic writings?)*

They also claimed to have recovered three detonators, battery cells, one meter of electric wire, photographs of important buildings, US $ 2,400, and one booklet titled, "Cry For Freedom Will Not Stop" published by Ikhwan Publications and issued by the Muslim Brotherhood. The booklet allegedly exhorted Muslims to take up arms to liberate Kashmir. (*Well, the dumb cops would like you to believe that three detonators, some batteries and just one meter of wire was all that you needed for making a bomb. Limited knowledge of the cops is understood but so limited imagination is shocking. By any chance, did they determine what sort of detonators they were? You cannot use just about any electrical detonator on any explosive. Plastic explosives, for example, are deliberately made rather insensitive. You cannot use a detonator for a plastic explosive that you would use for blasting nitrate emulsion explosives. Just for the information of the ignoramuses in the police, we would mention that electric detonators are classified in 4 classes depending on their electric properties.*

According to the European Standard (EN 13763-1) the denomination is class with subdivisions 1, 2, 3 and 4. The recommended minimum firing current for a single detonator is 0.6 amp for Class 1; 1.0 amp for Class 2; 2.2 amps for Class 3; and 6.0 amps for Class 4 detonators. To which class the three seized detonators belonged? Were the cells adequate to supply the required amperage of current? Were the detonators just right for that plastic explosive? That they cooked up stories in one thing; that the police leadership is so dumb that they could not instruct their subordinates to concoct even a lie properly, is another.)

The prosecution produced 14 witnesses, all of whom, barring one, were police persons. They parroted the above story. The defence proved that they were picked up from their respective places on the 25th and 26th April 1992, much prior to 29th April 1992, when the police claimed to have arrested them. In the intervening period, the defence argued that they were kept in illegal detention and a false case foisted upon them. **The Court noted that these documents filed by the defence witnesses "caused serious dent in the prosecution story"**. The prosecution was unable to explain how the defence witnesses could have filed applications and writs against the arrests in advance if the arrests were actually in fact made on 29th April 1992. Therefore the "rest of the prosecution story about recoveries from the accused persons on or at their instance on 29th April or after 29th April 1992...also stands in cloud of doubt." **Thus the Court acquitted all the accused**. ***It took them 10 years to get justice—life spoiled in bonus.***

2. State vs. Md. Amir Khan

[FIR Nos.: 790/1996; 70; 71; 117/97; 137/97; 249/97; 262/97; 191/97; 751/97; 752/97; 379/97; 260/97; 951/97; 752/97; 405/97; 746/97; 631/1997 Police Stations: Various Police Stations in Delhi, Ghaziabad, Rohtak and Sonepat Under Sections: 34, 120-B, 121, 121-A, 122, 320, 307, 435, 436 of IPC; 3, 4, 4(B), 5, 7 of Explosive Substances Act; 150 of Railway Act, Sessions Case Nos.: 51 of 1998/2004; 25 of 2006/2009; 18 of 2010; 111/98; 116/98; 95/98; 11/98; 100/98; 108/98; 109/98; 128/98; 357/2007; 115/98; 137/98; 113/98; 120/98; 104/1998, Date of Judgements: November 2000 to January 2012]

We have mentioned the horrifying saga of Amir Khan earlier. The cases against Md. Amir were spread across several states including Delhi, Uttar Pradesh and Haryana. Do not think that it was some joint operation of police of these three states. It was the machination of the Delhi police in the Capital; right under the nose of all is sacred to the democracy and governance in this country. Md. Amir Khan was acquitted in 12 cases between November 30, 2000 and August 17, 2001; in a span of just about eight months. In the remaining five cases, his acquittal came between March 16, 2006 and January 9, 2012; over a period of more than six years. The poor fellow spent the formative years of his life in jail. **In all, it took him nearly 14 years to get justice and get out of the jail. No one can dispute that his life was destroyed**. Who and how would you compensate for this loss?

Wake up, readers, this is important. *If someone is charged in as many as 19 cases, it would mean that the police genuinely believed that he must have done something. If he got acquitted in 17 of them, it means that the police were wrong in all of them. Since they were wrong in all of them, it means that the mistakes could not have been accidental. Different sets of officers could not have committed the same mistakes over a number of years. This means that the atrocity against this poor boy was institutional – nothing could provide a better expose' of the calculated brutality in which innocents have been implicated in false cases in the name of fighting terror than the case of Amir Khan. Who is responsible for this institutional atrocity? None but the police leadership*! They have no scope to argue that some mischievous subordinates did this.

Even if it is accepted that they did so, what were the scores of senior officers doing all these years? Why did each one of them meekly accept what their subordinates had told them? Why did they not question their lack of wisdom? Why no one applied any mind to the matter? There can be only three reasons. First, they are so dumb and ignorant in professional matters that they are incapable of applying mind to such matters and leave everything to their subordinates. Second, they actively colluded with their subordinates in committing these atrocities. Third, and most likely, both of these.

3. State vs. Khongbantbum Brojen Singh

[FIR No.: 93/02, Police Station: Kotla Mubarakpur, New Delhi, Under Sections: 121/121-A/212/201/120-B IPC; 3/5/20/21/22 of POTA, 12 PP Act, 10/13 UA (P) Act; 25 Arms Act, Date of Judgement: May 12, 2009]

In March 2002, the Delhi Police claimed that they had information that a terrorist belonging to the terrorist organisation Peoples' Liberation Army (PLA) of Manipur, namely, Brojen Singh @ Sony, was hiding in Kotla Mubarkpur with his accomplice, Ibotombi Sapan. They were arrested at their residence and the recovery of a loaded .38 Colt revolver tucked in the left waist belt of Brojen's trousers was claimed. It was further claimed that from a search of the house resulted in the recovery of "incriminating articles" such as a computer, a laptop, and Rs. 30,000 in cash.

It is instructive to see how the charges fell apart. The Delhi police had claimed that Brojen had given a confessional statement. The defence argued that the statement was recorded when Brojen had already been in custody for ten days so the accused could not be "considered free of police influence and the confession could not be taken to be a voluntary one." Incidentally, the disclosure statement recorded at the time of Brojen's supposed arrest on March 15, 2002 by an ACP and the confession recorded by a DCP under Sec. 32 of POTA were identical. The Court noted, "The entire statement is word by word including comma and full stop is exactly the same...It appears a humanly impossible conduct both for the person making such a confession or the person recording it that entire confessional statement would be exactly the same word by word." The Court accepted the defence argument that the DCP did not record the statement afresh but merely directed his PA to re-record the disclosure statement.

The Court also noted several problems in considering the material from the computer as evidence of Brojen's guilt—*one-month delay in sending the seized laptop and computer to the Forensic Laboratory. During the intervening period, the seized items and the seal remained with the police, thus tampering could not be ruled out.* The material cited by the police as indicative of Brojen's terrorist affiliations was not found to be incriminating. The Court asked how the following could be construed so as to refer to a terrorist organisation: "...to suppress our sentiments, the centre have even stopped paying salaries for 4-5 months to government employees. Even under such pathetic situation why people are still asleep." Most disturbingly, a file in the computer showed the timing as October 6, 2002; 04:58:17 p.m.—a time several months after the computer had been seized! Several files annexed as incriminating evidence could be found dated October 6, 2002. The prosecution argued that a revolver was seized from Brojen. The only independent witness to this seizure was the landlord. The Court held that his testimony could not be taken as independent since he could have been threatened by the police that he would be implicated on charges of harbouring a terrorist. Further, the arm seized was a Colt, not an illegal firearm. Why did the police not try and investigate how and where the accused acquired it? *(You expect them to have this much brains?)*

The real story is simple and shows how cold-blooded brutes the police could be. Brojen used to take part in agitations against AFSPA. As a result of this the police booked him along with other Manipuri youths in false cases. His preventive detention was quashed by the High Court and the quashing was upheld by the Supreme Court. The State did not release him in spite of the Court orders. He moved for contempt and the Supreme Court upheld the conviction of the senior officers of the State. This annoyed the state authorities to no end and they hit back when he came to Delhi along with his wife and child for treatment of his diabetes—he was implicated in the case to 'teach him a lesson'. The Court concurred with the explanation that since Brojen 'had been suspected as a terrorist by State authorities and he had already incurred wrath of authorities in getting their conviction in the contempt of court, the police got him targeted to become a victim of this crime.' **The Court acquitted Brojen of all charges.** ***It took the poor fellow seven years. You cannot help but notice the camaraderie which develops between the police forces of two states when it comes to tormenting an innocent citizen—an excellent example of the 'national' character of the police—from north to south; from east to west; they are all monsters of the same type.***

4. **State vs. Hamid Hussain, Md. Shariq, Md. Iftekhar Ahsan Malik, Maulana Dilawar Khan, Masood Ahmed, Haroon Rashid**

   [FIR No.: 40/50 and 132/04, Police Station: Special Cell, New Delhi, Under Sections: 121/121-A/122/123 and 120-B IPC, 4/5 Explosive Substances Act, 18/19/20/23 Unlawful Activities (Prevention) Act, 379/411 IPC, Sessions Case No.: 178/05 and 15/06, Date of Judgement: January 8, 2010]

This was one of the most fantastic stories woven by the police in which the imaginary web of terrorism were made to stretch as far as Pakistan and the Indian Military Academy! As usual, the police claimed that in the first week of February 2005 information was received that Lashkar-e-Toiba (LeT—*the ignoramuses in the police leadership do not know even the correct name of the organisation – Lashkar-e-Taiyyiba*) had set up a base in Delhi and that a person named Hamid Hussain (R/o Seelampur) was working for LeT in Delhi. It was further claimed that he had been frequently visiting Jammu & Kashmir, both to procure arms, ammunition and explosives as well to receive instructions from the LeT commander. He was 'ceremoniously' arrested at Mukarba Chowk—on the Delhi-Karnal bypass road—when he was supposedly coming from Jammu & Kashmir. The recoveries claimed from his air bag consisted of 22 cardboard packets containing 480 g RDX each. *(Don't you know, the police are so smart they can identify RDX from the mere sight of it – laboratory tests are for mere mortals!)*

From that point they cooked up more stories and committed more horrific atrocities. On March 6, 2005, supposedly acting on the information provided by the accused regarding his other associates, an 'encounter' took place at Uttam Nagar in which three militants identified as Bilawal @ Md. Shams (24 years; R/o Rawalpindi, Pakistan), Shahnawaj (25 years; R/o Sindh, Pakistan) and Shams @ Parvez (R/o Patna, Bihar) were killed. *(You know these Pakistanis can be identified from the mere looks of them – they have that archetypical look which you often see in third-rate Hindi films – long, thin face; sunken cheeks, trimmed beard; cruel eyes; black pathan suit; pink chequered scarf over shoulders; the works. Quite often they carry their passports with them so that the job of the police is made easier. Ha, ha, ha!)* According to the prosecution, the accused had revealed that these Fidayeen militants were planning to conduct an attack on the Indian Military Academy (IMA) Dehradun. *(Did you not note the sheer audacity of these guys? You see, these terrorists are such daredevils that, armed with a few guns only, a handful of them would attack an Indian army facility where thousands of armed security personnel are to be found!)* The matter did not end there because the rapacity of the police did not end. They claimed that further interrogation of the accused had revealed yet more names of accomplices in the IMA attack conspiracy, leading to their arrests. This brought the total number of arrests in this case to six: Hamid Hussain, Md. Shariq, Md. Iftekhar Ahsan Malik, Maulana Dilawar Khan, Masood Ahmed, and Haroon Rashid.

The entire case was marred by a lack of evidence to corroborate any nexus between the accused Hamid Hussain and Md. Shariq, or between the accused Iftekhar Ahsan Malik and Haroon Rashid and their connection with the slain 'militants'. The Court took cognizance of the fact that in spite of the photographs of the slain 'militants' available with the police, the latter made no attempt "to show the photographs to local residents to verify or substantiate whether the accused persons were at any time seen in the company or residing with the slain militants." In the absence of independent evidence to show any connection between the accused and the slain 'terrorists', the identification memos of those killed could not be relied upon as they were made at the behest of accused Shariq and Hamid Hussain. The Court dismissed the prosecution's reliance on the disclosure statements of these two accused. The disclosures were inadmissible evidence and could not be read against them particularly when nothing incriminating was recovered" from the search of their houses. The Court noted that "mere disclosure statement of the accused in the absence of anything concrete in the nature discussed above or mobile or telephone call records hardly inspires confidence."

The prosecution case against the accused Iftekhar Malik was that he had disclosed that he had arranged three passes for the passing out parade which was held in December 2004 and he had given two of these three passes to the slain 'militant' Shams whereas one pass was kept by him. The Court noted that the recovery of the invitation card of the 'passing out parade' of IMA, Dehradun proved nothing, because:

(a) There was no identification mark in the nature of any serial number or the name of the guest who was supposed to have attended the passing out parade;

'service to the people' was their creed, why did they not visit any other village in their whole life riding on a tractor trolley? We have seen them personally supervising the construction of the houses of politicians and getting very high posts in return. We have seen them offering to ride standing in a helicopter with the politician if no seat was available.

It is only an extension of such behavioural traits that makes the police leaders commit such ghastly crimes as fake encounters at the behest of politicians; or protect the kith and kin of politicians even if they are involved in heinous crimes like rape. *Gentlemen, police officers who do 'bad' or 'unprofessional' things do so not because they are compelled to do so by the politicians; they do so because they serve their own interests by doing those things.*

Is it not too well-known that there are a large number of officers who are known for their 'closeness' with politicians of different hues? Some of such officers are what we call 'committed' types (that is, those who are committed to one party); many of them have, however, been successful in wooing and seducing politicians of diametrically opposite hues also—thereby leading to our aphorism that 'there is nothing in India that cannot be had by 'manipulation' of the right kind'. Don't such officers, whether they have seduced one party or several, take pride in it? Are they not much sought after for that quality? They are the ones who can get things done both for the department and for individuals. They are the ones who can make or mar someone's career.

They are the ones who hold mini 'durbars' of their own at their homes or offices where people come and genuflect for favours small and big. They are the ones who decide transfers and postings, inquiries and punishments. They are the ones who can get files pushed up in record time, or get them buried forever. They are the ones who, when they speak with 'their' politicians, use tones which are acutely reminiscent of the Soviet Secret Police NKVD chief Lavrentiy Pavlovich Beria speaking to Stalin—whether it pertained to deporting someone to Siberia or awarding him a medal. Who can deny the omnipresence and omnipotence of such officers? As dear Brutus said: "If any, speak, for him have I offended." In an attempt to befool people that not all of them are corrupt (in every way; financially, morally, intellectually), some senior officers and service associations have taken a fancy to listing out the most corrupt officers. In our opinion, it is not necessary to list out the corrupt, the 'maha-corrupt', the 'ten top-most corrupt' and so on. These childish things only help to lose focus. The problem exists not on account of these 'toppers' only; those who scored 60-90 percent marks have also contributed greatly to the cause. ***Anybody in India who has his eyes and ears open and who has not buried his head deliberately in sand like an Ostrich must have seen in his 40-50 years or so of his life that it is not only the much-maligned 'netas' who have looted this country for the past over six decades—it is the well-known nexus of 'netas', bureaucrats (including police), criminals, businessmen, industrialists, and all those 'brokers' of power including the media houses and influential media persons which has systematically gang raped this country and its wealth.***

Sycophancy and the art of maintaining the nexus—manipulation of the system in general for their benefit—have been raised to such level that descriptions like 'crawl when asked to bend' sound like school kids' clichés. We do not think that there is any hope of redemption for a system that has a Faustus in every corner. And mind you, the politician is not the Devil; the Faustuses in the IAS and IPS are jumping to sell their souls to anybody who could further their selfish interests. The problem concerns the individuals, not the system per se; trying to blame the system is to deny the obvious truth.

A debate on how our model of democracy has been abused by the politicians is merely of academic interest; it will not lead you anywhere. Fortunately or unfortunately, that is the system we have. If the civil servants have any problem with the democratic system that the people of this country have adopted, they can go join the Naxals or some other group bent upon a bloody revolution to change the system. Politicians and politicking are an integral part of the democratic system. Bureaucrats have no right to label the politicians as inherently bad and seek to create a parallel system within the system. Politicians are as good or as bad as any one of us. There is no reason to believe that bureaucrats, merely because they have passed the UPSC exam, have more commonsense or are more reasonable than politicians. Intellectual capacity, even though its existence in the bureaucrats is highly doubtful, has nothing to do with personality traits. We have had numerous occasions to deal with a large number of senior officers who have been frighteningly unreasonable and completely bereft of commonsense besides being utterly cruel. On the other hand, class 8th pass politicians have often displayed more compassion, commonsense and reasonableness. There is one more factor to contend with. Politicians do not suffer an inferiority complex when they find that a junior officer knows much more than they do. We are aware of a PAR (Performance Appraisal Report) of a senior officer of 20 years of service in which his reporting authority observed, "He has great knowledge but he thinks that he is the only font of knowledge."

(b) The passing out parade had already been held on December 9-10, 2004;

(c) Passes for the parade were in effect taken away by the accused from the room of the public witness Sahil Pando 3-4 days after the parade.

The court reiterated that for the reasons cited above "the recovery of IMA passes ...does not lead to the inference that accused Iftekhar Ahsan Malik was involved in a conspiracy to mount a fidayeen attack on IMA."

The Court observed that the diary found on the accused also proved nothing against him: "The prosecution has failed to bring on record any evidence to suggest that the Quranic inscriptions found written in the dairy—admitted by the accused to be written by him—"in any way incited hatred, violence or called upon him or the Muslim Community to engage in *Jihad* or attack any military establishment." *(Praise be to the Court. The monsters in khaki sought to create entirely new types of offences. They have brought you closer to the concept of a 'thought crime' of George Orwell's '1984'. You might be thinking that your personal diary is for writing your personal thoughts and feelings because you are NOT going to make them public – as close as it can get to keeping them in your mind. No longer so, the cops say. You think that you merely thought and that was the end of it. No. The cops say that because you thought once, you would go on to act on that and commit some crime. In other words, thinking is a crime because the cops say that if you think, you will compulsively act too. And by any chance, do not commit the cardinal sin of writing anything from the scriptures.*

You write, and the cops come gunning after you. Thank God, they did not blame the Bhagwad Geeta for inciting people to murder after watching the 2001 film 'Aks' in which Manoj Bajpayee, playing the role of a psychotic killer says: "Na koi marta hai, na koi maarta hai; Ye mein nahi kahta, tumhari Geeta mein likha hai." Do not be surprised, dear readers. ***Dread the day when the stupid Indian cops also seek a ban on the Geeta and the Quran!*** *Some of you might recall that in 2011, state prosecutors in Siberia had filed a petition against 'Bhagavad-Gita As It Is' (a famous commentary on the Bhagwad Geeta by the founder of ISKCON, A. C. Bhaktivedanta Swami Prabhupada, claiming it sowed "social hatred" and called for "violence against non-believers." Eventually, the Court there threw it out.)* There was a gross discrepancy in seizing and sealing the hand-written slip (on which Malik had ostensibly received instructions from militants). The Court concurred with the defence that Malik was made to write the slip under threat and coercion while in police custody. Haroon Rashid was alleged to have been a financier of LeT activities. This was sought to be proved by the remittances of Rs. 49,000 he had sent as Farooq through Western

Union Transfer twice in January 2005. The second alleged piece of 'evidence' was Rashid's emails to his alleged LeT handler Abdul Ajiz. The coded emails revealed, according to the prosecution, Rashid's part in the IMA attack conspiracy. The Court was inclined to grant credence to Rashid's statement [u/s 313/281 CrPC] that he borrowed 2 lakh, including Rs. 1 lakh from his uncle to pursue a course in marine engineering in Singapore and when he realized that he had more money than required, he remitted the surplus to his father through above transactions. The alleged email evidence also fell flat when it was discovered that while the password to his email account was revealed to the police by Rashid on March 13, 2005, the printouts placed before the court were dated March 18. The Court emphatically said that "manipulation or tempering cannot be ruled out from 13.05.2005 to 18.05.2005...These emails bring out no evidence against the accused that he was involved in any conspiracy to fund terrorist activities or to plan an attack on IMA Dehradun". *The Court hauled up the prosecution for its total failure to put on record any evidence regarding the code words used by the accused to communicate with his alleged Pakistani LeT handler and how these were deciphered and what was their import or relevance in this case.*

The prosecution narrated that on March 12, 2005, a police team led by ACP Rajbir Singh took the accused Hamid Hussain to Welcome Area, Delhi. Hussain allegedly led them to house number JB 6/199, where the accused Dilawar Khan was identified as he stood outside his house. Dilawar Khan allegedly led the raiding party to recover a hand grenade. The accused thereupon led the police party to Baghwali Masjid where he identified the other accused Masood Ahmed, who was arrested. The latter's interrogation and disclosure statement led to the recovery of one Chinese pistol with 24 live cartridges wrapped in polythene. The Court questioned the prosecution as to why no effort at all was made to ensure the presence of public witnesses while effecting the alleged recovery of the pistol and cartridges; despite the area being densely populated and public witnesses being then available. **The Court observed: "Ex facie, the totality of facts and circumstances suggest that there is no case against the accused persons under the said charge. There is not even a mole of evidence against the accused for their engagement in any act of waging war against the Government of India."**

5. **State vs. Irshad Ahmed Malik**

   [FIR No.: 47/04, Police Station: Special Cell, Under Sections: 121/121-A/122/123/120-B IPC and 25 Arms Act, Sessions Case No.: 04/2009, Date of Judgement: November 8, 2010]

Once again the usual story, but this time the liars added a touch of central intelligence agency for that extra punch. The police claimed that in the first week of March 2004, the Special Cell received secret information through a central intelligence agency that a Kashmiri youth named Irshad Ahmed Malik, belonging to a militant outfit Lashkar-e-Toiba (LeT), had been making trips to Delhi for collecting funds for LeT. He had been receiving such funds through hawala transactions. Further, he was trying to set up base in Delhi. Then more specific information was received that Irshad Ahmed Malik would be coming to Delhi and staying in the Rajdhani Guest House, Bhogal, New Delhi. It was also gathered that he was carrying weapons with him. Of course, they claimed the recovery of a .30 pistol, eight cartridges and Rs. 2.75 lakh in cash.

The Court, however, emphasized that as a rule of prudence when police officials proceed to apprehend a person on information (that someone was to commit a serious crime) efforts should be made to enlist the presence of some independent public person so as to support the prosecution theory and for deposition by police witnesses to become credible. In the absence of such public witness, the testimony of police/official witnesses lack credibility and confidence. The Court noted that between the information received and the actual raid "there was sufficient time for the police to call some independent public witness to join that team before accused was captured." (*Needless to say, police officers avoid public witnesses like plague because under cross-examination they might blurt out the truth, exposing their misdeeds.*) The only public witness listed from the side of prosecution was one Ajab Singh. The police claimed he had been enlisted to join the raid party as he was in the vicinity buying some goods.

However, the particulars of the said public witness were insufficient. He was simply recorded as: Ajab Singh, S/o Bhagmal, resident of Kotla Mubarakpur. On top of it, the police reported that he could not be examined in Court as he was already dead. (*Ha, ha, ha! By God, can you beat the ingenuity?*) This led the Court to ask "What kind of sanctity can be assigned to such a witness when rule of prudence requires a public witness to be joined should be a respectable person of the locality or a public witness whose credibility could be found to be above board. Joining a person as a public witness only that person happens to pass through may not satisfy the requirement of some 'independent person' joined by the police to support its case." The police claimed to have 'definite' intelligence input about Irshad Malik's stay at Rajdhani Guest House at Bhogal. And yet, quite surprisingly neither before nor after the raid any police officer bothered to contact the Manager or some other senior staff to enquire if the accused had checked in or was likely to check in at the said hotel or had booked any room. The Court also registered the fact that nobody from the Rajdhani Guest House was made to join the investigation or even questioned later on. The Court wondered, why it should not remark that such enquiries and effort to enlist independent witness "was omitted by the police deliberately". The material allegedly seized was sent to the FSL one month later, forcing the Court to observe: "These create reasonable doubt in the authenticity of seizure bundles sent to FSL un-tampered."

The police had claimed that the money had been received by Malik through a hawala transaction from Chandni Chowk. The Court wondered as to why "no further investigation into such an aspect was carried out". The police could not escape by simply saying that the accused did not disclose the source of funds. *(Readers must note this. In thousands of cases, the police and the intelligence agencies speak of hawala transactions, but stop at that – you never get to learn anything more about them.)*

While passing the verdict, the Court cited the case of **State vs. Navjot Sandhu** (AIR 2005 SC 3820) – where these ingredients of offence under Section 121 IPC have been discussed by the Supreme Court – and **concluded that "by no stretch of imagination the charge of sedition can be said to have been proved against accused."** The Court repeatedly stressed that the prosecution story "did not inspire confidence", "lacked credibility", was "suspicious" and "doubtful and unacceptable". The Court also acquitted the accused under Section 25 Arms Act, as the prosecution miserably failed to prove that alleged arms and ammunitions were recovered from the accused. **The Court concluded that the entire operation of the Special Cell had been surreptitious, and blatantly violated all established legal procedures and norms.**

The Delhi Police filed a criminal leave petition (No. 208/2011) in the High Court. Honourable Judges G. P. Mittal and S. Ravindra Bhat dismissed the appeal and upheld the acquittal of the accused. **They remarked: "The investigating agency thus shifted the stand of the accused as per its own convenience to involve him in a serious case like waging war against the Government of India."**

6. **State vs. Saqib Rehman, Bashir Ahmed Shah, Nazir Ahmed Sofi, Hazi Gulam Moinuddin Dar, Abdul Majid Bhat, Abdul Qayoom Khan and Birender Kumar Singh**

   [FIR No.: 146/05, Police Station: Kapasahera, Under Sections: 307/353/186/489(c)/482/120-B/34 IPC, 25/27 Arms Act and 3/5 Explosives Act, Sessions Case No.: 24/10, Date of Judgement: February 2, 2011]

Once again, the police claimed that an anonymous informer had given information about the nefarious designs of two Kashmiri terrorists, Masood and Zahid and that they along with two associates, were ferrying a huge consignment of arms and ammunition into Delhi from Jaipur. Accordingly, the police laid a trap and after a chase involving firing from both sides and hurling of hand grenades, the terrorists were apprehended, thereby successfully averting a deadly terrorist attack. (*Wah, wah, kya baat hai! Badhai ho, sheron! Tussi kaamal kar ditta, paaji! Par thoda zyada jhooth nahin ho gaya?*)

The case crumbled from the very beginning. The cop concerned could not reveal the identity of the anonymous informer to the Court. Nor could he reply to why he felt no urgency to inform the IB or his seniors about the impending terror strike. **The Court firmly held that no one could be convicted on the basis of secret information which could be not be "tested on the touchstone of the cross examination by the accused".**

An army-type combat uniform was ostensibly seized from the 'terrorists' and traced by the police to a tailor in Gopinath Bazar in Delhi Cantt. The Court noted that the tailor was a stock witness of the police, appearing and giving evidence in many cases on behalf of the police. On closer examination of his testimony, the tailor conceded that he operated his shop from a pavement which left him at the mercy of police and MCD officials, and false testimonies were his way of paying the *hafta* to the police. He had actually been summoned to the Dhaula Kuan PS where poor Dar was duly exhibited to him.

A sketch of the Palam airport was apparently recovered from the pocket of Dar—a point used by the prosecution as proof of the terrorist conspiracy. The Court, however, noted that for the sketch to be kept in the pocket, it would have to be folded more than twice. The fact that there was a single fold longitudinally with no creases suggested that the sketch had been planted as an afterthought. Also, the police upon recovering the sketch made no attempt to either corroborate Dar's handwriting on the sketch, not to inform the Palam airport authorities about a possible terror attack. *(Brilliant! Such a serious thing was to take place and they did not inform anybody? Were they so dumb that they did not know that they could not even enter the airport without the permission of the airport authorities? Or, did they think that they could manage to fend off an attack on a huge facility like the airport with the handful of the men they had? The truth is that they did not want to involve anybody else in this farce because they ran the risk of getting exposed!)* It so turned out that along with the crooked cops, a major of the army intelligence was also involved in this sham. **The Court observed: "They [accused] are totally innocent and have been framed in this case by the aforesaid**

four police officers in order to achieve their personal gains and/or to settle petty personal scores, be that at the behest of one Major Sharma, whose attempts to persuade accused Gulam Moinuddin Dar to work for him in getting the militants surrendered in Kashmir were spurned by him (Gulam Moinuddin Dar) or to earn undue honours or awards for themselves."

The Court was scathing in its observations on the misconduct of the police officers, and needs to be quoted at length: "Viewed from any angle, the encounter alleged to have been taken place on the night intervening between 01.7.05 and 02.7.05, did not take place at all and an absolutely fake encounter has been projected. The story of the encounter was carefully scripted in the office of Special Staff, Delhi Police, Dhaula Kuan, by its main author SI Ravinder Tyagi with the assistance of SI Nirakar, SI Charan Singh and SI Mahender Singh. All these four police officers have acted in advancement of their self-interests in total disregard to the demands of their solemn duty. These four police officers whose duty was to protect and safeguard the citizens, have turned persecutors and tormentors...**These four police officers have brought utter shame and disrepute to the whole Delhi Police Force. In my opinion, there cannot be any more serious or grave crime than a police officer framing an innocent citizen in a false criminal case.**"

"Such tendency in the police officers should not be viewed or dealt with lightly but needs to be curbed with a stern hand. I, therefore, direct the Commissioner of Police, Delhi, to initiate appropriate enquiry against the four police officers...for the misuse and abuse of their powers as a police officer, as detailed herein-above. The enquiry shall be completed within three months from today, and report be submitted to this Court on the next date of hearing. The SHO, Police Station Kapasahera is also directed to register FIR against the aforesaid four police officers U/s 167 IPC and forward the same to the Addl. Commissioner of Police (South/West) who shall conduct investigation which shall be completed within three months from today and a report be submitted to this Court on the next date of hearing. A copy of the FIR shall be sent to this Court within one month from today."

On August 6, 2012, the Delhi High Court upheld acquittal of the seven alleged terrorists on the ground they were nabbed after a "fake encounter" in 2005 and were falsely implicated. A bench of Justices S. Ravindra Bhat and S. P. Garg upheld the acquittal, dismissing the police appeal against the trial court's verdict.

7. **State vs. Khurshid Ahmad Bhat**

[FIR No.: 122/05, Police Station: Special Cell, Under Sections: 121/121-A/122/123/120-B of IPC and Section 25 of Arms Act, Date of Judgement: March 26, 2011]

The police wove a story that information was received from a central intelligence agency that one Aslam Wani, hailing from J&K, was working as a courier for arms, ammunition, explosives and hawala money, and had set up base in South Delhi. In pursuit of this, Wani was arrested as he emerged from a service lane from DAV school side carrying an airbag on his shoulder—claimed recoveries included black colour explosive RDX in granulated form and ten electronic detonators, one 9 mm pistol with 10 live cartridges and 5 cartridges in the pistol. As if this was not enough, he was then claimed to have made startling disclosures about the grandiose designs of waging war against India involving the well-known Kashmiri Shabbir Shah, chief of the Democratic Freedom Party and one Khurshid Ahmed Bhat (a juvenile). Khurshid was arrested from Pampore, Kashmir and one .38 pistol, 72 live cartridges, and six live hand grenades, with one spare magazine of .38 bore pistol—and other incriminating objects such as a belt pouch, an ID card issued by the terrorist organization Jaish-e-Mohammed bearing Khurshid's photo and name, and a rubber stamp of the tehsil commander of Jaish-e-Mohammed were claimed to have been seized from him.

But, as we have been emphasizing all along, the cops are not only crooked but dumb too. While Aslam Wani was arrested on August 26, 2005, poor Khurshid was arrested nearly a month later from Kashmir on September 21, 2005. They also conceded that the newspapers had prominently reported the arrest of Wani. *(Was Khurshid so dumb that he could not even think of fleeing from the place after Wani was arrested? Or was he oblivious of the existence and arrest of Wani? If they were accomplices, he should have indeed kept track of Wani. Moreover, the main accused in the case, Shabbir Shah, while living publicly and freely in Srinagar, was not apprehended while the juvenile was arrested. The prosecution could produce no evidence to demonstrate that Khurshid had conspired with Wani to wage war against the nation.)* **The Court found the story unsustainable under scrutiny and acquitted Khurshid Bhat of all charges. The moral of the story is that the fiends in police would not spare even a juvenile in the pursuit of their nefarious designs.**

8. **State vs. Salman Khurshid Kori and Others**

[FIR No.: 96/06, Police Station: Special Cell, Under Sections: 121/121-A/122 IPC, 5 Explosive Substances Act and 18 UAPA, Sessions Case No.: 236/1/10, Date of Judgement: December 13, 2011]

In yet another sensational and concocted story, the Delhi police claimed to have arrested two alleged LeT operatives, namely Md. Alamgir Hussain and Abdur Razzaq Jiwon, and claimed to have recovered explosive substances from their possession. On further investigation regarding the source of these explosives (*You see, ye log maamale ki tah tak pahunchana chahate hain! Ha, ha!*), they arrested Salman Khurhsid Kori, Abdur Rehman and Md. Akbar Hussain also. Each accused was claimed to be carrying a bag, containing explosive sticks, detonators and hand grenades. These guys were projected as the infiltration of 'Jihadi' groups into the north-east, among Manipuri Muslims. It was touted as a pioneering effort by the Special Cell to crack LeT's network in the north-east. Interestingly, some of the claims made in press conferences—such as that Khursheed taking PULF leader Noora to Bangladesh for a meeting with LeT militants—were not repeated in the Court.

The Court observed that between the information received and actual raid there was sufficient time and opportunity for the police to call some independent public witness to join that team before the accused were captured. *The Court noted that "the entire case is based on the disclosure statements which are not admissible in evidence and the testimonies of the police officials who are interested witnesses."* The Court ruled that "mere possession of explosive substances cannot be tantamount to causing threat to the unity, integrity, security or sovereignty of India or to strike terror in the people or any Section of the people in India…so, the conviction merely on the indicative, to my view will lead miscarriage of justice."

In this case, the defence successfully proved that all the three accused named in this case were actually picked up by the police from places and on dates that were far removed from what they showed on record later. Each of the accused was picked up by the police from their native places in Imphal and several months before they were actually shown arrested from near Red Fort in Delhi. All this while, the accused were in the illegal detention and custody of the Special Cell. The prosecution could not produce any evidence to prove that accused at any point of time stayed or visited Jammu & Kashmir or had any connection with anybody there.

9. State vs. Maurif Qamar and Md. Irshad Ali

[Original FIR No.: 10/2006, Police Station: Special Cell, CBI's Case FIR No.: RC.3 (S)/2007/SCU.V/CBI/SCR-II, New Delhi (Dated: 27.07.2007), Under Sections: 121/121-A/122/123/120-B of IPC; 4/5 of Explosive Substance Act and Section 25 of Arms Act, Submission of Police Closure Report by the CBI: November 11, 2008]

This is an interesting case in which the lies perpetrated by the

This was a classic example of an officer suffering from an inferiority complex with another officer; a politician has no such hang-ups. Even if it is granted that the junior officer really thought that he was the only font of knowledge in the world, it was an 'internalized' thing; there was no way it could be commented upon. Did he ever tell the reporting officer that he thought that only he knew everything and that the reporting officer did not know anything? If he ever told only the former part and not the latter, it would still remain a childish bragging. The reporting officer had no case that the officer reported upon was a braggart and in spite of his tall opinion about himself, his performance was poor. The reporting officer never said that his performance was poor. There is no concept of thought crime anywhere in the world as yet.

Besides having a high opinion about himself, the officer could also have been thinking about doing some very obnoxious things with the wife of the reporting officer; the poor fellow should have realized that he could not possibly register a case against him for that. One must either accept a system or reject it. It is both illogical and immoral for those who are deriving the maximum benefit out of the system to start wailing like widows when it hurts them a bit. We accept the system as it is. If some civil servant has a problem with the political system India has given to itself, he must realize that short of a revolution which could purge the system and baptize it with blood and fire, no significant change can be brought. Most people of limited intellect fail to understand that while talking of bringing about changes is fashionable and de rigueur, it seldom results in anything real. It has never resulted in anything substantial. What do these morons expect? They have lived happily with a legal framework that is 150 years old without a whimper and they talk of change! Do they have any moral right to talk of change?

Anyone can analyze a record of the so-called changes that have been brought about—have they been of any help anywhere? *As far as the common man is concerned, he finds the police as inefficient, as corrupt and as oppressive as his ancestors found in the 19th century. Let us not waste time in farcical academic exercises. All that such exercises do is to provide employment to the seminar-wallahs for suggesting highly superficial and cosmetic actions (such as organizing more seminars on gender sensitization, image-building, and people friendliness, etc.) in the system that would still eventually leave sufficient loopholes intact.* Precisely for this reason, we do not have any reason to hope that things like State Security Commission, the Police Establishment Board or similar fancy devices would, in any way, bring any change in what the individuals in the service eventually deliver to the people.

Gentlemen, even an outdated system can deliver results provided the men charged with the system have a desire to deliver and strive hard to deliver it. This is not to suggest that an exercise in optimization cannot be attempted within the boundaries of a given system. Yes, it can be done, but the point being made is that it would remain a largely academic exercise only. ***The desire to deliver is more important than the means to deliver.*** In fact, it can be argued to the contrary that the desire to create an 'exclusivist' system that seeks to 'clip the wings' of the 'dirty' politicians has ulterior motives to garner a larger share of the booty than is possible with the politicians 'intimately' and 'mightily' involved with the system.

1.5 The Hoax of Lack of Resources and Modernisation

One of the oft-repeated pleas of police officers is that they have not been able to deliver the expected services because the police is not 'modernised' enough and lacks resources in general. It is extremely common for oldies in particular to launch into long narratives of how the police stations did not have enough stationery and how they were forced to ask the people to bring their own paper. Or that the police station jeep got only a few litres of petrol every month and they were forced to ask the people to fill the tanks. Bullshit!

You can bury the police stations under stationery and give them Mercedes Benzes—they would still be duffers! The crookedness of the police has nothing to do with what they have or do not have. They were duffers when there used to be just one motorcycle for the entire police stations; they are equally bad duffers when they have several motorcycles, Jeeps, Gypsies and Boleros in the police station. And for the sake of argument, even if it is accepted that the police lack resources; who is responsible for it—none but the police leadership! Why did they not fight for it all these decades? Are they supposed to only crib in private and do nothing at work?

What did they do when it was brought to their notice that their police stations do not have enough resources? Why did they not push the matter forcefully enough and tell the government that if the police are not given adequate resources, they would not be able to deliver, or it would lead to corruption? They never did that. Coming to the issue of modernisation, we would like to reveal that in spite of crying all the time most of the central funds allotted for modernisation of police forces across the country remained unutilised, according to media reports in May 2013. Home ministry records show that 14 of 28 states failed entirely to spend the centre's assistance in the form of

Special Cell, Delhi Police were so outrageous, so blatant that they were ruthlessly whipped by the CBI in some brilliant investigation. In February 2006, in a repetition of the familiar cock and bull story, the Special Cell of Delhi Police claimed to have 'arrested' two Muslim youth, Maurif Qamar and Md. Irshad Ali and charged them with being terrorists belonging to the *Al-Badr* outfit. The recoveries claimed included a .30 calibre pistol and eight live cartridges, three detonators and two timers from one guy and another pistol and eight live cartridges, and some 2 kg of explosives, etc. from the other guy.

As a result of a writ petition filed by Md. Kashif Ali (elder brother of Maurif Qamar), the Delhi High Court on May 9, 2006, ordered a preliminary enquiry to be conducted by the CBI, Delhi. In its preliminary report filed before the High Court on May 30, 2007, the CBI concluded that the Special Cell's version failed to answer many questions and sought a thorough and impartial investigation. The Court granted the same.

Investigations by the CBI revealed that both the accused, Maurif Qamar and Irshad Ali, were actually police informers who were assigned the task of infiltrating terrorist organisations in Jammu & Kashmir. When they refused to oblige the intelligence agency (IB), both were made to 'disappear' in December 2005. Then a missing person report was filed by Aqif Qamar, younger brother of Maurif Qamar, alleging that he had been kidnapped. Representations were also sent to the President, Prime Minister and Home Minister seeking directions to Delhi Police to trace Maurif Qamar. Alarmed at this, in February 2006 the Special Cell showed the arrest of Ali and Qamar, alleging that they were picked up by the Special Cell from Mukarba Chowk, on G.T. Karnal Road in north Delhi.

During the course of investigation, the CBI obtained and analyzed the Call Detail Records (CDR) of the following: (i) the two accused (Qamar and Ali), (ii) officers of the police team that allegedly conducted the raid leading to the apprehension and arrest of the accused and (iii) officers of the Intelligence Bureau (IB). Revelations from CDR conclusively nailed the lies, concoctions and frame-up indulged in by the Special Cell. *The analysis of CDRs between the officers of the Special Cell as well as those of IB and the both the accused conclusively proved that these officials (of IB and Special Cell) for long had been in contact with the two. Secondly, it established the fact that the duo were actually police informers or worked as 'source' (mukhbir) for IB. Thirdly, it shows a close connection between the date and time of the disappearance of the accused and the switching off, of their principal mobile numbers in use. The police just could not explain why the mobile phones of the accused were switched off for two months prior to their arrest.* The CBI's investigation further threw up startling facts and raised many questions. There was no record or documentary proof to show that the two accused were members of terrorist outfit Al-Badr. *Some of the Delhi Police and Intelligence Officers admitted that indeed the two accused were working for them as 'informers'.* There were no independent witness to the seizure of arms and ammunitions, even thought the arrest and seizures were made in broad daylight at a fairly busy intersection on G.T. Karnal road. How is it that the two bus tickets of the alleged JKSRTC were not seized on February 9, 2006 (arrest day) during Irshad Ali's personal search? How could the bus tickets be recovered from him next day, i.e. February 10, 2006? Moreover, the driver and conductor of the alleged JKSRTC bus (JK 02Y 0299) were not examined and their statements not recorded.

According to the police story arms and ammunitions recovered from the accused were delivered by Sheikh Pervez and Faiyaz Ahmed Radar, both residents of Batmaloo, Srinagar. However, investigations by the CBI revealed that the Special Cell officers made no attempt whatsoever to locate and interrogate the two alleged arms suppliers. The police made no efforts to trace how the weapons reached the accused. Instead, what they did was to simply obtain Non-Bailable Warrants (NBWs) from a court and send it to the SSP, Srinagar for execution. These NBWs could not be executed and were returned due to incorrect or nonexistent addresses. The police team eventually did go to J&K for the ostensible purpose of conducting an investigation—this was at a much later date on June 22, 2006 and they found nothing.

CBI's investigations revealed that both the accused, after being 'picked up' by the police in December 2005 were "thereafter kept in illegal detention" till February 9, 2006 when they were shown arrested as alleged terrorists. The CBI observed that the recovery and seizure of arms and ammunitions from Maurif Qamar and Md. Irshad Ali by SI Vinay Tyagi and claimed to have been witnessed by SI Subhash Vats and Ravinder Tyagi, "is false and that false evidence/record has been fabricated to implicate Irshad Ali and Muarif Qamar for an oblique motive." The CBI's Closure Report submitted in the court of the Additional Session Judge, S. S. Mohi on November 11, 2008 **categorically stated that far from being Al-Badr terrorists as alleged by the Special Cell, the accused were innocent men, framed and falsely implicated in the entire case by the Special Cell, which had planted fabricated evidence on these men.** The CBI recommended legal action against SIs Vinay Tyagi, Subhash Vats and Ravinder Tyagi for fabricating evidence and planting incriminating evidence.

These startling revelations brought into open the way in which such 'special' security agencies operate: kidnapping, framing innocents, planting pistols and explosives, and justifying their high-handedness in the name of fighting 'terror'. There is an aspect of it which is even more heinous—they are so immoral that they betrayed even those who had faithfully served them risking their lives for the nation. Such things happen at the behest of the police leadership even if it is only the subordinates who get punished because they are directly involved.

10. State vs. Gulzar Ahmed Ganai and Md. Amin Hajam

[FIR No.: 95/06, Police Station: Special Cell, Under Sections: 121/121-A/122/123/120-B IPC; 4 and 5 Explosive Substances Act and Unlawful Activities (Prevention) Act 2004, Sessions Case No.: 13/2007, Date of Judgement: November 13, 2009]

One proof of the intellectual bankruptcy of the police and their leadership is that they cannot even cook up new stories for every new case. They repeat the same old stories all over again. And if they ever try to be smart, they sure mess it up. In this case, the police claimed that one Md. Akmal, code named Abu Tahir, a resident of Pakistan and District Commander of the banned militant organisation LeT, had been sending his associates from Jammu & Kashmir to Delhi and other parts of India in order to collect arms, ammunitions and explosives as well as funds through hawala channels for terrorist activities—in short the whole gamut of terrorist activities. It was further claimed that one Mustafa had been sent by Abu Tahir to Delhi to indulge in terrorist activities and that Mustafa along with his associate would arrive from Dhaula Kuan by bus at Mahipalpur and would proceed to their hideout. As usual, the arrests were made.

One of the accused was identified as Gulzar Ahmed Ganai @ Mustafa; the second as Md. Amin Hajam. The recoveries were claimed to be two plastic lunch boxes: one with 8 slabs and the other with 7 slabs of yellow-coloured oil-based explosive from the bag of Gulzar; Md. Amin Hajam's shoulder bag was claimed to contain two silver coloured non-electric detonators wrapped in cotton which were placed inside white coloured socks; 12 wads of Rs. 500 each, containing 100 currency notes totalling Rs. 6 lakhs. It was proved in the court that the two accused were not arrested on December 10, 2006 but almost two weeks prior to that, i.e. on November 27, 2006 as they had come to Delhi for an excursion. They were kept in unlawful detention, beaten, tortured and then falsely implicated in this case. One Md.

Iqbal even testified that he was arrested by the Special Cell on November 27, 2006 and while he was in custody, he had met both of them on November 28 and thereafter for the next four or five days.

Many other holes were punctured in the police story. There was actually no bus service to the place on the day of arrest. None of the members of the police party presented as prosecution witnesses could describe the place of occurrence in a convincing manner—despite their claims that they remained at the spot for more than seven hours. *(How dumb they are?)* According to the police, the two accused had collected the explosives, detonators and the amount of Rs. 6 lakh from a hawala operator in Mumbai. There was not an iota of evidence as to how or in what manner the accused persons came from Mumbai and on which date. **Such information could have easily been obtained from the railways or the airlines, if such travel actually took place, concluded the Court, thus casting aspersion on the whole story.**

The prosecution also claimed that the accused were proceeding towards their hideout when apprehended but could not lead the police to their hideout. The Court termed this 'unfathomable'. Commenting on the casual investigation, the Court asked: "**So I wonder was it human mistake or something else. The moot point is: were the mistakes pointed out above bona fide or mistakes committed while attempting to cook up the entire story? These are the doubts which the prosecution fails to explain. It doesn't need divine eyes to see that when there are two views possible, the one favouring the accused should be adopted.**"

11. State vs. Imran Ahmed and Anr.

[FIR No.: 89/06, Police Station: Special Cell, Under Sections: 121/121-A/122 r/w 120B IPC; 17/18/20 of Unlawful Activities Act and Section 5 of Explosive Substances Act, Sessions Case No.: 32/2007, Date of Judgement: 26 April 2011]

The same old story was repeated in this case also. The police claimed that as learnt from secret information received from a central intelligence agency, a militant, code-named Khalid belonging to the LeT, had set up base in Delhi to channelize funds through hawala for the purpose of terrorism. The inputs revealed that the actual name of Khalid was Altaf and that his brother Imran, residing in Dwaraka, was collecting and transferring funds for terrorism under his instructions. Well, arrests were made and the usual recoveries of cash and explosives were claimed.

The Court emphasized that the prosecution had failed to place before it any "specific evidence, either oral or documentary or in any electronic form" that "could show that both or either of the accused are members of LeT or had any proximate or otherwise nexus with this organisation." **The Court further asserted that "just because a handful of police official of Special Cell of Delhi Police have given a tag of LeT Terrorists to two citizens of our country, this does not become a conclusive proof of their being terrorists...**The agency making such accusation is supposed to have substantive pieces of evidence..."

The Court raised some very uncomfortable questions: Why was Inspector Sharma not made a witness? While all witnesses deposed that Inspector Mohan Chand Sharma was assigned to the operation on and before November 16, 2006, his name was not even mentioned in the list of witnesses. The Court observed that the non inclusion of the name of Inspector M. C. Sharma in the list of witnesses could indicate only one thing: the "*Special Cell was not desirous of exposing this witness for the rigours of cross examination qua methodology and technology adopted in developing the claimed intelligence input.*" "**The clandestine manner in which the senior officers shirked from their role of taking over the investigation and becoming a witness in this case despite heading the entire operation", the Court concluded, "smacks that something was seriously amiss in the whole story."**

Once again, the fact that the Special Cell made no effort to ensure the presence of public witnesses in their operation, despite there being three hours between the supposed receiving of secret information at 3.30 p.m. and the alleged apprehension of the accused at 6.30 p.m., is "**indicative of the fact that the team was not keen at all in joining any public witness.**" *The use of private vehicles, the Court noted with displeasure, did not allow the Court to examine the log books of the Special Cell vehicles*. The investigation came to a grinding halt after the arrest, with the **Special Cell making no effort to trace the source of monies or explosives seized**. The Cell made no attempt to visit Imran's home in Dwaraka, or the company that employed him, or Ghulam's home in Azadpur. Most strikingly, the Special Cell did not engage the services of any explosives expert, which only proved in the Court's eyes that "Special Cell was not interested in joining any other person apart from its Special Cell team member." **In the absence of expertise, the Court wondered how, the Special Cell could claim in the rukkaa that black and white granulated material recovered from accused Ghulam was actually an explosive**. This material was sent to CFSL Laboratory after unexplained delay of 14 days on November 30, 2006.

While acquitting the two accused, the Court concluded that the

operation of the Special Cell had been clandestine, lacked transparency, violated all established legal norms and did not inspire confidence at all.

12. State vs. Md. Mukhtar Ahmad Khan

[FIR No.: 48/07, Police Station: Special Cell, Under Sections: 121-A/123/120-B IPC and 18/20/23 of UAP Act and 4/5 of Explosive Substances Act, Sessions Case No.: 48/07, Date of Judgement: April 21, 2012]

As usual, the police story was that secret information was received by Special Cell of Delhi Police that Abu Musab @ Tahir and Abu Hamza, both residents of Pakistan and District Commanders of LeT at Kupwara and Baramula in J&K, planned to carry out terrorist activity in Delhi on the directions of their Pakistan-based Chief Commander Abu Al Kama. Their plans were to be carried out by Mukhtyar (or Mukhtar), a native of Kupwara in J&K. This guy was arrested with the claimed recovery of 15 slabs of yellow-coloured oil-based explosive material (1.5 kg), two silver-coloured electronic detonators and one black-coloured timer besides, clothes, toothpaste, brush, etc. *(There is a universal agreement amongst terrorists that they would use these things only and if they did not, their licence to practise terrorism would be revoked by the ISI, Al Qaida, LeT or whatever.)*

The whole case was set into motion as a result of the so-called secret information received by the Special Cell in May 2007. The Court was surprised then that there was no specific date, time and place of receipt of such information in the records placed before it. Surely, the Court observed, the police were aware of the legal requirements of recording such information in writing. Not only is this a legal necessity but also a "harbinger of safety and fair play". ***Taking a very strict view of this failure of the Special Cell, the Court inferred "that either the story of receipt of input was introduced subsequently according to what suited the IO or else the inputs received were of different nature which was not placed on record as they might not had suited the line of investigation." The Court concluded that "there is something seriously amiss either with the claimed secret inputs or with the functioning of Special Cell."***

The Court first noted that "***no specific evidence, either oral or documentary or in any electronic form has been placed, proved or relied on record which could show that accused is a member of LeT or had any proximate or distant nexus with this organisation.***" Mukhtar's phone was claimed to have revealed the phone numbers of Abu Hamza, Abu Musab and Abu Saad, ostensibly, LeT leaders. The Court said: "*There is nothing on record to show that this phone belongs to the accused or was ever used by him for talking to any other member/ commander or Chief of LeT." Moreover, these numbers were operational in the State of J&K and not in Pakistan, whereas the chargesheet stated that the three LeT Commanders and Chief were residing in Pakistan and not in India.*

The Court threw out the charges made under Section 46 and 20 of UAP Act against Mukhtar. "***Just because a couple of Police Officials of Special Cell of Delhi Police have so deposed in their statements in the Court, accused Mukhtar cannot be given the tag of LeT Terrorist in the absence of any conclusive proof in this regard.***" Absolutely, they never made any attempt to take the accused to J&K to track and nab the source of the explosives during the police remand. Neither was any effort made to trace Shabir, who was supposed to receive the consignment of explosives from Mukhtar. The Court also noted that despite the claim of seizing 15 individual sausage shaped mounds of explosives, only 10 g each was lifted from two packets and sent for testing. Such a sample cannot establish conclusively that the entire 1.5 kg of material was explosive. The sample from the seized material was sent for testing only after a month, in violation of all settled legal norms—raising suspicions of tampering.

Above all, the so-called explosives expert examined by the Special Cell was only qualified in Physics and was not even a Chemistry Graduate! No wonder then that the report submitted by him was cryptic and did not indicate the purity percentage of explosives in the sample. He was not even aware of the classification of explosives into different classes under Schedule I of the Explosive Rules! All he knew was that explosives were of two types: high and low explosives! Further, the tests conducted by CSFL were primitive and obsolete. The Court felt it unsafe to rely on the "expertise and opinion" of the expert. The so-called forensic expert conceded that he prepared the report only on those parameters as dictated by the IO, failing to check the said sample for its strength, density, intensity, velocity, quality, temperature and percentage of its composition. The Court thus also questioned his independence.

Moreover, even though the expert was qualified in Physics and not in electronic devices and gadgets, he was made to give his opinion about the claimed detonators and timer. **The Court had "no hesitation in concluding that Expert Report appears to have been clandestinely prepared in a hurried manner without adhering to statutory rules and as such score very low on reliability scales."** The Court dismissed the prosecution contention that Mukhtar was setting up a terror base in Delhi. The valid passport, visa and ticket indeed prove that he was innocent rather than guilty. Simply because the accused was desirous of visiting Pakistan in order to see his relative and attend a marriage there, he could not be looked upon as a terrorist. Why was there no attempt made to trace Abu Musab, Abu Hamja and Abu Al Kama, alleged kingpins of LeT, whose names appear in the chargesheet? "**This goes on to show that these names were added in the investigation only to give colour to this case.**"

13. State vs. Md. Iqbal @ Abdur Rehman, Nazarul Islam @ Madhu and Jalaluddin @ Hamid @ Babu Khan

[FIR No.: 23/08, Police Station: Special Cell, Under Sections: 121, 121-A/122/123/120-B IPC, 18/20/23 UAPA; 4 and 5 Explosive Act, Sessions Case No.: 09/2009, Date of Judgement: November 19, 2009]

The police story was that in the first week of May 2008, intelligence inputs were received from a central intelligence agency that Pakistan trained outfits like Jaish-e-Mohammad and LeT along with HuJI of Bangladesh were conspiring to cause large-scale terror activities in Delhi. One Qamar @ Nata (allegedly a commander of HuJI) was planning to send trained terrorists of LeT to Delhi. One Abdur Rehman had been specifically asked to cause blasts in the capital city by Qamar @ Nata. This information was also supposedly revealed in the course of the interrogation of Jalaluddin who was in the custody of the UP police, arrested in connection with the Varanasi bomb blasts and other such blasts in the state. The secret information received by the Special Cell was not reduced into writing, and yet the officers deposing before the court could reproduce it verbatim after three years during the course of the trial. This was, in the Court's own words, "difficult to digest".

Abdur Rehman was arrested and the police claimed that he led them to the recovery of 3.1 kg RDX, a DCBA green-coloured timer and 5 silver detonators. During the course of investigation, Jalaluddin (in Lucknow jail) and another person, Nazrul Islam (then lodged in Jaipur Jail) were interrogated, and ultimately arrested in this case. **It was noted by the Court that no evidence was placed before the Court or recorded which would connect the accused with material or criminal conspiracy to wage war against the state**. Since Jalaluddin and Nazrul were in Lucknow and Jaipur prisons respectively at the time of their arrest, obviously no occasion to conspire could even have arisen. The only 'evidence' that the prosecution could produce were the disclosure statements that the accused belonged to terrorist organisation—and this confession was deemed inadmissible by Section 25 of the Evidence Act.

In this case, the FSL report confirmed the presence of RDX explosives. But the Court noted that there was an inordinate and unexplained lag of 27 days in sending the samples of the recovered items to CSFL for testing. During this period, the seal was not handed over to the public witnesses but remained with the investigating officer. In these circumstances, tampering with samples and case property could not be ruled out. This cast a long shadow over the authenticity of police claims about the recovery made. The defence argued that the public witnesses at the time of the recovery of explosives were planted. The court also noted that at the time of apprehending the accused at around 9.00 p.m., the police had failed to enlist any independent member of the public as witness, not even railway employees; though the alleged apprehension took place near a railway station.

It seemed strange then that the police managed to engage public witnesses at midnight when they went to make the recoveries. According to the police, it was Inspector M. C. Sharma who received the secret tip off and it was he who led the operation to apprehend the accused, and again, it was he, who informed the ACP of the arrest. And yet, the Court wondered, the prosecution had not felt the need to even list him as a prosecution witness. Neither was any explanation offered for this inexplicable omission of Inspector Sharma. Thus the court concluded that the case against the accused, even under the Explosives Act could not be proved. It therefore acquitted Abdur Rahman.

2.5 Where and How the Police Leadership Fails in Such Cases?

As we have been repeatedly saying, the police leadership has such morons amongst its ranks that there is a scripted pattern in all such cases:

- Secret information, which can never be verified or disclosed, leads the police to the accused.
- Public and independent witnesses are rarely joined in the actual operation, even when the accused are shown to be apprehended in public places with people present.
- Private vehicles are used in the operation doing away with the need of logs thereby making it difficult to verify if any such operation did really take place.
- The time and date of the actual 'picking up' of the accused is revealed in the subsequent trial to be of a much earlier period than that alleged in the police story. Illegal detention, a recurrent feature, is sought to be hidden from the court through blatantly concocted narratives.

- Seizure memos are often made in the PS/Special Cell office, and not at the supposed time of seizure, often in the same handwriting and ink as the FIR.
- Senior officers are protected from appearing before the court by not making them witnesses.

The reason is that they are intellectually incapable of thinking anything better. This is not a new phenomenon. The police leadership has been like that since the past 150 years. The only thing is that no one had exposed them as we are doing here. In the colonial past and even after that, there was a set pattern of words used for booking people under Section 109 CrPC. In the Persian-laden language used in the Hindi belt, it read like: '*Ba-neeyat irtakave jurm apni maujoodagi chhipaaye huye tha. Talashi lene par ek chakoo adad, fal aahani dasta chobi baramad hua.*' That is, he had concealed his presence with the intention of committing crime. Upon search, he was found in possession of a knife with wooden handle and iron blade. Hundreds of thousands of people across the country were booked under Section 109 with these words—as if there was a universal agreement by some magical means amongst all of them located thousands of kilometres away that they would invariably conceal their presence and carry such-and-such knife only, and that he would be excommunicated from the fraternity if he did something else to become a victim of Section 109. *The same phenomenon is evident in the false cases related to terrorism also for intellectual bankruptcy remains the same.*

The issue is not that the prosecutions failed in these cases; the issue is that the prosecutions failed because the entire edifices were built upon falsehoods. The leadership failed in its basic duty. In all probability, they colluded with their corrupt and utterly immoral subordinates in cooking up such falsehoods. If they did not collude, they failed in preventing them from committing such horrible atrocities. Why the system should need and provide for supervisory officers when they cannot do such elementary things? These are all high-profile cases supposedly related to national security and not some run-of-the-mill case. It was all the more imperative that they should have paid full attention to them—they were sure seen on TV bragging about the arrests and their role in thwarting the ugly designs of the terrorists—*taaki aap chain kee neend so saken!* Bullshit! Did their responsibility end with that byte on the TV? Cases after case, the same mistakes were committed. Even a fool can see that they were not incidental—they were deliberate. And when mistakes are made deliberately, they are no longer mistakes; they become outright *gunaah,* atrocities. Fabrication and frame-ups are not aberrations; they are the very body or foundation on which the entire police leadership is built up.

There is a very elaborate system of supervision at various levels built into the functioning of the police. When it comes to claiming credit for the work of their subordinates, the senior officers are only too happy to garner TV time and speak in terms of 'we'. It follows that they are, in equal measure, responsible for all the terrible mistakes that are subsequently pointed out by the courts. It cannot be a case of *'meetha meetha gap, kadwa kadwa thoo'*. For the sake of argument, even if it is accepted for a moment that at least some mistakes took place because of the stupidity of the subordinates, it implicates the leadership further. Stupidity exists and proliferates only if the leadership lacks the intellectual acumen to point out ignorance amongst the subordinates.

A supervisory failure entails many things. May be they are not very careful or meticulous. More probably, they are professionally simply ignorant and hence are intellectually unable to correct the mistakes of your subordinates. To correct someone's mistakes you must know more than him. In reality, the crooked subordinates are found teaching them the 'tricks of the trade'. The police leadership gets very jittery when such sensitive issues are raised because it exposes the carefully hidden fact that they do not know anything. There used to be a stock scene in old Hindi films and is sometimes found even now. The SP sahib or the Commissioner sahib, as the case could be, is found shouting at his inspector: *'Main kuchh nahin jaanta, 24 ghante mein ise kaise bhi kar ke laaiye'*.

Well, a classic Freudian slip—he could subconsciously be speaking the truth—the poor fellow does not know how it is to be done, but all he wants is the results! In his scholarly work 'Hitler As Military Commander', Maj. Gen. John Strawson, chief-of-staff to SHAPE (Supreme Headquarters Allied Powers Europe) and one of Britain's most brilliant military analysts, concludes that if the blame of the defeat of Germany is to be thrown on Hitler, the credit for Germany's victories is also to be given to him—and, by God, they were the most impressive in the history of Europe since Napoleon! So is the case here. If you take the credit for cracking a case and hog the limelight on TV, you are also responsible for all the crookedness that the courts could find in it later.

This takes us to the issue of the role of the media in the whole thing. Most of the journalists are utterly dumb. However, in the context of the police leadership, it has been found that very often many a wrong is committed in the pursuit of playing to the gallery and pampering the media. *The ignoramuses in the media create a public perception. The investigating agencies, instead of trying to unravel the truth, find the easy way out and do such things that would bolster the perception created by the media. That keeps everyone happy.* ***Innocent people have been framed and are being framed for various reasons—to claim a breakthrough when none exits; to settle scores; to teach a lesson; to buy favours, to dispose of petty informers past their usefulness; to 'help out' colleagues in other parts of the country; to please political masters; for self-aggrandizement; to cover-up extortion or other sort of exploitation. Each one of them reflects a leadership failure. In the process, they utterly destroyed the lives of so many innocent citizens. The sheer immorality of the act is appalling. They should be meted out the most stringent of the punishments departmentally as well as through criminal courts so that at least retributive justice is satisfied.*** Further, for all such cases of false prosecution the nation must think of a comprehensive compensation and rehabilitation package in terms of the judgements of the Delhi High Court in **Tasleema vs. State of Delhi** [161 (2009) DLT 660] and **Prempal vs. Commissioner of Police** [W.P. (C) 11079/2006 dated March 25, 2010].

The Andhra Pradesh Government has already made a beginning in this regard. But remember that punishing some subordinate officers alone will not root out the problem for the malaise lies deeper. The real therapy must begin elsewhere. It is the IPS officers who have encouraged these monsters who destroy the lives of innocent people. It is the IPS officers who have failed to take any action against them. It is they who need to be punished.

Chapter 3

Boundless Barbarity in all that they do

3.1 The Manifold Ways of Tormenting the People

The evils that beset the police are legion. However, we would list the important ones amongst them.

- **Unhelpful Attitude and Refusal to Work**: The cops are not there to help you. This country has evolved in such a manner that the cops are identified with a system that is supposed to rule, not a system that is supposed to serve. One thing they know for sure, quite like greedy doctors, is that one who has come to them is a man in distress. His is in an emergency and he cannot afford to argue. One thing which they enjoy most is the feeling of being in power which they get when people in distress are forced to grovel before them for help. At a psychological level, making people grovel before them helps their deep-seated inferiority complex by making them feel superior. What is the role of the police leadership in this? *The police leadership has utterly failed in making their subordinates work for the people.* In fact, much of the so-called power of the police is derived from their refusal to do what they are bound by the law to do. Since the common man cannot afford to go the courts all the time, he is at the mercy of the cops. The police leadership makes his job all the more difficult. *The police leaders are guilty of not only in failing to punish their subordinates, but behaving in a manner worse than them.*

Meeting Barack Obama could perhaps be easier; meeting senior police officers in India is infinitely more difficult. One who doubts this statement has obviously not tried it himself. The first hurdle is to get an appointment because if you go without an appointment, you will be shown the door ASAP. Try calling them up on landline in office (the number which is given in the departmental websites), and you would be told by somebody in a pompous tone that the sahib is constantly in meeting; or that he has gone in the *ilaqa* for God knows what. If the PA is somewhat educated, he would whisper that the *sahib* is 'on the conference table'! The so-called 'field officers' are found perpetually patrolling their jurisdiction (*ilaqa*) like artificial satellites—they are *field officers* and hence do not sit in the offices. Their cell phone numbers are almost a state secret but if you manage to get the number somehow and call on that, they have a simple solution for it—they simply do not pick up any calling number which they have not saved in the memory of the phone. The numbers which they have saved are those that matter to them—either their masters or those who oblige them. Send an SMS and they won't reply to it. If by mistake someone does happen to pick up the cell phone, he would growl menacingly 'I am in a meeting' and hang up. Try calling the residence and some stupid orderly would tell you that the *sahib* is in the bathroom. All senior officers suffer from *bahumootra* and spend a great deal of their time on the pot.

- **Conditional Dispensing of Service**: How can you make the cops work, if at all they may be made to work? There are only two ways. There are only two fuels that make this engine purr. The Indians are intimately familiar with both. It is either bribe or some recommendation or pressure from some quarter; politician, senior officer or whatever. Money is a simpler procedure. If you can, you must pay them. There is one problem with bribing, though. No, no, it is not related to vigilance or anti-corruption bureau. It is about the weight of money. *Once upon a time, the cops used to take bribe from one party and would do their work. Now they take money from both parties and do the work of that party which pays more. In other words, it is simple auction – the cops' services go to the highest bidder.* Bribing is therefore not a guarantee that your work will be done. The other option is to bring some pressure from somewhere—from anybody who is heavier than the cop—

get hold of some stupid *neta* (after all, that's their basic business), businessman (cops are often friendly with them because they pay so well and can also oblige in many other ways, such as lending their farmhouse for a little fling on the side), senior officer, or whatever. But remember that the cops grudge it—they might do their work under pressure but would resent losing the money. The next time they could be hostile to you.

- **Refusal to Register FIR**: This is so common a malady that every Indian knows about it. But we would like to advise you one thing. Never—for God's sake never—commit the cardinal sin of quoting them the Supreme Court judgements in the cases of **Lallan Chaudhary and Ors. vs. State of Bihar and Anr.** [on October 12, 2006, Appeal (Crl.) 1047 of 2006], **Aleque Padamsee and Others vs. Union of India and Others** [(2007) 6 SCC 171], and **Ramesh Kumari vs. State (NCT of Delhi) and Others** [(2006) 2 SCC 677] etc. that when a cognizable offence is disclosed, the SHO is duty-bound to register it—he is not doing you a favour. By God, if you do that, the cop might chuck you out and tell you to go to the Supreme Court and get it done from there. The cops have very fragile egos; you see—don't ever touch it. How are you going to raise the money to fight it out in the Supreme Court? And please remember, the senior officers would never help you. They would rather tell you that the SHO is conducting a preliminary inquiry to verify the veracity of your allegations. You may also be given a free lecture on the workload of the police and how they must prioritize. In fact, so used are the people to such atrocities of the police that their expectations from the police are consistently falling. Earlier, people used to get satisfied when police arrested somebody powerful or resourceful—that was justice enough to satisfy people who would not follow the trial or live long enough to see the result of it. If you have been reading about the investigation of all the scams these days, you would have noticed that now the people are satisfied even if the police merely question the powerful or resourceful—they know that nothing more would be done to them by the police.

- **Apathetic or Hostile Attitude**: Supposing the cops somehow agree to do your work. Thereafter your eyes will be opened to some unparalleled apathy. Yours might be the most heart-rending story but the cops remain unperturbed like Gautam

Buddha himself. Even in a rape case, they would try to persuade you to not lodge a complaint and enlighten you about the loss of social prestige that would ensue if you lodge the complaint. He is, of course, in no hurry. More often than not, he would pretend that he has to attend to some more important work and he would attend to your work only after that. Eventually, when your turn comes, the first thing he would do is to doubt the very veracity of your complaint. You must be telling a lie. If your matter is indeed serious, he would make you feel guilty for having landed in that problem or for having been a victim in the first place. At long last and may be several days later, when it comes to investigation, he would intimidate you with all sorts of procedural hassles—repeated visits to the police station for nothing in particular, recording of statements, and so on—to such an extent that you would regret having filed a police complaint in the first place. The failure of the police leadership lies in the fact that in spite of all this being too well-known and actually a butt of jokes in literature and films, they have done nothing at all to improve the situation.

- **Tweaking the Investigation**: Most people, who do not know the *andar ki baat* of the police, become happy at the police somehow registering an FIR. That's an illusion, my dears. For the common man, that's the end of it. But the job is not done yet—*picture abhi baaqi hai, mere dost!* The secret of the police lies further ahead—in what they do in the investigation and write in the case diary. Well, the courts could force them to register a FIR. But the courts cannot force them to conduct the investigation properly. The courts can comment on the investigation only after it is complete or in certain special cases, if the courts are monitoring the investigation. So the cops have complete freedom in what they call 'shaping the investigation'. As we have explained elsewhere also in the book, officers and crooked old-timers are highly valued for this skill. They are skilled in changing the entire course of investigation by doing certain things or not doing certain things—questioning some witness or not questioning him; creating bogus or 'stock' witnesses, sending something for forensic examination or not sending it; pressurizing the doctors to tweak the post-mortem reports (there have been instances when bullet wounds have been shown as those caused by spears—collapsing the whole case); 'planting' some evidence; destroying some evidence; and tutoring witnesses; etc. Never mind, such tweaking might get exposed later in the court but the damage is already done.

- **Abuse of Power, the Laws and the Legal Processes**: This country has more than 2000 laws, major and minor combined. There is not a single book in the country which has got all these laws in it. Then there are several thousands of judgements on most of them. Learning them all would require an extraordinary effort. Hence, even if you were interested in knowing the law, chances are that it is indeed possible to book you for the violation of some law. But the cops abuse the powers vested in them, the laws and the legal processes in more sinister ways. Later in the book you would find a whole chapter on this. Here suffices it to say that they can make your life miserable by getting you entangled in a legal cobweb in such a manner that you will have only four options left. And mind you, proving mala fide on their part is very difficult, time-consuming and costly. The first is to bribe them and get rid of the problem. The second is to suffer in silence and blame your *karma*. If you want to fight the injustice, the third option is to sell every last article in your house to pay some advocate—relief is still not guaranteed, however. The fourth is to commit suicide and hope the next life would be better. *Remember, the cops are not there to uphold the law; they are there to abuse the law. They are not the defenders of the law; they are the abusers of law.* We will explain with an example. You see, the primary objective of a private hospital is to fleece you and make money; that you might, by sheer chance or the Grace of God, get treated is only incidental. So is the case with the cops. *Their primary purpose is to make money and ingratiate themselves in many other ways; that, in the process, they might happen to oblige someone with money or recommendation, is purely incidental.* When it hurts their illegal earning, the cops become outright animals. In September 2010, a woman police officer of the rank of SP, Kalpana Saxena was dragged by her own subordinates in full public view on a busy Bareilly road, leaving her profusely bleeding because she had objected to extortion by three policemen in the name of routine traffic checking.

- **Implicating in False Cases:** With both the print as well as the electronic media abuzz with discussions on internal security almost every day and a generally vitiated internal security atmosphere with some terrorist attack taking place in some corner of the country, there is nothing easier than whipping up paranoia. The media and the cops would have you believe that sleeper-cells of the terrorists are everywhere, ready to be 'awakened' on a phone call from their handlers in Pakistan. *This means that there is nothing easier than implicating you on a false terror charge.* The police have a host of illegal firearms with them which they would plant on you and the media, ever so keen on sensationalizing everything would wholeheartedly support the juicy titbits dropped by the police. Rest assured, as we have consummately shown in another chapter, your life will be screwed for several years. You may recall the **case of Liyaqat Shah**. In March 2013, the Special Cell of Delhi police claimed that Liyaqat, a J&K resident, was apprehended from Indo-Nepal border area and had told his interrogators that he was a trained militant of the banned terror group Hizbul Mujahideen and was settled in Muzaffarabad in Pakistan Occupied Kashmir (POK). Liyaqat, on the other hand, claimed that he had come to surrender under the Jammu and Kashmir Government's rehabilitation policy. Both the J&K Government and the IB vigorously supported his version. With the integrity of the Delhi police clearly suspect in the matter, the case was handed over to the NIA. The Court granted him bail in May after the NIA probe did not find anything against him. The Delhi police claimed to have seized an assault rifle, several grenades, maps and dry fruits from a hotel in old Delhi where Liyaqat's would-be host had supposedly left them before running away. Late in June, the NIA found that even the CCTV footage which the Delhi police had submitted in its support was damaged. On June 05, in the Meeting of the Chief Ministers with the Prime Minister on Internal Security, the J&K Chief Minister Omar Abdullah took strong exception to the misdeed of the Delhi police and demanded stern action against them for implicating Liyaqat falsely and thereby jeopardizing the surrender policy of the Government. Here was a man coming to surrender as permitted by the Government and he was arrested for going to launch spectacular terror attacks in Delhi just before Holi? And is there anything easier than planting weapons?

- **Outright Illegal Acts:** There are many. One of the most prevalent is illegal detention. Every poor fellow in this country knows that the police can detain him in the police

molested or raped outright. In one case, the cops were so crooked that they raped the woman at her home and then produced her blood and semen stained innerwear for the man in custody to see. In another case, they produced the innerwear of a man's daughter for him to see.

- **Ill-Treatment of Friends or Relatives of a Man in Custody or Suspect**: A 'milder' version of the above, in which the male relatives of a man in custody or suspect are illegally detained, harassed or tortured.
- **Fake Encounters**: Once again, every Indian knows about fake encounters. Because the cops are dumb, they still concoct the conventional stories. Information was received that terrorists were hiding in such-and-such place or moving in such-and-such car to mount a deadly terrorist attack. Police party rushed there. The terrorists fired on them. The fire was returned and the terrorist died. Upon search, and AK rifle or Tokarev pistol (which the illiterate police officers call Star pistol, after the Star of the Soviet Union embossed on it), some ammunition, cash, dry fruits, a map of India or that town and terrorist literature was found from his possession. That terrorist could very well be you. You will be killed in cold blood and the cops will get medals. In many other cases, they do not bother to cook up so much of a story—you can be simply made to 'disappear' from the face of the earth—usually very much dead. If some questions are asked, they can very well say that they have no idea and for all they know, you might as well have renounced the world and become a *sadhu* in the Himalayas. There have been so many "disappearances" in Kashmir that there is now a term for women with missing husbands: they are called "half widows".

The ultimate blame for all such horrendous practices falls on the police leadership in general and the IPS officers in particular. The information given here is not a secret. Every poor Indian knows them and has suffered them in varying degrees. The police leadership cannot claim that they do not know these things. If they say so, they must be kicked hard on their ample derriere. Since they know it, and since such things continue to take place, it can only lead to the inference that they have failed to curb them. There are several reasons for their having failed—the most important of them is that they lack the moral authority to do so. They have been so intimately involved in the misdeeds of their subordinates and so corrupt that they lose all moral authority to take any action against the subordinates except in those cases where there is an outcry in the media. Quite often you would find the subordinates speaking of *upar se order*. Yes, they are correct. Orders for most illegal things are implicitly, if not explicitly, given by the senior officers. It is a different thing that when things heat up, they deny everything. It is only recently that an alert judiciary has started making them feel the heat of the law.

3.2 The Supreme Court Takes Notice of the Police Atrocities

Nandagopal, nothing but a suspected thief, was in illegal police custody in Annamalai Nagar in Tamil Nadu on suspicion of theft from May 30, 1992 till June 6, 1992. The cops beat him to death there, and also gang-raped his wife. The policemen had subjected his wife to repeated gang rape right before him with some women police personnel of the police station turning a blind eye to the deeds of their male colleagues. While dismissing the appeal by accused policemen Mahboob Batcha and others, a **Division Bench of Justices Markandey Katju and Gyan Sudha Misra** of the honourable Supreme Court described the conduct of the police as barbaric and said, "The graphic description of the barbaric conduct of the accused in this case shocks our conscience." Opining that murder by the police in their custody is "rarest of rare crime entailing death sentence," the Court said, "If ever there was a case which cried out for death penalty it is this one, but it is deeply regrettable that not only was no such penalty imposed but not even a charge under Section 302 Indian Penal Code (murder) was framed against the accused by courts below."

The Supreme Court warned the police that acts of custodial violence will not be tolerated as they cannot behave like the "oppressors of the people". The Division Bench of Justices Markandey Katju and Gyan Sudha Misra, while warning the police, said, "***Policemen must learn how to behave as public servants in a democratic country and not as oppressors of the people***". The court also directed that a copy of its order be sent to home secretaries and directors general of police of all states and union territories. They shall circulate the same to all police officers up to the level of station house officers with a directive that they should desist from indulging in custodial violence, the Court said.

NGOs 'Extra-Judicial Execution Victims Families Association of Manipur' through Neena N. and 'Human Rights Alert' through Babloo Loitongbam had requested the court to set up a Special Investigation Team to inquire into the extra-judicial killings in the state. Another petition by Suresh Singh through advocate S. Biswajeet Meitei alleged that continuance of AFSPA had led to a spurt in extra-judicial killings and sought its withdrawal from Manipur. In response to Manipur's alleged unaddressed extra-judicial killings, the NHRC in an affidavit said in the last five years, from 2007 to 2012, it had received 1,671 complaints/information regarding fake encounters. "The Commission in the last five years has awarded monetary compensation to the tune of Rs. 10.51 crore in 191 cases," it said in an affidavit. The Commission awards compensation in the range of Rs. 5-10 lakh to the kin of victims if it comes to the conclusion after inquiry that it was a fake encounter. Though the Commission's guidelines require states to complete mandatory inquiry reports within three months, many cases of alleged extra-judicial killings reported from Manipur have been pending with the NHRC since 2007 as the state has not provided the key investigation reports. Of the 68 pending cases, five incidents dated back to 2007, 17 to 2008 and 19 to 2009, the NHRC said.

In December 2012, appalled by the attitude of the Manipur government in responding to over 1,500 alleged fake encounter killings in the militancy affected state in the last three decades, a **bench of Justices Aftab Alam and Ranjana P. Desai** asked, "Is there a war going on within? Is this the attitude and orientation of a state to say that if they are killing my men, we will kill them?" *The Supreme Court, in fact, asked the Centre whether Rs. 5 lakh compensation awarded by National Human Rights Commission to the family was the cost of killing a person in a fake encounter.* It said the NHRC's report on 1,671 complaints of fake encounters, in which it found 191 to be true, was distressing to say the least. In April 2013, the report of a Judicial Commission headed by former Judge of the Supreme Court Santosh Hegde to the Supreme Court held that six sample cases they examined out of 1671 cases were actually fake encounters.

In November 2012, the Delhi High Court ordered the acquittal of two men wrongly sentenced to death in the 1996 Lajpat Nagar market blasts case. *The Court said that the prosecution had gone beyond "lapses and inefficiencies" to produce evidence whose "nature and truthfulness" were in serious doubt.* In this case, the wrong done to Mirza Nissar Hussein and Mohammed Ali Bhatt was so enormous that when the higher court set it right, the two men found themselves dramatically transported from their condemned world of despair and death to full life and liberty. In their judgement, **Justices S. Ravindra Bhat and G.P. Mittal** *made it a point to rebut the oft-used excuse in terror cases that the nature of terrorism makes it difficult for the prosecution to meet the "impossible standards" of proof demanded by the courts: "In matters of liberty, the weakness of the state surely can't be an excuse for lowering time-tested standards, especially in serious crimes where the accused stand to forfeit their life..."*

In a judgement of great import delivered in October 2012, the **Supreme Court overturned 11 convictions** under the Terrorism and Disruptive Activities (Prevention) Act (TADA), rejecting the prosecution's plea that it had committed only a technical error in overlooking a key safeguard of TADA. The Court's answer to this was that in the land of Gandhi, the means were necessarily inseparable from the ends. ***Rather than going after innocents and building cases on evidentiary quicksand—as it appears they have been doing in many cases—investigative agencies prosecuting terrorist crimes must learn to rely on improved technical and forensic evidence.*** At the end of the day, that is the only way to prevent the escape of real terrorists.

In March 2013, a woman was thrashed by Punjab police constables when she had approached them along with her father for lodging a complaint against harassment by a truck driver and his accomplices in Tarn Taran district. In another incident, Bihar Police had resorted to a lathi-charge and fired tear gas shells during a protest by contractual teachers outside the Assembly in Patna demanding regularization of their jobs and pay parity with regular teachers. Taking strong exception to the incidents of police beating protesting contractual teachers in Bihar and 'an innocent and unarmed woman' in Tarn Taran in Punjab, the **Supreme Court sought explanation** from the two states on the conduct of police personnel. Taking suo motu cognizance of media reports, a bench of Justices G. S. Singhvi and Ranjana Prakash Desai directed the two state governments to respond on the allegations of police brutality. The Court order stated: "***The contents of the news items revealed that members of the Punjab Police and Patna Police have mercilessly beaten an unarmed woman and teachers. Both the incidents have shocked the conscience of the entire nation.*** Unfortunately, the administrations of the Governments of Punjab and Bihar have not taken adequate steps for protecting the people against the wholly unwarranted action taken by the police at Tarn Taran and Patna."

The Bench directed the Punjab DGP to file his own affidavit on the action taken against policemen. Punjab's counsel submitted that a magisterial inquiry was on and the two accused policemen have been suspended. "Are we using colour glasses? The inquiry should have been over in 24 hours. Millions saw it (on TV). Was the lady a terrorist that she was beaten on a highway? What can ever justify beating a helpless woman with a stick? Does it not shock you? If the government was sincere, all necessary steps should have been taken the next day," shot back the Court. The Bench also asked the Bihar DGP to "explain the rationale" of beating the agitating teachers. Also questioning the

"conscience" and "sensitivity" of society towards its women, the Court regretted that nobody came forward to help these women when they were being assaulted.

Concurring with Attorney General G. E. Vahanvati's submission that there was a "systemic failure" requiring the Court's intervention, the Bench said "accountability" of senior policemen would be a "primary issue." Senior advocates Harish Salve and U. U. Lalit, who are assisting the court as amicus curiae, also said that punishing lower-level policemen would not serve the purpose and senior officers must be made accountable. That's precisely what we have been arguing all along in the book—the fundamental problem lies with the police leadership; it is their failure.

3.3 Punjab: A Case Study of Police Atrocities

The police atrocities committed in Punjab cannot be forgotten or overlooked merely because terrorism there has ended or abated—the end can never justify the means. The 2003 Amnesty International report "India: Break the Cycle of Impunity and Torture in Punjab" summarized the tactics commonly employed by police officers in Punjab: "Civilians were often arrested solely for being related to or living in the same village as members of armed opposition groups. Such civilians were often placed on an unofficial blacklist circulated to all police stations and were liable to be arrested again after their release on any occasion when there was a militant action in the area. Arrests often occurred when a quick solution for a case was needed or simply to fulfil an 'arrest quota'. Arrest procedures were frequently not followed and the arrest was often not recorded in the daily log of the police station, thus remaining completely unofficial and leaving detainees vulnerable to further abuses.

Detainees were frequently moved from one police station to another, or to unofficial interrogation centres, making it difficult for their families and lawyers to trace them. Torture was widespread and used both as a substitute for investigation and as punishment. The police routinely disregarded court orders to bring detainees before a court, and judges were threatened to deter them from taking action against the police. When detainees died in police custody, the police organised the post-mortems and the cremations before any independent investigation could be carried out into the cause of death." When terrorism was at its peak during 1984-1996 in the State, police personnel, whether the so-called police leadership or the lower ranks, were a law unto themselves and a very large number of them were involved in merciless killing of youth by branding them as terrorists for rewards and promotions in fake encounters. The bodies were quietly and stealthily cremated with no questions asked. Perhaps nobody would ever know the number of people who were killed in this manner, but you can rest assured that it is very large—even by the very conservative estimates of the National Human Rights Commission (NHRC). In 1995, after human rights activist Jaswant Singh Khalra released official records exposing the mass secret cremations perpetrated by the Punjab police in Amritsar district, the Committee for Information and Initiative on Punjab (CIIP) moved the Supreme Court to demand a comprehensive inquiry into extrajudicial executions throughout Punjab [Writ Petition (Crl.) No. 447 of 1995, **Committee for Information and Initiative on Punjab vs. State of Punjab and Others**, April 3, 1995]. When the Punjab police went on to make Jaswant Singh Khalra himself 'disappear', the Supreme Court eventually ordered the Central Bureau of Investigation (CBI) to investigate these crimes [order of the Supreme Court dated November 15, 1995, Writ Petition (Crl.) No. 497 of 1995, **Paramjit Kaur vs. State of Punjab and Others,** with Writ Petition (Crl.) No. 447 of 1995].

The CBI submitted its final report on December 9, 1996 [Order of the Supreme Court dated December 11, 1996, Writ Petitions (Crl.) Nos. 497 and 447 of 1995] limiting its investigations to Amritsar district. The CBI's report, which the Supreme Court sealed, listed 2,097 illegal cremations at three cremation grounds of Amritsar district—then one of 13 districts in Punjab [Order of the Supreme Court dated December 12, 1996, Writ Petitions (Crl.) Nos. 497 and 447 of 1995]. In December 1996, ***the Supreme Court referred the mass cremations case to the National Human Rights Commission (NHRC), observing that the CBI's inquiry report disclosed a "flagrant violation of human rights on a mass scale."*** The Supreme Court also entrusted the CBI with investigations into the culpability of police officials in the secret cremations case leaving "all the issues which are raised before the Commission" to the NHRC [order of the Supreme Court dated December 12, 1996].

The NHRC, which went through 2,097 cases of killing of youth and mass cremation of their bodies by the Punjab police during the peak of militancy in the State, ordered a relief of Rs. 27.94 crore to the families of 1,513 victims of such extra-judicial killings. The remaining bodies were not identified. The cases related to mass cremations in Amritsar, Majitha and Tarn Taran districts alone between 1984 and 1994. These include 195 cases where the victims were in deemed police custody and 1,318 others whose bodies were cremated by the police. A total of 532 bodies remained unidentified despite efforts by the NHRC from the date of remittance in December 1996. As far as the murder of Jaswant Singh Khalra himself is concerned, his family and friends refused to give up. At long last, a sentence of life imprisonment for five officers was **upheld by the Supreme Court** on November 4, 2011, a full 16 years after Khalra was cold-bloodedly murdered in police custody. He was tortured at Police Station Jhabal and shot dead there and finally his body was disposed of by them near the Harike Bridge, in river Sutlej. Earlier, the Punjab and Haryana High Court had stated 'we have no hesitation in coming to a conclusion that deceased Jaswant Singh Khalra was picked up from his house at the instance of Ajit Singh Sandhu SSP (since dead) by appellants Jaspal Singh, Satnam Singh, Surinderpal Singh, Jasbir Singh and Prithipal Singh.

K. S. Dhillon, a former Director General of Police, Punjab, wrote in "Fake Encounters and the Indian State" in *The Hindu* that there is little legitimacy for the kind of killings police and other security forces have been resorting to lately. Expressing concern at the approbatory affirmations that had greeted the Punjab police for their brutal handling of Sikh militancy, he notes that indeed the Punjab police could not have employed the shockingly repressive measures in the centrally-ruled State unless its leadership was sure of its full backing of the state. A large segment of Indian society too approved of its tactics, despite its deeply tainted operational record of kidnappings, disappearances, extortions and brutal killings, which left thousands of Sikhs traumatised and disabled for life. In fact, the Punjab police are believed to have refined the art and science of fake encounters to near perfection, right up to ferrying alleged terrorists from far off places in vehicles with fictitious number plates to home ground and then bumping them off.

He adds that if Vanzara (of Gujarat police, Sohrabuddin Sheikh fake encounter case) and other such encounter specialists are found to have accumulated assets worth several crores, one has only to look around Chandigarh and its satellite towns to marvel at the mansions, farmhouses and holiday resorts that cropped up in the aftermath of Punjab militancy. Yet those nightmarish happenings in Punjab remain shrouded in a conspiracy of silence for obvious reasons, although they have become a veritable model for anti-terrorism and counter-terrorism strategies, spawning a culture of state terrorism and hard policing all over the country. He laments that South Asian political and bureaucratic establishments are not averse to promoting the belief that encounters, fake or otherwise, are an acceptable mode of combating terrorism, militancy, mafia crimes and other such organised and ruthless criminal activity. Encounter killings have, thus, not only acquired substantial acceptability among many otherwise fairly discerning members of our civil society, the so-called encounter experts are also greatly lionised in films and other media.

Though the waning of terrorism in Punjab is to be attributed to many factors, we could analyze how the fake encounter business worked, if it worked at all to any extent? Let us face it. The reality is that killing people indiscriminately in large numbers frightens a much larger number of people. This severely restricts the potential recruits to the ranks of terrorists or insurgents. There are but few terrorists who completely renounce their family connections. You kill their family members and this mounts great pressure on them—they are left with but few options—stop their activities altogether and go into hiding; surrender; or flee the country altogether. In effect, they are neutralized. It was simply terrorism in reverse.

3.4 Torture, Horrible Torture

3.4.1 *Condemnation by the Supreme Court*

Torture is pervasive and a daily routine in every one of India's states, irrespective of whether arrests are made by the police, the paramilitary forces or the army. In the case of **Mohan Lal Sharma vs. State of Uttar Pradesh** [1988 (3) Crimes 122 SC], the Chief Justice of India R. S. Pathak had said, "We are gravely concerned at the increasing number of deaths which are reported of persons detained in police lock-ups." *Does it not reflect on the incorrigibility of the police leadership that a quarter of a century later also, the problem remains where it was*? Some people try to obfuscate the issue by bringing in the issue of figures of custodial deaths. Clever design, but does not stand before us. In fact, we need not bother about the figures of custodial deaths—we are talking of custodial torture. There may be some dispute over the figures of custodial deaths.

Even if the figures of the Asian Centre for Human Rights (14231 custodial deaths in ten years between 2001 and 2010) be at variance with the official figures, you must realize that it is only in a small fraction of the incidents that the victims die to become a statistic of custodial deaths—torture per se is ubiquitous. In **Dalbir Singh vs. State of U.P. and Ors.** [on March 2, 2009, Writ Petition (Crl.) No. 193 of 2006], the Supreme Court admitted, "*The dehumanizing torture, assault and death in custody which have assumed alarming proportions raise serious questions about the credibility of rule of law and administration of criminal justice system. The community rightly gets disturbed.*" Police torture has been relentlessly, inevitably, inexorably taking place in this country

since ages regardless of the political persuasion of the party in power. There have been many instances in which torture has been inflicted at the behest of political parties or politicians. But in them the basic motivation is 'pleasing the master' and they could perhaps be even odd cases. **A majority of the cases of police brutality that takes place on a regular basis, however, originates because of organisational compulsions for which the police leadership is responsible.** The individual's aberrations go on to exacerbate the situation but the original impulses are mostly organisational. However, there are cops who are, by nature, sadists and they commit torture for the sake of torture because it gives them pleasure. Others often commence torture because, in their perception, they are only trying to do their official job better. However, even such a character, once he embarks on that path, the demon lurking in his subconscious takes over. That his victim may even die because he beat him up relentlessly, is the result of his personality disorder—it has nothing to do with the police organisation. **The failure of the police leadership lies in the fact that it has done nothing to dispel the misconception that torture is a better or expedient way of doing the official job, or that the superiors would be pleased with supposedly quick results produced by torture. It has also not done anything to spot and weed out cops with such personality disorders**.

Torture which starts as what some would call 'coercive persuasion', soon becomes an activity which the cops start enjoying. It is at this stage that their latent sadism comes to the fore. Cops indulge in torture because it gives them a feeling of complete domination over the victim. He does not merely inflict pain on the victim, but also tries to destroy his 'will', his self-respect, his ego, his defiance, and his value system. What he really desires is the victim to grovel before him—make an abject surrender. The more pain one bears without grovelling, the more torture he is likely to be subjected.

There is extensive evidence that senior police officers, (and sometimes even executive magistrates in league with them), doctors and other state officials cooperate in the cover-up of such crimes or shield the police officers responsible from being brought to justice. Commenting on the brutal murder of a farmer in police custody for refusing to pay bribes to a police constable, the honourable Supreme Court had held in the case of **State of Uttar Pradesh vs. Ram Sagar Yadav and Ors.** [1985 AIR 416], "Police Officers alone, and none else, can give evidence as regards the circumstances in which a person in their custody comes to receive injuries while in their custody. Bound by ties of a kind of brotherhood, they often prefer to remain silent in such situations and when they choose to speak, they put their own gloss upon facts and pervert the truth. The result is that persons, on whom atrocities are perpetrated by the police in the sanctum sanctorum of the police station, are left without any evidence to prove who the offenders are. The law as to the burden of proof in such cases may be re-examined by the legislature so that hand-maids of law and order do not use their authority and opportunities for oppressing the innocent citizens who look to them for protect on. It is ironical that, in the instant case, a person who complained against a policeman for bribery was done to death by that policeman, his two companions and his superior officer, the Station House Officer." The Chief Justice made this observation after the Allahabad High Court had acquitted certain police officers of torturing to death a suspect in Uttar Pradesh on the grounds that there was insufficient evidence to prove the case beyond reasonable doubt.

The most serious failure of the police leadership lies in the fact that their first reaction is to deny what is known to be true to almost everybody in the country—that it is not happening in their jurisdiction—well, if it is not happening in everyone's jurisdiction, and yet if it is happening everywhere, you are obviously telling a plain lie. *By denying that torture occurs and failing to condemn it; by denying to even listen to complaints of torture; by failing to ensure that legal safeguards against torture are adhered to as a matter of routine; by failing to ensure that proper investigations are conducted into alleged human rights violations; by failing to constantly monitor what their subordinates do; by failing to punish the misdeeds of the subordinates; and by taking part in the cover-ups, generations of police leadership have to bear full responsibility for the persistence of a barbaric practice.*

3.4.2 *The Record of Castigation by the Courts Over Several Decades Confirms the Incorrigibility of the Police*

We would cite some old cases just to show that torture has been taking place since long and which proves that it is not only the current generation of police leadership which has failed; their predecessors had also failed in putting any check on this horrible practice. We have found that even those senior officers who would perhaps personally not torture someone, would not mind their subordinates doing so—a failure of leadership nevertheless. When Angadi Prabhakara Rao died in custody of the Chirala town police in Andhra Pradesh in April 1985, a **Judicial Commission** found that his death was a case of homicide and not suicide as the police had claimed. The Judge found that the executive magistrate, who had held an inquest into his death, was responsible for falsely certifying there were no visible injuries on the body of the victim. Instead, the Judge agreed with the report of the medical officer that there were 12 external injuries on his body and that the victim had died from blows on the stomach and the ribs. In October 1991 the **Supreme Court confirmed** such practices when it held that there were grounds to prosecute officials of the Department of Revenue Intelligence for causing the death of Ravi Narang, a 50-year-old businessman in their custody. Ravi Narang's widow had alleged her husband had been tortured to death and the Supreme Court ordered a District Judge to carry out an inquiry. His findings contradicted the inquest report of the executive magistrate which had attributed Ravi Narang's death to various causes including psychological shock, consumption of morphine, and a fight with another prisoner and a fall from the stairs. The Judge found that these factors did not cause his death, but that it was probably caused by shock "following a cobweb of injuries sustained through beating and torture".

Justice S. C. Deb, investigating the death of Mohammed Idris in Calcutta's Lal Bazar police station, had found that a doctor at Calcutta's Medical College Hospital had "falsely recorded that Idris had 'old' marks of abrasion on both wrist joints. He thus created false evidence which was not only an offence but was against his professional conduct" [**Deb Commission of Inquiry**, report published by West Bengal Government press, Alipore, 1989]. Justice Deb found that brutal injuries were inflicted on Idris at the time of interrogation. As reported in *The Telegraph* of October 3, 1991, the **Government of Andhra Pradesh** had suspended a civil surgeon of Karimnagar for issuing a false post-mortem report to "save the police". Uppuleti Chandraiah died in police custody on March 9, 1991 in the Husnabad police station. The police said that he had committed suicide. According to the fellow inmates he was beaten to death.

Falsification of medical records takes place much more frequently in non-fatal cases of torture. A **Supreme Court Commission** investigating allegations that Gunta Behn Ramji, a tribal woman from Gujarat, had been raped by police in January 1986 found sufficient evidence to conclude that four police officers and two doctors could be charged with "having hatched the conspiracy for destroying the evidence and thereby keeping the accused constables from being prosecuted in a court of law". Most Indians can recall one of the most notorious cases of police torture, the **Bhagalpur Blindings**, in which the police had blinded 33 young men (suspects and under-trials) over a period of one year (October 1979 to November 1980) in jail and in police stations by first piercing their eyes with a pointed object and then pouring acid into the mutilated sockets. Few of the 30 who were blinded had criminal records and, according to one commentator, no more than four had previously been charged with involvement in criminal activities. One victim, Suresh Sah, was apparently blinded as a punishment for refusing to work for low wages for local landlords. A police sub-inspector, a doctor and eight landlords were convicted in 1984 of a criminal conspiracy to blind him. Prakash Jha's film Gangajal was inspired by this ghastly incident—the police had reportedly told the victims that they were pouring Gangajal into their eyes to wash their sins. When the matter was taken to the Supreme Court amid nationwide outcry, a **bench headed by the then Chief Justice of India, Y. V. Chandrachud**, observed, "This court and the country awoke one day to the incredible fact that in Bhagalpur, undertrial prisoners were subjected to the most inhuman torture imaginable...There is nothing the court can do to restore the physical damage, which seems irreparable. But the offenders must be brought to book, at least in the hope that such brutal atrocities will not be committed again." Following a Supreme Court directive, each blinding victim was given a lump sum of Rs. 30,000 and, then, a monthly pension of Rs. 500 which was later enhanced to Rs. 750. In all, nine police officers were convicted for their part in blinding just five of the prisoners. No senior officer was prosecuted, although the CBI had reported that at least one had prior knowledge of the blindings and did not act to prevent them.

In **Kashmeri Devi vs. Delhi Administration and Anr.** [1988 AIR 1323], the appellant was the widow of a tonga driver Gopi Ram who had died in police custody. In 1986, two sub-inspectors accompanied by two constables visited the house of one Sudesh Kumar, and started beating him. On hearing his shrieks his maternal uncle Gopi Ram, tried to intervene whereupon the policemen beat him also. *Gopi Ram had been stripped and beaten with iron rods in the Patel Nagar police station, but the police had claimed that he had died of morphine and alcohol poisoning*! The Supreme Court, however, ruled that it was a prima facie case of deliberate murder of an innocent illiterate poor citizen of Delhi in police station and investigation was partisan.

Thiru Kathamuthu, aged 24 and a member of the All India Youth Federation and the Communist Party of India (CPI), was arrested in connection with a case of theft in the Union territory of Pondicherry. The day after his arrest in December 1986 he was taken to hospital with 94 percent burn injuries; he died shortly afterwards. The police claimed he had committed suicide by setting fire to himself, using matches and a kerosene stove. However, on September 7, 1989, eventually the **Supreme Court** agreed that he had died apparently on account of physical assault followed by burning of the body after drenching it with kerosene, and ordered prosecution against the concerned Station House Officer and constable of Dhanwantri Nagar Police Station. Senior police officers have frequently claimed that deaths in custody were the results of illnesses such as epilepsy, tuberculosis or heart failure, even when the victims were young and apparently healthy. In the case of T. Muralidharan, a navy man, the Vijayawada police claimed that an injury on his wrist was caused by rat bite! The lie was, subsequently, debunked by a **Judicial Commission**.

We are short of space here but interested readers can find a horrifying account of police torture from studies and publications like "Torture in India 2008: A State of Denial" [Asian Centre for Human Rights (ACHR)]; "Torture in India 2010" [ACHR]; "India: Break the Cycle of Impunity and Torture in Punjab" [Amnesty International, 2003]; and "Broken System: Dysfunction, Abuse and Impunity in the Indian Police" [Human Rights Watch (HRW)]. ***Readers must also keep in mind that the very few prosecutions that have occurred have almost invariably been the result of years of determined struggle by relatives of the victims seeking justice, rather than official initiatives by the police leadership to enforce the law and perform their bounden duty of securing justice for the people. If the Apex Court concluded that the investigation was partisan; it means that the superior officers had either colluded in the cover-up or it was an abject supervisory failure—they are responsible both ways.***

3.4.3 *The Demons Within and the Contrived Attempts to Justify Them*

As mentioned above, police torture is a complex phenomenon. Both organisational and psychological factors are involved in this and sometimes they get horribly mixed up. *Many police officers start believing that torturing is synonymous with being macho—a classical case of 'compensation' for their anxieties related to sexual inadequacy.*

A former editor of *The Washington Post,* Steve Coll, in his *work* 'On the Grand Trunk Road: A Journey Into South Asia' [p. 169] narrates how he had a revealing conversation with a very high ranking IPS officer who was hailed by the ignoramuses in the media as a 'super cop' in Punjab and was credited with eliminating terrorism in Punjab almost single-handedly. As Coll recalls, the top IPS officer downed at least seven whiskies in an hour. In his inebriated state he openly espoused a nihilistic outlook, viewing people as pawns of the state and the police as the essential tool for suppressing the rabble. In the sub-culture which the police have developed, excessive drinking is also regarded as a sign of being macho. Senior IPS officers just love to regale you with endless stories of how they used to go for fake encounters very early in the morning after a night-long orgy of hard drinking; and how this so-called super cop could finish a whole bottle of Black Label while driving from Chandigarh to Delhi. *A very curious justification offered very frequently by them is that the 'nature of the job' is such that it cannot be done without drinking*!

To say that the cops are 'control freaks' would be an understatement; they are actually power psychopaths. ***One of the most important things that drive them is the desire to wield absolute power over those who are bound by law into not resisting their illegal deeds. If they resist, they are branded outlaws. Thus, as far as the poor law-abiding citizens are concerned, it is a lose-lose situation.*** No class of people or category of society within India has ever been safe from the threat of police atrocities. As power go to their head, the definition of rabble mentioned by the so-called 'super cop' was 'liberalized'. Kirpal Dhillon, who became Director General of Police (DGP) in Punjab in July 1984, writes: "It was not only the masses who felt threatened by the activities of a lawless police—even judges, magistrates and senior IAS officers were apprehensive of their safety and well-being." For those who live on the fringes of society, only God can help for they lack both of the essential ingredient required to 'deal' with the police—money or 'connections'. *One of the anxieties consuming the police relates to social prestige arising out of an inferiority complex. Dumb and incompetent as they are, the police have no other claim to respect or authority. This makes them mortally afraid that abandoning their practices of torture and harassing the people through abuse of the process of law would result in a complete loss of the authority they wield.*

The intellectual bankruptcy of the police leadership lies in the fact that many of them try to even justify such inhuman deeds. Some of the facile excuses put forward include the following. That the police do such a high stress and filthy job—some deviation must be allowed for them. In fact, often they copy a dialogue from the films that the police have to deal with criminals and the scum of the society—this filth somehow rubs off on to them. That it is necessary to 'crack' cases. That it is necessary for national security. That but for it, you will never get prosecutable evidence. And finally, in a very condescending tone, they reveal that those 'academic types' who oppose it have no idea of how 'tough and complicated real policing' is. *In their perception, to be considered a 'practical' police officer, one must engage in all the illegal things including torture and extra-judicial killings. This is a sort of initiation rite in the Indian police sub-culture—you are formally inducted and acknowledged in the community only after you conform to their value system. Otherwise, you remain an outsider all your life.*

The oft-quoted excuses of bad working conditions, excessive workload, etc. are just not tenable and are a very poor attempt at hogwash. People live in this country in far worse circumstances. All of them do not become criminals. Similarly, the plea of short-cuts is not tenable. Those who advance it don't realize that if it were to be accepted, it would only lead to the conclusion that the leadership wants unrealistic results. The blame is, in any case, on the leadership. In fact, the argument amounts to saying that a poor man from a village working in a city and who lives away from his wife who lives in his village, is sexually deprived and hence he has no option but to become a rapist. Or, one who works hard in a factory but still finds it difficult to make ends meet has no option but to become a robber. As far as stress at work is concerned, we do not think that there is any job where there is no stress. Even the lowliest of the labourers is harassed to no end by his immediate supervisor. That's no excuse at all. *There are numerous occupations where working hours are longer. Still, they do not abuse the system – cops do.*

Police officers of all ranks have a very bad habit of misleading the aam aadami, the media and the academicians regarding their workload. It is all too common to hear that they work 24 hours a day and that if you bring an American policeman here, he would commit suicide in a day. One of us is an IPS officer and knows how farcical they are. The simple fact is that no human being can survive even a few days if he has to work for 24 hours a day – by God, it is a biological impossibility! Whom are they trying to fool? The reference to 'being on duty 24 hours' is true not only for the police but for all government servants. This phrase was found earlier in the Conduct Rules of government servants and is not to be confused with the Labour Laws that govern a factory worker regarding his working hours. *It only meant that a government servant shall not take up another gainful employment in his spare time.* However, government servants have a very despicable habit of misinterpreting it to project as if they are being exploited by the Government. The simple fact is that it only means that you are liable to be called for duty at any time and till such time that the 8-hour duty system is not formally enforced; you will not have a right to say that you are off-duty. The nature of the job of the police is such that, if there is a problem, it cannot wait for the concept of duty hours. The same thing applies to many other jobs as well – medical, paramedical, fire services, electricity department, irrigation department, you name it. Can the irrigation department afford to say that though there is a breach in an embankment threatening flash floods, they would not attend to it because they are off-duty? Can the electricity department afford to say that though there is a fire in the sub-station, they would not attend to it because they are off-duty? In the normal course, everybody gets adequate time to rest and discharge their family responsibilities. Problems do not crop up every day. *It is utter nonsense to say that the cops do not get any time for themselves or their families – they might actually be indulging in some perverse activities like extortion, whoring, torture etc. Such facile arguments may fool those academicians who do not know the police system inside out – not us.*

Similarly, blaming the colonial laws and various other colonial legacies for the horrible practices of the police is farcical. Yes, we are aware, how they influence and are responsible for many ills (such as the unwanted semi-military character; being the coercive arm of the power in place; the deep-rooted notion of being a part of the ruling system; disconnect from the people; physically isolating them in barracks; etc.)—but that's precisely the point. *The police leadership has summarily failed in even raising a demand that the colonial hangover ought to be corrected – simply because they are intellectually bankrupt.* The Law Commission of 1994 did point out that while a confession made by a person in police custody in not admissible in court of law as evidence under Section 25 of Indian Evidence Act. Section 27 lays down that if a person in the custody of a police officer makes a statement leading to the discovery of a fact, the same is admissible, whether or not it amount to confession. This generates an itch for extracting confession through torture. ***The point being made is that why is it that it was for the Law Commission to point it out—for something that has been there since 1872, why is it that generations of IP/IPS officers had not pointed it out? Either they must admit that they have been so dumb that it never occurred to them, or they must admit that they have been approving of torture.***

It takes both moral and intellectual courage to stand up against a system which is unjust. The police leadership obviously lacks everything needed to think on its own. This results in an obsessive desire to somehow come to 'belong' to the system. That's how the system gets perpetuated. ***The police sub-culture is nothing but demonic in which the most brutal get the most accolades and medals; are lauded as macho, super cop and what not; and do rise to the top. You must either be one yourself or must be seen as one vigorously supporting such characters. Illegal methods are not just the de facto lawful occupation of a police officer, but his preeminent duty if he desires to rise high and gain peer-recognition.*** The actual dirty job might often be done by the subordinate officers but they do it only because the seniors invariably approve of it and more often than not, try to protect them even when they might not have given direct orders for the misdeeds. And this is usually not a perceived 'moral' obligation—on the contrary, it is guided by purely materialistic considerations. ***Misdeeds of subordinates are sought to be covered up and the guilty protected because the very same subordinates have been the sources of their income and other gratifications. Perfect symbiosis—subordinates earn rewards, seniors earn accolades and gratifications.*** Let us hasten to explain that the police leadership cannot get away by arguing that the subordinates do all the mischief and they have no idea—the mischiefs are so utterly rampant that any denial of their knowledge would invariably mean that they have not only failed in supervision but are blind.

3.4.4 *How the Police Leadership has Failed in Addressing Some Key Legal Issues Related to Torture*

The Prevention of Torture Bill, 2010 [Bill No. 58 of 2010] was introduced in the Lok Sabha and passed on May 6, 2010. However, at the Rajya Sabha, the Government had to refer the Bill to a Parliamentary Select Committee. The Parliamentary Select Committee presented a revised Prevention of Torture Bill, in December 2010 after calling for inputs from stakeholders and testimonies from various experts including Asian Centre for Human Rights. To our knowledge, the new Bill has not been introduced in the parliament as yet. Readers may note that this too was in response to India having signed the UN's "Convention Against Torture and Other Cruel, Inhuman or Degrading Treatment or Punishment" on October 4, 1997. *But for that, in 150 years the generations of IP/IPS officers and all those illustrious characters in the ICS/IAS never felt the necessity of even demanding once that the nation must define torture so that it becomes easier to punish the violators. If this is not rank intellectual bankruptcy, what else is this?*

Now, even after the Prevention of Torture Bill having been revised, the police leadership has utterly failed in addressing the important legal lacunae in it. We will list some of them to show how application of mind has deluded the police leadership.

- The very definition of torture as used in the Bill is fraught with legal infirmities—for example, how in the world can anyone legally define mental pain or agony?
- It also uses the words 'for the purpose of obtaining information or confession'. This means that the Bill tacitly accepts that the law enforcer thus charged under the Act would have been acting in the discharge of his duty. That is,

he could not be accused of any mens rea (criminal intent) in the first place. And yet they have not provided for a situation to the contrary—in reality someone could be a pervert or sadist.

- Another fundamental issue is that the government or the law have not prescribed any procedure by which an accused is to be questioned or 'interrogated'. When no procedure has been prescribed in the first place, how can one be accused of violating something or transgressing his limits? Limits can be transgressed only when they are defined first.
- The word 'interrogation' has not been used in the CrPC nor defined in any judgement. Nobody knows what exactly can be done in interrogation. It has always been an implicit but not explicit concept. By definition 'investigation' means all the proceedings under the CrPC. This includes, for the purpose of this Bill, oral examination of witnesses (by putting questions to him), and recording of statements, medical examination, and summons to produce documents etc. Strictly speaking, anything else done would be a violation of law. Threat was ruled out in s. 163 (1) CrPC. Section 171 rules out 'restraint or inconvenience'.
- With the basic CrPC being so idealistic and strict, the correct way to address the problem of torture would have been to first prescribe all that can be done in investigation or interrogation besides what is mentioned by way of investigation in the CrPC and then to prescribe for punishment for not following the law relating to the modality of investigation. We can illustrate it with one simple example. Depriving someone of sleep is a simple way of torture, and it can be very severe too. Now the present CrPC is silent about the length of time up to which a person may be questioned. You could badly torture somebody by questioning him non-stop for 48 hours and not letting him sleep! Hence the length of the period to which a man can be questioned and the gap before the next session starts need to be defined and prescribed. There could be a whole battery of similar provisions.
- We do not think that the police leadership has had, at any time, referred to the Landau Commission report on torture or the debates in the Israeli Cabinet when they accepted it. Perhaps they might be aware of only the UN's condemnation of it. We may have our serious personal difference of opinion

with the Landau Commission but we do appreciate their intellectual honesty—at least they admitted something which has been practised for long and thought of legalizing it.

3.5 Sexual Violence and the Cops: Retrogressive Mindset and Absolute Insensitivity

3.5.1 *Create Hurdles at Every Step*

One woman is raped every 29 minutes, two women every hour; every day of the year in India. The figures, however, do not tell the complete story. The National Crime Records Bureau may relish analyzing them but analysis of rape statistics has nothing to do with the terrible trauma which the victim has to undergo. To her horror, the trauma only begins after she is raped. She suffers at the hands of everyone she encounters thereafter: a generally insensitive society which wakes only occasionally (as it did after Dec. 16, 2012 Nirbhaya case in Delhi) and then again slips back into slumber; doctors and nurses deputed to conduct the medical examination who are ignorant of the law and are utterly callous if not overtly hostile; a police force which has a curious mix of people at all ranks, some with highly retrogressive mindsets, some misogynists, and some simply insensitive; and lastly the horrors at the hands of the defence lawyers—all these violate every step she takes to seek justice. Most of the victims of rape or sexual harassment avoid going to the police because of their insensitive and harassing attitude.

The first point of contact in a police station, the duty officer, often dissuades a woman from registering the complaint of sexual violence. There is no need to narrate the reasons they cite because all of us in India know them. Readers may recall the infamous Gudiya rape case from East Delhi in April 2013 where a 5-year-old was brutally gang-raped by two men. The Gandhi Nagar police, in whose jurisdiction the incident took place, had been accused of making a bribe offer of Rs. 2000/- (yes, Rs. 2000/ only) to the victim's parents to hush up the matter. The in-charge of the police station was suspended after the incident was highlighted. An ACP rank officer was also suspended for slapping a girl who was protesting over the incident. Commenting about the attitude of the police towards rape victims and their families, a **Division bench of the Karnataka High Court** headed by the Chief Justice Vikramjit Sen observed in November 2012, "Until it happens to their families, they can't understand...I never understand why the police always take the side of villains. Whether it is Haryana or Karnataka, it is the same. No sympathy over the plight of women." A very curious feature of the distorted thinking of the police is that their first reaction to any incident of sexual violence is that one way or the other, the woman must have been responsible for it—either by choosing the wrong time to go out; by travelling in the wrong vehicle; by choosing the wrong company; by choosing to go to the wrong place; by choosing to wear what she wore; or by doing something which 'good girls' do not do. Retrogressive thinking is extremely common—only the degree might differ. They are all part of the same continuum: ranging from a fictitious concept of the violation of Lakshman Rekha inviting punishment; to 'dented painted women'; and that 'women should not venture out at night even if they have to'. Senior officers who blame rape on provocative dresses are merely senior versions of those brutes down the hierarchy who blame rape on the girl crossing her limits—for example, in going to discos etc.

You may recall how one DGP of Andhra Pradesh had infamously said that one of the factors responsible for rapes was modern women's preference for 'fashionable' dresses like salwar kameezes. "Rapes and murders are not strictly under the control of the police. I am telling you a frankly down-to-earth point. People are turning out to be more fashionable. Even in villages they are wearing salwar kameezes. All these provoke and this cannot be under the control of the police. So rapes increase or decrease..." The remarks reached the ears of Union home minister P. Chidambaram who categorically stated that the DGP was out of line. "The police are not the ones who should decide what women must wear. Each one in this country is free to wear whatever he or she wishes to wear. And I don't think there should be any kind of policing, certainly not by the DG of police."

At the lower level the retrogressive thinking becomes cruder. Sting operations conducted by many news reporters have revealed the disgusting mindset of the policemen across Delhi and the National Capital Region (NCR). And you can rest assured that the situation is almost exactly the same across the country too. Hidden cameras completely exposed the insensitivity of the cops about rape victims and rape cases. In a two-week long investigation, senior policemen in Delhi and the NCR were caught on hidden camera in interviews that will shock you. These policemen blame women on how they dress, how they behave, the fact that they drink or have relationships; it's the victim who is at fault, not the rapist, according to these cops.

In these secret recordings, the policemen have blamed the victims of having a "loose character". They also try to prove that the girl was actually a sex worker and the complaint of rape was made because there was a dispute over the payment. Another general tendency has been to prove that the girl knew the accused and the intercourse

was consensual—the complaint of rape was made because the relationship soured or it was found out by the family of the girl. If the victim is a minor, they often try to somehow manipulate the age so that she is shown a major and there is a better chance of passing the incident off as consensual sex. Many of them maintain that women from the north-east could not be true victims of forced sex as they are invariably involved in the flesh trade. Many of them are of the view that if a woman has consensual sex with one man, then she shouldn't complain if his friends also join in. In the Noida case of a teenage girl having been raped in a moving car, the police even revealed the identity of the victim, putting her future in danger. She had to drop out of school!

In this case, the 17-year-old girl was taken on the pretext of a birthday party, forced to drink alcohol, and then raped. Noida police had made public, not just her name, but even her address, in complete violation of set norms and tried to pass off it as a clerical error. The district SP also added that the victim "willingly" went with the accused and consumed alcohol, even as the victim said she was forced to consume liquor. That's where the failure of the leadership comes in to picture. *Tehelka* captured Sub-Inspector Malik on camera brazenly pinning the blame on the victim alone: *"Is case mein jo real baat hai, ladki vodka peene ki habitual hai. Usne vodka party mangi, Rs. 6,000 mein book ho gai. Physical relation ke liye 6,000 mange. Baad mein mukadma likha diya. Yeh real baat hai. Mere pass uske CDR call detail ka record hai; unka purana relation hai* (The real issue here is that the girl is a habitual vodka drinker and had asked for a vodka party. She then demanded Rs. 6000 for sex. When the money wasn't paid, she registered a rape complaint. I have her call records that establish she had a relationship with one of the accused.)

The cop knows everything, you see. How dare you ask him that having a consensual relationship with one boy does not mean that a girl deserves to be raped by four other men? Malik then proceeded to malign the character of the entire family, *"Is ladki ki ma ka pehle hi divorce ho gaya. Aur wo ek Yadavji ke saath baith gayi. Uski umar 48 hai, admi 28 saal ka. Saath mein do ladkiyan. Behekna to tei ho gaya. Nahi ho gaya?* (The girl's mother is divorced. She's living with another man from the Yadav community. She's 48 whereas the man is 28. It's inevitable the two daughters will be wayward, isn't it?) *"Ab jab 48 saal ki ma, 28 saal ke purush ke saath so rahi hai, do jawan ladkiyan dekh rahi hain, unko bhi zaroorat hogi. Sex is like hunger,"* he continued. (Now when two young girls watch their 48-year-old mother sleeping with a 28-year-old man, even they'll be aroused. Sex is like hunger.)

Her mother argues, "How can they claim she has registered the complaint to put pressure on the accused? If we were so interested in the money, wouldn't we have settled the matter without bothering to go to the police? It's the police who want to settle the matter. Which person, in the right frame of mind, will say something so outrageous and untrue? They are trying to malign her, though she is a minor the police say she is 19 years old to make their concocted 'drinking and loose character' theory appear more believable." The National Commission for Protection of Child Rights (NCPCR) took suo motu cognizance of the incident and chairperson Shanta Sinha said the Commission would seek "disciplinary action from the Uttar Pradesh government and the city SP for violating the Juvenile Justice Act under Section 21." Sinha also sent a letter to the state government and asked them to ensure that the guilty officials are punished. The NCPCR has also directed the state government to provide the victim security, medical aid, and legal aid.

3.5.2 *The Sickness in the Mind of the Cops*

In a two-week long investigation, **Abhishek Bhalla** *and* **G. Vishnu** of *Tehelka* posing as research scholars, *spoke to more than 30 senior cops in the Delhi-NCR region* across Gurgaon, Noida, Ghaziabad and Faridabad. *Here is a selection of the ugly mindset of the cops as recorded by their secret cameras.* Sub-Inspector Arjun Singh, SHO Surajpur Police Station, Greater Noida, opined, "*Ladkiya ek seemit daire main, seemit kapdon main nahi niklengi… to apne aap khichaon ho jata hai. Wo khichaon bhi aggressive kar deta hai ki kar do bas.*" (If girls don't stay within their boundaries, if they don't wear appropriate clothes, then naturally there is attraction. This attraction makes men aggressive, prompting them to just do it)." Sunil Kumar, SHO, Ghazipur, Delhi-NCR had it all sorted out, "Go to a pub in Greater Kailash, South Delhi, where there's free entry for girls. You'll find those who want to do 'it' for a thousand rupees. They'll drink and also have sex with you. But the day someone uses force, it's rape". Jangsher Singh, SHO of the DLF Phase-2 Police Station was also a believer of 'commercial' aspect. In connection with the investigation of the rape case of a 23-year-old pub worker, he knew everything, "*Isme kuch nahi hai. Chote chote bacche the… Do baar ladki ne baat ki ladkon se. Compromise karna hai toh compromise karlo. Ladki ne khud bol diya… money toh hai hi yaar. Money ke saath sauda kiya jaata hai.*" (This case is nothing. They were young kids. The girl spoke twice to the boys about striking a 'compromise'. It's all about money. It's only with money deals are stuck)." **The stereotyping is straight and simple: rape victims from poor backgrounds are looking for money, and the ones from affluent families are simply wayward and easy.**

Rajpal Yadav, Additional SHO of Sector-29, Gurgaon had his demographic and racial analysis ready, "*Yahan pe Darjeeling aur Nepal tak ki ladkiyan business purpose se ayee hain... wo jaatee bhade pe hain. Baad mein paisa nahi mila to rape case bata diya jata hai.*" (Girls from Darjeeling and Nepal have come here for business purposes. They go with men for money. Later, when the money is not sufficient, it becomes a rape)." **As *Tehelka* put it**, the Gurgaon gang-rape case appeared in the conversation of the Gurgaon Police only as a leitmotif of the girl's culpability. They captured conversations with the SHO as well as the additional SHO of Sector-29 Police Station, who otherwise have nothing to do with the ongoing investigation. Commenting on the girl's character, SHO Jagdish Prasad said: "In the recent DLF case, the girl is 27-years-old, the boys are 18 to 20-years-old. They are kids. She was dancing with these kids in the bar... I am telling you she induced them... The girl came and gave her phone number to them."

If Yogender Singh Tomar, Additional SHO, Sector-39, Noida, had his way, no woman should ever lodge a genuine complaint of rape, "*Aasaan nahi hota uske liye. Beizzati se sabhi darti hai. Akhbaar baazi se bhi darti hai. Asliyat main wahin aati hai jo dhande main lipt hoti hai.*" (It's never easy for the victim. Everyone is scared of humiliation. Everyone's wary of media and society. In reality, the ones who complain are only those who have turned rape into a business.) Additional SHO of Old Faridabad Police Station, and Ramesh Kumar, senior sub inspector, are convinced rape cases generally involve consensual sex, "*Hote hain par 70 percent aise hain, ki pehle sehmati ho gayi. Uske baad kisi ne dekh liya ya, usne paise dene se manu kar diya, toh woh balatkar ho gaya.*" (There are cases but 70 percent involve consensual sex. Only if someone sees, or the money is denied, it gets turned into rape.) One of them even told the amount involved. Satbir Singh, Additional SHO of Sector-31 Police Station, Faridabad disclosed, "*One lakh. Two lakh. Fifty lakh. Logon ko ye pata chal gaya hai ki ye achcha paisa kamaane ka dhanda hai... business hai. Income source dhoond liya hai logon ne. Aam baat hai... kharcha nahi hota. Money nahi hote.Gharwale kharch ke liye paise nahi dete.Wo phir razamandi se kaam chalta hai.*" (People have understood this is a lucrative trade for women; it's business. They've found an income source. It's common; you're short of money, your parents don't give you money to spend. You make compromises.)

Satbir Singh knew all about dressing and its 'side effects too, "*Agar koi bhi bacche ko kisi ladki ka shareer kapdon ke andar se dikhega to usme uttejna paida hogi...Ladkiya jo hai unko yahan tak yahan tak.* (He gestures to mean that women should cover their entire body, then carries on speaking)... *Skirt pehenti hai. Blouse dalti hai; poora nahi dalti hai. Dupatta nahi dalti. Apne aapko dikhawa karti hai. Baccha uske taraf akarshit hota hai."* (If a girl is wearing revealing clothes, it will encourage lewd thoughts in any kid. Girls wear short skirts. They wear a blouse that leaves nothing to the imagination. They don't wear dupattas. They flaunt their bodies. The kid naturally gets attracted to her.) Sub-Inspector Arjun Singh, SHO of Surajpur Police Station, Greater Noida, went a step ahead, "*Yeh (girl) itne kapde pehni hui hai; wo isiliye taaki log mujhse akarshit ho aur mere saath kuch na kuch kare."* (She is dressed in a manner that people get attracted to her. In fact, she wants them to do something to her.)

When it comes to gang-rapes, the general cop theory is that the victim must have been friendly with at least one of the perpetrators—that she must have agreed for sex with at least one of them while others merely piled in. Dharamveer Singh, Additional SHO at Indirapuram Police Station was categorical "*Rare hota hai ki ek ladki ko 10 ladke zabardasti pakad le... car mein bhi koi innocent ladki nahi gayi hai. Wahi gayi jo kisi ladke ke saath sambandhit zaroor hai."* (It's very rare that a girl is forcefully picked up by 10 boys. A girl who gets into a car with boys is never innocent. If she does, she definitely has a relationship with at least one of them.)

Where exactly the police leadership has failed in all this? Yes, we do agree that senior police officers cannot police what goes on inside the mind of their subordinates. Well, inside the depths of their minds, they could believe in anything. *But senior officers can and must ensure that the retrogressive mindset of their subordinates or their own mindsets do not affect their work.* Make sure that they keep it compartmentalized. And for God's sake, the police leadership should not waste anybody's time with their inanities. ***The nation can be spared the farce of some so-called 'sensitization' courses—these guys would improve when the leadership has the moral courage to punish them whenever the demon lurking in their subconscious slips out.*** *Yes, we agree that the law cannot force them to sympathize or empathize with the victims. But the law does expect them to be neutral, at the very least. Investigation cannot be impartial if the investigator has preconceived notions about how and why the crime would have taken place. This is the catch – this is the thing where the leadership has failed.*

3.5.3 *Blame Her for Everything She Does*

When it comes to clothes worn by the girls or their 'going out', the cops have their fundas clear. If it does not fit in with the concept of what the cop thinks a 'good girl' should do, then the victims are accused of "deserving" rape. The policemen argued that the victims should have "expected" rape when they wore "inappropriate" clothes or were out at night or went to pubs. What is 'inappropriate dressing' or 'indecent dressing and who has defined it? Rather, who has given the cops a licence to define it? Who are they to impose their version of morality on to the rest of the society? Are jeans or skirts 'indecent' and if so, why? Do the cops get excited by seeing a girl in jeans and then, to conceal their arousal, devise a theory that rapists should also be getting similarly aroused? Who has prescribed and under what law that if a man got aroused beyond a certain level, he would pounce and commit rape? Do the cops advocate a burqa? What do they think of the most traditional Indian wear, the saree?

Probably these guys have seen only their uncouth wives in sarees. They do not know that the stylishly designed saree-blouse combination is one of the most sensuous apparels in the world. Blaming jeans or skirts for rape is plain bullshit. Even if we accept for a moment that jeans and other 'inappropriate' clothing constitute provocations to rape then are they arguing that women in kurta-pyjama, salwar-kameez, or sarees should never get raped? If this is the case then there should be no rape case in rural areas because women are 'fully covered' there. If women in burqas do not get raped then there should be no rape cases in Muslim-dominated areas. But this is not true. Even if women wear "inappropriate" clothes, does it give a licence to someone to rape them? Is this the reality of 21st century India? In the "modern" society, don't women even have the right to decide what they should wear? Do the cops mean to say that the rapists or the molesters have a licence to behave in an uncontrolled manner—without caring two hoots for the law and societal norms?

Are the so-called 'moral' restrictions only meant for women? Are men not supposed to exercise any restraint? We remember one incident clearly. That was years ago. Once, a fellow IPS officer visited our house with his family. His son was a particularly nasty creature. However, instead of rebuking him, this guy kept on telling us, "*ab to ye kuchh todega!*" In retrospect, now we realize that cops, who try to 'explain' rapes, harbour precisely this mindset. The next thing to blame is the "inappropriate" behaviour of the women who get raped. If a girl goes to a party and is raped, she should not have gone there in the first place. Women who go to pubs or drink should "expect" rape because that's what men do after drinking in pubs. And God save the woman who herself takes a peg or so—she has no option but to get raped because that's what happens to women who drink. The woman who touches alcohol automatically gets a certificate of 'loose character'.

If they go to a pub then they slide a notch further below. Of course, the cops cannot be bothered with rapes that place within the confines of houses by their own relatives or neighbours; or where women of villages or slums get raped—they are regular crimes, you see! Rapes of minor girls are dismissed as aberrations.

The third thing to blame is the victim knowing the rapist beforehand. A general tendency amongst the cops is to try to prove that the victim knew the accused—and if she knew, then, at least for them, the corollary is that it must have been consensual sex which she is now trying to blame as rape for some 'other' reason. You don't expect the Indian police officers to have heard of something called 'date-rape', do you? Don't tax the poor fellows' brains so much—they might burst. How is he supposed to know that in numerous cases, the rapist is not some total stranger hiding in a bush or some dark alley ready to pounce upon an unsuspecting victim? How is the cop supposed to know that thousands of *bhabhis* in this country know their *devars* and *jeths*—and yet they get raped by them! The cops presume that if a woman knows someone, it means that the only relationship that can exist between them is that of consensual sex. If the cops are to be believed, one who knows a woman can demand sex as a right! What are the police trying to say? **Is it a crime to have a boyfriend? Should a woman not speak to any male in the world except her husband? Should they start behaving like the *purdah* women of two centuries ago? What would a poor girl do when she is raped by her classmates? Well, for this the cops have a solution—stop co-education! Ha, ha, ha!**

3.5.4 *If that Does Not Work, Shackle Her*

The peak of this sickening attitude reached with the 8 p.m. curfew for women imposed by Gurgaon police whereby women were asked not to go out after 8 p.m. Readers may recall that following two consecutive gang rape incidents in Gurgaon, some senior IPS officers sought to do something which they had never done before—applying mind. Well, when a car rusting in the garage since long is started, it may create all sorts of noises and give unexpected jerks. In such jerks, they issued many dos and don'ts for Gurgaon women to avoid eve-teasing and molestation.

What topped their list was the *diktat* that women should not be out in the public after 8 p.m. If they stayed at home, they would not be raped—how simple! You see, the police are all-powerful and they have the authority to issue such orders—who in the hell is talking of constitutional freedoms? They said the incidents of molestation and eve-teasing brought a bad name to the city and tarnished its image. You see, protecting the name and image of the city was far more important than protecting the women! Remember, the police are not for the citizens, they are for the city and its name! They did not stop at that. Shopping malls, pub owners and those running shops and commercial establishments were asked to not to keep women employees on duty beyond 8 in the evening. If women employees were to be detained on duty after that, they should obtain permission of the Labour department! The readers must appreciate that the cops have extremely limited intellectual capacity. They presumed that only working women got raped and non-working women would never have any occasion to step out of their homes in the night for whatever reason. In effect, a curfew was imposed for women after 8 p.m.

They added that if women employees were deputed on duty during the night shift, that is, after 8 p.m., their safe transportation from home to place of duty and vice versa will be the responsibility of the employer who will have to keep a daily record of the vehicle used, its registration number, time of departure, name of driver who was entrusted with the task of picking up or dropping the women employees. Plus, the place from where the women employees boarded the vehicle that is, parking place should have a CCTV camera there so that it could be ascertained that the woman was not lifted forcibly. In the other words, they intended to say that any woman now who is out after the official curfew of 8 p.m. would do nothing but 'invite' men to sexually harass her. It's your responsibility if you get raped—we told you, didn't we? Moreover, the responsibility of the police ended after 8 p.m. and the rapists could have a field day (or night) after 8 p.m. It amply proves that the police leadership is utterly dumb. We are saying so because it could not be passed off as the stupidity of some particular officers—the entire leadership failed in not having called for the explanation of the concerned. *Once again, the dumb cops thought that they have all the authority in the world and they can regulate the lives of the people in any stupid way they want. They made it worse by stating that if these instructions were not followed, then case will be registered against the pub and mall owner as well.*

The whole thing was so utterly illegal, so utterly beyond the powers of the police that we need not even comment on it. Anybody can understand it. In 2005, they had banned the so-called 'dance bars' in Mumbai and forced thousands of poor girls and their dependents into starvation. It took the sufferers eight years to get justice finally from the **honourable Supreme Court in July 2013**.

3.5.5 *Stop the Gimmicks, Please*

When the police get flak from all sides, they devise gimmicks. They can do only so much because to do something substantial is beyond their ken. Some of the measure suggested by the police leadership following the rapes in the NCR and Gurgaon included:

- All District Superintendents of Police have been told to report to the Director General of Police everyday if there is any case related to crime against a woman in their area of jurisdiction. (*What the DGP will do, sir – if he knows any secret remedy, he could tell that in advance. What is this obsession with monitoring except to placate someone?*)
- Set up anti-stalking help lines and instruct its police officers to act promptly in cases related to crime against women by registering first information reports. (*Sir, are they not legally bound to register FIRs anyway? Do you have to be told of such elementary things – haven't your cops ever heard of the Supreme Court judgements in this regard?*)
- Special training to tackle cases related to crime against women. (*What is that? How does training change attitudes?*)

The fact is the police leadership has done nothing besides such obviously facile things. They could not do anything because they are insensitive in the first place and intellectually bankrupt in the second. All they can think of is organizing seminars on gender sensitization! What action did they take against the insensitive cops exposed in sting operations? And, do they really have to wait for such sting operations? Sting operations serve to enlighten the common man because he has no other means of learning the ugly reality. Those who have spent several decades in the police must know such things. There is no excuse for not knowing unless they admit that they have been blind and deaf. In that case, they are not fit to continue in service. If they say that they knew, there is no excuse for not taking any action against those who have made the victims of sexual violence suffer more by their attitude and acts.

For the information of the ignoramuses, we may mention that as held in the case of **State of Karnataka vs. Manjanna** [AIR 2000 SC 2231] by the Supreme Court, a rape victim's need for a medical examination has been recognized as a "medico-legal emergency" and the doctor or hospital is now required to examine a victim of rape if she reports to the hospital directly, and voluntarily, without a police requisition. *But as we all know, this is not being done and senior police officers have not done anything to educate the people about it or to get the doctors punished who do not follow it. They should also know that as provided* *vide the section 164 (A) through Criminal Procedure Code (Amendment) Act of 2005 (6) in all other cases, her consent or her parents' or guardian's consent is necessary for the medical examination – the police or the doctors have no authority to force a medical examination merely because a police complaint has been lodged.* Yet, in hundreds of cases, they are forcing the medical examination upon the victim. It also provides that any registered medical practitioner can do the examination and a government doctor is not necessary. The same Section mandates that a medical examination must be carried out within 24 hours of the police receiving information, thus recognizing this as a medico-legal emergency and putting a time-frame for the investigating officer. Yet, in most cases, the cops still insist upon a government doctor and delay the matters for that, thereby prolonging the agony of the victim. That's where the police leadership has failed.

3.6 The Psychological Reasons of Incompetence and Perversity

The police have a particular propensity for attracting individuals who prove a menace at high levels of command. There are several theories in this regard. They are variously described as the 'bloody fool theory'; 'bone-headed leadership'; 'the long gallery of imbecility'; and 'the fate of the citizens being decided for them by idiots'. In fact, the very sub-culture of the organisation serves to accentuate those very traits which may ultimately prove disastrous. One such trait is authoritarianism. Authoritarianism, by its very nature does not brook dissent. Hence any sign of keenness or desire for self-improvement in professional matters on the part of anybody is frowned on as not 'good form', and a condemnable departure from tradition which bears the stamp of some mythical great officers in the past. *One, who seeks to improve himself or does not 'conform' to the general imbecility, is perceived as a serious threat to the organisation. Hence various methods are employed for preservation of status quo or perpetuation of stupidity.* They include harassment, denial of dues, making him a scapegoat, and everything that would discourage him from thinking differently. Through a skilful combination of self-interest, personal ambition, ignorance, obstinacy and crass stupidity, the greatest conformists reach the greatest heights.

Psychologists also point at some other characteristics of the police leadership which eventually culminates in incompetence and perversity. *Because they lack substance of any kind, they develop a morbid fascination with show.* This reflects, among other things, in their obsession with overtly visible symbols of subservience to authority. When it comes to manner of addressing, this has been taken to such depths that even a phone conversation starts with 'sir, sir, good morning, sir and dollops of 'sir' liberally sprinkled in the conversation after every sentence. In India, the morons have elevated 'sir' to a word where, with subtle changes in inflexion, it can be used in practically every sense—when they agree with the senior officer, they say 'sir' in response meaning they have understood it; when they are being rebuked, still they say 'sir' in response meaning they have admitted their mistake. In its versatility in the lingo of the cops, the word 'sir' occupies a status which in common English is matched only by the word 'fuck'. Senior officers love to tick off their subordinates about their manner of saluting, wearing of uniform, the tightness of the belt, the polish on the shoes, and so on. Some other characteristics include arrogance, vanity, and a compulsive habit of scheming and being dishonest.

The police organisation resembles the dinosaurs of a bygone age, huge in strength, massive in body, but controlled by a nervous system so sluggish and extended that the organism could suffer fatal damage before the tiny distant brain could think of, let alone initiate, an adequate response. A brain of that capacity naturally resists anything that might force it to exert itself. What it resists in itself, it resists in others also. That's how the organisation refuses to develop—any new idea, any innovation will be resisted with a wall of obstruction, compounded of burning jealousy, intense hatred, deep suspicion and legendary inertia. That's why in India you have a police that is still governed by a Police Act created more than 150 years ago and where the functioning of the police is essentially still the same as it was 150 years ago. ***In simple words, we can say that the police organisation suffers from a cult of anti-intellectualism***. Knowledge is a threat to their ego-defensive orientation, and is therefore rejected. And when there is no knowledge, the question of competence does not arise. What they claim to be 'knowledge' is actually a faith. Needless to say, this attitude towards knowledge rub off on those whom they see as purveyors of this dangerous commodity; this makes them openly suspicious and hostile towards "intellectuals". There is nothing more threatening to it than an 'intellectual' officer.

Precisely for this reason, most senior police officers have a predilection for holding fast to simplistic theories for very complex phenomena. That's how you find senior officers who swear that if beat patrolling is done on foot, there would be no crime. Most of them resort to meaningless catchphrases, to derision and finally to anger in the face of anything new. *Any opposition is levelled with the steamroller of 'experience'*. We have taken a re-look at this phenomenon in a later chapter. *A deep subconscious feeling of inadequacy haunts the police officers*. Much of what they do and what eventually becomes their second nature is a subconscious attempt to reduce that anxiety. As a general rule, snobbish behaviour betokens some underlying feeling of inferiority. It is a common characteristic of the social climber, of the individual with low self-esteem, of the person who feels threatened because of some real (or imagined) inadequacy. One important part of the inadequacy relates to masculinity.

Many of the youths who opt for a career in the armed forces and the police do so out of an underlying fear of being unmanly. Having said this, we request the readers to think of all those colonels, brigadiers and generals; cops and rather famous senior officers they have found with all sorts of weird moustaches—big and bushy; handlebar, horseshoe; and those acutely reminiscent of infamous dacoits of Chambal. *You will understand instantly why they chose such moustaches—all of them suffered from anxiety regarding their masculinity and wanted to allay their subconscious fears by an overt display of some secondary masculine characteristics. One of the reasons of rapes committed by the cops or their generally lascivious behaviour is this anxiety only—they want to reassure themselves that they are masculine enough.*

This also explains the aggressive behaviour of the cops. Individuals with fears of inadequacies are attracted to organisations which set upon them the seal of masculinity. *By being admitted to a society of men bent upon the most primitive manifestations of maleness—violence and aggression—the individual achieves the reassurance he requires.* The S.S. guards of the Nazis were not ideological fanatics, but inadequate 'little' men to whom the satisfaction provided by the S.S. Gestapo were tailor-made—all powerful father-figures, rigid rules of loyalty and obedience, and 'legitimate' outlets for their hitherto pent-up and murderous hostility. *As one of them had remarked, it was much better to be thought of as a hardened Nazi and brutal murderer than a sissy.* They hated in others what they could not tolerate in themselves. Hence it was that the weak, the old, the underprivileged, the cowed, and later the starving millions of the concentration camps suffered their fearful attentions. Apply this to the cops of India and you would understand why most of their atrocities committed are on the poor, the helpless, and the women.

It is for this reason that veiled, if not direct, references to women and sex make up a large part of the thoughts and speech of the cops. This is the reason that the police and the army resist, to the extent possible, the induction of women. As long as women are not there, they can boast that what they do is a 'man's job'. When people see that women could do that equally well, it makes them feel insecure.

Good leadership is synonymous with inspiring confidence in those who follow, and confidence is born of proven professional competence and results. Unfortunately, you can get everything in the police leadership but this. Not a single trait of good leaders is to be found in them. *They cannot pull their subordinates by force of character; they can only threaten. They do not stand by them when they are in trouble.* There have been numerous instances when, following a police firing if there was some Judicial Commission of Inquiry, senior officers present on the spot have refused to shoulder any responsibility and have thrown all the blame on the men who had fired. In other words, the police leaders do not assume even moral responsibility for something which could make it appear to their subordinates that they are taking some risk even metaphorically, if not literally and, by that act, stands out in front of the group. Talk to some old-timer and they would regale you with imaginary tales of how their subordinates followed them to the grave.

The truth is that, in that era, they could earn the subservience of their men even as they behaved them as they might have behaved towards pets because of the real and enormous social gulf which the rank and file perceived between themselves and their masters—not because of any other reason. Even domestic servants in that era were very loyal and you never heard of murders by domestic helps. *The social divide does not exist in such a virulent form any more and that's why the police leaders' continued habit of treating their subordinates like pets (feed them; groom them, pat them; and punish them) does not make them into any 'leaders' of their men – they remain merely senior officers with nothing but seniority to boast of.*

Chapter 4

Slammed by the Courts, Nowhere to Hide

4.1 Castigation Galore, Unequivocal and Unambiguous

4.1.1 *Courts to the Rescue*

The atrocities committed by the police in matters small and big are legion. However, our courts, the sentinels of justice, have repeatedly come down heavily on the police. ***In the following pages, we present a sample of the anguish and anger of the courts over police excesses. The courts have indeed done their duty towards the nation. Still, if the people are forced to suffer police atrocities, who has failed in its duty then? The police leadership, of course! It was incumbent upon the police leadership to take note of the scathing strictures passed by the honourable courts and institute corrective measures. Sadly, they have done nothing. Had they done anything, there would not have been such a sickening repetition of the same type of excesses all over the country.***

There are several reasons for their not doing anything. Being in the same service, we interact with scores of senior IAS/IPS officers as a matter of routine every day. We know that most of them are so utterly ignorant, so blissfully unaware of the happenings around them that they do not even know that the courts have been castigating the police in such unequivocal terms. This ignorance, in turn, stems from the supreme apathy which they nurture towards the acquisition of knowledge in any form. Knowledge is not on a premium in the service in any case. If an abject minority is vaguely aware of the strictures passed by the courts, they don't care. Most of them banish it out of their minds the moment they put down the newspaper—do not even remember reading the judgements! Often the first reaction is that it does not concern them directly; they would bother only when it concerns them directly. Obviously, no one cares about the system, in particular, or the Indian police, in general. They are too happy to be in the posts they occupy and making as much money as they can, as long as it lasts. Those who do not have such posts are all the time trying for such posts. *Thus basically we have only two types of IPS officers; those who have managed to land posts where they are furiously working to make as much money as they can, and those who are furiously trying to get such posts.* Who in the world has got time to think about the police department? It is every man for himself! ***That's where the leadership failed. They are not leading anything; they merely happen to be at such places in the hierarchical structure from where they are authorized to issue orders to many. But those 'many' do not matter to them unless they serve to increase their incomes or benefit them in some other way. It's time the nation seriously asked whether it really needs the police leadership, the IPS, when they are so pathetically incapable of providing any leadership at all!***

The instances of castigation of the police by the courts are legion. For lack of space, we cannot cite all such cases. However, the examples cited cover various instances from fairly representative samples. *That the honourable courts have had so many occasions to pillory the police in diverse cases shows that the police commit excesses uniformly—whatever be the matter, they would harass you. There is nothing situational, regional, or temporal about police excesses.*

4.1.2 *HC Fines State Rs. 6 Lakh for Illegal Police Arrests and Excesses*

In December 2012, the **Bombay High Court** slapped fines totalling approximately Rs. 6 lakh for illegalities and excesses committed by the police which included arresting a woman after sunset without following proper procedures, illegally keeping an elderly couple (about 65 years of age) in custody for 36 hours, and illegal detention of three persons. The elderly couple was illegally detained in a dowry harassment case. In the other case, a 56-year-old woman was arrested in a case of a cheque bouncing. In the third instance three persons were illegally detained in a Section 151 CrPC case. *A division bench of Justices Abhay Oka and Sambhaji Shinde allowed the state to recover damages awarded to the victims from the police officer concerned and also ordered departmental action against them.* Imagine, this could happen even after a battery of Supreme Court judgements on such issues? They are so famous that we find it difficult to imagine that the police leadership, in spite of its legendary ignorance, would not have heard about them. Then it can only mean that they have utter disregard for the orders of the honourable Supreme Court. If they say that they do not have disregard, it would mean that there is utter supervisory failure. They have either no control over their subordinates, or they do not care about what they do.

4.1.3 *HC Slams Probe in Amit Jethwa Murder Case*

Amit Jethwa, an environmentalist and a social worker, was shot dead by two assailants in Gujarat. It was suspected that he was killed at the behest of a powerful politician because Jethwa had filed several court cases against illegal mining in the Gir Forest area in which the politician was alleged to have a hand. In September 2012, while transferring the Amit Jethwa murder case to CBI, a **division bench of Gujarat High Court** highlighted how cops botched up investigation at every stage right from registering the FIR. *The order of the honourable High Court is important because it show how the police leadership kowtows before the politicians and how they throw professional integrity to the winds. No prizes for guessing why they do so? Obviously, to curry favours with the powers-that-be.*

The High Court found that the probe was not carried out in conformity with legal provisions. Citing the reason for handing over the case to CBI, the Court said, "The control exercised by one police officer of a very high rank, all throughout and even after the orders for further investigation by this court, provides sufficient ground to conclude that the investigation was controlled. And the line of investigation was determined and supervised so as to put to naught the allegations made and the suspicion raised by the acquaintances and family members of the deceased." The Court also highlighted that Additional DGP Mohan Jha was in control of the investigation from the day FIR was lodged. The Court also noticed that Jha remained reporting authority for the investigating officer Raghavendra Vatsa even when the probe was transferred on court order. The Court noticed that since the probe continued to be under Jha's monitoring and guidance, there was no possibility that probe could proceed further on any new line.

Besides, the Court highlighted the facts showing how the investigators—Sola police and the city crime branch, followed the leads by the accused after their arrest. Instead of working on suspicions expressed by witnesses and relatives of the victim, the cops chose to limit their probe to statements given by the accused persons. "A perfunctory investigation on the basis of statements of the accused persons themselves may not unearth the whole truth and meet the ends of justice. Therefore, it is imperative that proper and comprehensive investigation is undertaken by an agency which is not under the control of the state government," the Court said.

4.1.4 *Explanation on Police Brutalities an Eyewash, Says Apex Court*

In May 2013, a **three-judge Bench of the Supreme Court** comprising Justices G. S. Singhvi, Ranjana Prakash Desai and Sharad Arvind Bobde termed as an "eyewash" the explanation given in the affidavits filed by the Delhi Police and the Uttar Pradesh government in connection with the police brutality on a young girl and a woman protesting the rape of minors in the national Capital and in Aligarh. While the Apex Court had sought an explanation from the Delhi Police for a senior police officer slapping a girl protesting the rape of a minor, the UP Chief Secretary was directed to explain why a 65-year-old woman was assaulted by the police in Aligarh during a protest against the rape and murder of a six year old girl.

The Bench referred to several incidents of protest including the lynching of a rape accused in Nagpur in 2010 by a mob, saying the police inaction leads to such types of agitations. The Bench was not satisfied with their affidavits in which it was stated that the Delhi Police had already taken action by suspending ACP Bani Singh Ahlawat who slapped the girl and that the old woman, pushed by a police officer in Aligarh, was holding stones in her hand. "After such type of incidents, suspension takes place and in two to three months, the errant officials are reinstated," the Bench said while hearing the submissions and going through the Delhi Police affidavit. The Bench said "next time this type of incidents happen, the highest official will bear the brunt".

4.1.5 *Court Slams Gujarat Police Over Naroda Patiya Riot Case*

In September 2012, the Gujarat Police came in for **scathing criticism by a special court** for their handling of the riots at Naroda Patiya in 2002 and also initial probe into the ghastly incident in which 96 people were massacred. The designated court, which had earlier awarded extended life imprisonment to 31 accused, including BJP legislator Maya Kodnani, *came down heavily on the police for their "carelessness, insensitiveness and ineptness" in the handling of investigations into the worst post-Godhra riot case.* Judge Jyotsana Yagnik slammed the then Police

Inspector of Naroda, K. K. Mysorewala, who was also the first Investigating officer (IO) of the case: "While people were flocking the streets, Shri K. K. Mysorewala reported to the Control Room that "everything is okay (*'khairiyat hai'*).

The Court posed some pointed questions to police. "The question remains as to why the stone-pelters were not arrested then and there? Police could have caught the members of the mob on whom the police wielded baton/stick. The normal mentality of a mob is to run away if fired on. "Hence, the fact of firing by the police is doubtful. No cartridge has been found anywhere. One policeman with a revolver is sufficient to scare away many persons. Police could have cordoned off some members of the mob." Before the Supreme Court-appointed Special Investigation Team (SIT) took over and started re-investigation, the Naroda Patiya case had seen almost seven Investigating Officers, including five from State Crime Branch.

4.1.6 *Court Slams Police for Lax Probe into Suicide*

This is a classic case of the terrible ineptitude with which investigations are done and how the police leadership has failed in its duty of supervision. In April 2012, pulling up the Delhi police, **a Delhi Court** ordered proper investigation into the death of a man found with a bullet injury on the forehead in north Delhi, observing that no finger prints were lifted from the firearm used in the suicide. But that was not the end of their follies. According to the police, Ashish Pal's body, with a gunshot injury on his forehead, was found in his bedroom in Narela Oct. 26, 2008. There was a pistol in the right hand of the victim. The police filed a final report in the case, claiming that Pal committed suicide.

The Court observed that police failed to collect any document on record to suggest the reason for which Pal, a married man, committed suicide. The Court said that the photographs of the body showed that there was no blood on the wound, no part of the body was stained with blood and there was no blood found on the victim's hand holding the pistol. The court observed that the bullet, which allegedly killed Pal, was found after 10 days of the incident by forensic experts team from the mattress on which his body was found. The Court was surprised that there was no hole in the bed sheet on which the body was lying despite the fact that the bullet was recovered from the mattress under it.

4.1.7 *Don't Act Like Recovery Agents, HC Tells Cops*

The police are always eager to interfere in civil matters and either commit atrocities straightaway or make money by threatening the people that they would be implicated in criminal cases. Yet another obnoxious tendency of the police is to act as the servants of anybody who can pay them. In September 2012, the **Bombay High Court** slammed the Mumbai police for arresting a citizen and handcuffing him over a leave and licence dispute. "Are the police now acting as recovery agents?" asked a division bench of Justice Abhay Oka and Justice Sadhana Jadhav. "In normal circumstances, this could have been a civil dispute. In this case, an FIR is lodged, a man is arrested and he has to spend a day in the lock-up," said the judges, reminding the police that the court had recently ordered a compensation of Rs. 2.5 lakh in another case relating to illegal custody. "This is not a solitary case and is happening day in and day out in Mumbai. This has to stop," said the judges.

4.1.8 *HC Flays Attitude of Dindigul Cops*

In August 2012, in a strong indictment of police conduct, the **Madras High Court** Division Bench condemned the attitude of the Dindigul police in not registering a woman-missing case and directed the DGP to report to the court after taking appropriate action against the district superintendent of police and the concerned police inspector. A division bench of Justices K. Suguna and R. Mala was hearing the *habeas corpus* petition filed by one Gnanapragasam of Nilakottai seeking direction to the police to produce his wife missing since February. He alleged that a woman moneylender might have kidnapped her since she had borrowed money from her at high rate of interest.

"It is a specific stand of the petitioner that though three complaints have been given, no steps were taken by the Nilakottai police inspector or Dindigul SP. Not even receipt with regard to lodging of the complaint was given," the Court noted. It said the additional public prosecutor was saying that a complaint made on March 26 2012 had been registered, but the complaint was made by the moneylender himself, who is the suspect in this kidnap case. "When the moneylender approached the police, immediately police were taking action and enquiries were made....It is unfortunate that a private individual's complaint on disappearance of his wife from February was not taken on file and not even receipt was given," the court said, adding, "**It is unfortunate that for certain people alone, the police mechanism is functioning**". When the complaint was lodged against the moneylender, neither the complaint was registered nor a receipt given. "This shows the attitude and method of functioning of police," the court said. "It is very painful to note that the SP of Dindigul is a party to the habeas corpus petition...though three hearings were held, no steps have been taken by the SP", the court said. *We mentioned it above – the police act only for those who can bribe them.*

4.1.9 *HC Raps Cops for Shoddy Investigation in Corruption Case*

In June 2012, the Gauhati High Court came down heavily on the police for their shoddy investigation in a rather simple corruption case. The accused, a police constable, Prasanta Goswami, was caught red-handed by the Assam Police's CID while receiving gratification of Rs. 10,000 from a milkman in Guwahati, threatening him with a false case of selling adulterated milk.

Justice P. K. Musahary said, "It is simply disgusting and distressing that the investigating agency did not apply the modern scientific method as directed by the Apex Court and did not take up the matter in the right direction right from the stage of laying the trap and collecting materials against the accused person and probing the case." As per the Apex Court's order, the police must use phenolphthalein powder in a 'trap' case, something that was not applied in this particular case. This kind of powder if applied in small quantity to the currency notes, rubs off on to the hands that have touched it and then the presence of the powder on the hands of the suspect can be confirmed by a simple chemical test.

"The state police either lack proper training in detecting such crimes or they are negligent in performing their duties honestly in cases related to offering and accepting illegal gratification," the judgement said. Expressing 'serious' concern over the state police's negligence in proper investigation, the High Court order said: "It is a sorry state of affairs and the state home department is required to take corrective measures." "If such lapses are allowed to continue by the state, it will not be possible to convict and punish the accused person charged with any offence under Prevention of Corruption Act," the judgement said. ***As we have been mentioning, the police are either dumb or crooked or both.***

4.1.10 *HC Slams Cops for Taking Man to Police Station Over Traffic Rule*

Just mention traffic offences and the crooked cops start salivating. Most citizens and youngsters get their first taste of police in connection with traffic offences. Such is the terror of the police, so absolute is their power that people meekly pay up. But in October 2012, the **Bombay High Court** asked the police under which law citizens can be forcibly taken to a police station for traffic offences like not having their driving licence with them when stopped by a police officer? A division bench of Justice A. S. Oka and Justice S. S. Jadhav asked the police this question while hearing a petition filed by Kadar Solanky, a lawyer for allegedly detaining him for long hours after he was caught riding a bike without his driver's licence. Solanky had informed the policemen when he was caught that he had forgotten his licence at home. He had been willing to pay the fine immediately and produce the licence later. However, the policemen verbally abused him and forcibly took him to Bhiwandi police station, where he was detained for over six hours. He was later released, but only after he paid a fine of Rs. 3,000.

4.1.11 *HC Slams Cops Over Attack on Senior Citizen*

In February 2012, pulling up the police for failing to protect an elderly woman, a Division Bench of Justice V. M. Kanade and Justice P. D. Kode of the **Bombay High Court** directed the crime branch to register an FIR against the builder accused of assaulting a 68-year-old woman. *"An old helpless woman is assaulted. Is the entire police station supposed to help a builder? Senior citizens who have nobody to protect them. What has it come to in Maharashtra!"* said the Court. Anusuya Patil (68) had alleged that the builder Sandesh Gawadkar, his wife and 10-12 people assaulted her in the presence of inspector Vilas More, Dadar police station. Her complaint to the police commissioner did not result in anything substantial. The judges said a glance at a complaint discloses cognizable offences but the "police turned a deaf ear": *"Instead of registering an FIR, the police acted as mute spectators. Prima facie, it is clear that they colluded with the developer and not taken action,"* the bench said. They also ordered registration of FIR against More directed the police chief to conduct a departmental inquiry against him. *"Citizens have no rights. Police are there to help only builders and influential people,"* said Justice Kanade. *Once again, you can see that the police serve only the rich and the powerful and harass the poor.*

4.1.12 *HC Slams Gujarat Police Over Torture*

In June 2012, the **Gujarat High Court** initiated suo motu proceedings on the basis of a complaint sent by one Altaf Patel from Surat accusing cops of severe beating and giving him electric shocks on his private parts. The High Court asked the home secretary of the state to conduct an inquiry into the allegations and submit a report. As the government pleader submitted a reply and report from the home secretary and read it in the open court, Justice J. B. Pardiwala of the division bench stopped him saying that the government's report is completely incorrect. The Judge said that he could not even read in the open court what they (cops) had done with the youth in custody. Altaf Patel narrated how he was tortured by Vadodara's Special Operation Group (SOG). Patel named six police officials including then DCP of

Vadodara crime branch, Ajay. According to his complaint, in May last year, Varachha police in Surat summoned his younger brother Imrat for some inquiry, and from there Vadodara SOG took custody of him. Vadodara SOG called Altaf a few days later and took him also into custody. He claimed that SOG asked him to confess his role in a plot to make a drug peddler flee from the SSG Hospital. This was the second such incident of custodial torture, wherein HC has caught the administration on wrong footing. Earlier, in a case of custodial torture from Jamnagar, the **HC ordered transfer of the SP** and set up an inquiry.

4.1.13 *HC Slams Police for Not Granting Bail for Bailable Offence*

Anisha Bangera, Javed Shaikh and Karthik Kaushik were picked up from a so-called rave party. The cops had detained nearly 300 youngsters, including 59 girls. In this case and in other cases, many of the accused ended up spending nearly a week in custody, simply because police did not follow the law. Despite being charged with bailable offences under the NDPS Act, the police had refused to grant bail to them. They then approached the Sessions Judge in Alibaug, Raigad seeking anticipatory bail. However, there too, the court declined to grant them any relief, stating that since the offence was bailable, there was no need to seek anticipatory bail. For something so obvious, they had to go the **Bombay High Court** where a Division Bench comprising Justices A. M. Khanwilkar and A. R. Joshi ordered in June 2012, "The police have not facilitated the petitioners in availing of bail in connection with offences which are indisputably bailable..." *Does anyone still have any doubt about the way the police behave?*

4.1.14 *Not Everyone Who Believes in Maoist Ideology is a Terrorist*

As we have discussed at several places in the book, the bogey of fighting terrorism provides numerous opportunities to the police to satiate whatever perverse desires that might have been lying buried in their subconscious. The fight against terrorism gives them immense powers and more than that, at least, some societal approval for the time being. They literally start salivating when they get a chance to label someone a terrorist – there are rewards to be had and, courtesy some journalist friend, great coverage in the media. They have seldom bothered to furnish any proof; they simply called someone a terrorist and the people accepted it. The lives of hundreds of people have been spoiled by this fiendish act. Not any more as the Honourable Court has spoken. On October 3, 2012, a very important judgement was delivered by the Honourable **Bombay High Court**. The Bombay High Court granted bail to two people accused of being Maoists, saying it is "impossible to hold" that every person attracted to or influenced by the Maoist ideology "is to be treated as a member of a terrorist organisation".

Sushma Ramtekke and Jyoti Chorge were arrested by the Maharashtra Anti-Terrorism Squad for being a part of the Golden Corridor Committee—a group allegedly set up by the banned Communist Party of India (Maoist) to spread its message in urban areas. "A number of persons are influenced by and attracted to the Maoist philosophy because of the oppression of weaker sections of society. The applicants too, like a number of such persons, might have been influenced and impressed by the Maoist philosophy," the Court observed.

Justice Abhay Thipsay, while granting them bail, observed that committees appointed by the government to study the problem of Naxalites have found that it is the social, political, economic and cultural discrimination faced by the poor that drives them to the Maoists. "It is impossible to hold that all such persons are to be treated as members of a terrorist organisation, or that they are liable to be punished for having some faith in such a philosophy, or for having sympathy for those who propagate such philosophy," Justice Thipsay said in his judgement. The police had relied mainly on books and materials allegedly recovered from the duo to show that they were members of the banned organisation. But on this issue, the court observed that the material recovered was not banned under Code of Criminal Procedure or any other law. Noting that it would run against the freedoms guaranteed by the Constitution, the court said, "*That the possession of certain literature having a particular social or political philosophy would amount to an offence—though such literature is not expressly or specifically banned under any provision of law—is a shocking proposition in a democratic country like ours.*"

The Court observed that while the prosecution had taken lot of effort to show how the organisation posed a threat to the entire country, it could not show how the two accused were in any way actively involved. The Court said that the investigating agency had levelled a number of charges and general allegations against the accused, but there was no allegation that either of them had committed a terrorist act. Moreover, it said they did not have any evidence to show that the duo had conspired to commit a terrorist act, organise a terrorist training camp, or recruit anyone for terrorist acts.

4.1.15 *SC Slams Chhattisgarh Cops for Torturing Doctor*

In August 2012, reproaching "some megalomaniac police officers" who think they are the "law" and not its protectors, the Supreme Court slammed the Chhattisgarh police for torturing an Ayurvedic doctor in custody 20 years ago. It also ordered the police to pay a compensation of Rs. 5 lakh to the doctor for the "inhuman treatment" and "social humiliation" caused after posters describing him as a thief were put up. A Division Bench of Justices K. S. Radhakrishnan and Dipak Misra, while observing "it is luculent that the appellant had undergone mental torture at the hands of insensible police officials", directed the state to recover the compensation amount from the erring officers in equal proportions from their salaries. Though it took 20 years, justice was delivered nevertheless.

Mehmood Nayyar Azam, an Ayurvedic doctor who worked as a social activist in Chhattisgarh's Chirimiri district and led agitations against coal mafia, trade unions and corrupt police officials, was framed in a few false criminal cases in 1992. He was booked in a false case of theft of electricity and illegally detained on September 23, 1992 and beaten up. He was photographed with a banner declaring him as a thief and cheat. On his release, Azam learnt his photographs had been widely circulated in the area. The incident reportedly left a deep scar on his family life. Azam moved the High Court in 2001. A decade later, the Court declared the officers guilty but asked Azam to approach the state government for compensation. Not surprisingly, the state government rejected his representation in March this year following which Azam moved the Supreme Court.

4.1.16 *SC Slams Cops for Chopping off Man's Penis in PS*

In August 2010, taking a serious view of a barbaric act, the **Supreme Court** today sought response from three police personnel as to why they should not be awarded life sentence for chopping off the penis of a man in the police station. "How can you chop off the penis of a man? It is such a barbarian act. There is a limit even to nonsense. There is something called civilised behaviour," a Bench of Justices Markandeya Katju and T. S. Thakur observed, while dealing with the CBI's plea for enhancing the sentence of the accused policemen. In 1994 three policemen, SHO Sohan Singh, ASI Sumer Dhan and Kishore Singh took the victim Jugat Ram, an employee with a businessmen to the police station and chopped off his penis after subjecting him to torture. The police personnel, it was alleged, committed the gruesome act at the instance of the employer Bhairav Singh.

The Bench rejected the argument of the accused Kishore Singh, a constable with the Barmer Police Station, in Rajasthan's Barmer district that there was no evidence to establish their guilt. "You are all policemen. You have chopped of the penis of a man after bringing him into the police station. How do you expect some independent witness to speak against you policemen," the Bench asked. **The Apex Court further said that policemen cannot be allowed to go unpunished with such brutality.**

4.1.17 *The HC Sets Right the Injustice Meted Out to Seema Azad and Vishwavijay*

A classic example of the atrocity committed by the police – in this case the charge on this couple, human rights activists and journalists Seema Azad and her husband, Vishwavijay, was possession of seditious literature! The Allahabad police had arrested the duo on February 6, 2010 as Azad returned from New Delhi where she was visiting an international book fair. Her husband, who had gone to fetch her from the railway station, too, was arrested. They were charged under the Unlawful Activities Prevention Act. The prosecution claimed banned seditious literature had been found on the couple. It took them nearly two-and-a-half years to get justice.

Azad and Vijay, wife and husband, were given life imprisonment each on June 8 by a Sessions court. They were held guilty of being members of the Communist Party of India (Maoist). But a Division Bench of the **Allahabad High Court** Judges, Dharnidhar Jha and Ashokpal Singh, ruled in July 2012 that "no evidence of waging war against state was available", and granted them bail.

4.1.18 *Police Chief Told to File FIRs Against Four Special Cell Officers*

In September 2011, **Chief Metropolitan Magistrate** Vinod Yadav, acquitted all the accused in a case of cable theft after concluding that the police officers had framed them to extort money through threats to implicate the victims in a false case. The Court also directed the Police Commissioner to register a FIR against the Special Cell's Additional Deputy Commissioner of Police Ravi Shanker, Inspector Anil Dureja, Sub-Inspector Gajender, and Head Constable Hari Kishan under appropriate sections of the law. This was yet another 'feather in the cap' of the Special Cell, which has earned notoriety for all sorts of atrocities.

Expressing concern over the misuse of power by the Special Cell, the CMM observed: "**This case is a classic example of how and to what extent the police officers can go in framing persons, committing extortion and then make them suffer the ignominy of criminal prosecution by sheer misuse of power of investigation granted to them under the Code of Criminal Procedure**..."

Coming down hard on the investigating officer SI Gajendra, the

Court said: "The IO...in his zeal to frame the accused persons and in the process created false investigation record; tore off the investigation record; and extorted money from the accused persons by putting them in fear of implicating them in a MCOCA case." The CMM further noted that the policemen had demanded a huge bribe from the accused in their custody and also released some of them after getting bribed.

4.1.19 *Court Raps Cops for Trial of Wrong Man in Rape Case*

This takes the cake for being an excellent example of the utter depravity of the cops. In May 2012, questioning the police for ***putting a wrong man on trial in a rape case,*** **Additional Sessions Judge Kamini Lau** in Delhi asked the city's North-West district deputy commissioner of police (DCP) to take action against the erring officials for it. *The matter came to light at the time of recording of the statement of the victim who refused to identify the person facing trial as the real accused and told the judge that the one who had raped her was standing outside the court room and had threatened her not to depose in the case.* The Court pulled up the investigating officer (IO) in the case for not cross-checking the identity of the accused through the statutory Test Identification Parade (TIP).

"On the face of it, either Jai Kumar has been falsely implicated on mistaken identity perhaps only to work out the case or a deliberate attempt has been made to divert the allegations from Dinesh to Jai Kumar and perhaps it is for this reason that no identification was got conducted. It is this which makes the Court suspect the intent of investigating agency and the fairness of the investigation," ASJ Lau said. The Court observed that life and liberty of an individual is most "sacrosanct" and cannot be taken away by the state in the manner as done by the police in this case.

4.1.20 *Court Raps Police for Downplaying Crime, Charges Man with Gang Rape and Murder*

This was a particularly heinous offence in which, the court said, as the girl resisted the rape attempt, the accused Hitesh hit her on the backbone causing paralysis. The judge noted that after raping the girl in a moving car with his associate Monu, the accused "deliberately" caused the accident of the car by driving it into a ditch while jumping out. The victim died last year. And yet, for reasons which the readers can easily guess, despite medical records suggesting that the 15-year-old girl was raped, the police chargesheeted the accused only for the offence of attempt to rape and causing grievous hurt to her. In April 2012, **Additional Sessions Judge Kamini Lau** expressed anguish over the 'unprofessional and casual manner' of the Delhi police in chargesheeting a man allegedly involved in the gang rape-cum-murder of a minor girl for a milder offence of attempt to rape. "The chargesheet has been filed in a most non-professional and casual manner by invoking lesser offences. I am deeply anguished to note that till date the investigating agency has not even bothered to further investigate the aspect of cause of death of the girl," said the court.

We request the police leadership to do an honest introspection— by God, would you ever find such a diabolical, fiendish, and demonical savage, and such inhuman cops anywhere in the world as you claim to lead? No! And they are so, because you have failed in whatever you were supposed to do by way of leadership.

4.1.21 *Gagandeep Singh Case: Making an Accused of a Victim*

Gagandeep Singh, who was riding a motorcycle, had allegedly died after being hit by a car driven by sub inspector Jaspal Singh Bhullar in Sector-22, Chandigarh. According to Gagandeep's family, he had died when Bhullar allegedly jumped the red light and hit Gagandeep's bike on June 27, 2009. Pillion rider Mandeep Singh had received injuries during the accident. Bhullar, who was then in-charge of the Sector-22 police post, went on to file a case against Gagandeep and injured Mandeep Singh. The **Punjab and Haryana High Court** passed strictures against the Chandigarh police and on July 21, 2011 ordered Haryana DGP to conduct a re-investigation into the case.

4.1.22 *HC Asks Police Chief to Tender Apology for Harassing Man*

In March 2010, the **Delhi High Court** directed the city Police chief to send a written apology on behalf of the department to a man and his family for making him suffer for 15 years by registering false cases. Justice S. Muralidhar also awarded a compensation of over Rs. 5.32 lakh besides a cost of Rs. 30,000 for the litigation to Prem Pal and directed the police to pay the amount within four weeks. "*If the confidence has to be restored among the citizenry that the police is meant to protect their rights, then such expression of contrition by those at the helm is imperative,*" he said. The Court cautioned the officers "not to repeat such act in future" and directed the Police Commissioner to take note of the court's disapproval. Prem Pal had sought compensation for having faced harassment at the hands of the police, alleging the investigating agency had falsely registered 18 criminal cases, including a rape case, against him during 1991 to 2007. He also referred to the stricture passed against the Delhi police by a trial court while acquitting him in the rape case. Justice Muralidhar expressed his displeasure at the affidavits filed by DCPs H. M. Meena and Mangesh Kashyap for defending the acts of police and criticising the trial court findings.

In September 2004, the Trial Court had acquitted Prem Pal in the rape case, noting that the case was a "**glaring example of the poor in the country having no say and if they cry for justice their cries fall on deaf ears. They are made to suffer and pay by their life and liberty when they complain against police officials." The trial judge had also said "The police torture of Prem Pal has converted him into a living corpse.**"

4.1.23 *Delhi SHO Transferred After Court Stricture*

The victim Arvind had filed the complaint immediately after the accused tried to stab him in broad daylight during a religious procession, but the SHO did not register a case. Twenty one days later, a case for causing hurt was registered. In March 2003, a Court passed strictures against Kapasahera Station House Officer (SHO) for converting a case of attempt to murder into a lesser offence. The commissioner transferred the SHO, Virender Singh Chauhan, to district lines. The SHO is also accused of illegally releasing the three accused in the case. 'The accused were apprehended by a group of eye-witnesses. Instead of registering a case, the SHO released them.

4.1.24 *The 'Crackdown' on Baba Ramdev Rally at Ramlila Maidan*

In February 2012, the **Supreme Court** sternly pulled up the government and Delhi Police for the midnight crackdown in June 2011 at yoga teacher Baba Ramdev's Ramlila ground rally, saying the incident could have been avoided by more patient handling by the state. The Supreme Court directed the Delhi Police to register cases against police officials who indulged in destruction of public property and attacked the sleeping crowd. It has ordered disciplinary action against those police officials "who have exceeded the limit" and those who "didn't help to rescue the injured."

Baba Ramdev's rally was held to protest against what he called the government's inaction on the issue of black money. Thousands of the yoga guru's followers were present at the grounds when the Delhi Police swooped down to evict the Baba. Some of Baba Ramdev's followers retaliated. A woman, Rajbala, was among 30 people badly injured and she died later in hospital. **The Supreme Court had taken suo motu note of media reports purportedly showing the brutality of police action against Baba Ramdev's followers, including women and children, many of whom were reportedly sleeping at the time of the crackdown. The Supreme Court said that a sleeping congregation can't be called an unlawful assembly. The Supreme Court held that the police had acted in undue haste and that police**

restrictions at the Ramlila grounds on the day of the incident were unreasonable and unwarranted. The state, it has observed, could have avoided the clash by exercising patience. In its stinging indictment, the court said this was a glaring example of a trust deficit between the people governing and the people being governed.

The court observed that the real sufferer on that day was the public. The incident, the court said, was an assault on basic rights enshrined in the Constitution. It has ordered Rs. 5 lakh in compensation for victim Rajbala's next of kin. It has also ordered Rs. 50,000 for those were grievously injured and Rs. 25,000 for those with slight injuries. The court has ordered that 25 percent of this compensation must come from Baba Ramdev's trust as he was held guilty of negligence.

4.1.25 *'Murdered' Servant Produced in High Court!*

This is an interesting case which shows the utter depravity of the police—sometimes they produce the wrong man on a charge of rape; this time they charged people for a murder that never happened. On June 21, 2002, Sukhjit Singh, then a resident of Chhichhrewal village in Batala tehsil, was booked by the Batala police for having allegedly murdered his neighbour's servant Naresh Mirdha for having illicit relations with his two teenage nieces. Three of his alleged accomplices were also named in the FIR. On June 24, 2002, DSP Rachhpal Singh Ghuman even made a statement before the media, highlighting the achievement of the police in cracking the case of murder of the servant. Naresh was reported to have been killed in February 2002 but his dead body was never recovered.

Sukhjit Singh was let off only after he allegedly paid a hefty bribe to cops. After being released, he shifted base to Canada along with his two nieces as the honour and reputation of the girls had been "destroyed" by the police. However, even after moving to Canada, Sukhjit Singh continued to make frantic efforts to clear his and his family's name. Finally, the servant, the same whose murder had been pinned on Sukhjit Singh, was traced to his village in Jharkhand. Sukhjit Singh brought Naresh Mirdha to Chandigarh and his lawyer, Hemant Saini, produced Naresh before the High Court, which ordered that he be provided security so that the police, in order to justify the case, did not cause any harm to him.

In June 2006, taking note of the alleged high-handedness committed by the Batala police of Gurdaspur district in falsely implicating innocent persons in the murder that was never committed, the **Punjab and Haryana High Court** ordered a CBI inquiry into the matter.

4.1.26 *Cash-for-Vote Scam: SC Slams Delhi Police for 'Callous' Probe*

On July 22, 2008, three BJP members—Ashok Argal, Faggan Singh Kulaste and Mahavir Bhagora—had placed Rs. 1 crore cash in Lok Sabha alleging the money was given to them by floor managers of the UPA government to secure their support during the No Confidence motion after Left parties withdrew their support over the Indo-US nuclear deal. In July 2011, the **Supreme Court** slammed Delhi Police for its "callous" approach to the probe into the cash-for-vote scam of 2008. As the Delhi Police filed its status report on the investigation, the Apex Court said that it was not happy with it and pulled up the police on various fronts. The Supreme Court wanted to know why Delhi Police had not made even a single custodial interrogation in the case and that the investigation was not moving at a pace that it should have. It also slammed the police for giving only some stories in its status report.

4.1.27 *Court Frees Man Branded a Gangster, Slams Police*

As we have said repeatedly in this book, the poor are the most vulnerable and the easiest targets of police atrocities of all kinds. In India, there is no crime worse than being poor. The Delhi police had arrested a vegetable seller Rajeev under MCOCA and claimed that he was an associate of interstate gangster and contract killer Amit. In December 2011, he was freed by a Delhi court, which slammed the police for invoking a stringent law meant to deal with criminal gangs and keeping him behind bars without evidence. Rajeev, who was jailed for offences under the Maharashtra Control of Organised Crime Act, was freed by **Additional Session Judge** Sanjeev Aggarwal. "The investigating agencies are directed to be careful in future before invoking the provisions of the MCOCA against any individual without proper material and home work," the court said.

The Court observed that Rajeev was earning a living from selling vegetables and cleaning utensils at marriage functions. Judge Aggarwal said that during the investigations no evidence could be collected to establish any nexus between the organised crime syndicate, being run by accused Amit and Rajeev. The judge added that the accused had not generated any wealth in association with the crime syndicate. The court pulled up the investigating agency, saying that if they were not sure about the wealth generated by the accused from the fruits of his crime, 'what was the hurry to invoke the stringent provisions of the MCOCA, as it was an extraordinary act which curtails the life and liberty of an individual'?

4.1.28 *Differential Treatment of Accused: HC Slams CBI, Says it has Lost Credibility*

In April 2012, the **Rajasthan High Court** came down hard on CBI and observed that the agency has lost its "credibility" and is proving "counterproductive" to the aims and objectives with which it was established. The Court's remarks came in the wake of arrest of BJP MLA Rajendra Rathore by the CBI. Without taking any politician's name Justice Mahesh Chandra Sharma pointed at CBI's biased treatment towards accused in the Dara Singh fake encounter case.

"It appears that accused in same case are being given differential treatment by CBI. You people salute an accused, offer him tea and coffee and land him behind bars facilitating his judicial custody, whereas the same CBI gets police custody of other accused for the maximum time period in the same case. The aims and objectives with which CBI was established have been compromised and the CBI is proving counterproductive to these objectives and it's high time when the agency needs to be shut down."

The observations came on a criminal miscellaneous petition filed by Jagram, one of the police officers accused in the case. *The agency had faced criticism for not seeking Rathore's custody for interrogation and filing the supplementary chargesheet without any new evidence. When A. K. Jain, then ADGP (crime), surrendered before the court, the CBI had got a maximum remand of 13 days. "This is travesty of justice. An accused is languishing in jail for over 11 months and the CBI is all out to deliberately delay the trial.* An accused has a right to speedy trial, whether he will be punished or not is yet to be seen but he cannot be denied a speedy justice," observed the Court.

4.1.29 *HC Slams CBI's UT Branch, Hands Probe to Delhi Unit*

In March 2012, making it clear that the Court cannot "shut its eyes" to an "unabashed attempt to scuttle justice", the **Punjab and Haryana High Court** handed over the investigation of the controversial Chandigarh teachers recruitment scam to the Central Bureau of Investigation (CBI), Delhi branch. In an indictment and embarrassment to the Chandigarh branch of the CBI, a division bench of the High Court ruled that "*sufficient amount of suspicion has been aroused in the mind of the Court indicating a complete cover-up by the CBI Chandigarh branch*". The directions were passed today by a Division Bench comprising Chief Justice Ranjan Gogoi and Justice Mahesh Grover on a petition filed by one Karamjit Singh.

On the other hand Chandigarh Police, which has already submitted a chargesheet in the trial Court, has been slammed by the High Court for "shoddy investigation". The petitioner had moved the High Court seeking a CBI probe into the case. The scam allegedly involves the then Director Public Instructions (DPI), Samwartak Singh. After perusing the report of senior lawyer R. S. Cheema, *amicus curiae* in the case, the HC has ruled that "the CBI took a complete somersault and diluted its stand by saying that changes were arbitrary but not criminal so as to be sufficient to fix criminal conspiracy and that it was not established that candidates who were wrongly called for interview were finally selected and that change of criteria was not motivated". Also, the Bench took strong exception to CBI's silence in the case and its failure in not informing the Court of its investigation. "The CBI had been associated with the matter from the very beginning yet this fact was not disclosed to the Court till the time the enquiry report reached the Court and intimation received from a third person. This is a fact difficult to digest since the CBI was a party to the proceedings and its silence, therefore, is deafening to say the least," the Bench held.

4.1.30 *HC Slams Mumbai Police for Arresting Cartoonist on 'Frivolous' Grounds*

In September 2012, a Kanpur-based cartoonist was arrested on charges of sedition (***Readers must note this—charge of sedition for making a cartoon. Even the British, who framed this law, had never been so stupid***!). Subsequently, he got bail from the High Court. Later, a PIL was filed by lawyer Sanskar Marathe claiming Trivedi's arrest was illegal and unjustified. On this PIL, a division Bench of Justices D. Y. Chandrachud and Amjad Sayyed of the honourable **Bombay High Court** slammed Mumbai Police for arresting cartoonist Aseem Trivedi on "frivolous" grounds and "without application of mind", saying its action breached his freedom of speech and expression. "How can you (police) arrest people on frivolous grounds? You arrest a cartoonist and breach his liberty of freedom of speech and expression," said the Court. Observing that Trivedi's arrest was prima facie "arbitrary", the Court said, "We have one Aseem Trivedi who was courageous enough to raise his voice and stand against this, but what about several others whose voices are shut by police." *The Court clearly asked, "Why did the police not apply its mind before arresting him on sedition charges?" It added, "Today you attacked a cartoonist, tomorrow you will attack a filmmaker and then a writer. We live in a free society and everyone has freedom of speech and expression."*

4.1.31 *HC Slams Police for Not Acting Against Kanda*

We have repeatedly pointed out that the police serve only those who can pay them or those who are powerful. This ugly fact came out in

all its starkness in the case of a former Haryana minister Gopal Goyal Kanda accused of raping one of his employees Geetika Sharma, subjecting her to unnatural sex, and eventually abetting her suicide. In August 2012, rejecting an application for granting anticipatory bail to former Haryana minister Gopal Goyal Kanda; the **Delhi High Court** pulled up Delhi police for 'delaying the investigation' and making no serious attempt to arrest him. "This application appears to have been filed only to bring on record from the side of the police that the accused has gone underground and the police is unable to arrest him so that investigation gets delayed. This application is dismissed," Justice P. K. Bhasin said.

The Court said the vakalatnama, executed by Kanda on August 13, had been identified by a lawyer six days before it was signed by the accused. The Court said if Kanda himself had signed the vakalatnama then there was no justification for his brother, Govind Kumar, filing the bail plea on his behalf without authorization. Justice Bhasin observed that though the FIR in the case was registered on August 5 and co-accused Aruna Chadha was arrested on August 7; police merely issued a notice to Kanda to join the investigation. "Because of all these actions of the police, the concerned accused appears to be sitting comfortably somewhere..." he said.

4.1.32 *High Court Slams Police for Registering Criminal Case Against Activist*

Activists are another favourite target of the police for harassment. Generally these guys are poor but since they are educated and vocal, the police act against them with all the more vehemence. In March 2010, a year after a Thane resident Abdul Aziz Mukadam—an activist in the Vikrant Tower case—was booked for murder by the Mumbai police, the **Bombay High Court** came down heavily on them saying the investigation they carried out suffers from lack of credibility, fairness and commitments to bring offenders to book. A Division Bench of Justice B. H. Marlapalle and Justice R. Y. Ganoo transferred the case to the Central Bureau of Investigation (CBI).

Vikrant Tower was constructed by Shivaji Adak of Krishnai Developers on the land of Phoolabai Sarkale in 2005. Adak had failed to obtain development permission from the Thane Municipal Corporation (TMC) and thus attracted demolition. The Supreme Court recently ordered the demolition of Vikrant Tower. The process had started in 2005 itself—however, *the police booked him for murder in 2009 for two deaths that had taken place in 2005 even as no complaint against him was ever filed by any person.*

The judges, while taking the case away from Mumbai police, stated in their order, "If the criminal justice system in this country has to be set right so as to inspire the confidence of a common man, the police must be liberated from the clutches of the 'wanted interests', so as to belie the fast growing belief that the police are possessed by the lobbies of gangsters, builders and political dictates." The court added, "***We are at pains to note that the police officers before us have filed misleading and facts suppressing affidavits on oath and there is no room to believe that it was unintended.***"

4.1.33 *Hindu-Muslim Marriage: HC Frees Man, Slams Cops*

Inter-caste or inter-religion marriages also provide an excellent opportunity to the cops to give free rein to their deeply ingrained regressive social values. That's how you find the cops either supporting the khap panchayats or turning a blind eye to their depredations. In October 2010, one Aslam Khan, a class IV employee in the High Court's protocol section in Jammu and Priyanka Pandoh alias Shaheen, a first-year student of a private law college at Jammu, married before the Imam of a mosque at Sarwal. Hailing from two adjoining localities of Jammu city, they had an affair for the past three years and decided to marry when the girl turned 19. The girl supposedly had converted to Islam. Fearing reprisal from her family, the couple approached the **J&K High Court** on November 3 and appeared before Justice J. P. Singh the next day. The court fixed November 9 for the hearing, but a day earlier both of them were apprehended by the police from outside the Jammu airport following a complaint by the girl's mother, Sonia Pandoh. Both were reportedly going to board a Srinagar-bound flight. The cops arrested Aslam on charges of kidnapping and handed over the girl to her mother next day without even recording her statement and despite the HC instructions to produce her before it. *The moral of the story is that if you dare to marry outside your religion, the cops might put you behind bars on trumped up charges of kidnapping. In this case, this happened even as the man had taken the precaution of approaching the Honourable High Court beforehand.*

Eventually, the High Court came to their rescue and granted bail to the man who had been in police lock-up for three days on charges of kidnapping the girl and slammed the police for their failure to produce her before it. Justice J. P. Singh directed the SSP, Jammu, to make efforts to trace and produce the girl in the court on November 16, and took a serious note of the failure of the Pacca Danga SHO to comply with the directions to produce her in the court. The cops had the audacity to claim that the girl had already been handed over to her mother when the court's directions came. They did not produce the girl on the appointed date and Justice Singh noted, "I am concerned about the liberty and safety of a girl who had approached this court seeking protection." "**Two people had come for protection and you are trying to fiddle with the powers of the court. The SHO has been unable to trace a person whom he himself had handed over to someone without orders of the court. When you are not in a position to produce a person despite court orders, what protection will you provide to an ordinary man?**"

4.1.34 *Senior Citizens Held for Playing Cards, HC Slams Police*

Petty offences often provide good amusement and pastime to the cops to indulge in satiating their perverse desire of 'controlling' others and inflicting pain upon them. Going after small-time gambling is an extremely popular sport amongst police officers in general and young IPS officers in particular, even as they make good money from big-time gambling dens. In June 2012, Mumbai police was severely censured by the **Bombay High Court** for acting in a "high-handed" and "despicable" manner while arresting a group of mostly senior citizens playing rummy and bridge at Andheri gymkhana (not a shady place by any stretch of imagination). Suddenly, a team of policemen 'raided' the place and picked up the group for 'gambling'. They were detained overnight at the Andheri (E) police station and reportedly not allowed to eat. In the end, 17 people including two old women were charged while those with political or police connections were let off. The 17 later moved the court for relief and compensation.

A division bench of Justices V. M. Kanade and P. D. Kode quashed the FIR filed under the Bombay Prevention of Gambling Act against 17 people, including two women, and directed the state to pay a compensation of Rs. 1,000 to each of them. They also directed that an additional Rs. 25,000 be paid to each of the two women — Bina Gharat, 65 and Villi Wadia, 72 —who were arrested in violation of Section 46(4) CrPC. The law mandates that a magistrate's permission is needed to arrest a woman after sunset. "It is evident that the policemen acted in a very high-handed manner and did not follow proper procedure before conducting the raid," the judges said.

4.1.35 *'Anguished' Gujarat High Court Raps Cops for Framing Man*

In March 2012, the **Gujarat High Court** expressed "anguish" over framing of a youth in a drug-peddling case by Junagadh policemen. The court ordered inquiry and departmental action against those involved in this case. ***You will be surprised to learn of the depths to which the cops could fall, and how inhuman they could become in***

implicating somebody in serious charges like those under the NDPS Act, knowing it fully well that this law is very stringent.

In October 2009, one Mukesh Boricha was arrested on charges of peddling 170 gram of charas. This happened following information provided by one Krishnaba to a traffic constable Gul Mohammed, who allegedly intercepted him on bike and recovered the contraband. However, a Sessions court acquitted him the next year with observation that police could not prove the case against Boricha and the entire process of search and seizure was carried out illegally. The judicial findings were that a traffic cop does not have power to conduct such a search. The procedure as per the Narcotic Drugs and Psychotropic Substances Act (NDPS) was not followed as seizure took place in the absence of the mandatory panchas and gazetted officer. Police never placed call details despite court's demand. The bike shown as being used for peddling the material did not belong to the accused, but was chosen by cops from many vehicles parked in public place.

The state government challenged this acquittal order before HC, but a bench headed by Justice D. H. Waghela took a very serious note and ordered a departmental inquiry. In this probe, it was revealed that since the accused had refused to marry Krishnaba, the later falsely implicated him in drug-peddling case with the help of the cops. A Division bench of Justices Akil Kureshi and Sonia Gokani questioned the investigators on how they failed to spot fabrication. The HC confirmed the acquittal order and expressed "anguish over such arbitrary exercise of powers in complete disregard to settled position of law...As disciplinary proceedings are already initiated, it is expected that it would be pursued scrupulously to upkeep the faith of citizens in the justice delivery system." The High Court expressed displeasure at the way provisions of NDPS Act were violated rampantly in this case. "It is time and again held by the higher courts that for stricter punishment, scrutiny at every level correspondingly shall have to be stricter," the court observed. *If this is not supervisory failure, what else is this?*

4.1.36 *Assault Case: Court Raps CID Over Delay in Arresting Former MLA's Son*

Once again, this incident shows how the police go out of their way, to the extent of disregarding honourable Courts' orders, when it comes to serving their masters among the rich and the powerful. As we have repeatedly mentioned in the book, the police will not do anything unless they are given at least one of two things, namely, money or pressure. Money comes from the rich; pressure comes from

the powerful. The police, in effect, are the 'slaves' of the rich and the powerful.

Former Ulhasnagar MLA Pappu Kalani has several criminal cases—including murder cases—against him. His son Omie Kalani was allegedly involved in an assault on Sunil Sukhramani to dissuade his aunt Neetu Sukhramani from contesting from a ward in Ulhasnagar. This was because Omie's mother Jyoti had decided to contest from the same ward. Sunil Sukhramani approached the High Court demanding that the investigation of the case be transferred from the state CID to the Central Bureau of Investigation (CBI). **In August 2012, a Division Bench of Justices V. M. Kanade and P. D. Kode of the Bombay High Court pointed out that the CID had not arrested Omie despite his anticipatory bail application having been rejected by the High Court**. "The facts of the case disclose a sorry state of affairs. It is distressing that the state CID has taken no steps to arrest the accused," the judges said.

The court also took note of the fact that Sukhramani was assaulted for a second time after he approached the High Court, allegedly in the presence of policemen. **"You (police) arrest people where it is not necessary and put them in jail. But in serious cases like this where immediate steps have to be taken the police does not do anything. This is the problem with police," Justice Kanade said.** He added, "Such incidents send a wrong signal to society and create dissatisfaction. Some people are then tempted to take the law in their own hands. This must not happen—look at what happened at Azad Maidan (on August 11)."

4.1.37 *Bombay High Court Raps Thane SP for Inaction in Infant Abduction Case*

By the same logic, the police do not do anything for the poor. In this case, the child of a beggar was abducted and, as expected, the police did not do anything. In September 2011, the **Bombay High Court** rapped Thane's superintendent of police (SP) for failing to take action against those who had allegedly abducted a woman's infant in January and also against the police officers who "connived" with the accused by not opposing his bail. A division bench of Justice A. M. Khanwilkar and Justice P. D. Kode observed that they were "intrigued by the manner in which the superintendent of police has dealt with" the earlier directions of the court. In July, the High Court had directed the SP of Thane, P. S. Jadhav, to personally supervise the investigation into the abduction of Kaitul Ansari's son, Eid Ulla, who was taken away in January by three persons from Nalasopara railway station, one of whom was known to Ansari. Ansari, who makes a living by asking for alms at Nalasopara railway station, lodged a complaint with the police station on January 24 that a woman by the name of Sharli Charke had taken away her child when she (Ansari) went to attend nature's call. She even alleged that the police demanded Rs. 10,000 from her to lodge the complaint. (***You see, they could demand money even from a beggar!***) The Court had also asked the SP to submit a report on why no action was initiated by the police for bail cancellation of the accused after observing that it (bail to accused) "was possible because of the connivance of the investigating officer." The SP, on his part, had simply dismissed Ansari's grievance that the police connived with the accused who succeeded in getting bail. The court observed: "We are convinced that the superintendent of police has not at all examined all these aspects before discarding the grievance of the petitioner that the investigating officer had connived with accused nos. 2 and 3 who succeeded in getting bail from the concerned court."

4.1.38 *Court Rap on Police for Not Filing FIR*

Not registering FIRs is the most infamous atrocity committed by the police. We have analyzed it from a psychological angle. The phenomenon at work is the feeling of 'power' which accrues from it. Making somebody run a hundred times, gives the cop a high—he is so 'powerful' that people are obliged to beg him. At a subconscious level, this compensates for a deep-rooted inferiority complex. All sorts of excuses are put forward for not registering a case. Usually, they would say that they would conduct a preliminary inquiry first to find out whether a case is made out or not. But in this case, the cop said that though a case was made out, he needed permission from his superiors to register a case. In June 2012, pulling up Delhi Police for not registering an FIR for over a year on a complaint made by an elderly couple, a Trial Court, stating that it was pained to notice that a senior citizen has been subjected to harassment, directed Delhi Police Commissioner to file a report giving details of legal provisions that bar an officer from lodging the FIR without prior approval from superiors.

The Court was hearing the complaint of a septuagenarian couple, Uma Arora and her husband Santosh Arora—residents of east Delhi—against a property dealer and others for cheating them. They were being "harassed" and made to run from pillar to post for the past one-and-a-half-year just to get the FIR registered. Ordering registration of the FIR on the complaint of the 70-year-old man, *the Court took serious objection to a report of a police officer that though he was convinced that a case was made out, the FIR could not be lodged as an approval from the DCP concerned was awaited. "There exists no provision in the Code of Criminal Procedure which mandates or even requires the approval of any officer or the DCP before registration of the FIR. If the cognizable offence is made out and the IO is of the opinion that an FIR ought to be registered, police are bound to register an FIR,"* **Metropolitan Magistrate** Amitabh Rawat said.

4.1.39 *Court Raps Cop for Shoddy Murder Probe, Orders Action*

'Experienced and crooked' police officers are known for their ability to 'shape' investigations, that is, to manipulate the findings. This is done with the obvious motive of making money, often by siding with the accused who has greater reason to pay better. Readers must note that quite often the cops take money from both parties but eventually oblige only that party which pays more. In other words, the 'cop's justice' goes to the highest bidder. The rate, of course, depends on the gravity of the offence and the desperation of the parties. In September 2011, **Additional Sessions Judge N. K. Kaushik** in Delhi ordered action against inspector R. R. Khatana, saying he had tried to "raise unnecessary dust just to cause utter confusion and hide the truth". Noting that there was a string of lapses in the probe conducted by Khatana in the murder of west Delhi resident Hitender Singh, the court said, "It appears the inspector made it a point, in a calculated manner, may be in collusion with the accused, to ensure the failure of the prosecution's case during investigation itself."

4.1.40 *Court Raps Police for Falsely Implicating Man in a Case*

The sentiments expressed above found mention in another case. Twelve years after a truck driver allegedly crushed a man in a hit-and-run incident, a city court acquitted him, saying the police had falsely implicated him in the case. **This case is an example of how padding up is done by the investigating officer, by using false witnesses/evidence, so as to give a hit-and-run case, a shape of complete and proper investigation, Metropolitan Magistrate Prashant Sharma said while acquitting the accused Rishi Pal.**

The incident dates back to February 16, 2000, when Pal, driving a truck, allegedly hit a bike-borne man, Narender, in Moti Bagh area and sped away. The police had claimed to apprehend Pal after a chase. The police had chargesheeted Pal under Sections 279 and 304-A of the IPC for rash driving and causing death by negligence. The court described the testimonies of the prosecution witnesses as unreliable and untrustworthy. Believing the defence version of the story that the accused did not commit the crime in question, the court said, "**Rather, he was stopped by the police official on Shanti Path and later on falsely implicated in this case.**" *How heinous!*

4.1.41 *Dhruti Patel Death Case: High Court Raps Navsari Cops for Destroying Evidence*

No marks for guessing why the police manipulate investigation of cases. To make money, silly! The **Gujarat High Court** came down hard on police in Navsari when it stated that they had tried to destroy evidence in Dhruti Patel death case of March 26, 2012 in which her mother-in-law and sister-in-law are accused. Justice Anant Dave refused to grant bail to the accused on the ground that the investigation in the case had already been tampered with and if the applicants are released on bail at this stage, they may tamper with the evidence and influence witnesses and the investigation officer. The HC also stated that a thorough and impartial investigation by an independent agency like Central Bureau of Investigation (CBI) was required to be done. "**The court will be failing in its duty if it does not record that the filing of the charge-sheet by the investigation officer is based on deliberate and considered mischief to shield the accused, for which, the complainant is free to take suitable action in accordance with law,**" the order said.

The HC also considered observations of the trial court that the inquest panchnama and panchnama of the scene of offence were tampered with, no table or stool was found in the bathroom standing upon which the deceased reached the curtain pipe at a height of 6.4 feet to tie the towel. The court also considered the trial court's observation that the towel using which Dhruti hanged self has not been taken as 'muddamal' (circumstantial evidence) and not sent for forensic examination. The court also made serious observations about the 14 injury marks on the body of the deceased. ***The moral of the story is that if you have enough money to buy the police, they will be your dutiful servants and will do their very best to protect you even from a murder case.***

4.1.42 *Adarsh Scam Probe: Bombay HC Slams CBI for Inaction*

The natural tendency of the police to protect its masters or whoever is connected to that class is almost universal and is found even with the so-called premier investigating agencies of the country. In March 2012, the **Bombay High Court** came down heavily on the Central Bureau of Investigation once again for not initiating significant action against accused in Adarsh society scam despite gathering sufficient evidence against them. A Division Bench of Justice Mujumdar and

Justice R. D. Dhanukar questioned the CBI, "Why haven't you arrested anyone despite gathering incriminating evidence against the accused persons?" The court accepted the names of eight persons who, according to the CBI, have 'benami' flats in Adarsh society. The names were submitted to the court in a sealed envelope. The court perused through the contents of the sealed cover and asked the CBI, why no action has been taken against them. Justice Mujmudar, without revealing the names, hinted that some of the eight persons named by the CBI are serving government officials. "The fact that you have zeroed in on these names means that you have evidence against them. So what action have you taken against them," he asked.

The court also slammed the CBI for not intimating respective departments of the serving government servants, who were named as accused in the case. It directed the CBI to inform the government departments and share details in a sealed envelope with those departments recommending departmental inquiry against the accused. To all the criticism on the lack of arrest in the case, the CBI informed the court that specific sanctions are required to execute the arrests. However, the CBI had no reply to a question posed by the court, "Have you even asked for a sanction on anyone's arrest?" The CBI responded by saying that it would make the necessary arrests at the time of filing the chargesheet. The court, however, refused to accept its statement and observed that this was not the procedure followed in other cases.

In the Adarsh Scam, as you would recall, R. C. Thakur, a retired defence estates officer, along with Brig. (Retd.) M. M. Wanchoo, conspired with defence services officers, state government officials and others with the intention to illegally get the land allotted in favour of Adarsh cooperative housing society in which they were members. The concerned public servants abused their official position, manipulated and fabricated records to get the land allotted. In 2003, Thakur and Wanchoo and another member Gidwani further entered into a criminal conspiracy with Ashok Chavan, the then Revenue Minister of Maharashtra. Chavan agreed to include civilians as members in the society with the ulterior motive of making his relatives members in the society. P. V. Deshmukh, while working as deputy secretary, urban development department, in conspiracy with Thakur and other members of Adarsh, fraudulently communicated to the Chief Engineer Building Plan, Municipal Corporation of Greater Mumbai that No Objection Certificate (NOC) was granted by the Ministry of Environment and Forest though no such NOC was ever issued by the ministry.

4.1.43 *Bofors Case: Court Slams CBI on Quattrocchi: 'Bias, Mala Fide, Cart Before Horse'*

The Bofors case is well-known. What is not so well-known is the attempt of the CBI to shield the 'powerful' accused. We should not be surprised—after all this is the national character of the police to serve the 'rich' and the 'powerful'. *Slamming the CBI for "mala fide", "bias" and not pursuing properly the extradition to India of Bofors case accused Ottavio Quattrocchi, a Delhi Court said the agency's move to first withdraw the Red Corner Notice (RCN) against the Italian businessman and then seek withdrawal of his prosecution was like "putting the cart before the horse".* The CBI has put the cart before the horse by taking off the red-corner notice against Quattrocchi before this court could decide on the withdrawal of prosecution," he said.

As records of extradition proceedings in courts in Malaysia and Argentina and how Quattrocchi withdrew money from bank accounts in London were produced, **CMM Vinod Yadav** did not hold back his criticism. "I am prima facie convinced of the mala fide and lack of good faith of CBI. I completely agree that there were certain mala fide intentions in the case and there is no doubt about that. Appeal was not filed in Argentina against dismissal of the extradition plea and then fictitious bank accounts were opened only to withdraw the money," the CMM said. He accepted the contention that extradition proceedings were not properly pursued or might be "pursued with a bias."

4.1.44 *Amusement-cum-Theme Park Scam : Protecting the Powerful*

As mentioned above, protecting the powerful like a faithful dog is in the genes of the police, the CBI being no exception. In August 2012, rejecting the closure report filed in the multi-crore amusement-cum-theme park scam in Chandigarh, the **Special CBI Court** minced no words in raising eyebrows over "no investigations" done by the CBI "regarding financial status" of the then UT Administrator Gen. (Retd.) S. F. Rodrigues, his son in law Patrick Kerr and his then ADC Nirvikar Singh. Referring to an official communication sent by the CVC to the Director, CBI in October 2009, the Special CBI Court Chandigarh held "the Commission was of the view that thorough evaluation of available documentary evidence regarding involvement of senior officials of Chandigarh Administration was required. The role of Administrator, Chandigarh was not free from suspicion". Those in dock are former UT Advisor Lalit Sharma; former UT Home Secretary Krishna Mohan, former UT Director (Tourism) Vivek Atray and Unitech Amusement

Ltd. The three were booked on charges of corruption. However, the CBI on April 16 had filed a closure report in the case. Slamming the premier investigating agency for not carrying out thorough investigation, the special CBI Judge held that key facts were "wrongly overlooked" by the CBI.

The Special CBI Judge Vimal Kumar gave a host of reasons for rejecting the closure report by CBI. They include improper valuation of land for assessing fixed annual licence fee; non participation of M/s. Unitech Limited at Expression of Interest (EoI) stage; non tracing of file of EoI by M/s. Unitech Amusement Limited; ignoring of M/s. Unitech Amusement Park Limited which had participated at EoI stage; and accepting bid of M/s. Unitech Limited having no experience of similar project were wrongly overlooked in investigation. The concluding paragraph of the judgement reads "keeping in view the importance of matter as well as dealings of public servants in financial matters, acceptance of closure report dated April 16 shall lead to loss of public faith in the public administration. So, the closure report cannot be accepted".

In the detailed order, Vimal Kumar, special CBI Judge termed the entire bidding process to M/s. Unitech Limited by the bureaucrats as "unnatural". The son-in-law of the Administrator was alleged to be the middleman in the two projects. The judgement also reads that "no investigation regarding the financial implications of the agreement in favour of M/s. Unitech Limited was carried out to know about the loss to public exchequer". Elaborating on the "liberal" role played by the three bureaucrats, the CBI Court has held that the "official accused initially dealt with all bids liberally and subsequently acted strictly and rejected bid of M/s. DLF". "It is unnatural that after M/s. DLF Limited was found to be successful in first stage and financial bids were called, the financial bid was not opened on basis of technical objection". Referring to a noted Supreme Court judgement, the special CBI Court has ruled "it is well settled principle of law that governmental action is routed through individuals. Hence, they should be answerable for illegal acts."

For the lay reader, the important point to be noted is that so many lapses in investigation, and that too by a premier agency like the CBI, cannot be passed off as genuine mistakes. If they are genuine mistakes, then they do not deserve to be called a premier agency. And if they are not genuine mistakes, it can only mean that they were committed intentionally and knowingly to save the 'powerful' accused.

4.1.45 *Gujarat Minister Murder: All Accused Acquitted Due to Blinkered and Washed Up Investigation*

In August 2011, the **Gujarat High Court** dropped murder charges against all the 12 accused in the killing of former Gujarat Home Minister Haren Pandya. Haren Pandya, former Minister of State for Home in Gujarat, was shot dead on March 26, 2003, near Law Garden area of the city when he had gone for a morning walk. The CBI had stated in its chargesheet that the murder was carried out to avenge the 2002 riots. The 12 accused were found guilty by a POTA court in 2007 and seven were sentenced to life imprisonment. A Division Bench of the High Court comprising Justices D. H. Waghela and J. C. Upadhyay said the investigations by the central agency in the case were "washed up, blinkered and had left lot to desire." Criticizing the CBI, the Court further said the investigating officer should be made accountable for such lapses which have caused injustice to the accused and wastage of public resources. It said the investigation agency could not prove murder charges. Hence the conviction by the Trial Court, where the accused were convicted of murder with criminal conspiracy would not survive hence the order is set aside. The court, however, said that they can be convicted for criminal conspiracy and attempt to murder.

4.1.46 *National Rural Health Mission Scam: HC Rap Leaves CBI Red-Faced*

In August 2012, a Division Bench of the **Allahabad High Court** came down heavily on the CBI for its failure to take the probe into the NRHM scam to its logical end. The CBI had submitted its report before the court seeking to conclude the probe into the NRHM scam, the two-year-old murder case of two chief medical officers and a suspected case of suicide of a medical officer. The CBI could nail down only a few kingpins in the NRHM scam. It also failed in bringing the accused to book in the murder cases. Nor has it been able to establish the motive behind the murder.

The agency was roped in to investigate, following allegations that the state police was trying to hush up the probe. "We think Uttar Pradesh Police are better than the CBI," the Court said, leaving the CBI officials in the court red-faced. "It has been over a year since the CBI launched probe. But the agency failed in both the cases, despite seeking time from the court thrice. Last time also, the agency sought three months' extension for concluding the investigations...and **when it submitted the report, the court was just short of throwing it into the dustbin,**" the Bench said. "You have not been able to make progress even an inch ever since your last request," lamented the court.

4.1.47 *The ISRO Espionage Case: Justice at Long Last*

The infamous ISRO spying case is a classic example of how the lives of even respected people could be totally destroyed by implicating them in absolutely false cases. It took them full 18 years to get justice. In this case, the motive was not the usual desire for money, but the desire to sensationalize the matters by invoking a 'spy ring' in an otherwise placid state like Kerala; and the desire to claim credit for having done a great professional job by busting a great 'spy ring' when there was none. This was one case in which the police and the media fed each other; the media went ballistic, cooking up all sorts of spicy stories and conducting a trial of its own; the police claimed credit for all those revelations.

The ISRO 'espionage case' burst upon the national scene on November 20, 1994 when a Maldivian woman, Mariam Rasheeda, was arrested from a hotel in Thiruvananthapuram on charges of overstaying after the expiry of her visa. In the days that followed, the story took a startling turn. The police said she was a spy, and not just for one country—she was said to be an intelligence agent for Russia, the ISI and the international rocket technology mafia across the world. *(By God, quite an achievement for a mere high school pass woman!)* The Kerala police had alleged that, as inferred from the alleged confession of Mariam Rasheeda, ISRO scientist Dr. Nambi Narayanan along with a colleague and four others, including the two Maldivian women, had transferred certain secret documents on India's space programme to foreign countries. On November 30, 1994, a team of policemen barged into the house of Dr. Nambi Narayanan, a senior scientist with Indian Space Research Organisation (ISRO), and arrested him. He now claims that he was detained illegally for three days and tortured in the process of interrogation.

The police reportedly fed the media 'conspiracy theories' about India's space technology being smuggled out by a network of scientists like Narayanan and spies like Mariam Rasheeda and another Maldivian woman, Fauzia Hassan. Regular hints of a 'honey trap' angle or the use of sleazy sex in luring the scientists were subtly dropped. Every morning, Kerala's newspaper readers woke up to new spicy bits on the two women and the lifestyle of Narayanan and others. They simply lapped it up—a great source of excitement in a place where usually they don't get any news other than dharnas, demonstrations and protest actions. The case was first investigated by state police and later handed over to the CBI, which found that no espionage as alleged had taken place. The CBI filed a closure report in a special court in Ernakulam along with a recommendation for action against the police officers who had fabricated the story. When the CPM-led LDF government came to power, it withdrew the go-ahead given to the CBI and ordered a reinvestigation. It had made it an issue against the Congress government while in opposition, and once in power couldn't be seen backtracking. The reinvestigation was approved by the High Court in December 1995. The CBI went to the Supreme Court against it, and in 1998, the Apex Court quashed the reinvestigation. On September 7, 2012, a Division Bench of the **Kerala High Court** ordered the government to pay an "interim compensation" of Rs. 10 lakh—as ordered by the National Human Rights Commission in 2001 while hearing a petition for Rs. 1 crore in damages filed by him to Nambi Narayanan for being falsely implicated in the case.

The CBI had in early 1996 itself exposed the sensational lies and half-truths leaked out by investigators of the Kerala Police and the Intelligence Bureau and published with spicy embellishments by a section of the local media. But by the time the Supreme Court confirmed its findings, the victims of the "false case" had paid a heavy price. It played havoc with the lives and careers of two scientists of the Indian Space Research Organisation, S. Nambi Narayanan and D. Sasikumaran, and it destroyed the lives of four others, Bangalore-based businessmen K. Chandrasekharan and S. K. Sarma and Maldivian women Mariam Rasheeda and Fauzia Hassan. The standard plea of the police officers was that "The CBI's report did not say that the case was fabricated, but it only pointed out the flaws in the procedures adopted by the local police. Such flaws do happen. Action could be taken only if any officials intentionally fabricated any evidence," and that "Should investigation officers be punished every time courts acquit the accused in various cases." But this, even if true, could not undo the untold miseries inflicted upon the victims. *As we have been arguing all along, saying sorry at the end of torture does not help the victim*. Nambi Narayanan points out, no one had bothered to examine some professional issues: "What was the alleged cryogenic technology which the scientists could pass on to a woman who had studied up to 10th standard, and could it really be so cryptic that it could be handed over in a carry bag? What was the evidence that he had made any illegal money in the process—his assets were never looked into."

4.1.48 *Lajpat Nagar Market Blast Acquittals*

In November 2012, the **Delhi High Court** set free two men facing death row for the 1996 Lajpat Nagar market blast, saying the Delhi Police had failed to furnish even the "minimum standards of proof" in the case. "In matters of liberty, the weakness of the state surely can't be an excuse for lowering time-tested standards, especially in serious crimes where the accused stands to forfeit their life," the Bench said. A Trial Court had awarded death sentence to three persons and had sentenced another to a life term for carrying out the blast in which 13 people had died and 38 were injured. *An HC Division Bench comprising Justices S. Ravindra Bhat and G. P. Mittal, however, tore apart the police story, saying the probe was "inefficient", "casual" and "slipshod". The Bench added that the Trial Court had "glossed over" these deficiencies while sentencing the accused.*

The Court acquitted Mirza Nissar Hussain and Mohd. Ali Bhatt alias Kille, both arrested soon after the blast in 1996. The two were dubbed militants of the Jammu and Kashmir Islamic Front (JKIF) and awarded death sentence by the trial court. The High Court also upturned the death penalty for another accused, Mohd. Naushad, converting it to a life term. It, however, upheld the life sentence given to Javed Ahmad Khan alias Chotta Javed.

In its 232-page judgement the Honourable High Court virtually conducted a retrial, painstakingly pouring over the entire evidence including statements, witness testimonies, disclosures, exhibits etc. to conclude the probe was shoddy and riddled with glaring inconsistencies. It flagged the "grave lapses" of the police and the prosecution such as lack of proof connecting some of the accused with the bombing, failure to hold TIP of articles and the accused, as well as the places where the articles were obtained.

Questioning the nature of the evidence produced by the police, the court wondered why the statement of vital witnesses wasn't recorded or why a conduit, who allegedly supplied arms in the case, was not arrested. *It said this underlines "not only lapses and inefficiencies, but also throws a question mark on the nature and truthfulness of the evidence produced". The Judges were unsparing in their criticism of the police citing the complete absence of any daily diary (DD) entries to corroborate the movement of the police, inability to collect easily available documents like authenticated copies of the reservation chart or provide details to prove telephone calls were made. All this, the HC said, betrays a "slipshod approach".*

The *Times of India*, took the following view: "The fact that so many of those accused of terror have been subsequently let off by the courts raises serious questions about the quality of investigations by our police forces. Such a high rate of acquittals can mean only one of two things—either many innocents are wrongly being accused by police of these grave crimes or those who are guilty are being allowed to get away because police are unable to establish their guilt. Either way, it is a matter of serious concern. It could be argued that the conviction rate for other crimes too is not too good, but that is hardly a consolation. Ideally, all investigations should be better conducted, but at the very least we should ensure that terror cases are dealt with more competently.

Remember, such cases fall in the category of what are popularly described as high profile cases. The police leadership is intimately involved in them at all stages. They are found splattered all over the media, giving interviews and sound bites, and generally back-slapping each other. The same leadership goes into hiding when courts bash up the police investigation. Many of them, in fact, go on to shamelessly blame the subordinates. What could be a better example of the utter lack of ethics in the police leadership?

Chapter 5

Abuse of Laws and Legal Processes to Harass the Common Man

5.1 Why it is so Serious a Matter?

The abuse of laws and legal processes is a very serious matter because, as the abuse is being committed, the citizen has no immediate remedy. Yes, he can always go to court later but that takes both time and money. How many people can afford to go to court? Suppose the police arrest somebody unjustly or seize something unjustly under Section 102 CrPC, there is no remedy available to the citizen except going to the court later. Meanwhile the damage is done. The courts have passed severe strictures against the misdeeds of the police in the past and many of them have been cited in this book. But that has not prevented the police from committing the sake outrages over and over again. The second option for the public is to approach the senior officers in the hope of some quick action but almost as a matter of rule, they disappoint. We have never come across any instance in which the senior officers intervened effectively and in time to stop some abuse of law by their subordinates. In fact, many violations are, done at the behest of the senior officers. The police are, in fact, the principal violators of the law and they get away with impunity because of the failure of the leadership.

5.2 Abuse of Preventive Powers Under Sections 151, 107, and 109 CrPC

Section 107 expects the citizen to execute a bond for keeping peace—you have not committed an offence but the authorities could believe that you might. Section 151 empowers a police officer to arrest you if he comes to know that you have a design to commit a cognizable offence. Section 109 expects a citizen to execute a bond if it is believed that he is taking precaution to conceal his presence and that there is reason to believe that he is doing so with a view to committing a cognizable offence. As you can see, they are very powerful sections and for that reason, they are some of the most abused sections.

The Delhi police had arrested Anna Hazare in August 2011 just in front of his residence in Mayur Vihar, nearly 10 km away from the JP Park, where prohibitory order under Section 144 of the CrPC was clamped while there was no prohibitory order anywhere near his residence. A **Division Bench of the Supreme Court comprising Justices P. Sathasivam and B. S. Chauhan** *came down heavily against the "misuse" of preventive detention powers holding that the authorities were liable to be prosecuted for violating the fundamental rights of the detained citizen.*

The Apex Court said that a police officer could make the arrest under Sections 107 and 151 of the CrPC only if "he has come to know of a design of the person concerned to commit any cognizable offence." "A further condition for the exercise of such powers, which must also be fulfilled, is that the arrest should be made only if it appears to the police officer that the commission of the offence cannot be otherwise prevented. Section 151, therefore, expressly lays down the requirements for exercise of the power to arrest without an order form the magistrate and without warrant..." "If these conditions are not fulfilled and, a person is arrested under Section 151 CrPC, the arresting authority may be exposed to proceedings under the law for violating the fundamental rights inherent in Article 21 and 22 of the Constitution," the Court held.

"The objective of Sections 107 and 151 of CrPC are of preventive justice and not punitive. Section 151 should only be invoked when there is imminent danger to peace or likelihood of breach of peace under Section 107. An arrest under Section 151 can be supported when the person to be arrested designs to commit a cognizable offence," the Supreme Court explained. The court said that any immediate action by the authorities under Sections 107 and 151 could be resorted to only in a situation when it "appeared to be absolutely necessary to deal with the threatened apprehension of breach of peace promptly." "The jurisdiction vested in a magistrate to act under Section 107 is to be exercised in emergent situation," the Apex Court said, adding that if the person arrested was able to prove that his detention was without reasons and had violated his fundamental rights, he was also entitled to claim compensation from the government.

The scope of Section 107 of the Code of Criminal Procedure was discussed at length in the famous case of **Madhu Limaye and another vs. Sub-Divisional Magistrate and others** [AIR 1971 SC 2486]. The Supreme Court had held that this section was aimed at persons, who caused a reasonable apprehension of conduct likely to lead to a breach of the peace or disturbance of the public tranquillity. This provision is in aid of orderly society and seeks to nip in the bud conduct subversive of the peace and public tranquillity.

Under Section 107 the Magistrate takes action when he has formed an opinion that a person is likely to commit a breach of peace or disturb the public tranquillity and that there is sufficient ground for proceeding against him. He cannot start proceedings merely on information. If the information is not sufficient, it will be his duty to hold further inquiry and satisfy himself that it is a fit case where action should be taken because sufficient grounds exist. It is after the Magistrate has taken these steps that he can proceed to make the order under s. 112. It would make his action purely administrative if he were to pass the order for an interim bond without entering upon the inquiry and at least prima facie inquiring into the truth of the information on which the order calling upon the person to show cause is based. Unfortunately, this is observed more in violation than in compliance. The cops harass the citizens with this to no end—and, of course, with the active connivance of the police leadership. In the view of many senior officers, the number of proceedings initiated against the citizens is one of the parameters on which they judge the performance of their subordinates, particularly at police station level. The courts have had numerous occasions to pillory them. But the mules refuse to learn.

In **Ganesh Kumar Sharma vs. State and Another** [5 April, 2011, Criminal M.C. No. 3157/2009 and Crl.M.A. 10606/2009] proceedings under Section 107/150 CrPC were initiated against the petitioner because he had a dispute with his tenant! The petitioner had let out a shop at House No. 2, Satnam Park, Chander Nagar, Krishna Nagar to the respondent tenant. He had got an eviction order also from the High Court. The tenant went on to threaten to kill him. He informed the PCR. The PCR did not respond. He also lodged his complaint by e-mail to the Commissioner and the DCP concerned. Nothing happened. When he persisted, the police booked him under s. 107 CrPC! Anyone can see how they must have lied before the magistrate and misled him. The Delhi High Court observed that even though there was a dispute between the landlord and the tenant, it is difficult to infer in the absence of any cogent evidence that the members of public were affected by the alleged exchange of hot words between the petitioner and the tenant or there was any possibility of the breach of peace or disturbance of public tranquillity, particularly when the petitioner himself has informed the PCR by giving a telephone call—the 107 proceedings were quashed.

In the case of **Purshottam Ram Agarwal and Ors. vs. State** [August 26, 1969, AIR 1970 Pat 293] the Circle Officer, Sahebganj Achal in the district of Muzaffarpur informed the Sub-Divisional Magistrate, Sadar Muzaffarpur that the petitioners and their father, Shankar Prasad Agarwal were going to open a daily market and that if they were allowed to open a daily market, the Government market would be totally finished resulting in a loss of five to six thousand rupees per annum to the Government. *The Circle Officer, accordingly, requested the Sub-divisional Magistrate to take immediate necessary action under s. 107 CrPC even though he did not even talk about any apprehension of breach of peace!*

Nobody thought that every citizen of the country has got fundamental right as guaranteed by Article 19 of the Constitution of India to carry on any trade and business. The Patna High Court unravelled the truth. The truth was that the *thekedars* (contractors) of the government market did not want the other market to open. They started physically preventing the shopkeepers from going there. In the circumstances, if some of the petitioners abused them, it could not be said that they were responsible for a breach of the peace. Really it was the contractors of the Government market who should have proceeded against. No marks for guessing why the police had favoured the other contractors!

The court further observed: This case provides an instance justifying that sooner, the executive and judicial powers even in respect of preventive matters, such as proceedings under Sections 144, 107 and 145 of the Code are completely separated, the better.

In the case of **Rajender Singh Pathania and Ors. vs. State of NCT of Delhi and Ors**. [August 12, 2011, Criminal Appeal No. 1582 of 2011], the matter was that the appellants (two) and the respondents (two) had been fighting with each other in an intoxicated condition. For this they were booked under s. 107/151! The appellants got the proceedings quashed by the Delhi High Court. The Delhi High Court was so angry that they even ordered a CBI investigation. The Supreme Court upheld the quashing but did not agree with giving it to the CBI. The Supreme Court once again emphasized that the object of the Sections 107/151 CrPC are of preventive justice and not punitive. S. 151 should only be invoked when there is imminent danger to peace or likelihood of breach of peace under Section 107 CrPC. An arrest under s. 151 can be supported when the person to be arrested designs to commit a cognizable offence... A further condition for the exercise of such power, which must also be fulfilled, is that the arrest should be made only if it appears to the police officer concerned that the commission of the offence cannot be otherwise prevented. If these conditions are not fulfilled and, a person is arrested under Section 151 CrPC, the arresting authority may be exposed to proceedings under the law for violating the fundamental rights inherent in Articles 21 and 22 of Constitution. [Vide: **Ahmed Noormohmed Bhatti vs. State of Gujarat and Ors.** (AIR 2005 SC 2115)].

In **Satish Chandra Sarkar vs. Emperor** [January 15, 1912, (1912) ILR 39 Cal 456], the case was that Satish Chandra Sarkar was in Nattore or its vicinity, and was said to be hiding himself in order to avoid observation, and there was reason to believe that he was connected with anarchist agitation and conspiracies for the purpose of committing dacoity and other crimes, and whereas he had no proven means of livelihood, and could not give a satisfactory account of himself, he was called upon to execute securities. Proceedings were taken under Section 109.

A Division Bench of the Calcutta High Court comprising Justices Holmwood and Sharfuddin ruled that the charge that the accused was concealing himself in order to avoid observation was no offence at all. The second allegation that the accused was connected with anarchist agitation and conspiracies for the purpose of committing dacoity and other crimes could constitute no ground for a proceeding under s. 109. The prosecution had not made out that he was taking any particular steps to conceal himself for the purpose of committing any offence. The Court pointed out that the fact that he had previously been connected with any criminal conspiracy or might still be in correspondence with any criminals outside the jurisdiction, would not be relevant in a case under s. 109.

For the charge that he had no ostensible means of livelihood, and that he could not give a satisfactory account of himself, the Court held that as long as a young man out of employment was staying in his father's house, and that father was a man of substance, able, if necessary, to support him in the joint family, he could not be said to be without ostensible means of subsistence. As regards the account he is asked to give of himself, the Court held that the Magistrate has exceeded his jurisdiction under s. 109. The account he had given of his presence in the limits of the Magistrate's jurisdiction was quite satisfactory. He had fled for fear of a warrant directed against him in a specific case. That warrant having been withdrawn three months ago, he has ventured to return to his home, though he kept to himself, as was natural and we think proper, in strict seclusion from curious enquiries. The proceedings were quashed.

5.3 Abuse of the Prohibitory Powers Under Section 144 CrPC

There would be hardly an Indian who would not have heard of this. With the objective of preventing, or tending to prevent, obstruction, annoyance or injury to any person lawfully employed, or danger to human life, health or safety, or a disturbance of the public tranquillity, or a riot, of an affray, this section permits the authorities to order you to abstain from a certain act or to take certain order with respect to certain property in your possession or under your management. The honourable Courts have never had any doubt as to when this section can be used or ought to be used. However, in spite of such elaborate and eloquent pronouncements, the police leadership continues to defy them and abuse the powers. The Supreme Court dwelt at length on this in the cases of **Superintendent, Central Prison, Fatehgarh vs. Ram Manohar Lohia** [January 21, 1960, 1960 AIR 633] and **Dr. Ram Manohar Lohia vs. State of Bihar and Ors.** [1966 SCR (1) 709]. In expounding the phrase 'maintenance of public order' the Court said that one has to imagine three concentric circles.

Law and order represents the largest circle within which is the next circle representing public order and the smallest circle represents the security of the State. 'Public order' is synonymous with public safety and tranquillity; it is the absence of disorder involving breaches of local significance in contradistinction to national upheavals, such as revolution, civil strife, war, affecting the security of the State. The Court made further fine distinctions. The words 'public order and 'public tranquillity' overlap to a certain extent but there are matters which disturb public tranquillity without being a disturbance of public order. A person playing loud music in his own house in the middle of the night may disturb public tranquillity, but he is not causing public disorder.

The s. 144 confers powers to issue order absolute at once in urgent cases of nuisance or apprehended danger. The Court cautioned that the gist of action under s. 144 is the urgency of the situation and its efficacy in the likelihood of being able to prevent some harmful consequences. It is not an ordinary power flowing from administration but a power used in a judicial manner and which can stand further judicial scrutiny. As it is possible to act under the section absolutely and even ex-parte, the emergency must be sudden, and the consequences sufficiently grave. Ordinarily the order would 'be directed against a person found acting or likely to act in a particular, way. A general order may be necessary when the number of persons is so large that the distinction between them and the general public cannot be made.

Everybody is aware of the Ramlila Maidan incident in which the police unlawfully used force on the followers of Baba Ramdev and drove them out of the place in a most blatant abuse of power. An incensed Supreme Court took suo motu cognizance of the matter. In Re-**Ramlila Maidan Incident Dt... vs. Home Secretary and Ors**. [February, 23, 2012, Suo Motu Writ Petition (Crl.) No. 122 OF 2011], the Apex Court explained that s. 144 deals with immediate prevention and speedy remedy. Therefore, before invoking such a provision, the statutory authority must be satisfied regarding the existence of the circumstances showing the necessity of an immediate action. *The Court reiterated that such a provision can be used only in grave circumstances for maintenance of public peace. The efficacy of the provision is to prevent some harmful occurrence immediately. Therefore, the emergency must be sudden and the consequences sufficiently grave.* It observed that it was evident from the order passed under s. 144 itself that the people at large, sleeping in tents, had not been informed about such promulgation and were not asked to leave the place...There was utter confusion and the gathering could not even understand what the real dispute was and had reason to believe that police was trying to evict Baba Ramdev forcibly. At no point of time, the assembly was declared to be unlawful. In such a fact-situation, the police administration is to be blamed...Thus, the present is a clear cut case of Human Rights violation.

The Apex Court further noted that there was no gossip or discussion of something untrue that was going on. To the contrary, it was admittedly an assembly of followers, under a peaceful banner of Yogic training, fast asleep. The assembly was at least, purportedly, a conglomeration of individuals gathered together, expressive of a determination to improve the material condition of the human race. The aim of the assembly was prima facie unobjectionable and was not to inflame passions. It was to ward off something harmful. (That) such an assembly is necessarily illegal cannot be presumed, and even if it was, the individuals were all asleep who were taken by surprise altogether for a simultaneous implementation and action under Section 144 CrPC without being preceded by an announcement or even otherwise, giving no time in a reasonable way to the assembly to disperse from the Ramlila Ground. To the contrary, the sleep of this huge crowd was immodestly and brutally outraged and it was dispersed by force making them flee hither and thither, which by such precipitate action, caused a mayhem that was reflected in the media...Can such an attempt be permitted or justified in the given circumstances of the present case? Judicially and on the strength of impartial logic, the answer has to be in the negative as a sleeping crowd cannot be included within the bracket of an unlawful category unless there is sufficient material to brand it as such. The facts as uncovered and the procedural mandate having been blatantly violated, is malice in law and also the part played by the police and administration shows the outrageous behaviour which cannot be justified by law in any civilised society.

You can see how frequently it is abused—the police leadership would just not be able to fit all those thousands of situations when they apply it in the criteria described therein—of course, you do not expect the poor sufferers to be able to slug it out every time in the Supreme Court.

In **Acharya Jagdishwaranand... vs. Commissioner of Police, Calcutta** [October 20, 1983, 1984 AIR 512], the Calcutta police had been issuing repeated orders under s. 144 prohibiting procession or assembly of more than five persons. Aggrieved by this, the Anandmargis went up to the Supreme Court. The Apex Court noted that it is not legitimate to go on making successive orders after earlier orders have lapsed by efflux of time. The proviso to sub-section (4) of s. 144 which gives the State Government jurisdiction to extend the prohibitory order for a maximum period of six months beyond the life of the order made by the Magistrate is clearly indicative of the position that Parliament never intended the life of an order under s. 144 of the Code to remain in force beyond two months when made by a Magistrate. The scheme of that section does not contemplate repetitive orders... *Thus the clear and definite view of this Court is that an order under s. 144 of the Code is not intended to be either permanent or semi-permanent in character.*

5.4 The Unlawful Business of Shoot-at-Sight for Violation of Curfew Orders

It is extremely fashionable among young as well as old officers to issue shoot-at-sight orders for violation of curfew. For your information, there is nothing called curfew in law—prohibitory orders under s. 144 are popularly known as curfew. For the edification of the ignoramuses in the police leadership, the word curfew comes from the French phrase 'couvre-feu' which means 'cover the fire'. Originally, the word was used in the context of describing the time of blowing out lamps and candles. In Middle English it came to be adopted as 'curfeu' and later it became 'curfew' in modern English.

These officers do not know that the shoot-at-sight business is utterly illegal under any circumstance. Disobedience of an order lawfully promulgated is made an offence by s. 188 of the Indian Penal Code, if such disobedience causes obstruction, annoyance or injury to persons lawfully employed or if such disobedience causes or tends to cause damage to human life, health or safety or causes or tends to cause riot or affray. It is punishable with simple imprisonment for one month or fine of Rs. 200 or both. There is nothing called shoot-at-sight in law—either by the police or by the military. Kick them hard in the back if they ever use this word and do not forget to make it a solid one.

In the case of **Jayantilal Mohanlal Patel vs. Eric Renison and Anr.** [February 6, 1974, 1975 CriLJ 661] the Gujarat High Court had made it very clear 39 years ago that "the law and order forces of the State of Gujarat have no authority to shoot at anyone for a mere breach of the curfew order and, therefore, the executive directions contained in the 'Important Announcement' in so far as they direct the threat of such an action are void and unlawful. We direct the respondents by a writ of mandamus to instruct their law and order forces civil or military to forbear and desist from shooting at anyone for a mere breach of curfew order or from taking any such action. Rule is made absolute to the aforesaid extent." ***If someone does it even now, it would only prove our contention that the police leadership is so dumb that two generations have passed in the period of 38 years but all of them continue to remain as dumb as ever.***

5.5 Abusc of the NDPS Act

The NDPS Act (Narcotics, Drugs and Psychotropic Substances Act) is one of the most abused laws. The abuse of this Act becomes all the more serious because it provides for very stringent punishments. The usual form of harassment under this Act is to show the recovery of some drug like heroin in the possession of the person. The amount shown to have been recovered is almost always very slightly more than the maximum quantity prescribed under the Act the possession of which would not attract punishment. For example, for heroin, as prescribed in the notification issued vide S.O. 1055 (E) dated October 19, 2001, if the quantity is 5 grams, the cops would show the recovery of 6 grams or at best 10 grams. ***Now this fact in itself is enough to indicate that the recovery in all such cases is a planted one—do you think that by some agreement, all the junkies and drug peddlers across the length and breadth of the country have decided to keep only this much quantity on their persons.***

5.6 Abuse of Law in the Name of Combating Terrorism

The threat to internal security is often distorted because there are many vested interests involved. Organisations have their departmental interests. Cry wolf and you get more funds; get more powers; expand the organisation; create more posts for senior officers; and above all, manage to stay relevant even if they have done nothing to justify their existence. Internal security has therefore become a big business of its own, a racket in fact—hundreds of traders are surviving and flourishing selling useless gadgets to the dumb police leadership because there are thousands of crores of rupees to be spent in the name of modernisation and internal security. In February 2013 it was disclosed that states will be given Rs. 12,378 crore till 2016-17 for modernisation. The business of internal security also provides survival to a battery of self-styled experts in the media and the academia. Their only qualification is verbosity. Fickle-minded police officers like to consult them as they find themselves not up to scratch with words. In any case, when they have raised the bogey of internal security and have also obtained great resources in the name of it, they have to somehow justify it. That's where the abuse starts. They have to keep on showing arrests of people whom they label dangerous terrorists and then spoil their lives. The arrests are, of course, farcical. Elsewhere in the book we have debunked all such cases.

In **Bhim Singh, MLA vs. State of J&K** [(1985) 4 SCC 677] the honourable Supreme Court had proclaimed: "Police officers who are the custodians of law and order should have the greatest respect for the personal liberty of citizens and should not flout the laws by stooping to such bizarre acts of lawlessness. Custodians of law and order should not become depredators of civil liberties. Their duty is to protect and not to abduct." In **People's Union for Civil Liberties and Anr. vs. Union of India** [December 16, 2003, **The vs Unknown on 26 March, 2002]**, the Apex Court observed: "The protection and promotion of human rights under the rule of law is essential in the prevention of terrorism. Here comes the role of law and Court's responsibility. If human rights are violated in the process of combating terrorism, it will be self-defeating. Terrorism often thrives where human rights are violated, which adds to the need to strengthen action to combat violations of human rights. The lack of hope for justice provides breeding grounds for terrorism." *Alas, the exact opposite of that has been happening.*

5.7 Abuse of the Law Pertaining to Abetment of Suicide

This law (s. 306 IPC) makes the cops salivate – instant gratification, immediate publicity and above all, no detective work needed to find the culprit. Suicides become a God-sent opportunity to harass and fleece. They take money from the victim's side for slapping the abetment charges; they take money from the other party for not slapping the charges. The other side is also made aware that thenceforth they would be issuing press notes everyday containing juicy titbits to malign their reputation. If there is a suicide note, perhaps there could be some justification for invoking s. 306, but the cops are found invoking 306 cases on the allegations of relatives or the media also. A worker is dismissed. He commits suicide. The owner or manager of the company is arrested by the police for abetment to suicide. A debtor unable to pay the debt commits suicide; the creditor is arrested for abetment to suicide. Whenever a suicide takes place, the media in particular and the society in general is overcome by a desire to expiate its feeling of guilt by blaming someone.

How do you tolerate such terrible atrocity? Wake up, before it's too late, and you find yourself behind bars. Tomorrow, any employee, subordinate, spouse or friend can blackmail you, "Promote me or else...!" "Marry me...or else!" A girl commits suicide. The cops ask you, "What did you say to her before she committed suicide!" You tell them, "Go to hell! It's all over between us!" "You are under arrest", the cop hollers. In another situation, a failed student commits suicide. Police go to the school, "Who corrected his paper and what did you tell him?" the teacher says, "I reprimanded him and told him that he was a disappointment to his parents." "You are under arrest", he is bluntly told. What actually constitutes abetment to suicide has been clarified in a number of judgements of the High Courts and the Supreme Court. Yet the tyranny of the police continues unabated.

In **A. K. Chaudhary and 2 Ors. vs. The State of Gujarat and 2 Ors.** [September 9, 2005, (2006 CriLJ 726)], the Gujarat High Court referred to the earlier decisions of the Apex Court in the cases of **Swamy Prahaladdas vs. State of M.P.** [1995 Supp (3) SCC, 438]; **Mahendra Singh vs. State of M.P.** [1995 Supp (3) SCC 731]; and **Ramesh Kumar vs. State of Chhattisgarh** [AIR 2001 SC 3837], and observed as under: Even if we accept the prosecution story that the appellant did tell the deceased 'to go and die', that itself does not constitute the ingredient of 'instigation'. The word 'instigate' denotes incitement or urging to do some drastic or unadvisable action or to stimulate or incite. Presence of mens rea, therefore, is the necessary concomitant of instigation. It is common knowledge that the words uttered in a quarrel or in a spur of the moment cannot be taken to be uttered with mens rea. It is in a fit of anger and emotional. The High Court cited the case of **Hans Raj vs. State of Haryana** [2004(12) SCC, 618], where the Apex Court had observed as under: One of the circumstances which has to be considered by the Court is whether the alleged cruelty was of such nature as was likely to drive the woman to commit suicide or to cause grave injury or danger to life, limb or health of the woman...It also cited other judgements: 'If on one or another issue the spouses are often quarrelling it is the usual wear and tear of the married life, and certainly that would not lead any one to end his/her life. One would bring end of his/her life if he/she is put to the compelling or alarming circumstances with no opinion. The prosecution has, therefore, to show what was the apple of discord so as to determine about abetment...With regard to the past quarrels also it is not made clear in what context, and who was at fault? The party at fault if ultimately facing frustration of his/her plan goes to the extreme, i.e. suicide the opposite party cannot be blamed and held liable. In different words, if extremity is one's own creation, and the opponent is blamed, it would amount to roguery supplants justice... The ingredients for abetment for suicide would be satisfied only if the suicide is committed by the deceased due to direct and alarming encouragement/incitement by the accused leaving no option but to commit suicide.' ***The law is very clear. The courts have done their duty. Only the police leadership has failed. And remember, very few people can afford lawyers like Mr. K. T. S. Tulsi who had appeared in the case of A. K. Chaudhary.***

5.8 Abuse of the Powers to Arrest

There is a great social stigma attached with arrest in the minds of the common people. Most people would avoid even being summoned to the police station; they would die of shame if they were to be arrested. The cops know it too well and exploit it. In the famous film Pakeezah depicting a bygone era, the director has tried to show the exact opposite of reality. The hero Rajkumar is taken to the police station after he had a tiff with some loafers. After learning his identity as a Forest Officer, the *daroga ji* lamented, '*Aaap jaise baa-rutba shakhs ka thane aana achcha nahin laga.*' Well, such *darogas* are found only in films—not in real life!

Arrest has been literally the bread and butter of the police. Much of the money they make is made by abusing the powers to arrest. The powers are wielded both ways—they can decide to arrest somebody when it is really not warranted, or they may decide not to arrest somebody even when his arrest is warranted—in both situations, the parties concerned may be squeezed to fill the pockets of the cops. However, for the edification of the people and the ignoramuses amongst the police leadership, we may inform that as ruled and clarified by the **Supreme Court in December 2010**, arrest should be the last option in a criminal investigation. A Bench headed by Justice Dalveer Bhandari added that unnecessary incarceration of a person violated the fundamental right to personal liberty and, so, arrest should be restricted to times when it is imperative keeping in mind the facts and circumstances of the case.

The Bench said: "Personal liberty is a very precious fundamental right and it should be curtailed only when it becomes imperative according to the peculiar facts and circumstances of the case." It added that anticipatory bail to a person should continue till the conclusion of a trial and no conditions should be imposed on the accused to surrender for obtaining a regular bail. The Apex Court made the remarks while granting anticipatory bail to Siddharam Satlingappa Mhetre, a Congress leader allegedly involved in the killing of a BJP worker on September 26, 2009, in Maharashtra. Mhetre had moved the Supreme Court after the Bombay High Court dismissed his anticipatory bail plea. The Apex Court said it is a common knowledge that a large number of under-trials are languishing in jail on charges of committing minor offences.

The honourable Supreme Court confirmed what we stated in the beginning of this section: "A great ignominy, humiliation and disgrace is attached to arrest... Most people do not make any distinction between arrest at a pre-conviction stage or post-conviction stage." It said the courts' practice to grant anticipatory bail with conditions like asking the person to surrender before a court for regular bail was contrary to the statute and ruling set by a Constitution Bench.

The tragedy of this country is that, in spite of such lofty orders of the honourable Supreme Court, given the intellectually bankrupt police leadership which we have, the police still continue to detain people without maintaining any record and torture them during such illegal detentions. The right of the arrestees to be produced before a magistrate within 24 hours of the arrest is also continues to be grossly violated. Further, there is no safeguard if the police arrest someone without warrant or simply pick up and detain in the lockup without any record and torture the detainee. The police have a thousand tricks up their sleeves to manipulate the technical safeguards devised by the Court—it can manipulate the arrest witness by influence or intimidation; influence the doctor examining the detainees; and can even intimidate the victim of torture not to testify against the police before the doctor or the magistrate. Moreover, at many places the Director of Health Services have not finalized the panel of doctors to whom the arrested persons shall be forwarded for medical examination immediately after arrest and during their detention.

Guidelines regarding arrests are not being followed because arrests or threats of arrest are major sources of money. Register a crime and proceed to arrest—that's way, baby—who bothers about collecting any evidence. Some Mr. X, out of nowhere, says that you did such-and-such thing and by God, you must have done it. Given the social stigma which arrests carry in India, who would not pay to avoid arrest?

In 2009, Section 41(1)(b) of the Code of Criminal Procedure was amended and Section 41-A, providing the conditions for the arrest of persons who had been accused of offences where the maximum punishment is lower than seven years imprisonment, was inserted. Finding however, that these new provisions were not being followed in spirit, the Allahabad High Court in re **Shaukin vs. State of Uttar Pradesh and Others** [2011 (75) ACC 763)], on September 15, 2011, ordered the Director General of Police, Uttar Pradesh, to send a circular to all police officers to ensure strict and honest compliance with these provisions. The Court however, did not let the matter rest there but proceeded to explain the import and meaning of the amended provisions and to illustrate where the accused could be arrested straightaway on lodging the FIR, and where immediate arrest may not be needed.

The Court clarified that immediate arrest may be appropriate where the accused has not been named in the FIR; or where the co-accused have been picked up or arrested while committing a crime and has named another person as also having participated in the crime, whose custodial interrogation may be necessary, and the police officer is of the opinion that the disclosure furnishes credible information or gives rise to reasonable suspicion for inferring that this accused whose arrest is sought could also be involved; or looking to the nature of the crime and the background of the particular accused, there are chances that such an accused would abscond or not respond to a notice under Section 41-A to appear. Likewise, where the accused whose arrest is sought appears to be habitually engaged in committing crimes or appears to be participating in some organised crimes, and there is the probability of the accused repeating the offence, then it may be necessary to arrest such accused without delay.

Pulling up police officers for not following the law in spirit, the Court also directed that a police officer should not mechanically and routinely write down in the case diary that there is a likelihood of the accused running away, or presume that the accused would not respond to the notice to appear under Section 41-A, or that he would tamper with the evidence, unless there are strong reasons with concrete material for taking such a view, and this satisfaction along with the concrete reasons for taking the view need to be spelt out clearly in the case diary before the accused is arrested. The High Court also made it clear that in the event it found that the accused who are wanted in cases punishable with up to seven years imprisonment are being arrested in a routine and mechanical matter, without the existence of the conditions necessary for arresting them as mentioned in Sections 41(1)(b) and 41-A, the Court would have no hesitation in summoning the concerned police officers or even the superior police officers and they may even have to face contempt charges. The Court even threatened disciplinary action against errant police officers found persistently arresting people in such matters in violation of these provisions.

In most places, however, the orders are being freely violated. The law is being followed more in the breach and the police leadership is principally responsible for not doing anything to correct it. There is one very simple way of checking our contention. Any fool who doubts it can check the arrest figures/crime registered since the order and he would find that there is no significant change. People are still being arrested at the same rate and the grounds of arrest as stipulated in the law are not being recorded. If you arrest a person now without following the conditions laid down in the amended s. 41, the arrest would become a wrongful confinement within the meaning of Sections 340 of IPC punishable under s. 342 thereof. But we are not aware of any instance when a cop got punished thus for violating the law.

It is also very wrongly believed by many ignoramuses amongst the police leadership that chargesheet cannot be filed without arresting the accused. In many CBI cases, chargesheets are filed without making arrest. And we are not blaming the leadership without reason—let them face it—how many Police Headquarters have issued detailed circulars following the amendment? *Have the people at large been informed through state police websites about their enhanced rights and contact points for getting their grievances if any, in this regard redressed? And if they have circulated and if their subordinates are still violating it, what action they have taken? Fact is, and we are personally aware, most of the time, the senior officers themselves pressurize their subordinates for indiscriminate arrest in order to gain brownie points with the public and the media for these characters regard arrest as the culmination of investigation and half the punishment for all practical purposes.*

5.9 Arresting for Being a Member of a Banned Outfit

Arresting people and claiming that they are members of a banned organisation is another favourite excuse of the police. As it is the

MHA website lists some 32 organisations as banned. The cops can easily fit you in one of them. The whole thing is actually absurd. What are the criteria adopted for determining that someone is a member of a banned organisation? Do they expect him to be in possession of a genuine identity card issued by the organisation? Or do they think that his ideological sympathies with the organisation are enough? Should that be the case, hundreds of thousands of intellectuals would be behind bars for harbouring ideological sympathies. Or do they require someone to be supplying weapons to the organisation? Would they arrest somebody even if he just happened to supply food to the organisation—knowingly or unknowingly? Luckily, the honourable Supreme Court came to the rescue. Members of banned organisations cannot be treated as criminals by police till they indulge in or incite violence, the **Supreme Court has ruled in February 2011**. The Apex Court's ruling is part of a judgement acquitting Arup Bhuyan, convicted by a Guwahati court under the now lapsed anti-terror law Terrorist and Disruptive Activities (Prevention) Act. Bhuyan was a suspected member of the outlawed secessionist outfit United Liberation Front of Assam (ULFA). "**Mere membership of a banned organisation will not make a person a criminal unless he resorts to violence or incites people to violence or creates public disorder by violence or incitement to violence**," a Division Bench comprising Justices Markandey Katju and Gyan Sudha Misra said.

The trial court had convicted Bhuyan based on his confession to police, admissible as evidence under TADA. Bhuyan had appealed in Supreme Court. Allowing his petition, the court said his conviction was based on "a very weak kind of evidence" and could not be sustained in the absence of corroborative material. On the confessions, Justices Katju and Misra expressed strong views. "As is well known, the widespread and rampant practice in the police in India is to use third-degree methods for extracting confessions from the alleged accused. Hence, the courts have to be cautious in accepting confessions made to the police by the alleged accused," the Bench said. "Torture is such a terrible thing that when a person is under torture, he will confess to almost any crime. Even Joan of Arc confessed to be a witch under torture," the Court added.

5.10 Abusing the Powers of Preventive Detention Under the Dreaded MCOCA

The abuse of preventive detention is well-known. The Constitution Bench of the Apex Court, in the case of **Prakash Kumar alias Prakash Bhutto vs. State of Gujarat** [(2005) 2 SCC 409] reproduced the observations made in the case of **Kartar Singh** [1994 (3) SCC 569]: "It is true that on many occasions, we have come across cases wherein the prosecution unjustifiably invokes the provisions of the TADA Act with an oblique motive of depriving the accused persons from getting bail and in some occasions when the courts are inclined to grant bail in cases registered under ordinary criminal law, the investigating officers in order to circumvent the authority of the courts invoke the provisions of the TADA Act. This kind of invocation of the provisions of TADA in cases the facts of which do not warrant, is nothing but sheer misuse and abuse of the Act by the police."

Preventive detention orders were passed against Ramakrishnan and six others in Tamil Nadu. Their offence? Selling expired drugs! A **three-judge Bench of Justices Markandey Katju, S. S. Nijjar and Gyan Sudha Misra of the honourable Supreme Court** quashed the detention and said: "Preventive detention is, by nature, repugnant to democratic ideas and an anathema to the rule of the law. Article 22 (3) (b), which permits preventive detention, is only an exception to Article 21. An exception is an exception and can't ordinarily nullify the full force of the main rule, which is the right to liberty under Article 21." Laying down the guidelines, the Bench said: "Whenever an order under a preventive detention law is challenged, one of the questions the court must ask while deciding its legality is: Was the ordinary law of the land sufficient to deal with the situation? If the answer is in the affirmative, the detention order will be illegal. In the present case, "Surely, the relevant provisions in the Indian Penal Code and the Drugs and Cosmetics Act were sufficient to deal with this situation." The Bench also said the possibility of a person being released on bail even when no bail application was pending could not be a ground for preventive detention.

In **A. K. Roy, etc. vs. Union of India and Anr.** [1982 AIR 710] the Supreme Court held that laws of preventive detention cannot by the back-door, introduce procedural measures of a punitive kind. Detention without trial is an evil to be suffered, but to no greater extent and in no greater measure than is minimally necessary in the interest of the country and the community.

Yes, we are very much aware, as it was held in the case of **Sanjay Dutt vs. State** [(1994) 5 SCC 410], that merely because a statute is likely to be abused cannot be a ground for upsetting its constitutionality or construction. The constitutional validity of the MCOCA has been upheld, but the fact remains that the abuse of MCOCA is well-known—it has been used by the police basically as a tool to make getting bail nearly impossible. *Under the MCOCA, a person is presumed guilty unless he is able to prove his innocence. The abuse of this* *law has devastated hundreds of lives and families.* Even if a court eventually throws out the case and the confessions allegedly made before a police officer above the rank of the Superintendent of Police or Deputy Commissioner of Police, the accused has already spent months to years behind bars because securing bail is next to impossible. The real sufferers are the poor small fries whereas the big fish remain very much cozy and intact. *Police officers argue that the MCOCA has put the fear of the Lord in the underworld. In our considered opinion, this is a sweeping and unproven generalization. There is not enough evidence for it.* Chhota Shakeel's property in Mumbai was attached in the Milind Vaidya case, when he was named a prime accused in the plan to kill the Shiv Sena member. It has not made a difference to Shakeel, as he continues his lavish lifestyle in countries that are accommodating him. Attaching, and later auctioning, nearly 20 properties of Dawood Ibrahim under TADA in the 1993 Mumbai blasts case has made even less of a difference to him, if reports of his ostentatious lifestyle in Karachi are anything to go by.

Nor has MCOCA managed to drastically reduce the phenomenon of extortion, extortion-related killings by the underworld or any other activity of the criminal gangs. The arrest of Bharat Shah has not diminished the financing of Bollywood by the underworld. *Moreover, prosecution of police officers later found guilty of abuse of their authority is notoriously difficult and that's how the abuse continues unabated. Yes, safeguards are very much there but it is not within the means of a vast majority of Indians to hire top quality legal help to defend themselves.*

It was stated in the case of **The State of Maharashtra vs. Jagan Gagansingh Nepali** [Criminal Appeal No. 20 of 2011 with Criminal Application No. 798 of 2011**]**, the Bombay High Court held that the purpose behind enacting the MCOCA was to curb the activities of the organised crime syndicates or gangs. Unless there is *prima facie* material, firstly, to establish that there is an organised crime syndicate and, secondly, that organised crime has been committed by any member of the organised crime syndicate or any person on behalf of such syndicate, the provisions of MCOCA cannot be invoked. The HC "cautioned police officers and designated courts from misusing MCOCA" and directed them to "enforce it effectively" within the meaning of the "legislative intent." And the HC said the legislative intent clearly was to curb organised crime.

The HC gave examples of how its interpretation of the "organised crime" would not mean that MCOCA is slapped in regular crime cases. For instance it said, "A property dispute between two brothers in which a deadly weapon is used would not attract MCOCA' and nor would it mean that a fight over tap water would. But when a "politician is killed at the behest of another politician by using the underworld, it could mean that the gang is doing it to gain political patronage from the one who one who sought the killing" and also "if a leader of one gang shot dead the head of another syndicate it could be for gang supremacy" and would fit under MCOCA. Even when a trial witness is killed or one gang member may kill another to promote his own interest and thus attract the stringent law which does not allow bail easily and attracts death sentence.

In **State Govt. of NCT of Delhi vs. Khalil Ahmed** [April 23, 2012 Crl. Rev. P. No. 42/2012 and Crl.M.A. No. 975/2012], MCOCA was slapped on Khalil Ahmed who was alleged to have threatened Qamar Ahmed who runs a trading company in Old Delhi and demanded Rs. 10 lakh. This man had more than 34 criminal cases against him since 1985 to 2009 and had been chargesheeted along with other persons. The High Court, however, pointed out that the prosecution had failed to ascertain as to whether the offences committed therein were related to organised crime or not. Therefore, the prosecution failed to establish that the respondent has committed an offence either as a member of organised crime syndicate or on behalf of such syndicate.

Commenting on the issue of applying the MCOCA, in the case of **Dr. Mahipal Singh vs. CBI and Anr.** on 21 May, 2012 [May 21, 2012, http://indiankanoon.org/doc/156255189/], the Delhi High Court had pointed out that the cause of action for invoking MCOCA is the continuing unlawful activity undertaken by a person singly or jointly as a member of an organised crime syndicate or on behalf of such syndicate in respect of which more than one chargesheets have been filed before a competent Court within the preceding period of 10 years and the Court has taken cognizance of such offence. Readers are well aware as to how the police try to circumvent it when they unjustly slap MCOCA on some first-timer. They rope in some other notorious gangster with him and claim that while he does not have any chargesheet against him in the past, the gangster has had. Usually, the courts throw it out but how many people can afford to slug it out in the court.

In **State of Maharashtra and Ors. vs. Lalit Somdatta Nagpal and Anr.** [(2007) 2 SCC (Crl) 241], commenting on applying the MCOCA for alleged violation of Sales Tax and Excise Laws, their Lordships held: "To apply the provisions of MCOCA something more in the nature of coercive acts and violence in required to be spelt out so as to bring the unlawful activity complained of within the definition of "organised crime" in Section 2(1)(e) of MCOCA."

A two-month investigation by **Ajit Sahi** and **Rana Ayyub** in 2010 for the *Tehelka* magazine found that MCOCA has only pinned the small fry while failing to nail real gangsters. This painstaking investigation not only thoroughly exposed the crookedness of the police in implicating the helpless but also rendered yeoman service to the cause of the victims of police excesses. *They showed, with enough proof that this law has been abused to devastate innumerable innocent lives from long incarcerations in jails because the law allows confessions of the accused made before police officers to be admissible as evidence, and makes bail virtually impossible to obtain. Most of them* lived out the nightmare of MCOCA spending sleepless nights on their jail beds, only to be freed after months or years because, simply, there was no evidence against them. These have included the mighty as well, such as former Mumbai Police Commissioner R. S. Sharma—no less. Even the Supreme Court said Sharma seemed to have been wrongly accused. Wrote the Apex Court: "We are furthermore of the opinion that the restrictions on the power of the Court to grant bail should not be pushed too far." MCOCA is harsher than POTA and TADA. It was meant to curb only mafia gangs, but it has been badly subverted. In the following we will discuss some of the cases investigated by them. ***You can see how indiscriminately, how brutally, how mindlessly MCOCA was applied on people coming from diverse backgrounds and how eventually the honourable courts rendered justice to them. Who is responsible for this if not the police leadership? They are principally and squarely responsible for destroying the lives of these people.***

The victims of the abuse of MCOCA include:

A Recruiting Agent: *Shah Alam worked* as a recruitment agent, sending out semi-skilled workers hungry for better paying jobs in the Middle East. He was charged with harbouring one of the alleged gang members after the murder of one Ajit Diwani in 2001 and giving him Rs. 15,000 and booked under MCOCA. Shah Alam spent three-and-a-half years in jail. Still he was lucky, because his co-accused had spent eight years before **Special MCOCA Judge** R. G. Avachat, in a voluminous judgement delivered in September 2009, acquitted six of the seven accused. The MCOCA judge found no evidence to link Upendranath, the man Shah Alam was said to have sheltered, with the murder in question. The case fell after that.

A Businessman and a Squash Fan: In July 2006, Mahendra Agarwal was booked under MCOCA allegedly for operating on behalf of one of Mumbai's absconding underworld dons, Ravi Pujari and threatening one Brijlal Tiwari. Tiwari was a resident of an 8,000 sq. m. shantytown that Agarwal had acquired in the north Mumbai suburb of Andheri East by paying off its residents with a view to pulling it down and replacing it with a modern building. But despite moving heaven and earth and hiring the best lawyers, Agarwal cooled his heels in the cell for 65 days. After that period, Mumbai's **Special MCOCA Judge** Abhay Thipsay freed him and his associates on bail. The prosecution had claimed that Agarwal had called up Tiwari and threatened him from the landline in his Mumbai office on a particular day. Agarwal submitted documents such as his passport and airline tickets proving that on the date he is alleged to have threatened Tiwari, he was holidaying in Europe with his wife, daughter, the daughter's fiancé and his parents. In his judgement, the Special MCOCA judge noted that there was no evidence against Agarwal; not even phone intercepts or records of Agarwal's alleged calls.

Moreover, none of the six accused, including Agarwal, had ever faced a single criminal charge. The Mumbai Police tried to get around this shortcoming by making mafia don Pujari an accused in the case. The police said the fact that there were more than two criminal cases against Pujari in the past 10 years was enough to incriminate Agarwal and the other five. But the prosecution could not even produce any phone records or transcripts of phone conversations linking Agarwal and the other accused with Pujari. The police could also not explain why Agarwal's phone was not tapped, even after receiving Tiwari's complaint that the builder was allegedly threatening him. Surely, if the police had wiretapped his phone, they would have found all the evidence they needed to connect Agarwal with the underworld.

Alleged to be a Shooter for Chhota Rajan: In July 2005, Fareed Tanashah, a software engineer by training, was booked under MCOCA for threatening Mumbai-based businessmen for extortion. His is a classic case of bungling by the dumb cops and their dumber senior officers. Tanashah was not convicted in any of the five MCOCA cases that had been brought against him before this particular case. In this case, the **Special MCOCA Judge** observed that he was arrested a day before the complaint that was lodged against him with the Mumbai police. The prosecution claimed that the police had found seven mobile phones in the possession of Tanashah as well as with his alleged accomplice Malhotra, when the duo was arrested in New Delhi. But the defence successfully argued before the judge that this fact is not reflected in the *panchnama*—the list of seizures prepared in front of witnesses—filed at the time of the arrests. "There is no such material to indicate direct involvement of [Tanashah] in any of the crime much less the crime in question," the court said.

A Former Mumbai Police Chief: Ranjit Singh Sharma was arrested on December 1, 2003, less than 24 hours after he retired from the IPS. They booked him under MCOCA as an accused in the widely publicized case of what the news media dubbed the 'Telgi fake stamp paper scam'. Abdul Karim Telgi, a native of Karnataka, was arrested in 2001. He was found to be the kingpin of an audacious illegal scheme in which he installed presses to print fake government stamp papers worth tens of thousands of crores of rupees and sold them liberally across India for over a decade before being busted. As Police Commissioner in Pune in 2002 and as Police Commissioner in Mumbai in 2003, Sharma was accused of abetting Telgi's scam by favouring two policemen investigating the case and who, in turn, were found favouring Telgi. Also, an IAS officer said he had seen Telgi and Sharma having tea in Sharma's room in 1995. Police also claimed that Telgi had admitted in a narco-analysis test that he had paid Sharma off.

Sharma contended that the case against him was cooked up. But the special MCOCA court rejected his bail plea, as did the Bombay High Court. Sharma was to stay in jail for 11 months, until the **Supreme Court** granted him bail. "Unless a nexus with an accused, who is a member of the organised crime syndicate or an offence in the nature of organised crime is established," the Supreme Court said, "...the appellant [Sharma] cannot be said to have conspired or abetted commission of an organised crime." It also rejected Telgi's narco-analysis test. In June 2007, Chitra Kiran Bhedi, **Special MCOCA Judge** in Pune, discharged Sharma without sending him for trial. The judge slammed the prosecution and instead raised questions at the investigation. "The fact," wrote the judge, "that he [Sharma] was instrumental in unearthing this scam cannot be lost sight of."

Many senior police officers were castigated in this case. The judge unequivocally slammed Subodh Kumar Jaiswal, heading the SIT: "Jaiswal in his 1½ years of investigation has not done anything against Telgi. No significant recovery of stamps, no recovery of printing machines was made... He had not arrested the brothers [when he found them with Telgi at his flat]." The judge also slammed the SIT for not moving against S. M. Mushrif, who had opposed naming Telgi's wife and son as accused in the case: "It appears that [the] prosecution is deliberately indulging in choose and pick policy. Mr. Mushrif against whom serious allegations are made by his colleagues and even superiors is left untouched." On the allegation that Sharma was responsible for illegally letting Telgi out of jail, the judge said Telgi "enjoyed comforts" in Mumbai even before Sharma became Police Commissioner on January 1, 2003. "M. N. Singh was Commissioner of Police, Mumbai when Telgi was in custody of Mumbai Police from

28.10.2002... No questions are asked about any commission or omission in this substantive period. On the contrary, the applicant [Sharma] is dragged [in] for alleged minor acts." The IAS officer who claimed to have seen Telgi in Sharma's room in 1995 is now embroiled in a case arising out of the scam. He had been Superintendent of Stamps for Maharashtra during the time Telgi operated his illegal business. A court has ordered that the IAS officer be investigated for complicity.

The Man Who Kept a Beard: After growing a beard to mark his Haj pilgrimage in 1988, the businessman Asif Khan came to be known by the nickname 'Asif Dadhi'. He was arrested and booked under MCOCA in 2000. It was a case of mistaken identity. It so happened that the police were looking for a realtor, also nicknamed Asif Dadhi, who they claimed was involved in deals with absconding mafia don Chhota Shakeel. That did not deter them from charging the poor businessman for having paid shooters in a murder case.

Khan had never seen the inside of a police station. But he could not get bail. After 17 months, the court accepted his plea. The police failed to provide any evidence, not even the SIM cards the accused had allegedly used, though the police claimed they had arrested the gangsters "red-handed" while talking on mobile phones. The judge threw out the case. He shaved off his beard and vowed to stay clean-shaven forever. Three years passed. In 2004, police claimed that funds that Shakeel was sending from Pakistan to pay the legal fees of several of his gang members arrested in Mumbai were being disbursed by Khan. Flustered, Asif Khan went underground. When he learnt he could be declared an absconder, he surrendered after three months. As per the law, the police must file charges in the court against an accused within 90 days of his arrest. When they did not do so in Khan's case, the judge granted him bail.

A year went by since his arrest. In September 2005, Mumbai Police submitted a five-page application before the MCOCA judge saying they had found no evidence against "Mohammad Asif Mohammed Rafiq Khan alias Asif Dadhi". The police also took printouts of the call records of Khan's two landline phones and mobile phone. "A study of these printouts shows the accused [Khan] had neither made nor received calls to/from gangsters of Chhota Shakeel," they told the judge. Sales tax records of his medical shop were scrutinized and "nothing adverse [was] noticed." "There [were] no major deposits or withdrawals" in his and or his wife's bank accounts. "Nothing incriminating was found" in his house. His employees and partners were interrogated. "Nothing incriminating [was] noticed." "There is no evidence to send him on chargesheet in the present case," the police application concluded. It asked the judge to discharge Asif Khan.

A Jobless Drifter: Some jeweller in Bombay was assaulted. A man with no permanent job, Sajid Syed was arrested in October 2006 by a wing of Mumbai Police known as the Anti-Extortion Cell. The police claimed he had made phone calls to one of the two accused who had attacked the jeweller. All three were arrested seven months after the attack on the jeweller. Police claimed they were henchmen of gangster Faheem Machmach, who reportedly absconded from Mumbai in the 1980s and is said to live in Dubai. Police say Machmach is the right-hand man of the dreaded don, Chhota Shakeel. So MCOCA inserts itself. The police bumbled in the case from the beginning. The story was that Jay and Rahul had attacked the jeweller in the shop in the presence of his assistant and a woman customer. All of them contradicted each other in the court regarding everything—who attacked whom and with what.

The police never asked the doctor that operated the jeweller if the wound was from a chopper or a knife. The jeweller reportedly received phone calls while still at the hospital, threatening him for ransom. His brother, wife and daughter, too, received such calls. The police never examined his three relatives; nor did it offer them as prosecution witnesses. As already mentioned, the police did not take voice samples of Sajid or Rahul, so there was no way to know if they made those calls. The Judge threw the case out the window, acquitting all three of the accused. He said the prosecution had even failed to prove that a violent attack on the jeweller took place in the first instance.

A Perfume Mixer and a Construction Site Supervisor: The brothers Abrar Azmi and Anwaar Azmi were arrested allegedly for being gangsters of Faheem Machmach, threatening and extorting money in his name. On February 1, 2005, nine days before their arrest, a local woman had complained to the police that the brothers had accosted her and her daughter in broad daylight on a busy street. She said the brothers threatened they would have Machmach order her and her family killed. Once the trial began, the case began to unravel. Admittedly, the complainant was a controversial local leader known as a troublemaker. (She passed away before the trial concluded.) In cross-examination, her daughter and son—who claimed to have witnessed the alleged crime—admitted that their family and Faheem Machmach's had long been hostile neighbours.

They also admitted that their mother had had a long association with the police. On February 1, 2005, the day of the alleged crime, she had met the local DCP, who had asked his subordinates to act on her complaint. The question arose, if the Azmi brothers were indeed gangsters of Machmach, shouldn't the police have registered a criminal case against them the day the complaint was made? Instead, the police took eight days to register the case. "There is substance in the submission by the defence that this delay might have been used for shaping up the case against the accused and Faheem Machmach," wrote **Special MCOCA Judge** M. R. Bhatkar in her order of November 2007, acquitting all the accused. The judge noted that not once in those eight days did the police meet the complainant to investigate her complaint. In those eight days, not once did the complainant go back to the police to follow up on her complaint. "The entire incident took place for 12 to 13 minutes," wrote the judge. "How could the police not get any independent witnesses?" The prosecution claimed the Azmi duo was involved in "criminal activities such as threatening, abusing, assaulting people and recovering money for Faheem Machmach. But when asked for evidence, it offered the oral claims of none other than the complainant's son and daughter. When the court asked for specifics of the Azmi brothers' alleged activities—such as the names of people extorted from and dates—they could offer none. Both admitted they had never received any calls from Faheem Machmach. The Azmi brothers could walk free only after 33 months and 15 days in jail.

A Housewife: On March 20, 2004, two activists of the Vishwa Hindu Parishad (VHP) were attacked and killed in a shantytown in Powai with swords and sharp weapons. Gangubai, who had married a Muslim man, found her family members arrested. Three months later, she was also arrested for giving money to three of the accused and sending them to hide at her brother's place. They were not booked for murder—only under MCOCA! The prosecution said that the family was actually a gang: the "Sher Bahadur Akram Khan gang". In December 2006, more than two and a half years after the family members' arrests, the **High Court** struck down the charges under MCOCA and ruled that the family be tried under the IPC. Said the High Court: "The mere fact that the accused are related to each other and have committed offences either individually or jointly, would not, in our opinion, lead to the inference that the accused formed an organised crime syndicate." Once the double murder case went to trial under the IPC, as should have been done in the first place, bail was given to Gangubai because she was not accused of murder but only of being an accessory after the crime. She walked free in February 2007, having spent more than thirty-one months behind bars. The judge said there was "absolutely no evidence" to show that on the day of the murders of the VHP activists, Gangubai had given Rs. 2,000, as alleged, to three of the accused and sent them to her brother's.

One Who was Caught in a Shootout: D. K. Rao was caught in a shootout in 1998 and brought to hospital. He spent 11 years in jail until being released on bail in October 2009. Hailing from Karnataka, Rao's real name is Ravi Mallesh Vora. The story is that the police found in his pocket a business card giving his name as D. K. Rao. It stuck. Rao was sent to jail and made an accused in the case arising out of the shootout. Yet, while being a jailbird, beginning in 1994, police filed more than 25 cases against Rao, for crimes that range from armed robbery to murder. He has even had cases registered against him in far away Goa. Since then, Rao has been acquitted in most cases. But never could he get out of jail, until his luck changed for the better—under MCOCA. The judge threw out the MCOCA charges and ruled that the accused be tried under the regular IPC. Seven years after Misal's murder, a Pune city judge acquitted all the accused, including D. K. Rao, in January 2009. Even after 11 years of holding him, including in several MCOCA cases, the police have yet to prove the charge that D. K. Rao is an underworld operative.

A Cinematographer: Bhushan Satam, a cinematographer, is the son of the gangster Guru Satam, who fled the country 20 years ago. Bhushan, who works as a cinematographer in Hindi films, claims that he has not seen his father since 1989. In 2006, Mumbai Police arrested Bhushan and claimed he was linked to his father's extortion bid. The police said Guru Satam had plenty of chargesheets against him since the 1980s, and since these were his men, they should be tried under MCOCA. He spent 10 months in jail till he was acquitted. The judge's order is, in fact, a stunning exposé of a frighteningly inept prosecution. The police did not even bother to say how Bhushan was linked with the phone call that his father allegedly made to the builder. Shockingly, the builder could not even recognize the voice that the police purported belonged to Bhushan's father. There was no evidence that Bhushan instructed the other accused for their various roles in the alleged crime.

The investigation was full of stupidities. One police officer deposed that he arrested an accused and then went with him to his house to seize firearms. But an independent witness who police took along to the arrest said the accused opened the door, whereupon he was arrested. One witness turned out to be an electrician plying his trade—without a municipal licence—from the pavement outside the office of the police unit investigating the case. The judge noted the man regularly fixed the wiring at the police office.

The Case of Iqbal Kaskar, Brother of Dawood Ibrahim: Iqbal Kaskar returned to India from Dubai in March 2003. He was arrested at the airport and booked under MCOCA. Police said Kaskar was working for his brother, Dawood Ibrahim, and forced property owners to sell to him cheaply to build a shopping mall. Fine. For the sake of argument, one might accept that he was in league with his notorious brother. But the question is why the hell could the dumb cops not prove the charge against him. After a trial lasting over four years, in 2007, the **Special MCOCA Judge** M. R. Bhatkar acquitted Kaskar, saying the police failed to provide any evidence against him. So inept was the prosecution that while the judge said there was evidence to link Kaskar with the other accused who had been found guilty, there was no evidence to prove that Kaskar had participated in the crime of threatening the original property owners. The judge slammed the police for creating the charges against Kaskar because he was Dawood's brother. "In the eyes of the law each person has an independent status unless any criminal connection is brought on record," she wrote. "A person may be closely related to any known wanted accused in the underworld; however it is not sufficient circumstance to prove him guilty under MCOCA."

Quite often the police leadership laments that they could not successfully prosecute a dreaded criminal because no one would give evidence against him. Well, readers would be amused to learn that in this case, shockingly, even some police officers turned hostile. DCP Pradeep Sawant said he did not "recollect" giving any report against Iqbal Kaskar in respect to his intercepted telephone conversation "disclosing that it was a threat [the] to security of [the] state". The judge wrote that the phone conversations between Kaskar and others "do not reveal any threat or pressure or violence showing [an] attempt or use of threat, pressure, coercion, intimidation or any kind of violence on any person..." The Investigating Officer of the case, ACP Shankar Kamble admitted that he "did not have anything to prove that Iqbal Kaskar has made any pecuniary benefits of transactions made between them." What was the police leadership doing in such cases? ***Of course, it is quite possible that Kaskar is indeed connected with Dawood Ibrahim's 'organised crime' activities. If that is true, then MCOCA, at least in this case, has entirely failed in its stated purpose, that is, to finish off the underworld.***

5.11 Persecuting the Poor to Please the Powerful

An ideal example of this is the abuse of the s. 66-A of the Information Technology Act. Readers may recall how two girls were arrested in Palghar near Mumbai in November 2012 for questioning the shutdown in the city on the day of Shiv Sena chief Bal Thackeray's funeral on a social networking site. The first girl, a 21-year-old BMS student, had posted this message on her Facebook profile: "People like Thackeray take birth and die daily and people should not observe bandhs". Her friend, a Botany student who graduated this year, had simply pressed the 'like' button. Incensed by this 'blasphemous act', a mob of 2,000 Shiv Sainiks ransacked her uncle's Palghar hospital on Sunday night. Though the girl, who belongs to the minority community, later apologized and even deleted the message, the damage was done. "The mob damaged medical equipment and even ransacked the operation theatre," said a doctor from the hospital. Some patients were injured in the violence. The arrests of the girls sparked outrage across the country. Press Council of India chief and former Judge of the Supreme Court Markandey Katju wrote to the Chief Minister and demanded immediate action against the policemen involved. Finally, the Supreme Court had to intervene in the matter.

Justice Katju wrote, "To my mind it is absurd to say that protesting against a bandh hurts religious sentiments. Under Article 19(1)(a) of our Constitution freedom of speech is a guaranteed fundamental right. We are living in a democracy, not a fascist dictatorship. In fact this arrest itself appears to be a criminal act since under Sections 341 and 342 it is a crime to wrongfully arrest or wrongfully confine someone who has committed no crime." "Hence if the facts reported are correct, I request you to immediately order the suspension, arrest, chargesheeting and criminal prosecution of the police personnel (however high they may be) who ordered as well as implemented the arrest of that woman, failing which I will deem it that you as Chief Minister are unable to run the state in a democratic manner as envisaged by the Constitution to which you have taken oath, and then the legal consequences will follow," he further wrote. The mail was also posted on his blog, Satyam Bruyat.

When the CM did not reply to his email but only forwarded it to what appears to be an official, Justice Katju responded with a second email which said, "Please realize that silence is not an option for you in the matter. Therefore, I once again request you to tell me, and through me the entire nation, why this arrest of a woman was made in Mumbai just for putting up an apparently innocuous material on the Facebook, and what action you have taken against the delinquent policemen and others involved in this high-handedness and blatant misuse of state machinery." Subsequently, the girls were let off and two cops were suspended. ***Remember, you cannot even shout a slogan when somebody belonging to the powers-that-be is around—by God, you are a security threat and, by implication, a threat to national security***! Entertaining a PIL on the subject, the **honourable Supreme**

Court echoed the public outrage over the high-handed night-time arrests of two girls, "The way the children were arrested and treated like criminals outraged the conscience of a major section of society. The way things were done needs some kind of consideration though the serious charges against the two girls appear to have been withdrawn," the bench said. It added that the arrests were in violation of the Apex Court's guidelines prohibiting the arrest of women after sunset. "They were arrested after sundown and for a bailable offence? So the might of police was activated by a mob," the Division Bench of Chief Justice Altamas Kabir and Justice J. Chelameswar said.

The Court also took note of the arrest of a professor in Kolkata for circulating a cartoon which took a dig at West Bengal chief minister Mamata Banerjee. The PIL drew the attention of the honourable Court towards many other instances that include the arrest of professor of chemistry Ambikesh Mahapatra from Jadavpur University for posting a cartoon concerning a political figure on social networking site (April 2012); arrest of Air India employees V. Jaganatharao and Mayank Sharma by Mumbai police for putting up content on social networking sites against a trade union leader and some politicians and kept in custody for 12 days (May 2012); and arrest of businessman Ravi Srinivasan by Puducherry police for making allegations against a TN politician on a social networking site (October 2012).

The Hindu editorial, "Unfriend the Thought Police" said: "What stands out in this episode, and similar ones earlier, is the readiness of the police to make arbitrary arrests and cloak their censorial actions using a combination of Indian Penal Code sections that have no place in a free country, and the infamous Section 66-A of the Information Technology Act which deals with offensive messages. It mattered little to them when using Section 505(2) of the IPC on promotion of hatred, ill-will or enmity, that their case grossly fails the test of *mens rea*, or intent. After all, what can be illegal about expressing an opinion about so public an event as the complete shutdown of the country's financial capital?...The rise of community websites as networks of hope for the average citizen is obviously discomfiting many in authority. The capacity of the medium to name, shame and embarrass far exceeds the ability of the high and mighty to control it. Their response has been to use the police to settle scores with some, and thus send out the message to the majority. Brazen misuse of the power to arrest continues, because there is no significant penal outcome.

Commenting on the Puducherry arrests, *The Hindu* wrote in its editorial 'An Attack On Media Freedom' (November 2, 2012): "The arrest of a Puducherry activist for alleging on Twitter that the Union

Finance Minister's son had "amassed more wealth than Vadra" is a disturbing reminder that the Information Technology Act is serving as a convenient tool to curb free speech...What is particularly shocking is that it took only an email complaint from Karti Chidambaram for a posse of policemen to practically drag the 'India Against Corruption' volunteer out of bed at dawn and place him under arrest...Also, it must be emphasized that defamation—which is what Karti Chidambaram might plausibly accuse the IAC activist of indulging in—is essentially a civil matter...It is inconceivable that journalists would be summarily jailed for printing or broadcasting the many allegations that people in public life routinely make."

It is interesting to note how the police leadership failed even in this case. In July 2013, the Bombay High Court chastised the administration for not launching criminal proceedings against police officers in the illegal arrests of two Palghar girls over Facebook posts. A division bench of Justices S. C. Dharmadhikari and S. B. Shukre was hearing a PIL calling attention to the delay in action on an inquiry report. The state had suspended superintendent of police (Thane Rural) Ravindra Sengaonkar for making a "hasty arrest" and police inspector Shrikant Pingale of Palghar police for "creating false records". Further, additional superintendent of police Sangramsinh Nishandar was "issued a letter of displeasure for failing to prevent falsification of records". When additional public prosecutor Jayesh Yagnik submitted that a departmental inquiry into the charge of falsification of records is underway, Justice Dharmadhikari asked, "Are you of the opinion that they should be proceeded against only departmentally? You feel it is not a punishable offence?" The Judges questioned why the law was not set in motion if a report had established distortion of records. "What would you do if an ordinary citizen does this? There cannot be a different law for common citizens and police officers." The Court cited the inquiry report's conclusion that shifting blame on juniors was unacceptable. "You don't proceed against superiors. Somebody is supposed to supervise and monitor. They may have not done it directly. Their failure to monitor may invite displeasure," said Justice Dharmadhikari.

Readers may also recall the incident of denial of Salman Rushdie from attending the Jaipur Literary Festival. The police asked the organisers to ask Rushdie to stay away and allegedly backed it up by encouraging rumours of paid assassins being dispatched from Mumbai, something the Mumbai police denied. *In other words, they had concocted a false intelligence report*. Further, the leadership of Rajasthan police chose to remain silent even as the obscurantist had a field day.

The legally correct thing for them would have been to warn all those threatening violence and take suitable preventive measures. They did neither because they would not take any *panga* with those who are powerful. Let us hasten to add that we are not admirers of Rushdie—we are mentioning the case for other reasons. Such a thing could happen to anyone and for a different reason. The issue is that on the pretext of law and order the police did not act against the law-breakers.

Though the police leadership is intellectually incapable of giving any sound explanation for their misdeeds, yet the most often quoted argument is that maintaining law and order is their first priority. Fine, but at what cost? Would law and order be maintained at the cost of law itself? Suppose a mob is threatening to do something utterly unlawful, such as hanging the boy and girl who had committed the sin of an inter-caste marriage. What would the police do? We have seen innumerable circumstances of this type in our lives and career—most often the police try to placate the mob. They do not take any action against them—they merely plead with them or beg them. Quite often they ask them to not do anything till they are there and then fell free to do whatever they wanted.

5.12 Donning the Mantle of Moral Police

On a sociological plane, the police represent the epitome of the value systems of orthodoxy and conservatism—be it Bombay's streets; Bangalore's pubs; Delhi or Gurgaon's nightspots; Goa's beaches; Valentine's Day celebration; the archaic patriarchs of the khap panchayats; the plight of a molestation victim who might have worn what the stupid cop thinks to be 'ultra modern or provocative'; or the issue of a girl going out for a matinee show with her boyfriend; *the police in India, cutting across all sorts of boundaries, behave worse than the matriarchic mothers in law or patriarchal fathers-in-law found abundantly in the TV serials depicting stinking rich families in some imaginary semi-urban area.*

Some of them actually genuinely believe in the orthodox value system. But the problem of some of them is different. They can actually not tolerate anybody enjoying life. If a boy is with a girl, they immediately become jealous. When they were that age, they could not even talk to a girl. How come this guy is enjoying life? If they see boys and girls going to pub, they become jealous again. They too drink and drink heavily, but in some seedy places, their homes or in the homes of their friends. And when they drink, they know that they have no culture of drinking or understanding of alcohol; they drink merely to get drunk. Girls should not appear attractive. Actually, they are fighting with themselves when they say so. *They become 'sexually' terribly disturbed by seeing girls who appear attractive – the problem is that they cannot give any expression to their arousal. This conflict reflects in their blaming the girls. A great perverse pleasure is derived in busting the so-called 'rave parties' and insulting the young men and women.*

We can look at such perverse activities from another angle also. Is moral policing of this type actually important? We have a thousand tasks of far greater importance to attend to. On one hand, the police leadership keeps on crying at various forums about the lack of resources and on the other hand, the resources that they have are wasted on such high publicity and low impact activities. *Fact is the cops use these drives to hike their extortion rates – the availability and consumption patterns of any 'party drugs' are scarcely affected.*

If these perverts have their way, you cannot hold hands in a park with a member of the other sex (forget about kissing or other forms of PDA – public display of affections) – for the cop, you are indulging in indecent behaviour in public. You cannot wear what the cop from his semi-urban or rural background thinks is ultra modern, revealing or provocative clothes. You cannot marry outside your caste, religion or inside your gotra – if you choose to elope, for God's sake never dare to step in that village again. You cannot go against the dictates of what the powerful, influential and rich in your area say for anything – after all, they are the respected elders and guardians of morals in the society and the police men are their loyal dogs. If they say that some woman is a witch and must be lynched because two kids of the village died of diarrhoea recently, you better keep quiet.

Though the activities of the Mumbai ACP Vasant Dhoble which led to an outrage across the country, are but one small example, there are certain professional issues that need to be discussed because such things are allowed to happen with the blessings of the police leadership. In connection with his raid on the famous Shiro nightclub in Worli alleging it was flouting rules, IBNLive had reported that his team was armed with a video camera and began videotaping the venue scaring away customers. Later he charged the restaurant for being 'overcrowded'! Why was the video camera carried? What evidence was supposed to be recorded that could not be adduced in some other manner? If at all it was necessary, why it could not be recorded by a secret camera? Two women arrested from a restaurant by Dhoble, who has also been accused of calling partying women "prostitutes", have already sued him for defamation. Pune-based industrialist Tehseen Poonawala produced a video that showed Vasant Dhoble, harassing four foreign tourists, herding them into a police van, aided by constables. The women, said to be German, refuse to get in, demanding an explanation as to why they were being detained, but are eventually led into a police van even as one of them cries while others repeatedly ask, "But what have we done?" Dhoble and his constables then took them to a police station for "verification" and to "record their statements" for which the women were detained for an hour. *The professional issue is under what authority the police think that they can conduct 'verification' on just about anyone. What exactly is that 'verification' and what do they seek in that?* In fact, in one of our celebrated research papers, 'The Law Of Passports In India: A Legally Untenable Attempt To Incorporate Some Draconian Provisions In The Name Of Security As Well As To Satisfy Some Populist Demands' in Indlaw [http://crimes.indlaw.com/search/articles/?76959ec2-e607-4a68-b05a 795cc453dee0], we have shown that even in the so-called verification for passports the law has not defined what exactly one must verify. ***Why did the police leadership not object to such things? The reason is that they do not have sufficient professional knowledge to point out such mistakes.***

We are aware that some fools in the police leadership invoke a plea that people like Dhoble have had been only mechanically applying some law, however archaic it be, and that there is nothing illegal in his acts—if someone has a problem with the laws they should seek amendment in the law. *Yes, the people will demand change in the law because everything in the country is done in their name, but this argument actually amounts to an admission that they have failed as leaders. If everything is to be done mechanically, subordinates could do it very well—why do we need senior officers then?* Leaders must always look at the larger picture and use their considered discretion—that' exactly what differentiates them from the cops on the streets. ***Senior officers must think—but unfortunately that's what they don't do—they want the 'people' to think while they relax. Does the nation pay these guys for relaxing?***

The *Times of India* editorial 'Madness In Mumbai' warned: "A Talibanesque police force running riot can cause grievous economic harm to Mumbai as well. The city is one of India's top entertainment and tourism hubs. But it can hardly remain so if authorities assume the role of moral vigilantes and attempt to shut down partying and nightlife. To stop such vigilante-ism from seeking the cover of the law, Maharashtra's archaic rule book must be upgraded in consonance with rapidly changing times, to meet 21st century standards." Maharashtra's former DGP K. Subramanyam called it unfortunate that law enforcement agencies were victimizing law-abiding people over issues as trifling as drinking without a liquor permit. "We catch hold of people who do not have Rs. 5 permits to consume alcohol. But even a permit holder can consume liquor and create a scene." Senior counsel S. G. Aney said, "I recognize the state's duty to enforce prohibition. But how do drinking permits become an effective means to that end. It finally remains one more unthinking attempt to provide some activity to government officers and the police."

5.13 Wrongly Invoking the Law Related to Sedition

Writer Arundhati Roy, Hurriyat hawk Syed Ali Shah Geelani and some others were booked in November 2010 on charges of sedition by Delhi Police for their "anti-India" speech at a seminar in New Delhi. According to the complaint, the accused made the 'seditious' comments at a convention in October last year on 'Azadi—The Only Way'. The filing of the FIR came following a directive from a local court on a petition filed by Sushil Pandit who alleged that Geelani and Roy made anti-India speeches at a conference on "Azadi-the Only Way" on October 21. Roy and others were charged under Sections 124-A (sedition), 153-A (promoting enmity between classes), 153-B (imputations, assertions prejudicial to national integration), 504 (insult intended to provoke breach of peace) and 505 (false statement, rumour circulated with intent to cause mutiny or offence against public peace. These sections were read with Section 13 of the Unlawful Activities Prevention Act of 1967.

Roy and Geelani had shared the dais with Maoist sympathizer Varavara Rao and others. Geelani was heckled by the audience. Reacting to the court order, Roy said that perhaps they should posthumously file a charge against Jawaharlal Nehru and cited 14 instances where the first Prime Minister has said about "the question of accession in any disputed territory or state must be decided in accordance with wishes of people. S. A. R. Geelani, who organised the seminar and faces charges of sedition, said the filing of charges were actually a diversionary tactics to divert attention from truth. He echoed Roy's view that if someone is charged with sedition in this issue, they should also register cases posthumously against Nehru and former Union Minister Krishna Menon who had expressed similar views.

In February 2011, Delhi Police told a court that the probe against Hurriyat hawk Syed Ali Shah Geelani, writer Arundhati Roy and four others in a case of sedition for their alleged anti-India speeches, was still inconclusive. In a status report, filed in the court of Metropolitan Magistrate Navita Kumari Bagha, the Station House Officer (SHO) of Tilak Marg Police Station said that the probe in the case has not concluded. In July also the city police told a Delhi court that it was yet to complete its probe into the sedition case. It would be advisable to give a brief overview of the correct legal position regarding sedition so that the people of the country may see how stupid the cops have been. The concept of sedition went through several ups and downs during the colonial rule as well as in independent India. The Federal Court had held one view; the Privy Council quite opposite to it. Then the Supreme Court deliberated upon it in several cases. The position was, however, finally settled in the case of **Kedar Nath Singh vs. The State of Bihar** [1962 AIR 955] by a five-judge bench of the Apex Court. Incidentally, the word "Sedition" does not occur in Section 124-A of the Indian Penal Code or in the Defence of India Rule. It is only found as a marginal note to Section 124-A, and is not an operative part of the section but merely provides the name by which the crime defined in the section will be known.

In Kedar Nath's case, the Court observed that any written or spoken words, etc., which have implicit in them the idea of subverting Government by violent means, which are compendiously included in the term 'revolution', have been made penal by the section in question. But the section has taken care to indicate clearly that strong words used to express disapprobation of the measures of Government with a view to their improvement or alteration by lawful means would not come within the section. Similarly, comments, however strongly worded, expressing disapprobation of actions of the Government, without exciting those feelings which generate the inclination to cause public disorder by acts of violence, would not be penal.

In other words, disloyalty to Government established by law is not the same thing as commenting in strong terms upon the measures or acts of Government, or its agencies, so as to ameliorate the condition of the people or to secure the cancellation or alteration of those acts or measures by lawful means, that is to say, without exciting those feelings of enmity and disloyalty which imply excitement to public disorder or the use of violence...A citizen has a right to say or write whatever he likes about the Government, or its measures, by way of criticism or comment, so long as he does not incite people to violence against the Government established by law or with the intention of creating public disorder. The provisions of the sections read as a whole, along with the explanations, make it reasonably clear that the sections aim at rendering penal only such activities as would be intended, or have a tendency, to create disorder or disturbance of public peace by resort to violence.

5.14 The Abuse of Section 498-A IPC

The Section reads: Whoever, being the husband or the relative of the husband of a woman, subjects such woman to cruelty shall be punishable with imprisonment for a term which may extend to three years and shall also be liable to fine. ***This law, merrily abused by unscrupulous people by filing false cases has been leading to humiliation and imprisonment of even innocent people. All of them succeed only with the active connivance of the corrupt police officers who have made it into an excellent extortion racket.*** Asha-Kiran, a large group of several thousand families, in its study 'Indian Dowry Law (498a): Myth vs. Reality An Investigative Report' published in 2006 reveals that with an estimated 40,000 such accusations per year and an average of 5 members of the husband's family implicated in each of these 498-A cases, about 200,000 people are directly affected by these accusations. The number of such cases is increasing by about 20 percent every year. Many senior citizens who have never been to the police stations or courts in their lifetime are dragged into jail without investigation and then into court cases that span several years. Many women in the husband's family are abused by the process. Many in the husband's family lose their jobs/earnings. Let us be very clear. We are not concerned with the constitutional validity of the law; we are concerned with the devious ways in which it is abused.

There are several reasons for which the law is abused. Some of them are:

- Extortion: Get-rich-quick-scheme to extort large amounts of money
- Prior Relationship: Wife has a prior relationship, and cannot get out of it. She marries to satisfy her parents, and then misuses 498-A in order to obtain a divorce
- Adultery: Women who indulge in adultery or are caught in adultery use 498-A as a bargaining tool
- Domination: Wife wants the husband to abandon his parents and siblings, and have total control over his finances and social behaviour, including his lifestyle
- Fraudulent Marriages: In which the bride (and her family) hides her education level or mental health; and when is justifiably asked to free the person who has gone into marriage without knowing the full facts; she files a false 498-A case.

The honourable Courts have delivered numerous judgements to bring succour to the victims of the abuse of this law, but the naked dance of the cops' atrocity continues unabated. In July 2012, taking note of the increasing dowry-related complaints, a **Division Bench of Justices T. S. Thakur and Gyan Sudha Misra of the Supreme**

Court ruled that a casual reference to the names of family members of the husband in the FIR filed by the wife without any allegation of their active involvement in the offence will not justify a case against them. The Apex Court said courts should be cautious in implicating family as the wife sometime wants to settle scores arising out of teething problems or "skirmish of domestic bickering".

Earlier also, the Supreme Court in **Kans Raj vs. State of Punjab** [2000 CriLJ 2993] had said that "for the fault of the husband the in-laws or other relatives cannot in all cases be held to be involved. The acts attributed to such persons have to be proved beyond reasonable doubt and they cannot be held responsible by mere conjectures and implications. The tendency to rope in relatives of the husband as accused has to be curbed." In **State vs. Srikanth** [2002 CriLJ 3605], the Karnataka High Court had also ruled, "Unless there is specific material against these persons it is downright wrong on the part of the investigating authorities to indiscriminately include the whole of the family as accused persons."

In the case of **Sushil Kumar Sharma vs. Union of India and others** [Writ Petition (Civil) 141 of 2005], a Division Bench of Justices Arijit Pasayat and H. K. Sema held that "the object of this provision is prevention of the dowry menace. But as has been rightly contended by the petitioner many instances have come to light where the complaints are not bona fide and have been filed with an oblique motive." In such cases acquittal of the accused does not wipe out the ignominy suffered during and prior to trial. Sometimes adverse media coverage adds to the misery". Merely because the provision was declared constitutional and intra vires, it did not give licence to unscrupulous persons to wreak personal vendetta or unleash harassment, the judges said.

The Bench called upon the Legislature to find out ways of dealing with those who made frivolous complaints or allegations. Until then, courts would have to take care of the situation within the existing framework. "The object is to strike at the root of dowry menace. But by misuse of the provision a new legal terrorism can be unleashed. The provision is intended to be used as a shield and not an assassin's weapon. If [the] cry of "wolf" is made too often as a prank, assistance and protection may not be available when the actual wolf appears", the Bench said.

In August 2010, in the case of **Preeti Gupta and Another vs. State of Jharkhand and Another** [Criminal Appeal No. 1512 of 2010] a Division bench of Justices Dalveer Bhandari and K. S. Radhakrishnan of the Supreme Court had plainly told the government to take a relook at the anti-dowry law by sending a copy of the judgement to the Union Law Minister to initiate the process—Section 498-A of Indian Penal Code—saying it has been misused by women to lodge false or exaggerated complaints against husbands and their relatives accusing them of cruel behaviour. Such is the level of exaggeration of cruel behaviour on the part of husbands and their relatives that "to find out the truth is a Herculean task in a majority of these complaints", said the Court. Advising extreme caution in dealing with such complaints, the bench said courts must take pragmatic realities into consideration while dealing with matrimonial cases. In **Jasbir Kaur vs. State of Haryana** [(1990)2 Rec Cri R 243], the Punjab and Haryana High Court had observed, "It is known that an estranged wife will go to any extent to rope in as many relatives of the husband as possible in a desperate effort to salvage whatever remains of an estranged marriage."

In **Savitri Devi vs. Ramesh Chand** [2003 CriLJ 2759], the Delhi High Court observed without mincing any words: "These provisions were though made with good intentions but the implementation has left a very bad taste and the move has been counter-productive. There is a growing tendency amongst the women which is further perpetuated by their parents and relatives to rope in each and every relative including minors and even school going kids nearer or distant relatives and in some cases against every person of the family of the husband whether living away or in other town or abroad and married, unmarried sisters, sisters-in-law, unmarried brothers, married uncies and in some cases grandparents or as many as 10 or 15 or even more relatives of the husband...*To leave such a ticklish and complex aspect of proposition as to what constitutes 'marital cruelty' and 'harassment' to invoke the offences punishable under Sections 498-A/406 IPC to a lower functionaries of police like Sub Inspectors or Inspectors whereas sometimes even courts find it difficult to come to the safer conclusion is to give the tools in the hands of bad and unskilled masters.*

Once a complaint is lodged under Sections 498-A/406 IPC whether there are vague, unspecific or exaggerated allegations or there is no evidence of any physical or mental harm or injury inflicted upon woman that is likely to cause grave injury or danger to life, limb or health, it comes as an easy tool in the hands of Police and agencies like Crime Against Women Cell to hound them with the threat of arrest making them run here and there and force them to hide at their friends or relatives houses till they get anticipatory bail as the offence has been made cognizable and non-bailable. Thousands of such complaints and cases are pending and are being lodged day in and day out." **In Saritha vs.**

R. Ramachandra [(I) (2003) DMC 37 (DB)], the Andhra Pradesh High Court observed: "*This is nothing but misuse of the beneficial provision intended to save the women from unscrupulous husbands. It has taken a reverse trend now*...It is for the Law Commission and the Parliament either to continue that provision (Section 498 IPC) in the same form or to make the offence a non cognizable one and a bailable one so that the ill-educated women of this country and their parents do not misuse the provision, to harass innocent people for the sin of contacting marriage with egoistic women. We have no hesitation to hold that if this situation is continued any longer the institution of marriage and the principle one man for women will vanish into their air." There is a battery of other judgements also in which the courts had commented on the abuse of the law.

In August 2010, it was reported that in a note addressed to the state chief secretaries, the government has asked the police and courts to handle matrimonial disputes and complaints of harassment for dowry with utter care and caution. In cases of matrimonial disputes, the first recourse should be to mediate between the warring spouses and their families. They can file charges under Section 498-A of the IPC only where conciliation efforts have failed, and when there is a prima facie case under Section 498-A and other laws. ***Well, readers must be aware that such direction notwithstanding, the depredations of the police continue and the police leadership has done nothing at all to even curb it—what abject failure! It can, of course, be inferred that it is not simple apathy—the cops must obviously taking their cut in the extortion.***

5.15 Abuse of the Provisions of the Motor Vehicle Act

The MV Act is another thing which makes the cops start salivating. Traffic is one of the major sources of income and is often considered to be relatively clean money which is not tainted with blood. There are numerous judgements which show how the police misuse the laws. The most often abused section of law pertains to drunken driving. They catch you, take you to a pathetic-looking government doctor who smells your breath and then ceremoniously proceeds to write that you have consumed alcohol. The lower courts might even convict you for that.

The High Courts, however, have repeatedly pointed out that that Section 185 demands one to be driving a vehicle under intoxication, whereas consuming alcohol and intoxication are two different things. Clause (a) of Section 185 of Motor Vehicles Act provides punishment for driving, or attempting to drive, a motor vehicle has in his blood alcohol exceeding 30 mg. per 100 ml. of blood, detected in a test by a breath analyzer. It is therefore necessary that a breath analyzer test to that effect should be performed. The evidence of the doctor as described above is therefore held to be insufficient and the charge under s. 185 is held to be not proved. The abuse of the MV Act can be seen from the case of **Joseph, Aged 26 Years vs. State of Kerala** [on 31 October, 2008, Crl.M.C. No. 3384 of 2006] where the Traffic police, Kochi had charged even the passengers of an auto rickshaw under Section 188 of the MV Act (the section reads: a person who abets the commission of an offence under Sections 184, 185 or 186 shall be punishable with the punishment provided for those offences) claiming that they were urging the auto driver to drive rashly! The Court threw it out. *Some of the numerous judgements in which this principle has been reiterated are listed below. Yet the police persist in the harassment of the citizenry.*

Abdul Gafoor S/o Muhammed vs. The State of Kerala [on June 10, 2010, Crl.M.C. No. 3223 of 2005]; **R. Venkobarao vs. State** [Criminal Revision Petition 1159/2007]; **Bineesh. P.O., S/o Late ... vs. The Assistant Sub Inspector of** ... [on June 10, 2008, Crl.M.C. No. 2113 of 2008]; **G. Ramulu Alias Venkat Ramulu vs. APSRTC Hyderabad** [on July 15, 2010 C.M.A. No. 1647 of 2003]; **Jyothish S/o Unnikrishnan vs. The State of Kerala** [on October 16, 2009 Crl.M.C. No. 3225 of 2009]; **K. P. Santhosh Kumar vs. S.I. of Police** [on March 11, 2008 Crl.M.C. No. 924 of 2008]; **Krishnaprasad S/o Venugopal vs. State of Kerala** [on January 3, 2008, Crl.M.C. No. 3549 of 2007]; **N. Babu S/o Narayanan, Aged 53 vs. State of Kerala** [on January 2, 2008, Crl.M.C. No. 3813 of 2007]; **Robert P. Thomas @ Lalichan vs. Sub Inspector of Police** [on July 19, 2010 Crl.M.C. No. 2720 of 2010]; **Saidalavi Aged 28 Years vs. State Of Kerala** [on January 10, 2007, Crl. M.C. No. 10677 of 2002]; **Sebastian, K.M. Aged ... vs. Unknown** [on June 23, 2008, Crl.M.C. No. 1926 of 2008]; and **M. Rajavalse vs. State by Circle Inspector of** ... [1999 CriLJ 58].

In **Shibu vs. State of Kerala** [2006 (4) KLT 747] it was held that as per Section 203 of the Motor Vehicles Act what is required to be conducted is breath test and not blood test. Blood test is enabled only in cases falling under Section 204(1)(a) or (b) of the Motor Vehicles Act namely only in cases where it appears to the police officer on breath test that there is presence of alcohol in the blood or when the offender when given an opportunity to submit to breath test has refused, omitted or failed to do so.

5.16 Abuse of the Law Related to Prostitution

Most IPS officers, and we have seen it hundreds of times ourselves, derive some sort of perverse pleasure in harassing the poorest of the poor in this country—the prostitutes. We were particularly amused by one officer in Agra physically chasing and catching some of them when he was SP (City) there. The local newspapers, intellectually bankrupt as they are, praised it as an act of dedication to duty and 'field work'! Here was the self-proclaimed moral guardian of the society bent upon ridding it of the one of the oldest evils! That accepting money for sex is considered a crime is based on their own distorted notions of sexual morality. Women are blamed for not maintaining chastity as if only they are responsible for maintaining the morals of the society.

It appears that hundreds of IPS officers seem to be unaware that prostitution, per se, is not an offence. Still, they get frequent raids conducted on cheap hotels (often near railway stations and bus stands) and harass innocent citizens. If somebody is sleeping quietly with a woman or the woman of his extramarital affair, what is your problem? Is there any law which says that one can have sex only within the confines of marriage? Is there any law which says that an unmarried person cannot have sex with some woman? Is there any law which says that the woman who stays with a man in a hotel room must necessarily be his wife? Is there any law that even if you are sleeping with your wife, you must always carry your marriage certificate with you – otherwise how do you prove that she is your wife? The cop can very well argue that she is a whore. Is there any law that a thulla can demand you to prove that the woman with you is your wife? And yet they have been doing it since ages and the police leadership has singularly failed in checking this tyranny. ***There are several reasons for this. One is, of course, the failure of the leadership in restraining their stupid subordinates. The second is the lure of the cheap publicity they get from dumb journalists. The third is, of course, the money which they extort from such hotels regularly.***

In spite of the fact, that the police are blatantly on the wrong side of the law, they harass millions of even good people who, because they cannot afford costlier hotels, choose to stay in such hotels. May be you can recall a hilarious scene from the Kareena Kapoor-Shahid Kapoor starrer 'Jab We Met' when the cheap hotel they had been staying in Ratlam was raided by the police in the dead of the night. Readers, if any one of you who has ever stayed in one such hotel, you would know the sheer terror of a police raid at the hotel.

Broadly speaking, there are three categories of sex workers. The first are the poorest of the poor street sex workers. They are homeless and live and even sleep at the roadside without shelter from sun or rain. They could perhaps be found soliciting in public—usually even they don't solicit in public because they often operate from near roadside *dhabas* and their potential customers know it by word of mouth that they are available. The second category is sex workers who have their own homes but they go to hotels or lodges for the act. Usually they also do not solicit in public because they are informed of the customer by the pimps who are present at the hotels. Call girls or girls provided by escort services are merely big city and high-priced versions of this category. The third category is those who entertain clients in their own homes with or without the help of agents. A variation of this is those who work either at or through the help of beauty parlours, massage parlours etc.

It is clear that any commercial sex worker who is not soliciting in public cannot be prosecuted. The cops must know what is meant by solicitation—unfortunately either they do not know or pretend to not know. Merely because a poor woman is standing at a bus stand, it cannot be inferred that she was soliciting. This was discussed by the Bombay High Court in the case of **State vs. Premchand Kubchand** [AIR 1964 Bom 155]. The honourable Court noted that the word 'solicit' has not been defined in the Act and hence referred to the Oxford and the Webster's dictionaries. The Court said it means to urge, entreat or importune, or to accost a man for immoral purposes. The Court noted that whether the urging or accosting is by the prostitute herself or by any other person can make no difference to the criminality of the act. Thus the Court held that it has been overlooked that persons other than the prostitute could urge or accost others for purposes of prostitution and indeed it is not unoften that" the soliciting is indulged in more by the mobile middleman than by the prostitute herself.

How can a poor woman who lives under some plastic sheet by the side of a dhaba be presumed to be soliciting when it is well-known to all the truck drivers eating at that *dhaba* that some women are to be had there? The sex may take place in her shed or in the trucks. How does it become an offence under the Act? There is no solicitation by the prostitute herself or by any pimp. Yet these hapless women are harassed by the miliions. Police arrest them at will and fabricate false cases against them—if they don't take a case under the ITP Act (Immoral Traffic Prevention Act) then they take a case under s. 294 IPC which deals with obscene acts or under some section of the state's Police Act. Many of them are arrested as soon as they manage bail somehow.

Gentlemen, the Act is intended to protect women from being trafficked, that is, coerced or forced to participate in selling sex. The Act punishes anyone maintaining a brothel, living off earnings of prostitution and procuring, inducing, or detaining for the sake of prostitution. Why do the cops harass someone who is already harassed so much by life? The cops not merely arrest them or prosecute them, it is not uncommon for them to be beaten up, insulted, their money and jewellery snatched, and threatened with eviction. Anyone can check the statistics – the number of pimps arrested is far less than the number of prostitutes arrested, even if one presumes that one pimp arranges for several prostitutes at a time.

The police turn a blind eye to the real traffickers or those responsible for the exploitation of the women. There is no good reason for the cops to gloat over the convictions they get and claim that the courts supported their version. The fact is that convictions under these sections are immediate, as sex workers often confess to the charge to expedite the proceedings, a better option than being detained to await trial and lose earnings. In effect, a law aimed at protecting women is being used to harass them. The importance of prevention of trafficking is irrefutable, but the entire focus of the enforcement of the ITP Act has shifted towards eliminating prostitution rather than prevention of trafficking in persons. Thus the real criminals from whom the policemen take much bigger money than what they take from the poor women continue to enjoy life whereas the poor sex workers are crushed further.

The cops try to justify their general raids on cheap hotels by invoking Section 15 of the ITP Act which gives power to search without warrant. The section never intended to provide for a general raid on any hotel near the railway station. The logic of having received the so-called credible information cannot be stretched like this. If you extend the logic this way, any residential home also where more than one woman is residing, can be raided claiming that they had received the so-called credible information that the premises were being used as a brothel – certainly, the law never intended it to be so. Does it mean that no family with two women or more is safe from police raids? Certainly not. The police leadership has failed in stopping its misuse or even pointing out the potential for abuse. Why don't the cops carry out raids on the residences of their own colleagues where more than one woman could be staying?

There are numerous judgements in support of what we stated above. The position that commercial sex work per se is not illegal was made clear in the case of **T. Jacob vs. State of Kerala** [AIR 1971 Ker. 166]. The same position was taken in **Sangeeta and Anr. Vs. State and Ors**. [1995 CriLJ 3923] also. In **Dhanalakshmi vs. Unknown** [1974 CriLJ 61] it was held that a perusal of the definition of the word "brothel" would clearly indicate that the place must be used for purposes of prostitution for the gain of another person or for the mutual gain of two or more prostitutes. The phrase 'for purposes of prostitution' postulates plurality of instances of prostitution. A single instance, in my view, would not suffice for the purpose of prostitution, for the definition mentions the word 'purposes'. This means that if a single woman entertains a man at her home, it is not an offence. If a woman gets her clients over email or phone, she cannot be said to be soliciting in public. Now you can see how call girls are harassed.

Smruthy D/o Sivanand vs. State of Kerala [Kerala High Court, on November 12, 2010, Crl.MC No. 2601 of 2010] was an interesting case. The police had alleged that a man and a woman were indulging in sexual intercourse in a Santro car which was parked on the side of a public road. As you know, the cops harass even those boys and girls who might be sitting close to each other in a park. In this case, the cops argued that it was a public place and charged them under Section 7 and 8 of ITP Act. The Court held that to attract an offence under Section 7, prosecution has to prove that second accused was carrying on prostitution and the first accused was found with the second accused in any premises within the notified area as provided under the Act. The court further cited **Radhakrishnan vs. State of Kerala** [2008(2) 2 KLT 521] which had defined the meaning of prostitution and held that in order to become prostitution there should be the offering of her body by a female for promiscuous sexual intercourse for hire, whether in money or kind. The word 'promiscuous' means indiscriminate. The import of the word 'promiscuous' is that the woman or girl offering her body, offers it for hire to anyone who desires it for sexual intercourse. In other words, the woman is available to be shared without any discrimination. In this case, there was no offer of her body for sexual intercourse to anybody by the first accused. Hence, for the sole reason that petitioners were found engaged in sex in a car parked on a public place, neither an offence under Section 7 or 8 is attracted.

Sometimes the cops argue that they were trying to rescue girls trapped in prostitution. In **Tara vs. State** [on April 13, 2012, W.P. (Crl) 296/2012], the Andhra Pradesh police came to Delhi, armed with a search warrant issued by the Principal Judicial First Class Magistrate, Anantapur claiming to rescue a large number of minor girls under Sections 16 and 17 of the ITP Act who had been lured with false promises and introduced into prostitution. A Division Bench of the Delhi High Court held that the coercive manner in which the police dealt with the victims was offensive of their rights under Articles 14 and 21 of the Constitution of India and transportation, without consent, of petitioners amounted to treating them as less than human beings and belittling their dignity. The High Court also cited the Apex court in the case of **Budhadev Karmaskar vs. State of West Bengal** [on August 2, 2011 Criminal Appeal No. 135 of 2010, orders dated 14.02.2011, 02.08.2011 and 24.08.11] whereat it was held: "Sex workers are also human beings and hence they are entitled to a life of dignity... Providing short stay homes to sex workers is hardly a solution to their problem. They must be provided a marketable technical skill so that they can earn their livelihood through such technical skill instead of by selling their bodies. Merely sending them to homes is sending them to starvation...The so-called Homes run under the Government sponsored projects virtually operate as prison houses..."

Chapter 6

Professional Issues that the Police Leadership has Failed to Address in 150 Years

In this chapter we discuss some of the professional issues which should have been discussed by the police leadership because, for various reasons, they have a great deal of ambiguity in them. In 150 years, generations of police officers have failed to discuss them because it demands application of mind and which they do not have. The list is only illustrative and not exhaustive. A separate book will be required if we have to discuss all such issues.

6.1 Use of Force in Dispersing Unlawful Assembly

6.1.1 *Historical Reasons of the Grey Areas*

When the law was enacted it envisaged an ideal situation and very fondly, in a manner quite characteristic of the Victorian era, presumed that things would always be like that only—unfortunately the reality of India has belied that fond expectation. The law pertaining to use of force in dispersing an unlawful assembly envisages an ideal situation where the policemen and the magistrate stand together in one group before an unlawful assembly/riotous mob and following the orders of the magistrate, the police party charges and disperses the mob—end of the matter. This has hardly ever happened in post-independence India.

When the law is viewed in its historical background, as discussed so eloquently in the case of **Rex vs. Pinney** [(1832) 5 Car and P (254)], it would become clear that the English law presumed that the responsibility of taking a decision would *always* be that of the magistrate and fault would not be found with the policemen. The English policeman of that era was supposed to be so dumb, so bereft of intelligence that he was not even issued with a weapon. It was the duty of the magistrate to issue him with the weapon for a specific duty and then collect it back. The magistrate was supposed to embody the brain and the policemen were supposed to embody the brawn. The law also presumed a priori that a magistrate would always stand by what he had ordered there.

This clarity of roles got horribly mixed up in India when following the Second Law Commission comprising John Romilly, John Jervis, Edward Ryan, R. Lowe, C. H. Cameron, John. M. Macleod and T. F. Ellis et al., the British introduced the CrPC for India. These characters used the phrase 'executive magistrate or police officer' and left the confusion forever. The historical fact is that they were, at that time, under the fond impression that the magistrate would be a man of honour and the police officer would be either completely dumb or a 'loyal' man who would consider it infra dig to fight for his rights—and hence there would never be any conflict. There is no reason to believe that Macleod and company were infallible or that we are forever doomed to remain bound with their wisdom or lack of it. There is no reason that we must necessarily live with the shortcomings of the CrPC as made by these gentlemen. What does it take to amend it? If we can amend the Constitution a hundred times, we can do this also. After all, it is an important matter having a bearing on the police and the people both. But the police leadership has traditionally been so dumb that they have not even demanded for its amendment.

6.1.2 *The Problems That Arise on Account of the Grey Areas*

Supposing both a police officer above the rank of sub-inspector and an executive magistrate are available, who will be in command and responsible for the decision taken? It has not been clarified anywhere. Their assessment of a situation may differ. Whose view shall prevail and under what legal authority? It is only a popular presumption that the magistrate's view shall prevail—there is no clear judgement on that. If that has to be the magistrate then no responsibility must be fixed on the police officers. But it does not happen in real life. What a police officer/CPMF officer is supposed to do when there is a difference of opinion with the magistrate? Is he supposed to retreat unilaterally or is he supposed to exercise his right of self-defence? Or is he supposed to use the authority that is vested in him by Section

129 or vide MHA notification No. J.II-9/74-ADM (PERS-II/GPA-I) dated July 27, 1976? Supposing he withdraws, will it be treated as desertion or not? He should be told the exact circumstances under which he can retreat.

What are the forces supposed to do if a magistrate slips away on some pretext at a critical moment and resurfaces again after the police have used force on their decision? After all, unlawful assemblies could materialize at scores of places and it may not be possible for the government to deploy magistrates at every place. The law does not admit of anything called a sector magistrate. The law envisages a magistrate who is physically present at the spot in such a manner that he can see and evaluate a situation or himself.

Given the fact that in practice, deployments are quite spread out, and that mobs emerge simultaneously from scores of places and attack the forces, making it impossible for a magistrate or a sub-inspector to be available at all the places, what protection is available to personnel junior in rank to sub-inspector if they are obliged to use force? Do they have to plead self-defence all the time?

There is one more complicating aspect of it. We are all aware that very frequently, central forces are deployed along with the state police—you have the CRPF, the BSF, the army, the RAF and what not. In a situation where the CPMF (Central Paramilitary Force) are deployed along with the state police, what the CPMF should do when there is a difference of opinion regarding the assessment of a situation between them and the state police, or between the methods they consider it proper to adopt and the methods for which the state police officers might insist. The CPMF officers might maintain that the situation warrants use of lethal force—the state police might not. Whose opinion shall prevail? Are the CPMF obliged to blindly accept the opinion of the state police even if that results in casualties amongst their ranks? Which law says so? This is a fundamental issue because it is intimately related to a quintessential question: "Are the CPMFs merely providers of (dumb) manpower or are they a professional counter-insurgency-cum-law and order maintenance force which have their own methods and work ethic?" For decades such delicate issues have been brushed under the carpet in the name of maintaining coordination or synergy.

All such eventualities and uncomfortable questions which we, as a system, have been deliberately leaving unanswered for more than 150 years or leaving it to the discretion of the poor semi-educated constable, must be foreseen and answered. But the police leadership has meticulously shied away from this—basically because they are

intellectually incapable. It is unfair to leave them on the judgement of the officers in the field if the system itself cannot muster the intellectual and moral courage to answer them. The leadership should have seen to it that subordinate officers and men are not asked to assume responsibilities or take decisions for which they are not legally or even intellectually equipped. But that was not to be.

6.1.3 *Grey Areas When the Magistrates Do Not Behave in an Ideal Manner*

It has happened innumerable times throughout the country that an executive magistrate who is on duty, refuses to give the order to use even non-lethal force, not to speak of lethal force. The law, it needs to be understood clearly, never stipulated orders in writing and the magistrates have been taking advantage of it. A written order could perhaps serve the purpose of a somewhat better legal defence should the magistrate backtrack later but it is not a legal requirement. More often than not, the magistrates deny having given oral orders also; even for written orders there have been instances when they have, to save their skins, claimed in subsequent inquiries that the orders were obtained from them under coercion. The courts are silent on how they would view a situation if the magistrate argued later that his signatures were obtained under coercion, he never gave a verbal order or that his orders were misunderstood. *Why has the police leadership not agitated against this for the past 150 years?*

The issue of the legal validity of command and control is a fine legal point and needs to be understood carefully. Suppose a platoon is spread in a length of even 60 m on a curved road and if at one end of the road a section comes under attack, the platoon commander or the magistrate who is out of sight at the other end of the road cannot be legally said to be exercising command and control over that section. The section of men for all legal purposes is on its own. Command and control exist only when each person being commanded can, with his senses see and hear the commander clearly and understand him. Command and control for a legal purpose cannot be exercised by remote control. Even if the platoon commander or the magistrate is in wireless or cell phone communication with the section at the end, the legal position is that he was not a direct observer of the proceedings and therefore he could not be a judge of the situation. When the matter goes to court or before a judicial commission of inquiry, they will ask questions like—in the din of the rioters could the man even hear correctly what was being said by the commander from that distance (the commander or the magistrate could have shouted 'fire mat karo' and the man could have heard 'fire karo' as the 'mat' was drowned in noise at that moment—quite like *'Ashwatthama Hataha iti, naro va kunjaro va'* of the Mahabharat); could he even see the commander/magistrate clearly, and so on.

6.1.4 *Legal Position on the Myth of Minimum Force and Maximum Restraint*

The police leadership, particularly when it is trying hard to please some political dispensation, gives a clarion call for exercising maximum restraint and using minimum force. There are numerous instances when officers have been punished by their still senior officers for not observing this. Most of these ignoramuses do not know that the popular notion of exercising maximum restraint and using minimum force has actually no legal basis. It was held in the cases of **Pancham Lal vs. Dadan Singh** [1979 CriLJ 1018 (para-8)]; **Akhilesh Prasad vs. Union Territory of Mizoram** [AIR 1981 SC 806]; and **Commissioner of Police and others vs. Manoj Sharma and another** [on October 3, 2007] that the officer on the spot would be the best judge of the degree of force which would be required to control a particular situation. It was also held that it is quite different from sitting and calculating in a cool and serene atmosphere of a court room dissecting the acts and counter-acts alleged by parties.

In the case of Manoj Sharma, the Court summed up the position in the following words: "Once law enjoins a duty upon an officer and gives him power to perform the duty, it gives enough discretion to the officer to take decisions necessary for the performance of his duty. Section 129 gives power to the Executive Magistrate and other officers to give command to the unlawful assembly to disperse and where it is seen that unlawful assembly is determined not to disperse, the power has been given to the police officer to disperse such unlawful assembly by use of force. How much force is necessary to disperse the unlawful assembly has to be the decision of Executive Magistrate or the police officer concerned. This decision is to be taken on the spot assessing the situation and the assessment of the situation has to be of the officer concerned. If there are 10 different persons in similar situation, they may have different assessment of the situation and may devise upon different methods of use of force. Since, the opinion of 10 persons may differ, it cannot be said that one person is right and another person is wrong or the assessment of 'X' would have been correct and assessment of 'Y' would have been incorrect. In a situation of maintenance of law and order decisions are to be taken instantly and there is not enough time for reflection. Such decisions are to be taken by the officer in-charge of the situation. The decisions about the kind of force to be used, where it is to be used, how much force is to be used are required to be left to the discretion of the officer. If this discretion is not given, no unlawful assembly can ever be controlled. A police officer, who is required to control the unlawful assembly, cannot take into consideration the purpose for which the assembly has gathered. An unlawful assembly is unlawful assembly irrespective of the fact whether the people have assembled for a good cause or a bad cause. Neither there is a golden scale of quantum of force to be used, nor can such a yardstick be laid down by the Courts. The quantum of force to be used has to be determined by the officer concerned, the Court cannot substitute its own opinion or decision about the quantum of force which should have been used."

We also agree that there should be no wanton use of force. But the legal position raises two questions. *How and why they have punished police officers for not observing their clarion call for exercising maximum restraint and using minimum force. Secondly, if they feel so strongly about it, why did they ever not try to challenge these views of the honourable courts? Of late a notion is taking hold that the police must use lethal force only in self-defence when their own lives are in danger or when their own camps are attacked. The law does not provide for any such discrimination but it has actually been stated several times by the political leadership that the police must not use lethal force when public property is being damaged – even when government offices, buildings, and their own vehicles were set on fire; it was said that you could always get a new vehicle. Why has the leadership never sought to clear the air on this?*

The police are neither obliged to nor expected to 'play' with the rioters in the name of a 'tactful handling'. The so-called tactful handling is often a pretext for not acting sufficiently or resolutely. The law does not permit any discretion in this regard. If there is an unlawful assembly, it has to be dispersed for if the system does not do so, it would be failing in its constitutional duty. The legal position is that before any force can be used, three pre-requisites are to be satisfied. Firstly, there should be an unlawful assembly with the object of committing violence or an assembly of five or more persons likely to cause a disturbance of the public peace. Secondly, such assembly is ordered to be dispersed, and thirdly, in spite of such orders to disperse, such assembly does not disperse.

The practice of indulging in a day-long '*ding-dong*' battle with the rioters is legally incorrect. The law does not permit the police to 'play' with the rioters or engage them in a 'holding operation'. The law is straight on this. If there is an unlawful assembly, the system is obliged to disperse it and ensure that it remains dispersed. If the police are not dispersing the unlawful assembly decisively, it would lead to the conclusion that the police lacked the will to disperse them or that the system, for whatever reason was deliberately soft on the rioters. The law does not accept the plea that the police 'played' with the rioters because they did not want to aggravate the situation. The law permits a judicious use of force.

The object is to disperse the unlawful assembly for good and not allow it to assemble again. If the unlawful assembly is assembling again and again, it would only mean that the dispersals have not been proper. It also means that the system has, without saying so in many words, accorded them a degree of legitimacy which they do not have by any means. Legally speaking the system has no discretion with regard to an unlawful assembly. If there is an unlawful assembly, it has to be dispersed and dispersed decisively. The system has no legal right to say that it would tolerate such-and-such behaviour from the mob but no further.

In other words, the system cannot say that the police would remain a mute spectator or would block the stones with their shields if they only threw stones at the police from a distance of 50 yards but it would react if the stones were to be thrown from a closer distance. The system cannot say that it would tolerate if the mob carried sticks in their hands but would react if they carried swords. The system cannot say that it would not ask the police to disperse the mob as long as the swords carried by the mob were only brandished but would react if they threw petrol bombs or acid. The system cannot say that it would tolerate as long as the rioters only broke the glasses of the government vehicles by throwing stones but would react if they set fire to the vehicles. The law does not accord any such discretion to the system. Any such notion that has taken ground is based on ignorance of law.

These are dangerous examples of legal ignorance. They have been mentioned here because even if they are not stated in so many words, quite often such sentiments have been tacitly implied. After all, do not we hear it all too frequently: "They are only throwing stones? You are covered from top to bottom in protective gear. Why you have to use force at all?" In the eyes of law, this is a terrible mistake. The law does not envisage that an unlawful assembly has the right to throw stones on the police and that the police have an obligation to stand like Buddha simply because the system has also given them some protective gear. Throwing stones collectively or even individually is actually an attempt to murder and there are several judgements to that effect.

The law does not envisage that the right to protest extends to the limit of violating prohibitory orders, assaulting public servants on duty and damaging public property. In a democracy, people have a right to register their protest against the government for whatever aggrieves them but which law or provision says that in the process they can make murderous assault on policemen with stones and other implements and damage public property? If they are allowed to do so, the impression which the rioters themselves derive is that they have a right to do so. In fact most rioters genuinely believe that while taking up a gun could perhaps been an offence, rioting is not.

6.1.5 *Legal Position on Identifying the Most Deserving Target(s)*

Yet another fallacy is that police must fire only at the most deserving targets. This concept, taught to generations of police officers, is not only illegal; it is beyond simple scientific sense too. There is no way a police officer or a magistrate from a distance may judge as to who in a mob of over a thousand is the ringleader or the real troublemaker. The fact is that it is not required either. Once again, moral concepts must not be mixed up with legal concepts. The legal position is that each member of an unlawful assembly would be held vicariously liable for the crime committed by any member of such assembly if it was proved that the offence was committed pursuance to a common object.

Further, a mob is a dynamic object and not a collection of static targets. People within a mob are moving all the time. There is no reason to believe that the ringleaders of the mob would necessarily be standing right in the front of the mob with their chests puffed up, challenging the police. The simple fact is that people keep on moving within the mob; it is not possible to shoot a person who is standing or moving behind the cover of even a couple of persons even though he might have been identified easily by his features or clothes. Above all, the average policeman is not a sharpshooter in any case. It is therefore eminently possible that people other than the so-called ringleaders would be hit if fire is opened. Firing which is precise like a surgeon's knife does not exist in real life.

6.1.6 *Legal Position on the Manner of Firing*

Since long, senior officers have been insisting that policemen must fire from a kneeling position and that the fire must be directed below the waist. 'You should not shoot to kill' is the watchword. Where is the law for it? Nowhere! There is no legal sanctity of such pseudo-moralistic ideas. It is both amusing and a confirmation of the intellectual bankruptcy of the police leadership that such ideas have held ground since 1926!

These guys do not know that firing from a kneeling position is a relic of the 18th century when the front line of the famous 'English Infantry Square' had to necessarily kneel so that the line in the rear could fire simultaneously from a standing position. Thus firing from a kneeling position is a historical relic of an exactly opposite desire—to deliver the maximum volume of fire simultaneously. Even if a man is made to kneel, it can never be ensured that the barrel of his rifle will be only at such-and-such degrees from the horizontal—who will measure it there and with what? Thus even a man who is made to fire from the kneeling position can also hit a man in the head.

In the heat of the moment when the men of the forces are under great stress and fear of being lynched, there is no way it can be guaranteed that the barrel of the weapon shall always be exactly horizontal or dipped below horizontal—he is not firing on a firing range for practice—he is firing to save his life or the lives of his comrades. It is a matter of simple trigonometry that if the elevation changes by even 2 degrees, the bullet will go exactly 1.75 meters up at a distance of 50 meters. This means that a bullet that it aimed at the feet of a six-foot tall man will hit him in the head if the elevation of the barrel changes by just two degrees. It must be kept in mind that the gun is held in human hand and not in a vice—the human body is not a block of concrete—the hands do tremble in stress or otherwise too and what it takes to change the elevation by just two degrees?

The police leadership has never had the intellectual acumen and moral courage to inform the nation that while they would try everything to not 'shoot to kill' the effect of fire is unpredictable and people could well be hit fatally. Once a bullet leaves the muzzle, it is on its own and no longer under the control of the man who fired. Whom it will hit and where it will hit depends on the behaviour of the target which is by no means a stationary target, a crowd being a dynamic thing. Somebody in the mob might duck and could get hit in the chest or head. The same argument applies to tear gas shells or rubber bullets/plastic pellets also. Where is the law that says that they must only be fired at 45 degrees or more?

6.1.7 *Other Myths*

There are several other myths pertaining to the management of law and order and for which the police leadership has never applied any mind. One such myth relates to the minimum strength of deployment. As far as the legal position goes, there is no legal sanctity attached with the magical figure of a company or a platoon. Fixing of strength would therefore be arbitrary in any case. The critical legal issue is that if a man in a small detachment uses lethal force in self-defence because only his small detachment was in danger of being overwhelmed in a 'localized' fashion with the other detachments faring relatively better, the system should not find fault with him on account of the fact that he had not been a part of a larger detachment or that he did not seek orders from a magistrate.

If we accept that extended deployments are inevitable, we must also accept two things simultaneously and provide for them:

- That each component of the deployment cannot have an officer of the stipulated rank or an executive magistrate with it;
- That even if there is such an officer or the magistrate somewhere near or far (which could be anywhere from 50 m to 200 m depending on the situation and the locality), he cannot be legally presumed to be actually in command and control of the deployments for the simple reason that he is not a direct observer of the proceedings and that in the din and confusion his orders, if any, cannot be unmistakably understood by the men.

If we do not accept this then the extended deployment would become wrong—for both things cannot be true simultaneously. At the same time, it is vital that fault should not be found on procedural grounds.

The other myth relates to the strength of the armed component. The entire business of 1/3rd armed component and 2/3rd lathi-wielding/ tear gas component is administrative fiction or convenience—there is no legal sanctity attached to it. The concept of 1/3rd armed component had some relevance when the mobs were not expected to be so hostile or violent as are found today. It also presumed that the space and the situation would be such that the 2/3rd lathi-wielding component would remain compact together and right in front of the eyes of the magistrate with the 1/3rd armed component waiting in the rear—that sort of ideal situation is perhaps never encountered. To make lathi-wielding men face murderous mobs armed with all the things ranging from stones, sticks, acid bulbs, Molotov Cocktails, iron rods, chains, axes and other sharp-edged weapons, is to condemn them to death.

Yet another myth relates to the use of protective gear. We have frequently heard a mistaken argument that the rioters were unarmed and yet the police used force on them. This is a terrible fallacy. Suppose there is a detachment of 3-4 policemen deployed to block or cover a lane. They could easily be surprised by a group of just 10 unarmed men and beaten to death, their lathis notwithstanding. It is all a matter of effecting surprise and overawing them with sheer aggression. In fact a group of 10 unarmed men which succeeds in isolating a policeman and pounces on him, can pin him down by their sheer body-weights. They do not have to be martial artists to kill the fallen man—ten kicks in the abdomen or groin of a fallen man may well kill him by rupturing the spleen or inducing vasovagal shock if he is hit even once in the testicles.

If the purpose is only to put policemen in armour and not let them do anything, they could as well sit inside the camp. The law expects the police to disperse an unlawful assembly and not hide. The protective gear is to meet contingencies and that too to some extent. It does not protect against all eventualities. The average policeman does not have the dexterity of Bruce Lee in wielding his shield. It can be easily demonstrated that just two men can engage a policeman in such a manner that a stone hits him and hits hard. One could engage him by throwing so that the attention of his shield is diverted to the lower side whereas the other could surprise him with a throw on the upper side. Nowhere in the world are the policemen trained in the art of wielding the shield with such dexterity so as to protect them from a barrage of stones coming from multiple directions simultaneously. In the Medieval Age, soldiers spent years practising sword-fighting with shield in one hand and yet in the battles hundreds of thousands of them got killed in sword-fights alone! Most people do not realize that when one has the shield in one hand, he can use the lathi with one hand only and that not only restricts its freedom of movement, it also greatly reduces the force with which it can be wielded. A man armed with a lathi and shield cannot protect himself against a group the members of which pounce him from several directions. It is nothing but a myth.

6.2 Failure to Address the Legal Issue of Deaths at the Hands of Police

On February 6, 2009, in the case of **AP Civil Liberties Committee (APCLC) vs. The Government of AP** and others [W.P. No. 15419/2006], a five-judge bench of the AP High Court ruled, among other things, that:

- Where a police officer causes death of a person, acting or purporting to act in discharge of official duties or in self-defence as the case may be, the first information relating to such circumstance (even when by a police/public official; whether an alleged perpetrator is named or not) shall be recorded and registered as FIR, enumerating the relevant provisions of Law (u/s 154(1) CrPC), and shall be investigated (u/s 156/157 CrPC).

- That the existence of circumstances bringing a case within any of the Exceptions in the Indian Penal Code including the exercise of the right of private defence (a General Exception in Chapter IV IPC), cannot be conclusively determined during investigation. The opinion recorded by the Investigating Officer in the final report forwarded to the Magistrate (u/s 173 CrPC), is only an opinion...The Magistrate (notwithstanding an opinion of the Investigating officer, that no cognizable offence appears to have been committed; that one or more or all of the accused are not culpable; or that the investigation discloses that the death of civilian(s) in a police encounter is not culpable in view of legitimate exercise by the police of the right of private defence), shall critically examine the entirety of the evidence collected during investigation to ascertain whether the opinion of the Investigating Officer is borne out by the record of investigation. The Magistrate has the discretion to disregard the opinion and take cognizance of the offence u/s 190 CrPC
- That a magisterial enquiry (inquest) (u/s 174 to 176 CrPC) is neither a substitute nor an alternative to the obligation to record the information as FIR and to conduct investigation into the facts and circumstances of the case and if necessary to take measures for the discovery and arrest of the offender (s) (u/s 154(1), 156 and 157 CrPC).

In simple words, it meant that murder case would have to be registered for all deaths at the hands of police whether in the so-called 'encounters' or in law and order management. Aggrieved by this, the AP Police Officers Association filed an appeal in the Supreme Court. On March 4, 2009, **a three-judge Bench of the Supreme Court** comprising Chief Justice K. G. Balakrishnan, Justice P. Sathasivam and Justice J. M. Panchal stayed the aforesaid order. Mr. Harish Salve, appearing for the appellant AP Police Officers Association, said that going by the High Court order, cases would have to be registered even against those police officers involved in the Parliament attack and against the NSG commandos in the November 26, 2008 Mumbai terrorist attack. He said no police officer would be able to counter terrorist or subversive elements. The Bench issued notice to the State and other respondents including the AP Civil Liberties Committee (APCLC), the petitioner in the High Court. There are important questions of law involved in the whole affair. Whether police officers were entitled to claim protection against investigation and prosecution for acts (using lethal force) supposedly done in the course of their duty and whether such acts would constitute a cognizable offence?

Where exactly do we draw the line between duty and 'not duty'? Taking bribe, while sitting in the office is not a part of duty, for example. But when security forces go into jungles for anti-Naxal operations and fire, where do we draw the line between duty and not duty? Who is supposed to delve into the mind of the police officer to ascertain his intent before he has committed the act? Whether in the event of any injury or death to a person arising out of exchange of fire between such person and police officers, the only defence available to police officers would be private defence or something else too?

How will we protect the citizens against the 'murders' by police in fake encounters and in 'wanton' firings if some blanket protection is given to police officers? The HC order, if interpreted literally, would not give any immunity to police officers involved in exchange of fire while dispersing an unlawful assembly and would be treated on a par with any civilian who uses force in his self-defence. ***However, what is most lamentable is that the police leadership of the country is pretending to be completely oblivious of such an important matter.*** The matter is, however, hanging fire since then. The case has not come up for hearing at the time of writing this book and thus a very vital question of law that will have a bearing on the fate of those hundreds of thousands of police men involved in anti-Naxal and other counterinsurgency operations, still hangs undecided.

6.3 Legal Issues in Counterinsurgency Operations

Counterinsurgency or anti-terrorist operations are the in-thing these days. Nine states are said to be affected by Naxalism—every other day some very high level meeting is held or some high-power committee is appointed, whatever they might mean. The police forces of these states are undertaking anti-Naxal operations. Some 82 battalions of CRPF are deployed in these states besides 15 of the BSF, 5 of the ITBP and 5 of the SSB. Then, of course, we have J&K where some 60 battalions of CRPF are deployed to assist a disproportionately large state police. We have some 36 battalions of the CRPF in the north-eastern states also. Ask them what they are doing and they would say 'operations'. Half the police leadership earns its bread, butter and medals through this route. Even those who don't, claim a sort of birth right over 'operations'. ***Every IPS officer, by virtue of being an IPS officer, claims to be an expert in 'operations' and has some valuable advice or opinion on that. And yet, as we will show in this section, the police leadership is so intellectually bankrupt that they have, over the decades utterly failed in addressing some of the most fundamental issues pertaining to counterinsurgency operations. In fact, the issues have never been raised at all.***

6.3.1 *Definitional Problems*

The first question that arises in the context of counterinsurgency operations is have we even defined insurgency and terrorism in a strict legal sense? Unfortunately, no! And yet we are undertaking counterinsurgency operations on such a large scale! *The police leadership could, of course, not be bothered with this. Bothering requires mind and that is in short supply.* The Supreme Court deliberated on the definition of terrorism in the case of **Madan Singh vs. State of Bihar** [on April 2, 2004, Appeal (Crl) 1285 of 2003] and admitted that it is not possible to precisely define terrorism. In the case of **Zameer Ahmed Latifur Rehman Sheikh vs. State of Maharashtra** [on April 23, 2010, Civil Appeal Nos. 1975-77 of 2008] it was held that although the term 'insurgency' defies a precise definition, yet, it could be understood to mean and cover breakdown of peace and tranquillity as also a grave disturbance of public order so as to endanger the security of the state and its sovereignty. It was also held that the Constitution thus requires a line, perhaps only a rough line, to be drawn between the fields of public order or tranquillity and those serious and aggravated forms of public disorder which are calculated to endanger the security of the State.

The current Unlawful Activities (Prevention) Act 2008 Amendment [UAPA-Section 15] describes terrorist act but the definition leaves a great deal of scope for interpretation. *What exactly it is that threatens the unity, integrity, security or sovereignty of India or is done with intent to strike terror or likely to strike terror in the people or any section of the people in India or in any foreign country?*

Let us leave the question of intent. Intent resides in the mind and you cannot penetrate that. For legal purpose it is only the intent inferred from the attendant circumstances that matters. The critical question therefore is how do you distinguish a terrorist act from other crimes or crimes that are committed in pursuit of passions like communal, regional, racial, religious or social hatred? Suppose there is a massacre of people of a certain community, religion, region, or caste. Such crimes of varying degrees are committed in large numbers. Even third-rate goondas freely use bombs and firearms. Well, they also threaten the socio-political fabric of the country—would you call them terrorist acts? The Indian Penal Code has Sections 153-A for promoting enmity between different groups on grounds of religion, race etc.; 153-AA for carrying arms in processions; and 153-B for imputations or assertions prejudicial to national integration. Would they be called terrorist acts? ***The simple legal issue is what exactly are the parameters on which you decide that a certain violation of***

law is actually intended towards the nation-state of India as a political entity and it is only incidental that some citizens happen to be its victims; or conversely, that a certain crime is intended towards only individuals and had nothing to do with the nation-state of India? It is only a matter of interpretation! The police leadership has, of course, not burdened itself with such complex issues.

6.3.2 *How Do You Undertake Counterinsurgency Operations?*

The definition of terrorist acts in the UAPA does not really help in devising a legal framework for counterinsurgency or anti-terrorist operations. How do you go about it? If a crime is committed in front of your eyes and you give hot pursuit to the terrorist and then engage him in a fire fight, it's fine—you can always say that he refused to surrender, shot at you too and you fired in self-defence. What happens when this is not the case? After all, you cannot keep on waiting for some terrorist strike to take place and that may not be often. Further, you may be late in reaching and the terrorist might have decamped in the meantime. Then you may have to undertake some pro-active measures—what they commonly and wrongly call as 'offensive operations'.

How can you carry out cordon and searches, mount raids or lie in ambush? Under what authority of law and what provisions? You cannot invoke a plea all the time that you had some secret information? For the sake of argument, even if it is accepted that you had some information, what permits you to shoot? To put it very simply what is the legal authority under which you hunt a terrorist and shoot him down? What exactly are you supposed to do before a terrorist or insurgent has committed an act which, by some contrived interpretation of the Section 15, you determine to qualify for a terrorist act? He may be a member of what could have been described as an 'unlawful association' for the purpose of the Act, but the mere fact of his being a member of that unlawful association does not entitle him to be shot at and killed. So what do you do?

Even the Armed Forces (Special Powers) Act [AFSPA] speaks of 'use of armed forces in the aid of civil power' and 'contravention of any law or order for the time being in force'. The contravention of which law one could be talking about in the context of counterinsurgency operations is not at all clear. 'What exactly', they are supposed to be doing is not defined anywhere. Since 'contravention of any law or order for the time being in force' is vague enough, the only tangible thing is 'public order'. Since the plea of public order cannot be easily invoked for the so-called offensive or pro-active counterinsurgency operations, the legal position is that it is not at all clear as to what exactly the police and the central forces are supposed to doing by way of counterinsurgency operations and under what legal authority? We are purposefully refraining from using the word 'encounter' in this discourse because it has not been defined in law anywhere.

There is no legal basis for any pro-active or offensive operation. Let us envisage a situation where the police or the central forces (henceforth addressed as 'forces' for simplicity) are in a jungle in an area or state where they have, by their own admission, the problem of terrorism or insurgency. Suppose they see some people armed with weapons. What exactly are they supposed to do then? The existing legal system has not yet provided for any clear direction in this regard.

One possible way could be to challenge them and then proceed according to their response. If they open fire, one could retaliate in self-defence. It needs no explanation that challenging or demanding surrender is not a practical proposition in counterinsurgency operations. It can be done perhaps in urban situations where, the concerned persons are known to be hiding in some dwelling or place. You challenge in a jungle, they shoot first with automatic weapons and you drop dead before you have managed to cry 'Ayyo, Amma'! What does one do with people who do not respond to the challenge, do not open fire either, and start running away? Obviously, the law does not permit shooting at them.

There is, presently, only one legal provision under which fire may be opened and that is self-defence. We have doubts whether the IPS officers are really conversant with the law of private defence but we may inform that it is really difficult to prove. However, we must emphasize that proving the exercise of the right of self-defence is extremely difficult. It is easy only when someone on the side of the forces is injured. If nobody is injured then a doubt will be cast by the other side and the very heavy onus will be that of the forces. Hence, the legal fact is that even if the forces have opened fire after having been fired upon and if they kill or injure, unless they have recovered a dead body with a firearm, it will be very difficult to establish it prima facie that they had fired and killed in self-defence—even then, there is a good possibility of an allegation that the weapon is a planted one. It is quite possible and it happens innumerable times in anti-Naxal operations in particular that the comrades of the dead man take away his weapons—weapons are precious for them.

There is no legal validity of lying in an ambush and firing unprovoked upon the terrorists even if they happen to be armed. The weapons that they are armed with could be illicit but that does not give the legal authority to open fire. A violation of the Arms Act does not permit shoot to kill. Similarly, when one is searching a village or a house, the fact of seeing an armed person does not provide the authority to open fire. Perhaps one could argue that there was intelligence information about the presence of terrorists and that's how he opened fire. This does not hold legal water. Intelligence, however great, has no legal value and visual identification of a terrorist is still not sufficient to give any authority to shoot.

These are some of the legal lacunae which must be addressed to provide a sound legal footing for counterinsurgency operations. The police leadership has utterly failed in even raising such issues at the appropriate forums, not to speak of addressing them. There are infinite legal complications in deciding the fate of the men of security forces who happen to kill somebody whom they had thought to be a terrorist or insurgent but from whom they could not recover a weapon.

6.3.3 *No Weapons Policy, No Rules of Engagement*

The Indian police and army officers (how can you leave them behind) are so dumb that they have not even been able to decide what weapons they would or should use in counterinsurgency operations. This is intellectual bankruptcy at its best. We are not concerned with or commenting on the reasons, whatever they may be, of using or not using certain weapons because that could be a matter of government policy. We are only pointing out the illogical nature that is inherent when the position is so ambiguous. For example, the Indians seem to have a great reluctance in using machineguns from helicopters whereas the fact is that tactically it would be an extremely effective step and save hundreds of the casualties of security forces. Firing from the air, however, is a great taboo for reasons best known to somebody else. Some people argue that air power should not be used against your own people.

But the same people do not have any moral compunction in using the same machineguns on the ground—never mind that the victims' bodies do not find any difference whether the bullet came from the air or the ground. In fact, they use much more powerful weapons also. They do not have any hesitation in using 40 mm grenades launched by UBGLs, medium machineguns, automatic grenade launchers, 51 mm mortars, 81 mm mortars (which fire shells of 4.2 kg to a range of nearly 5 km and have an effective bursting area of about 40 meters), and Carl Gustav Recoilless Rifle (CGRL)—the CGRL is actually an anti-tank weapon and they use it for human targets!

Mortars are notorious for inaccuracy. What accuracy can be

expected from fin-stabilized shells fired from smoothbores? Even jungles per se are not desolate areas—people are found in jungles for grazing cattle, agricultural purposes, picking up forest produce of all kind and for various other purposes. They could well be killed or injured by such fire. A shell could land in some hamlet and obliterate it. What would you do then?

They would use the Unmanned Aerial Vehicles (UAVs) to observe the area of operation from the air so that the targets may be killed better, but they would not shoot from the air. If they use something, the question is why; if they refuse to use something, the question is again why? Unless they answer it, anybody can see the contradiction inherent in their position.

Their reluctance to fire from the air seems to imply that they have some unstated desire to fight what they consider to be 'fair' in which there is no great disparity of power—some sort of pseudo-ethical issue. But the same morons are found only too eager to lay an ambush and kill an unsuspecting enemy—do you think that this is fair? Quite often insurgents have only muzzle loading guns. Is it fair to shoot at them with modern automatic weapons? Certainly not, and if they have such an insistence on '*dharmayuddha*' they might as well start wrestling with the enemy instead of shooting at him. Obviously, the imbeciles are contradicting themselves. In other words, they do not have anything like **'rules of engagement'** for counterinsurgency operations. We do not have any problem whether you fire from the air or not; whether you fire 81 mm mortar; and whether you would use tanks or not—it is their sweet will and prerogative; after all, they had used tanks and artillery also in the Operation Blue Star. We are only saying that, for God's sake, first please create a clearly defined, logical and legally tenable framework for the 'rules of engagement' in counterinsurgency operations.

This saga of legal lacunae continues in some other spheres of the business of counterinsurgency operations also. Take the sentries, for example. While there could be hundreds of thousands of sentries deployed in terrorism and insurgency affected areas in the country, at no place, the poor man's rights and duties are clearly defined. *The police leadership has never bothered to discuss the situation when a sentry who finds that there is some suspicious movement outside his post; that the suspicious movement is likely to be a man who could be carrying a weapon or explosives; that he does not respond coherently to challenges; and that he could kill him if he left the security of his post. What is the poor sentry supposed to do?* Should he challenge the intruder to warm the hearts of some dumb old-timers with '*tham, kaun aata hai*'. By God, what is he supposed to do if the man is really a terrorist but responds to the sentry's challenge with the answer of '*dost*'. Should he let him come near? What is the sentry supposed to do if the visitor is allowed to come close and is then found fumbling as if to take out a grenade from his pocket. The sentry shoots at him. Later it is found that he was only trying to take out his ID! What mechanism does the sentry have to distinguish friend from foe? None! Suppose the sentry is not satisfied with the response of the intruder and since the intruder does not show any intent to go away, he opens fire on him. The law, as it stands today, would blame the sentry if the man was found to be unarmed.

Similarly, there is no legal framework available as to how troops must operate when the terrorists could be in a village mixed with innocent people. Should there be a system of warning—but this may help them escape, a cordon notwithstanding—they may simply drop their weapons and walk away with the villagers. What if some villagers vacate but some others refuse to? What is the law that could compel them to leave their homes? What happens if a fire fight starts even as some innocent people are left there? What plea would be taken if some innocent guy gets killed? One may argue that he was caught in crossfire. But the counter argument would be that you could have killed innocent people and then claimed that they came in crossfire. In other words, the whole issue of someone coming in crossfire needs to be given a legal examination or else it would always be regarded as a contrived lie.

This is not merely an academic exercise in legal niceties. In fact, such issues have never been raised in this country in such an erudite manner. This is necessary because the police leadership has not had applied enough intellectual capacity and analytical mind to certain vital legal issues that have been left in grey areas—and particularly so for counterinsurgency operations.

6.3.4 *Legal Aspects of the Business of Dialogues, Peace Talks, and Ceasefires with Terrorists*

Many in the police leadership seem to have great faith in the power of dialogues which we so proudly flaunt. The problem is that they equally proudly flaunt their belief in the rule of law as well. Now the law does not permit any dialogues, peace talks or ceasefires with terrorists or insurgents—the very people whom the system does not tire of describing as criminals and grave threats to internal security. One can go through the Code of Criminal Procedure and other statute books word by word—nothing permitting this would be found. The nation-state, the upholder of law, does not indulge in a dialogue, peace talk or ceasefire with any criminal; it is not supposed to. The very foundation of the nation-state rests upon the premise that those who violate the law shall be punished according to the law.

What is the legal validity of the so-called interlocutors, mediators or whatever? None! They do not have any legal powers to take any decision or make any assurance on behalf of anybody. In India, private parties can indulge in what is known as ADR (alternative dispute resolution) that could be non-binding and non-adjudicatory, or binding and adjudicatory. The former involves negotiation, conciliation, mediation; the latter involves arbitration—the official machinery can do neither with a criminal. How could they ignore (or condone?) the murder of the two policemen when the release of the Sukma collector Menon, kidnapped by the Naxals, was sought through negotiations? Not even a demand was made that their murderers be handed over. It was taken for granted. The cops could die. It is their job to die. The mighty leadership of the police sits on too high a pedestal to bother itself with such trivial issues. ***Does the police leadership not know the law? If they know, why did they not raise the issue***?

6.4 The Business of 'Joint' Counterinsurgency Operations

6.4.1 *The Intrinsic Irrationality of the Concept of Joint Operations*

In the business of counterinsurgency operations, the most popular words today are coordination, liaison and synergy. Everything can be solved with more coordination, better liaison and greater synergy. From this flows the concept of joint operations—in other words, whenever some stupid terrorist is to be killed, everybody (that is, the state police, the CPMFs, the Rashtriya Rifles, the Assam Rifles, the Indian army) must all pitch in together. The army and the Rashtriya Rifles (RR) insist on keeping the operational command to themselves and one has to fight with them if it has to be otherwise. Well, such a concerted effort could perhaps be necessary if the terrorists were very strong; a great amount of firepower was needed and one of the forces, on its own, would not have it. In other words, you supplement each other when you are singly not enough—the old clarion call of *'saathi haath badhana; ek akela thak jaayega'*. Why should you have it when one agency, on its own, is adequate? Yes, forces should not be working at cross purposes but it does not mean that they should not be conducting operations independently when they can. This clarion call of something called 'synergy' is a great hoax. As we will show shortly, this practice is fraught with serious complications and the police leadership has not had enough mind to apply to it.

Nobody knows how this utterly stupid practice started. Some people say it emanated from some unwritten order of some chief minister. Well, since when do verbal orders or platitudes become a law? Unfortunately, the police leadership thinks so. The legal fact is that when the central forces like the BSF, the CRPF, and the RR were deployed, their exact role was never precisely defined in any order—yet another example of the ad hoc manner in which things have been done in this country. We all know the oft-quoted phrase 'in the aid of state government'. What exactly they were supposed to do and the mechanics of what they would do, has never been defined anywhere. Ad hocism rules. Woe betide the officer who dares disturb the traditions established by sheer ad hocism. He would be roundly accused of having spoiled the much-flaunted 'synergy' of the forces.

Now we come to the professional issues that have not been addressed. The simple issue that has not been addressed is that in a joint operation, who will decide as to which agency and which officers have to do what—and who will judge as to what was the contribution of different officers/personnel for deciding upon the issue of gallantry medals? Operations do not mean that one has only to do some firing practice there. How exactly operations are conducted, is a separate subject in itself and our earlier books on the subject may be referred to. Here, suffices it to say that critical decisions need to be taken regarding various steps, such as, the positions from where the fire is to be delivered; the nature of fire; the manner of house intervention; using weapons other than small arms and so on. In real life, the army/RR officers start throwing weight around claiming that they have better training and relegate state police/CPMF officers and men to a secondary role. The practice has been that they keep the state police for filing the FIR after the operation, and relegate the CPMF to the outer cordon duty. They take all the critical decisions.

They decide how and when house intervention is to be done. They decide when and how the house is to be blasted (which they usually do and pass off as the house having been gutted in the exchange of fire—by God, since when have bullets become capable of starting fires), and so on. Is that acceptable? Paramilitary and state police officers merely hang around there trying to hide their embarrassment. Those who are shameless enough, even try to appear important before TV channels without doing anything important. Does the system spend thousands of crores of rupees on training, equipping and keeping the central paramilitary forces so that they may eventually do the outer cordon duty, that is, essentially *chowkidari*. What happens then to their pretensions of being counterinsurgency forces? Not one CPMF/state police officer can rightfully lay a claim to a medal on the strength of having done the *chowkidari* or having filed the FIR.

6.4.2 *The Farce of the Gallantry Medals*

The corollary of this is that all the medals awarded in such so-called joint operations are farcical. In any case, what can be expected from a system where gallantry medals have literally been looted by the hundreds on ridiculous citations like: "He went to the place in his bulletproof Gypsy and supervised the operation from it?" Someone managed to get a medal for killing a third-rate criminal in an open field who, for the purpose of the citation was described as a dreaded criminal. Well, the 'dreaded criminal' was so impoverished that he was said to be firing from a muzzle loader gun (and not any better weapon) that was shown to have been recovered from him! Of course, no one in the police leadership had the intellectual capacity or knowledge to argue that it takes so much time to reload a muzzle loader that after he had fired the first shot, the criminal could have been beaten senseless with shoes, not to speak of bullets. If they don't admit their ignorance, they will have to admit complicity in such frauds!

A separate book can be written on this massive fraud of gallantry medals but here we will cite only one example from what is already in the public domain. Rediff.com and *The Hindu* had reported on March 20, 2010 that a **Division Bench of the Andhra Pradesh High Court** had asked the state home ministry to reconsider its decision, taken in 2003, to honour three senior IPS officers with gallantry awards, as they were given sans the minimum verification of recommendations by the state government. The bench comprising Justice G. Raghuram and Justice G. V. Seetapathy, disposing the public interest petition of lawyer K. N. Rao, criticised the manner in which the state government had recommended the names of the three officers and the way in which the central government awarded them the medal without minimum verification. Observing that the way the home ministry dealt with the issue had put the prestige and integrity of the medals in jeopardy, the Court asked the central government to reconsider the awards. The Centre's contention that it went by the recommendation of the state government was not accepted by the Court. The allegation was that the three insurgents were arrested from another state, brought to the concerned state in a helicopter and killed in a fake encounter. It was also alleged that those three officers were not even present in the forest where those chaps were killed—one of them was actually on leave that day to attend a marriage! The state government had ordered a probe in the matter after some IPS officers lodged a complaint. But the inquiry was reportedly dropped in 2007 after the officers concerned claimed that they were present on the spot of the encounter, but their names were not included in the records on the grounds of security! By God, that's way to screw the system!

The *Times of India* had also published an interesting story in this regard on August 16, 2011. It claimed that following the High Court order, state government sources told the ToI that they had written to the Centre offering to withdraw their recommendations, but that there was no response from the Centre. "A former DGP was said to have played a role in the Centre not pursuing the re-opening of the grant of the awards as the issue was said to be creating a lot of bad blood between the IPS officers in the state," said the sources. According to the *Times of India,* the case was subsequently closed with the High Court leaving it to the discretion of Centre. The links are given in the bibliography and interested readers can read them.

The stupidity of joint operations does not end with medals having been claimed fraudulently. Even the recommendations of medals are supposed to be joint ones—there is a strange concept that recommendations of one agency should have the concurrence of the other. Incidentally, the army or the RR never seeks anybody's concurrence. Anyone can see how illogical the business is.

There is no reason or logic that one agency can sit in judgement upon the other. How can they be, particularly given the well-known problem of inter-agency rivalry and organisations fighting bitterly for their respective turfs? How can somebody else speak on another force and, if so, on what authority? Do they know more than the other guy? In fact, officers of other agencies may have strong personal likes and dislikes of officers from other forces. There is no reason to believe that they would be objective and impartial. No agency has a legal or logical locus standi to comment on the performance of the personnel of other agencies. From a quasi-legal perspective, since medals have a bearing on career, if the DGP of a state can sit in judgement upon a paramilitary officer's gallantry, he could very well write his CR also. Since we do not have a system of dual reporting authorities for CR, how we can have this system for medals? A strange logic was advanced by some people in the defence of this affair of seeking concurrence. The idea was that a claim to medal would be strengthened if essentially the same claim is made by two or more different agencies. Let us analyze it closely. What is the basis of such a presumption? The basis is an unstated belief that the chances of something being true are higher if more than one person is saying it. This so-called basis itself is erroneous and illogical. Truth is something absolute in character and is not dependent on the number of persons for or against it. Millions may be wrong and one lone man could be right and vice versa. When such a basis is put forward, it is also presumed that while one agency could lie, two agencies would not lie together or would be less likely to lie together. This is also a notion which has no foundation. There is no logical reason to believe in it. Nothing prevents two agencies from lying together. In fact, the stronger the personal bonds between the officers of two agencies, the more likelihood of lying together. *In effect, the system depends only on the personal relationships and on nothing professional. Personal relationships are paraded with the embellishment of the so-called coordination, liaison and synergy.*

The very premise of seeking to buttress a claim by a similar claim or testimonial by an equally fallible and human agency is illogical. Corroboration, in any matter, has any value when it is made by an independent and uninterested party. There is no value of corroboration by an interested party. In this business all the parties involved are interested parties. Moreover, their officers are the product of the same system and the society and suffer from the same weaknesses and foibles. They are all equally likely to lie; both individually as well as collectively. And let us not forget that two lies together cannot make up a truth. But remember, since the parties concerned in the operations are the only parties present at the spot, there is no locus standi for any 'absent' third party (like some intelligence agency) to offer any views. In the end, the system does not have a foolproof (or even logical) way of ascertaining amidst all sorts of claims as to who could be telling the truth, untruth or partial truth. The failure of the police leadership lies in the fact that it has never applied any mind to evolving a logical, fair and just system which may ascertain the truth.

The secret of the business of concurrence lies elsewhere. Actually, it is in this business of seeking concurrence that the so-called coordination, liaison and synergy really come into play—they are all euphemistic expressions for plain old sucking. The business of concurrence has been reduced to a mutual admiration club as long as everybody is telling the same lie—it is used both to get medals for undeserving persons and also to deny them to those who might be regarded as inconvenient. The moment there is any problem with this so-called coordination, you come across hilarious situations in which agencies make wildly different recommendations.

We have full details of a proposal for recommendation of medals (and, on a personal level, we can share it with proof to anyone who dares doubt this) in which the paramilitary officers had waxed eloquent about their having taken the lead in an operation and their exemplary bravery. These guys did their best to appease the district SP and even prepared a joint recommendation which was signed both by the SP and the commandant. Unfortunately, they did not coordinate, liaise or synergize sufficiently well with the relevant guys in the PHQ who were 'close' to the DGP. The DGP had his own list of favourite people whom he considered fit for the medals—they were not to be found in the joint recommendation of the SP and the CPMF's commandant. The version of the operation prepared by the DGP of the state had relegated the role of the paramilitary force to laying the 'outer cordon'. Well, since the two diametrically opposite positions could not be true simultaneously, it became a problem that could never be reconciled. *There was a deeper issue involved. If the DGP was correct then the paramilitary officers had purposefully and in sheer greed exaggerated their role; if the latter were correct, the DGP would be guilty of being unfair and denying the due share of credit to the paramilitary officers. One would be guilty of collusion in a farce; the other would be guilty of suppression of facts to harm someone.*

Chapter 7

Counterinsurgency Operations Expose the Achilles' Heel of the Police Leadership

7.1 Why Counterinsurgency Operations have Floundered in India?

Counterinsurgency operations are the in-thing these days. Hundreds of thousands of men of various state police forces and paramilitary forces have been deployed exclusively for counterinsurgency operations. Some have been wasting their lives in Kashmir; some in the north-east; and the remaining are having a tough time in anti-Naxal operations in the jungles of central India. Every IPS officer, by virtue of being in the IPS, thinks himself to be an expert in counterinsurgency operations and has some very valuable opinion on that. We will puncture the balloon right here.

One of the most important reasons of anti-Naxal operations not producing any worthwhile results in spite of a very heavy investment of manpower and resources is the absolute ignorance of the police leadership in counterinsurgency operations. Otto von Bismarck had said, "Fools learn from their own experience; I prefer to learn from other people's experiences." Nobody should waste his energies reinventing the wheel. Now insurgencies and counterinsurgency operations in jungle and urban terrains are very complex subjects. Before you venture into it, you should have had a painstakingly thorough study of all the strategies and tactics developed by some of the best forces in the world who have acquired this knowledge in a period stretching a century—from the jungles of Philippines, the Pacific Islands, Malaysia, and Borneo to Vietnam; and from the streets of Stalingrad, Berlin, Ulster and Beirut to Grozny. Respect it; this is a lesson that has been learnt at the cost of nothing but sheer blood of millions. And then you must subject that knowledge to a critical analysis to find out how much of it is applicable to circumstances unique to you and to what extent you have to develop your own theories. The police leadership in India does not have any institutionalized mechanism for imparting this valuable knowledge anywhere, not to speak of developing new knowledge. They might give fancy names to some courses and seminars—examine their contents and you would find them hopeless beyond measure. Gentlemen, no poor bastard ever won a war by making Power Point Presentations; you win a war by blood and guts, and above all, by mastering the art of warfare, the real McCoy. When it comes to the crunch, if you have to fight and fight damned well to survive and win, you got to know the nitty-gritty for yourself.

The tragedy of counterinsurgency operations in India is that vast resources have been placed at the disposal of those who are simply not fit to command—who do not have the slightest idea of combat. A very large number of men and great material have been made available to them because this large nation-state should be seen to be doing something. Unfortunately, the people of this country, in whose name everything is done and whose money it actually is, have no idea of the capabilities of the people who are entrusted with these resources. Since resources are given, the police leadership also has to be seen to be doing something. Now, bereft of any knowledge of counterinsurgency operations, what they can do? So they simply, blindly push the men into the jungles. The poor men have no idea of what to do. They are supposed to fight with an elusive enemy, without any intelligence, plan, or methodology having been developed for combat in such situations. As a result, they fall back on their commonsense which is of little use. ***The police leadership is therefore guilty of both the heavy casualties that their own men suffer as well as the innocent people who get killed at their hands. The real insurgent has a hearty laugh sitting somewhere else.***

7.2 The Reality of Anti-naxal Operations

7.2.1 *The Men, the Cost, the Results*

Let us face the facts. We will first show that counterinsurgency operations of this country have been a massive failure. Then we will analyze the reasons of this failure and examine how far the intellectual bankruptcy of the police leadership is responsible for that. In 2006, the Prime Minister described Naxalism as "the single biggest internal security challenge ever faced by our country". By mid-2013, the nation had come to deploy 107 battalions (that is, about 134,667 men @ 1151 men per battalion) of central paramilitary forces (CRPF-82; BSF-15; ITBP-5; and SSB-5) in the Naxal-affected areas. Then we have the state police forces (district police, district armed reserve, armed police battalions and women police) of the respective states. We take the strengths of the police forces for the year ending 2012 from the National Crime Records Bureau's 'Crime in India Statistics 2012'. They are: Andhra Pradesh (96989); Bihar (66645); Chhattisgarh (42975); Jharkhand (57013); Madhya Pradesh (76763); Maharashtra (185667); Odisha (45368); Uttar Pradesh (183155); and West Bengal (88366).

Now to get an idea of how many of these are deployed in Naxal-affected districts, we refer to a publication called 'Guidelines of the SRE (Security Related Expenditure) Scheme' of the Naxal Management Division, Ministry of Home Affairs. The districts under the SRE scheme have been chosen on the basis of Naxal strength and activity there. The total number of SRE districts is 106: AP (16 out of 23); Bihar (22 out of 38); Chhattisgarh (16 out of 27); Jharkhand (21 out of 24); MP (1 out of 50); Maharashtra (4 out of 35); Odisha (19 out of 30); UP (3 out of 75); and West Bengal (4 out of 19). For the sake of simplicity, let us assume that the police forces of the states are evenly distributed in their districts. From this we can get the approximate strength of the state police which is deployed in the Naxal-affected SRE districts. This comes to: AP (67470); Bihar (38584); Chhattisgarh (25467); Jharkhand (49886); MP (1535); Maharashtra (21219); Odisha (28733); UP (7326); and West Bengal (18603) or a total of 258823 policemen.

Now the police force in a district has to do myriad jobs—law and order duty, traffic duty, investigation, etc. Obviously, the entire police force of a district cannot be deployed for anti-Naxal operations. Once again, for the sake of simplicity, let us assume that just 10 percent of the police force in a district is deployed for anti-Naxal operations. That gives a figure of 25882 persons. Add that to the paramilitary forces and you get a figure of 160549 persons doing anti-Naxal operations. That is over 1.5 lakh soldiers! Before we will analyze the returns of this deployment, let us have a look at the state of anti-Naxal operations from figures. We use two sources. The first is the authoritative South Asia Terrorism Portal; the other is the Naxal Management Division, MHA. The figures given by the SATP in its website are very exhaustive with details of important incidents also and are available for the period 2005 to June 23, 2013 at the time of writing this book. The web page of the Naxal Management Division, MHA gives merely the 'official' figures without any details of incidents and that too for the period 2008 to 2012 only. Naturally, we do expect some difference between the two but we will go by the figures of the SATP for good reasons. Just to illustrate the point, the Naxal Management Division, MHA claims that in 2008-2012, 1,089 security personnel were killed; the SATP puts this figure at 1,035. The Naxal Management Division, MHA puts the figure of the Naxals and civilians killed in this period at 764 and 2,570 respectively; the SATP puts it at 1,101 and 1,658 respectively. Readers can notice that while there is not much variation about the number of security forces personnel killed because that is easily verifiable, there is considerable variation in the number of civilians killed. Readers can guess the reasons for it.

You may also keep in mind that in any combat, the number of security forces personnel injured is at least three times the number of personnel killed.

The SATP figures for the state of anti-Naxal operations are as follows:

Year	Civilians killed	SF killed	Naxals killed
2013	95	58	78
2012	146	104	117
2011	275	128	199
2010	626	277	277
2009	391	312	294
2008	220	214	214
2007	240	218	192
2006	266	128	343
2005	281	150	286
TOTAL	2540	1589	2000

Now, for the moment, let us not bother about the trends. Let us look at the overall figures instead. In nearly eight-and-a-half years, the security forces have killed 2,000 Naxals whereas the Naxals have killed 1,589 security forces personnel and 2,540 civilians—a total of 4,129 persons. We should not forget that protecting the civilians is also the responsibility of the nation state. It is because the nation state is failing somewhere in providing security to the citizens that the Naxals are able to kill so many civilians. It cannot be argued that we are concerned only with the casualties of the security forces. This means that on an average, the Naxals are able to kill about 2 persons for every man they lose (exactly 206 for 100).

Even if you consider only the casualties amongst the security forces, they are able to kill 126 Naxals for 100 of their own killed. This extremely poor kill-ratio is just not acceptable anywhere else in the world. **All over the world, the minimum they accept in counterinsurgency operations is eight insurgents killed to one of their own. The British SAS operated at about 23 insurgents killed to one of their own.** View it from the point of view of the total number of Naxals operating and the depressing picture would become clearer. Regarding the total number of armed Naxal insurgents, we have estimates by the intelligence agencies and the media. They could be highly speculative too. There seems to be only one recent official statement in this regard. "As per available inputs, the total strength of armed cadres of Naxalites is around 8,500," the Minister of State for Home Affairs, Ajay Maken, had told the Rajya Sabha in a written reply on August 11, 2010. He added that as many as 21 left wing extremist groups were indulging in acts of violence. Earlier, the Ministry of Home Affair's Annual Report 2004-2005 had put the figure at 9,300. Bhavna Vij-Aurora, writing in *The Outlook* had estimated the number at about 10,000. Gautam Navlakha, writing in the *Economic and Political Weekly*, estimated the cadre strength of the CPI (Maoist) to be about 10,500. In July 2010, *The Economist* had estimated the total number of Naxals to be anywhere from 10,000 to 20,000. The highest estimate came from Philip Bowring in the *International Herald Tribune* which put the figure at 20,000. Thus it is seen that even by the most inflated estimates, the number of armed Naxals would not be more than 20,000.

For these 10,000-15,000 guys we have over 1.5 lakh of security forces personnel actively deployed on anti-Naxal operations and they have managed to kill only 394 Naxals in the past two-and-a-half years (2011 till mid-2013) while losing 290 of their own besides letting 516 civilians killed. In effect, we require 407 security forces personnel to kill just one Naxal. Remember that insurgencies are dynamic phenomena. The Naxals keep on recruiting people. This means that, in effect, there has been practically no damage to the Naxals.

Now let us look at the cost of anti-Naxal operations—and it turns out to be frightening. According to the NCRB's Crime in India 2012, on an average, it costs Rs. 3.32867 lakh (about Rs. 3.33 lakh) to keep one policeman in the states. The cost for the central paramilitary forces would be slightly different but approximately the same. This means that the nation is spending Rs. 5,344.15 crore (about Rs. 5,344 crore) on anti-Naxal operations—and that excludes the cost of arms and ammunition, vehicles, fuel, medical treatment, etc. ***For the past two completed years (2011 and 2012), the forces killed 316 Naxals. This*** *comes to about Rs. 16.9 crores per Naxal killed. That's a very costly supari, isn't it? The inescapable conclusion is that the anti-Naxal operations, viewed and judged purely as a military venture, are simply not working—the nation is obliged to deploy a painfully large force and spend through its nose to kill a handful of insurgents. Any professional army of the world would be appalled at this state of affairs*. You can compare the deployment of our forces for anti-Naxal operations with that of the number of soldiers deployed by the ISAF (International Security Assistance Force) in Afghanistan as on June 24, 2013. The figure for the forces combined from as many as 48 countries stands at 97,920 with the USA contributing 68,000 of them for the entire nation of Afghanistan!

The state of anti-Naxal operations can also be analyzed from the angle of recoveries. Most of the firearms recovered, whenever they are recovered, are actually crude country-made firearms (such as even muzzle loaders, called 'Bharmaar' in their parlance; 12 gauge shotguns; 9 mm Sten guns; and even .315 rifles, all made locally). There has been an old but thriving industry in Bihar and parts of Uttar Pradesh where such weapons have been manufactured on a large scale since decades. Very few of the recovered weapons are good factory-made weapons like AK rifles, SLRs or INSAS rifles. On the other hand, the forces have not been able to make any dent on the easy, almost effortless availability of emulsion explosives to the Naxals which they seem to have by the tons!

7.2.2 *Fighting an Enemy About Whom They Know Nothing*

Obviously, something is very wrong somewhere. In the following, we will figure that out. A word of caution is considered necessary here. Numbers do not reflect the whole picture in counterinsurgency operations. More important than body count or recoveries made are the questions that are often left unasked: "Has the nation made any dent on the Naxal movement? Have we been able to weaken the movement materially? Are the Naxals on the run? Have we been able to strike at their vitals? Have we been able to disrupt the sources of supply of their arms and ammunition? Have we been able to disrupt their financial support systems? Have we been able to make them lose their popular support whatever it be and however extensive or limited it be? Have we been able to make any inroads among the people from whom they draw their cadres? The era of protests of the late 1960s promising the romance of a Red revolution is long over. Occasional downturns apart, economies in general are booming and nation-states are stronger than ever. As such there is very little on the world horizon that could inspire people to take up arms to defeat the leviathan of modern nation-states. With apparently such discouraging trends in view, do we know what it is that keeps practically illiterate young men and women in India join the Naxal movement even now knowing well that life therein would be very tough and that, at least in their lifetimes, they would not see 'The Internationale' being sung from the ramparts of the Red Fort?" The answer to all these questions is, unfortunately, very much in the negative—and that's the tragedy of anti-Naxal operations in the country. The IPS leadership is hugely responsible for this state of affairs.

The stark reality of the hollowness, the vacuity of anti-Naxal operations is that even after suffering Naxalism for the past 45 years, the nation is still not able to answer two fundamental questions: what are the sources of strength of the Naxal movement; and what are the weaknesses of the Naxal movement? The nation does not have any answer to many other important questions also. The nation does not know how the Naxals manage supplies of arms and ammunition. Surely we don't wish to delude ourselves with saying that they are fighting only with the arms they had looted from the police in the past, such as in the Nayagarh incident. Bulgarian-made RPG-7s have been recovered in Aurangabad, Bihar in March 2012. They are also found using Garand semi-automatic American rifles. While the rifles themselves could be of the Second World War vintage, the ammunition is not. This means that the Naxals do have some supply channel open to foreign countries about which we don't know anything.

We do not know what are their finances and from where do they raise funds? Is it only from extortion or is there some other source? More importantly, where do they spend it? This is important because the figures of their annual earnings generally touted in seminars is very high—several hundred crores per annum. If they have this kind of money, how do they spend it, where do they spend it? Interrogations of surrendered and arrested Naxals reveal that most of them are paid very meagre amounts by way of salary by the organisation. The food they get is of the most basic kind. There is so far no evidence to suggest that senior Naxal leaders have been squandering the money in luxurious living somewhere. Then how do the Naxals deal with the critical issue of popular support? Is it only the proverbial fear of the gun or is there some genuine popular support? Finally, how do they keep on getting fresh cadres? They cannot get recruits from a population which is only terrorized and tortured by them. The fact is that the nation does not know anything about any of these questions. No agency can claim that it knows anything about them. The answer has to be in the negative because if the nation had answers to any one of them, certainly something could have been and should have been done in respect of some specific things in all these years! If some agency says that it knows something, it would be guilty of not having done anything so far.

7.3 A Confused Police Leadership Blunders on

7.3.1 *Groping Blindly in the Dark*

We have analyzed a very large number of anti-Naxal operations of various magnitudes launched jointly by the central paramilitary forces and the state police forces (that is, security forces in general) in all the Naxal-affected states. Though the security forces undertake various types of missions such as short range patrol, long range patrol, so-called 'road opening', area domination exercise and the like, for the purpose of this book, we have considered only those operations which were supposedly based on specific intelligence. In general, it meant that the intelligence machinery (both central and state) had furnished information to the security forces that Naxals were present at such-and-such location, and the security forces were supposed to go there, hit them and arrest them or kill them.

The analysis of the operations brings out some striking findings. It is found that in most (read nearly all) of the operations the security forces could not force the Naxals to fight on their terms. In fact wherever they went, the Naxals were not to be found anywhere near that place at all. Reason? There has never been any intelligence worth its name. The troops go into jungles because they are supposed to undertake operations, and obey they do, groping blindly in the dark—theirs not to reason why but to do and die! We call it jungle bashing—their situation is like that of a boxer who has been blindfolded. Even if, by some chance, some Naxals happen to be in the area, they refuse to fight superior forces and simply melt away. If at all they have to open fire, they open fire when they decide that it is advantageous to do so. That is, they fight on their terms, not on the terms of the security forces. When the security forces chase them in jungles, they run to villages; when they are chased in the villages, they run to the jungles. And the nation can never have so many security forces that they could man all of this vast country simultaneously at all times—that's how the cat and mouse game has been going on!

It cannot be said that the response of the troops to the intelligence input was ever slow or that the troops could not maintain adequate surprise. The troops almost never find Naxals in a disadvantageous position where they could take them by surprise. Had the Naxals been there in an advantageous position instead; had they known about the movement of the forces; had the forces lost surprise, the Naxals could have laid an ambush for the troops or at least planted IEDs. Even such events happen rather rarely. The Naxals are not itching to fight. They fight only when they calculate that they can inflict casualties profitably. If they did nothing of the sort means that they were not there in the first place.

The intelligence community cannot argue that their information was correct; the Naxals were there but ran away when they saw the forces. No, it is not so. Whenever, wherever there is a group of humans, it does leave some trace of its presence such as disturbed ground or vegetation, food items, Gutka pouches, evidence of cooking, some piece of paper, and the like. In most of the so-called operations not even such things are found—this can only mean that the Naxals were never there in the first place.

We strongly maintain that the nation cannot run away for long from the inescapable fact that most of the information which is passed on to the forces in the name of actionable intelligence is nothing better than pure guesswork at best or outright cooked up stories, at worst. Bereft of any actionable intelligence, the whole gamut of anti-Naxal operations is best described by a vernacular saying that we are 'trying to kill fish by beating water with a lathi'. Operations have therefore been reduced to essentially taking chances with their luck and an exchange of fire takes place basically when the Naxals have miscalculated something – not because the security forces forced them into it. Most of the time the exchange of fire in non-ambush situations or when the initiative has been that of the forces, is actually a cleverly executed rearguard action by a couple of Naxals to allow the main body or leaders to escape safely – an action straight from Mao's dictums.

The sort of intelligence reports which flood the system, fall basically into two categories; either speaking vaguely in terms of information regarding 'the presence or movement of some Naxals in such-and-such area (which happens to be quite large)' or trying to give 'precise' and sensational information that the Naxals are at such-and-such coordinates. Reports of the first category are of no operational value anyway and are created merely because the intelligence community wants to be seen to be producing some intelligence almost every day; reports of the second category are created because they want to be seen to be producing intelligence of operational value also—unfortunately, they often turn out to be wrong. The more sensational a report is, the more likely it is to be false. Since they are not intelligent enough to concoct credible lies, they tend to speak such things which happen to tie them in knots rather. For example, they often speak of fortifications made by Naxals. One must ask a professional question: "Why should the Naxals build permanent fortifications in the first place?" It is against the very basic principles of guerrilla warfare and insurgency to try to hold ground and defend a location against much stronger forces. Temporary fortification of stone boulders can be understood as a tactical need in case a longer stay becomes necessary at some place—that is simply a part of perimeter defence. However, building a permanent fortification to slug it out does not make sense because the guerrilla can never match the firepower of the forces. The intelligence agencies cannot take refuge in the plea that the 'source', 'agent' or 'informer' had told so and they are not responsible if he had lied. It is the responsibility of the intelligence community to 'process' information by asking such questions—and they would be guilty of displaying a singular lack of critical intellectual capacity in not being able to ask such questions.

7.3.2 *Why They are Clueless?*

Intelligence for anti-Naxal operations is poor because there is no human intelligence (HUMINT) worth its name. *The intelligence agencies cannot honestly claim that their informers have 'penetrated' the ranks of the Naxals. If they had, there could have been some specific intelligence-based operations with spectacular successes. Since there are none, it means that their so-called informers do not have any penetration of the Naxal groups.* ***In any case, the intelligence community does not hail from Mars—their failure is the failure of the police leadership.***

Tactical intelligence of operational value can be provided by only those who have a direct access to the Naxals. Now the question is who could have such access and how would they be won over so as to become 'conscious sources' or 'conscious agents'? The usual response to this question by the intellectually bankrupt police leaders is that they could tap the Naxals' logistic providers, such as those who supply them with rations, etc. There is a practical problem in this. Approaching such people directly is not possible. The first reason is that often they are committed supporters and cannot be won over easily. The second is that they are themselves often under over-watch by the Naxals. The third is that even if one of such persons is won over, he cannot be a regular source of intelligence. May be he can betray once, give information and get way with that. However, if he repeats, he can always be identified by a process of 'successive logical elimination' that the leak could have taken place only through such-and-such person. Such persons are often located deep (thereby making it difficult to contact them regularly) and at times are smart enough to use cut-outs themselves. Raising 'sources' (agent-running) that have some 'direct' (or 'primary') penetration in terrorist outfits is the most difficult job in intelligence. In such situations, most of the intelligence actually happens to come from 'fringe contacts', and is often secondary or tertiary. As a result, the agencies usually end up contacting the lackey (*chamchaa*) of the lackey of the lackey of the man in contact with the Naxals. This makes the intelligence (if at all it comes) stale, distorted (in the classic manner of Chinese Whispers), badly delayed and of little actionable value.

Bereft of HUMINT, the intelligence agencies have fallen into the 'bad' habit of depending too much on technical intelligence (TECHINT) which in the Indian context boils down mainly to interception of telephone calls. In places like Kashmir where the terrorists use mobile phones in very large numbers, TECHINT is rather good. In the areas and jungles affected by Naxalism where the mobile coverage is very poor anyway, not so many mobile phones are used and hence the input from that corner is also proportionately poorer. Moreover, since there has been so much loose talk about interception of phones that even the Naxals know that this takes place. As a result they deliberately plant misleading information over their phone conversations and send the forces on a wild-goose chase.

7.4 The Follies and Foibles of Jungle Combat

The police leadership is forcing hundreds of thousands of men into jungle combat without knowing a word about it. As discussed above, we know they have not read anything on the subject. The tragedy is they do not even know the vast amount of professional literature that is there in the world and that needs to be read. Most officers have only exotic notions about the jungles and jungle warfare—shaped largely by Hollywood films—and they are highly reluctant to question them because they do not question anything anyway. Most of them think that jungle combat is what John Rambo did in 'Rambo: First Blood Part II'. Some other notions make the jungle appear a place where venomous snakes crawl everywhere—and you are not a true-blooded jungle warrior unless you catch them by the tail, dangle them upside down for your buddies to see, roast them over open fire and eat them regularly! If you are more macho, you must cut off the cobra's head and drink his blood! A popular refrain is that the Indian troops are not well-versed in the art of jungle warfare or operating in the jungles—clearly implying, if not insinuating outright that fighting in the jungles is a secret art in which only Rambo or those tribal people excel—Rambo, because of his out-of-the-world training from the Green Berets and the tribal people because they have been born and brought up there. Many of them are heard saying that the Naxals do not carry any provisions with them whereas the troops lose their mobility because of the weight they carry in their rucksacks. We know a large number of officers who insist that the troops should be able to 'live off the land' (as the Naxals supposedly do in their fanciful notions), that is, survive on whatever they can forage from the jungle (scorpions, leaves, berries, etc.); drink even contaminated water from anywhere; and be able to walk barefoot tirelessly for an unlimited length of time. By God, soldiers are supposed to fight; that's their primary task—not to waste their time in ensnaring a solitary bird by an improvised snare. Even if you catch a bird, it would not suffice for even two guys—you are many times that! You are not a camper; and you are not on a mission to prove that you can survive eating three earthworms or four locusts a day. Fighting in jungle is different from survival in the jungle—such myths and notions have no scientific basis. *In any case, my dear sirs, even if we accept that there is something wanting in training, what you, the leaders have done to help it?*

Whenever troops are attacked and casualties take place, senior officers start the blame game – the blame is almost as a matter of rule shifted on the poor constables that they did not follow the SOP (Standard Operating Procedure)! As if the SOP is some sort of *Rambaan* which will ensure your victory in any situation, however grave that be. Ask them where the SOP is and they would have no answer. For the information of the readers, no SOP of any kind exists anywhere. In fact, there should not be a SOP because every situation is different and there cannot be a one-size-fits-all type of response. Either the SOP should be so elaborate as to provide for all types of situations, or there should be none. The truth is that, there is not even a training manual which could tell the troops the basics of how to fight in jungles. The troops do not have the slightest idea of the science of combat in jungles. They fight by instinct and not by training. ***Everybody speaks of counter-ambush drill. The usual refrain is that the troops should follow the counter-ambush drill. Fine, but where it is or what it is? What exactly is that the troops are supposed to do when they are ambushed? Where has it been printed? Nowhere! Can anyone of the worthies in the IPS tell what counter-ambush drill is? And why should it be a drill? Is it some mysterious one-size-fits-all technique which can be used in any situation? Ambushes can be laid in several ways—for that matter, do they even know those different ways?***

For that matter do the police leaders know anything about other professional aspects of jungle combat such as, security and movement in jungles; planning for defence in jungle; point, flank, and rear security; combat patrolling in jungles; travelling, travelling over-watch and bounding over-watch; basic techniques of patrolling; fire and movement; observation during day and night; night combat; the actual science of engagement with the enemy; combat techniques of fire and fire formations; fire team formations; different types of ambushes; laying and executing ambushes; the scientific principles of countering ambushes in various situations like when the entire force is not caught in the kill zone and when the whole of a force is ambushed; counter to the classic linear ambush; counter to the famous L-formation ambush; counter to the V-formation ambush; Rhodesian cover or Drake shooting; general principles of counter-ambush action for vehicle convoys; scientific organisation of a vehicle convoy so that it may fight credibly; counter-ambush techniques for convoys; counter-ambush for a blocked road; convoy defence against mines and booby traps; techniques of assaulting a position which has some prepared defences; counter-sniper or sniper defeat techniques; scientific principles and practices of camp defence; and scientific design of 'defensive fighting positions' and the method of firing from them? This should not be regarded as some game of one-upmanship but in the interest of the nation, we sincerely advise them to read '**Jungle Warfare: An Ultimate Handbook**' and they will see it for themselves what they need to know about jungle combat.

We have never come across any IPS officer who knew even a modicum of these vital things. Those who do not have any knowledge by themselves, expect the troops to fight without knowledge and yet come out with flying colours! How unfair, how unethical! The men have never been told the techniques because the officers never knew them in the first place—the officers have a bad tendency of leaving it to the 'boys' because it is considered infra dig for the officers to even know such things, not to speak of doing this—a very clever way of covering up their ignorance. They have to do higher level things like planning, you see! The poor 'boys' have no idea of what to do in any case and they fall back on their commonsense, natural reactions or what they have seen in war movies. That's why casualties occur and everybody tries to cover them up in so many ways.

Some particularly obnoxious fools in the police leadership have started advocating small-team operations. That is, a couple of guys sneak into the jungles and kill a whole bunch of Naxals. This is called the 'super commando solution to the Naxal problem'. If they had excellent commandos like Rambo, they would have finished off the Naxal menace a long time ago. This is what happens when people watch too many third-rate Telugu or Tamil films! In real life, small teams get butchered. The strength of the team for an operation must be decided only on the basis of METT-TC (mission, enemy, terrain, troops available, time available and civil considerations), not on some fool's notions of bravado. Poor buggers never understand that a clever enemy does not have to engage their mythical super-commandos into a frontal battle and discover, to his horror that man-to-man, the commandos are better fighters. Once the enemy finds out that the commandos are in the jungle without any rear support, he has only to engage them in small battles of attrition and wear them out—once they start running low on ammo, they are easy meat. Giving them a fancy name of 'hunter-killer team' would not save their asses from getting shot up.

Perplexed by the problem, many senior officers have started swearing by anti-tank weapons like the CGRL. Ignoramuses call it the Carl Gustaf Rocket launcher instead of Carl Gustaf Recoilless Rifle. They hope that this would do what rifles could not do. Poor thing! *This was designed by the Swedes in 1949 as an anti-tank weapon, and our IPS officers want to use it against human targets like Naxals!* Where in the world are you going to get a clear line-of-flight in the jungle for even 100 meters? Then the warhead of the CGRL hasn't got a 'smart fuze'—it was designed to explode on hitting the armour of a tank. Unless it hits a wall made of stones, it is likely to simply penetrate through most other barriers without exploding. The result is that you may not get detonation of the warhead where you need it. Moreover, it is absurd to even think of using a 14.2 kg weapon in anti-personnel role in the jungle. Who is going to carry it when every man is already loaded with 20-25 kg on his back? Further, one warhead weighs 3.2 kg—how many of them can be carried to justify the carrying of the 14.2 kg weapon? So is the case with the AGL (Automatic Grenade Launcher). Nowhere in the world foot soldiers carry it—it is as a matter of rule, mounted on helicopters or vehicles because then only you can have sufficient number of grenades to fire in automatic mode. That's how it was mounted famously on the UH-1 Huey and Mi-24 Hind helicopters or the Humvee vehicle. Foot soldiers cannot carry that load. *But our dumb police leadership insists on the poor troops carrying it in pain for fear of disciplinary action – even if they carry a few grenades only to fire from an automatic weapon*!

7.5 A Misplaced Faith on High or Exotic Technology as the Panacea

Flummoxed by the situation, many police leaders seek refuge in high technology in desperation and hope that it would be the panacea for all the operational ills. Unfortunately, it does not help. A large number of officers swear by the extremely costly UAVs (Unmanned Aerial Vehicles). Of course, you don't expect the police leadership to know that the optical or even thermal camera of the UAV cannot penetrate jungle foliage or tree canopy—do you? These are complex matters of physics—why should they bother with them? Their idea is that the UAV will take images of the jungles from which they will be able to spot the insurgents and then the forces on the ground will rush (with a lusty cheer?) and finish them off! Unfortunately life is not so simple! The UAV serves its purpose in high altitude land surveillance and maritime patrol missions where there is no obstruction to the field of view. But the jungle is a different story. The optical cameras mounted on the UAV can only see what a human eye can see—and human eyes cannot penetrate the tree canopy. The problem of locating men hidden in a jungle by observing from the air therefore defies a technical solution.

Many officers have still not been able to understand that the Naxals have figured out the fatal weakness of the MPV (Mine Protected Vehicle) a long time ago, as evident from one of their papers in their military magazine *Awam-e-Jung* in 2005. But the police leadership requires some experts to do the thinking for them! Some other weird solutions to the Naxal problem include the use of Belgian Shepherd (Malanois) dogs to sniff out explosives. Poor fellows do not know that they are good only for settings like an airport where they have to sniff a suspect baggage only once in a while and where they get time to rest periodically. They cannot be expected to march 40 km into the jungles sniffing every inch of the floor all along its track. Some officers have gone to the extent of suggesting using a tractor for snagging and pulling out IED wires from the sides of the roads and have even sanctioned tractors for their units! Omigosh!

On the other hand, they have never projected the requirement of useful systems like Bunker Defeat Munition or the M72 LAW for taking on prepared defences; commando mortars; and hand grenades like P2A1 or Type 86 because they have not even heard of them.

7.6 Ignorance about Anti-terrorist Operations in Urban Terrain

7.6.1 *Failures, Lack of Professional Knowledge and Unaddressed Problems*

Fighting in urban areas is a very complex affair. Unfortunately, the police leadership in India has absolutely no idea of the subject. One of the reasons that our counter-insurgency operations in urban areas invariably result in heavy collateral damage is their ignorance of the science of fighting in urban areas. Whenever the Indian forces have been obliged to operate in urban areas, they have fumbled and messed up. Their first exposure to urban combat was during the Operation Blue Star at the Golden Temple Complex in Amritsar in 1984. They messed it up so badly that eventually howitzers and tanks had to be called in and there was extensive collateral damage, both to religious structures and innocent lives—hundreds or even thousands of people according to some estimates, were killed in the Operation. Subsequently, the repercussions were so heavy that Indira Gandhi was assassinated and thousands of innocent people were killed in the communal riots that erupted in Delhi and elsewhere. ***In almost all the operations the Indian forces have undertaken against terrorists in Kashmir, they invariably end up blasting the entire house with explosive charges after suffering a few casualties mainly because they do not know the science of house intervention.*** This habit of blasting houses has actually led to a great deal of alienation there and has thus complicated the problem as no one, not even a child, ever believed in their pet theory of some brick-cement house catching fire from small arms fire touted for the benefit of ignorant journalists. Everybody knows that bullets don't start fires or collapse walls.

Obviously there is much to be learnt. Unfortunately, the police leadership has utterly failed in learning anything. The Bombay 26/11 attack took place 24 years after Operation Blue Star. Entire world knows how we fumbled in killing a handful of terrorists. The terrorists fought pitched battles with the security forces and could be overcome only by 29/11 after over 54 hours of fighting. The incident utterly exposed the unpreparedness of the Indians in urban combat, particularly when the opponent happened to be well-armed and also with some cover. At least 173 people, including at least 22 foreign nationals, had to lose their lives and at least 308 people were injured. At the Nariman House, the NSG were called in to insert commandos in the building by helicopter amidst much fanfare, a first in the history of counter-terrorism in India. Still, the terrorists succeeded in killing all the hostages in the Nariman House!

We have analyzed all the incidents of terrorist attacks in an urban setting and we find that whenever any terrorist attack has taken place in any public building or some camp of the security forces, utter confusion has prevailed and there has been no methodical response—everybody who has a rifle, fires wherever he can, more to relieve himself of the anxiety, not at the terrorist. The Indian security establishment and the police leadership are completely flummoxed when they are faced with something unexpected. Ask any Indian soldier what he would do and he would say: "*fire ka jawaab fire se denge*", that is, he would retaliate bullets by bullets. Ask any officer what he would do and he would say: "*position le ke fire karenge*", that is, they would take up positions and fire. That's the end of it. *They have no idea where they would be firing if the terrorists are concealed because the police leadership has never developed any system and procedures for combat in such situations.*

As is the case with jungle combat, the police leaders know nothing about the professional aspects of urban combat such as, pie technique of visually clearing an area; unit movement down a street; crossing danger areas; selecting initial entry and breach points; techniques for clearing a building between floors; clearing a basement; room entry techniques; the buttonhook technique; the crossover technique; the modified technique; the pie-slice technique; the high-low technique; the limited penetration technique; and physical security. Most morons in the Indian armed forces know of only one way – approach the house in an armoured vehicle, lob explosives inside and blast the house! Once again, huge experience has been gained by other forces in the world and a voluminous amount of literature has been produced. This should not be regarded as some game of one-upmanship but in the interest of the nation, we sincerely advise them to read **'The Ultimate Handbook of Urban Warfare'** and they will see it for themselves what they need to know about urban combat.

Once you study you would find that the solutions found feasible and workable in the context of house interventions by the professional forces are vastly different from what you see in films and which has distorted the perception of the police leadership. House intervention in Hollywood films is a most thrilling affair with the SWAT (Special Weapons and Tactics) teams in their swanky gear working with clockwork precision and eliminating the opposition without as much as even the mirrors in the room cracking. Real life is, however, vastly different from reel life. Most of the SWAT procedures that have been developed by American police forces are good only for situations that they encounter most of the time. They expect handgun wielding criminals who might be holding hostages. They do not expect heavily armed crazy terrorists willing to die in the first place. That's why they lay so much emphasis on a regulated use of force so as not to harm the hostages or other innocent persons trapped therein. That's why they talk of using frangible bullets. Leave such amateurish stuff for those dumb guys who copy the Americans blindly – they have no relevance in anti-terrorist operations where real terrorists operate. House intervention is one field where training and scientific methods evolved after endless hours of research and practice must take precedence over your natural reactions. Those who try to imitate films end up very seriously dead; those who go by natural instincts also follow them to the mortuary.

7.6.2 *How Intellect Shrinks and Stupidity Explodes*

The police leadership has a habit of desiring simple explanations and simple solutions – no one has the patience or the intellectual capacity to grapple with complexity. Knee-jerk reactions have taken such complete control of the collective psyche of the leadership that the system is utterly unable to think beyond the last method of attack. Before 26/11 the Indian security establishment thought in terms of bombs planted on bicycles, scooters or cars. Bombay (26/11) was basically a rifle-cum-grenade attack. Then the police leadership hurriedly presumed that all future attacks would also be rifle attacks and hence the demand that there should be commandos in all the major towns. Fine, you may have it. The next attack could again be a bomb attack. What would the commandos do then? You may station the commandos in major towns; the terrorists would attack small towns. You may deploy police in places of religious worship; the terrorists would attack markets. You deploy them in markets; they would attack cinema halls. You deploy cops in cinema halls; they would attack malls—the list is endless.

A few Sikhs could successfully bomb the Air India plane Kanishka. Is there any law that nobody would do that again? What is the defensive preparation for that eventuality? Yes, airport security has been tightened since then. But that's largely show, not substance. The security does practically nothing for what goes in the cargo hold of the aircrafts. A bomb can be easily smuggled in that and exploded in mid-air to bring the aircraft down. The only problem is that the bomber too would not be able to get off the aircraft—so what, they can always find some fool who would be prepared to give up his life in return for glory as a 'martyr' or compensation to his family. Remember, Arthur Hailey's 'Airport'? The airport security has no system to check those who enter the airport building as passengers. At any time hundreds of people are to be found before the counters in the lobby.

Terrorists can come legitimately to the airports as passengers, enter the lobby with their weapons in the luggage and simply open fire on them with automatic weapons and kill hundreds there besides damaging the computers and other equipment and thereby rendering the airport dysfunctional for quite some time—great propaganda value! All those scores of security forces personnel whom the imbeciles in the police leadership deploy so ceremoniously at the airports would not be able to do a thing in such a situation because they will have to shoot at the innocent people also from amongst whom the terrorists would be firing at others. In other words, what happened at the Chhatrapati Shivaji Terminus in Bombay in 26/11 can happen at any of your airports. ***No one in the police leadership has the intellectual capacity to realize that the terrorist is not short of methods of attack. The police leadership refuses to understand that there is no way in which every possible target in the country could be protected unless***

you recruit three-fourths of the population in the security forces to protect the remaining one-fourth round-the-clock in three shifts!

When it comes to explosives, the dams of stupidity burst forth. Many of the senior officers genuinely believe that the terrorists have invented such mysterious explosives which they can make on board aircrafts using innocuous ingredients. The ingredients will be smuggled in bottles of cold drink etc. and the explosive will be made in the toilets of the aircrafts. After that they will blow up the aircrafts in mid-air. Many believe that the terrorists are able to make 'deadly explosives' from things as simple as hair bleach, nail polish remover and battery acid. The stupidity does not end there.

Another popular belief is that if there is a bomb blast, ammonium nitrate and RDX must have been used. (*By God, it appears that the only explosive terrorists now use is RDX because Al Qaida has decreed that any terrorist using any other explosive shall be excommunicated from the fraternity and his licence to practice terrorism shall be revoked!*) As we have shown at length subsequently, the so-called forensic experts are as dumb as the senior police officers. That's how we find forensic experts who identify the explosive material used in the 'landmine' as ammonium nitrate. (*Yeah, just ammonium nitrate and you did not know all these years that it was a bloody explosive? These fertilizers must be banned! We support organic farming!*) The terrorists are able to make 'high intensity' explosives with substances as simple as aluminium powder. (*Looks like even paint shops will have to be closed! Next they will make explosives out of thin air!*) The terrorists have made explosives which also release poisonous fumes after explosion, thereby invoking a chemical warfare aspect to it. (*Now these guys are really getting nasty, isn't it? Adding insult to injury – as if the blast itself was not enough?*) They use a timer circuit called ABCD timer in their time bombs. (*Ever heard of it; even if you have a Ph.D. in electronics? And you thought the ISI was teaching them English alphabet?*) They have only to carry a couple of LPG cylinders in a car and crash it – they will be able to blow up entire airport buildings.

The IED (which was no bigger than a cricket ball), if it had succeeded in exploding, would have demolished a three-storey building. A major tragedy was thus averted. (*Thank God! Had it been of the size of a football it would have taken the entire town down!*) The explosive used in the pressure cooker bomb was a high explosive as well as incendiary and that's why it had set the train compartment ablaze. (*You know, what these American scientists will ever invent? The ISI knows how to invent explosives! They are the real master blasters! And you thought a master blaster is a batsman?*)

Another bogey raised by the senior police officers is that our forces are failing in their counter-terrorist mission because they do not have the latest weapons and gadgetry. The leadership and their equally dumb friends in the media keep on lamenting how impoverished the Indian forces are. By God, the real thing to lament about is their intellectual impoverishment. Indian forces are fumbling in their fight against terrorism because they are dumb, not because they are badly ill-equipped. ***The police leadership wants to hide its incompetence in both strategic and tactical spheres behind an alleged lack of fancy weapon systems.*** Quite like adolescents, they are fascinated by gadgets. When they watch foreign channels or surf the Internet, they get to see a lot of gadgets being used by foreign forces. Since they are intellectually incapable of understanding the complexities of counter-terrorism, they latch on to the fanciest objects—gadgets fit the bill perfectly. Then the general refrain becomes: if we had such-and-such thing, we would have wiped off these jokers a long time back.

Little do they realize that fancy weapons are either simply fancy weapons or an adolescent's fancy—having a fancy weapon does not mean that you will win in all combats; not having a fancy weapon does not mean that you will lose all combats. For example, it does not really make any difference whether you are pouring out 30 rounds in 3 seconds (at the rate of 600 rounds per minute from a rifle) or 2.6 seconds (at the rate of 700 rounds per minute from another rifle)—the human targets in front of you will not be able to tell the difference—you cannot say that the target can take evasive action if the rate of fire is 600 rounds per minute and cannot take such evasive action if the rate of fire is higher—human reflexes are, in any case, far slower. And for the duffers' kind information, when you take into account the fact that anyone of the bullets could be fatal, the difference becomes even more insignificant.

In the context of urban combat, the next bastion of stupidity of the police leadership is the so-called VIP security. VIP security is something that has been given the status of a sacred religion amongst senior police officers who look up to these organizations as some sort of divine authority. By God, many myths owe their origin to the practices adopted by these bodyguards. The police leadership does not know that the job of a bodyguard is a lowly one—a completely de-intellectualized one—the dumbest of the men, in fact, make the best bodyguards. If looks could kill, they would sure kill—white loose trousers, knee pads, swank goggles, a trademark dumb zombie-like expression and the works. The rest, as we see below, is all crap. The police leaders and these bodyguards are so dumb that they never realized that the very rationale of using a sub-machinegun for VIP security is utterly wrong. Dear sirs, the so-called VIPs are generally to be found and likely to be attacked only amidst a gathering of people—you cannot afford to pour in a high volume of fire there indiscriminately and kill innocent persons! In fact, you need a weapon like the SIG-Sauer P226 pistol there which can deliver accurate fire. What is the advantage of a range of 200 meters that you may get with the P90? None whatsoever! In VIP security you do not engage an enemy at this range. One who decides to attack the target at that range will take precautions to conceal oneself too or make a provision to get away immediately after firing his shots. Similarly, why do you require armour piercing bullets—where on earth are you going to encounter armour wearing terrorists and why? Won't they be making themselves all the more conspicuous by that whereas the primary objective of a terrorist should be to appear as inconspicuous as possible? And for God's sake, if at all you are obliged to fire on full auto for whatever reason, you are supposed to concentrate on firing. Would you have the time to look whether any rounds are remaining or not? What purpose does it serve then to have a transparent magazine in the weapon? A manufacturer introduces some juvenile thing and the duffers are smitten by it.

The police leadership has done nothing to address all these vital issues. If this is not a failure of the leadership, what else is?

Chapter 8

Ignorance in Forensic Matters and the Miscarriage of Justice

8.1 A Religious Faith in Experts Who are Not

8.1.1 *The Nexus of the Ignorant and the Charlatans*

Bereft of any other source of information and allergic to any kind of reading, senior police officers derive their notions and beliefs from films or TV serials. In Hollywood films and TV serials, the moment the cops trace a hair, a bullet fragment or a fingerprint, the game is over. The bad guy is locked up ASAP. The TV show "CSI" (for Crime Scene Investigation) in the USA has fostered the so-called 'CSI effect'. Its counterpart in India could be called the 'CID' effect after the hugely popular serial 'CID'. Incidentally, in the Indian serial 'CID' there is only one forensic scientist who is a veritable one-man army—he is ballistics expert; a forensic medicine specialist; a forensic chemist; a forensic toxicologist; a forensic anthropologist; a forensic biologist; and you name whatever else. Of course, it is not for the viewers to question how could a man become a specialist in all these specialities? Such on-screen stupidities have come to possess public imagination to such an extent that public expectations from the forensic sciences have been unrealistically elevated. Senior police officers are also victim of the same phenomenon. What is there in the world that the ACP Pradyuman Singh and Dr. Salunkhe cannot solve? And if they can solve, why cannot the characters in real life solve? Viewers-turned-jurors want quick forensic tests with absolutely definitive results. "The CSI effect has caused jurors to expect crime lab results, far beyond the capacity of forensic science," wrote Jim Fisher, a former FBI agent and retired professor who taught forensic science at Edinboro University of Pennsylvania, in his 2008 book entitled 'Forensics Under Fire: Are Bad Science and Duelling Experts Corrupting Criminal Justice?'

These days it is quite fashionable amongst police officers to make some reference to forensics. It is de rigueur to take the help of forensic experts. Police officers, particularly those who are consumed by a desire of being called modern, have an almost religious reverence for forensic methods. Many of them have a peculiar habit of tom-tomming forensic reports—the very words 'forensic report' are pronounced in such a menacing manner as if they carried some threat. *As it happens with all matters religious, the problem is that they do not even think of questioning their beliefs.* We have spoken of the lack of critical faculty in the police officers at many places in this book. Never is this more evident than in the case of forensic methods. *There are two reasons of their not questioning it. First, they do not have a desire to question something which they regard sacred. Second, one must have some knowledge to question something. By themselves, they do not know anything about forensics. A realization that they do not have any domain knowledge makes them lean on some other support. This 'other support' is found in the form of the so-called forensic experts. The wisdom (or lack of it) of the expert is never questioned. There is nothing more convenient than leaving something in the hands of others.*

This is actually an escape mechanism. The police leadership has no desire of learning anything on its own. Ignorance helps. When you do not know anything, you are saved the trouble of asking any questions either. Somebody else must carry the burden of learning. Throw everything on him and let him decide. In forensic mattes, this burden is passed on to the so-called 'experts', as the burden of knowing law is passed on to the public prosecutors. Never mind that the so-called forensic 'expert' could be a mere science graduate, or that he could not have had any specialized training or expertise in a particular forensic discipline. *For the police officers, as long as someone is employed in the FSL, even if he is a janitor, he is an 'expert'.*

What they do not realize is that neither the experts are real experts, nor is the so-called science practised by them an exact science. The biggest casualty in this morass of ignorance is justice—very frequently, there is grave miscarriage of justice because forensic methods were incorrectly applied or incorrectly interpreted.

In this chapter we will reveal several startling new facts and bust a couple of myths related to the business of forensic science. The first myth is about the expertise of the so-called forensic experts. We show that they are not the experts they pretend to be. *At times their knowledge is suspect; at some other times their professional integrity is suspect – quite often, both are suspect.* The second is that what is touted as forensic science is not really a science – it is merely a collection of some techniques. The third is that some of the best scientists in the world have shown most of the popular techniques of forensic science to be unreliable.

Charlatans are found in all walks of life, especially in activities where there is some scope of making money, but forensic science is particularly prone to it because the field is relatively nascent and few people work in it. *Fact is, the so-called forensic experts in India are some of the biggest duffers in the whole world. And still, the police leadership depends on them – what could be a bigger tragedy? Why? Because these guys do not even know that anything better exists in the world.*

As far the discipline of forensic science is concerned, the less said the better. The standard for M.Sc. degree in forensic science in universities across the country is so hopelessly poor that it pains our very souls. Science graduates of any discipline can join it and it is expected that they would master the intricacies of ballistics; chemical analysis; fingerprints; hair and fibre analysis; explosives; arson; serology, document analysis; and even computer forensics! Omigosh! The situation in respect of forensic medicine is equally bad. It receives the lowest priority amongst the subjects of medicine. In all the medical colleges of this country, from the most backward to the top-most, the only books which kids pursuing MBBS degree course study for forensic medicine are two archaic books, namely J. L. Modi's 'Medical Jurisprudence and Toxicology', and C. L. Parikh's 'Handbook of Forensic Medicine'. No reference books are studied and often they are just not found in the libraries.

These two are utterly archaic and actually very low-level textbooks having been published decades ago. An enormous development has taken place since then. *The tyranny of ignorance continues unabated because except us nobody has even raised this issue.* Since the lawyers also who acquire some interest in forensics, do not muster courage to study a word beyond Modi's book on their own – it becomes the ultimate word in Indian courts – close to the words from Scriptures. That's how miscarriage of justice takes place – the police officers; the lawyers; the so-called experts; the judges; nobody knows beyond Modi and Parikh, and which have innumerable factual errors. Had the police leadership known better about forensics on their own, they could have at least pointed out the shortcomings. But that was not to be.

Autopsies in India are generally performed by government doctors. With the knowledge of forensic medicine they have from their graduation programme, nothing more than the most rudimentary conclusions can be drawn from the autopsies—a miscarriage of justice at that stage itself. Even those conclusions are drawn in the most questionable way. Moreover, the duty of performing post-mortems is assigned by rotation amongst available doctors and thus all sorts of medical practitioners including ophthalmologists, paediatricians and gynaecologists also get to perform autopsies. We know hundreds of them personally. By their own admission to us, not one of them has ever even touched the dead bodies brought for post-mortems. The bodies are cut open by the lowest level attendant available (often under the influence of liquor), and it is he who 'dictates' the findings, shouting them to the doctor sitting in the corner. If the doctor sahib is a very keen type, he may grant a cursory look to the dissected body, otherwise the job of the doctor is only to sprinkle a little bit of old school jargon in the report dictated by the attendant so that it appears written by a professional.

8.1.2 *A Case Study of the Post-mortems in the Shopian and the Bhandara Deaths*

Gentlemen, that's how we have reached the pathetic situation that we describe below. In 2010, in a place called Shopian in Kashmir, exhumation was performed on two dead bodies that had been lying properly buried according to Islamic rites (that is, without any coffin) in wet ground for exactly four months. This was a case in which it was alleged by the public that the two young women were raped and murdered by soldiers. The dead bodies were found in shallow waters of the river Rembiara within hours of the deaths. The doctors taken from Delhi by the CBI who conducted the exhumation proceeded to perform the thoroughly discredited 'two-finger test' in the vaginas of the decomposed bodies to decide whether they were raped or not! Omigosh!

That's not all. Since it was a case of suspicious deaths and in view of such serious allegations amidst mounting public uproar, two post-mortems had already been done before the bodies were given a proper burial. In this case, the CBI claimed that one of the doctors involved in inspecting crucial evidence had, at one point, falsely claimed to have used her own vaginal swabs to prove that the two were raped before their death. The CBI said that Dr. Nigahat Shaheen had claimed to have used a glove in her dustbin to prepare the swab to prove rape on Asiya Jan (17) and her sister-in-law Neelofar Jan (22). "Shaheen's claim turned out to be false when the swab was matched with her husband's blood sample," said CBI DIG Satish Kumar Golcha. Dr. Nigahat works at the Pulwama district hospital had conducted the second post-mortem on the victims. She had reportedly admitted before the CBI that she had sent fake vaginal swab slides for forensic examination. She also revealed that she had done so at the instance of then chief medical officer and deputy medical officer. The J&K HC directed the CBI to reveal details of the Shopian probe only to the Court and share nothing with the media. The strictures came after reports in a section of the media quoted forensic experts as saying that one of the victims had died a virgin, thus ruling out rape.

The CBI probe found that both the teams of doctors that had conducted the first two post-mortems had lied in the post-mortem reports. The first team of doctors termed the death of Asiya Jan as due to cardio-vascular arrest and that of Neelofar due to neurogenic shock. The second team of doctors from Pulwama claimed there was sexual assault on Asiya and death following haemorrhage and shock due to bleeding from multiple injuries. In case of Neelofar, the second team had claimed, it was death by neurogenic shock following sexual intercourse.

The CBI probe questioned the entire process suggesting that doctors had assembled a piece of the heart and termed it to be parts of lungs. Besides, the second team of doctors fudged the vaginal swab samples. It belonged to neither of the women. Dr. Nigahat Shaheen did not tell CBI from where she collected the samples.

The CBI report quoted medical opinion of the AIIMS doctors that conclusively said the deaths had taken place "due to asphyxia as a result of ante-mortem downing". It said the lacerated wound on Asiya's forehead was not sufficient to cause death. The theory of drowning was based on the presence of diatoms—a test that has already been discredited elsewhere in the world. We have debunked the diatom test a little later in the chapter.

The CBI eventually filed a chargesheet against six doctors, five lawyers and two civilians, including the brother of one of the women who died, for fabricating evidence. The CBI report accused the 13 of hatching a criminal conspiracy to direct public anger against security forces. Besides the deliberate bungling in the vaginal swab samples, two doctors were charged for wrongly mentioning the lacerated wound on the frontal portion of Asiya Jan's head as incised wound. He was also accused of falsely opining on the cause of death as hemorrhagic shock and bleeding from multiple injuries in case of Asiya Jan and neurogenic shock in case of Neelofar Jan.

Thus, in this case, not one but three post-mortems had messed up. Well, what does it tell you about the professional competence and ethical standards of the doctors who conduct post-mortems—the charge of destroying or tampering with evidence will obviously not address the much larger issue of the professional misconduct which casts a shadow on the entire business of post-mortems—and which the police leadership swallows hook, line and sinker.

The dumbness of the doctors who assume the mantle of so-called forensic experts is also evident from a case of March 2013 in Bhandara, Maharashtra. According to police, three sisters, aged six, nine and 11 years, who went missing since February 14, were allegedly raped and murdered by unidentified persons in Murwadi village in Lakhni taluka of Bhandara district, nearly 70 km from Nagpur. Their bodies were found dumped in a farm well on February 16. The post-mortem was performed the following day at the Bhandara district government hospital. According to the reports of the forensic team of Bhandara government hospital, the youngest girl had a major injury in her anus. She also had scratch injuries on her inner thighs. The hymens of all the three girls were found to be ruptured too. The eldest sister had injuries below her elbows. They found no bleeding from the vaginas of all three. The chemical analysis and swab tests conducted did not reveal any trace of semen. There was no semen on the dresses.

The flustered cops tried to apply whatever little mind they had. They opined that the girls were likely to have been raped and killed before being thrown into the well. "The findings of the chemical analysis," said a police source, "suggest that the girls had consumed the water of the same well where their bodies were recovered. It means they were alive when brought to the well. The injuries seen on the girls are ante-mortem too." Bhandara SP added a fresh dimension to the case stating that the forensic team of the district hospital did not mention the cause of death. Police also felt that the absence of semen could mean that the perpetrators were 'well prepared' with condoms. The day of the disappearance of the girls, February 14, also coincided with Valentine's Day. Even for a God forsaken village like that, the police felt that it was possible that the elder girl was summoned at a place by someone she knew (hinting at a Valentine's day date—note it, a date, a rendezvous in that backward village, and that too by an 11 year old girl!) and she had taken the sisters along from the school. The police also claimed that eldest girl, in November last year, had planned to leave her place for Nagpur along with two other friends after being scolded by mother. A section of the police felt that she was a "mysterious character"—whatever it meant. The cops also tried to question several youngsters who used to take the girls for a spin on their bikes for fun. "It could also be a case of Valentine's Day turning ugly," said a police source. We have ourselves spoken in confidence with several police officers of the area and they had a simple solution to a complex case—the 11 year old girl was precocious; that she was sort of 'loose character'; that she used to go out with boys; that she had a tendency to run away from the home because the mother had scolded her once; and that on the fateful day she had gone for some fun with boys at that isolated place where things did not go exactly as planned; the boys lost control and raped not only her but the other two also; and that after the rape, murder of all of them became inevitable as the girls could recognize the boys. Simple!

Then another panel was constituted. This panel comprised the forensic heads of Mumbai's KEM and JJ Hospitals, Dr. Harish Pathak and Dr. S. D. Nanadkar, and the former director of the forensic department of Delhi's AIIMS, Dr. T. D. Dogra. They ruled out rape and sexual assault. Dr. Harish Pathak told ToI that, based on the evidences collected, the panel has "conclusively" shown to the state that the three sisters had "walked up to the well", which means they were not murdered but were thrown in. The panel concluded it was death by drowning. This finding was, once again incidentally, based on the thoroughly discredited diatom test. Did it make any sense for the girls to commit suicide that way? They were country girls and knew wells of that type? And if someone threw them inside the well, there should have been some reason for it. But, you see, these doctors who perform autopsies are like demigods; why should they bother about the question of the three girls committing suicide that way? "We have concluded that there has been no rape. There were no vaginal or anal injuries. There were merely organs protruding due to decomposition, which the doctors who conducted the post-mortem had interpreted as injuries," Pathak said. Pathak further added that the bodies did not have any vital reactions or swelling, which should have been present if they were assaulted. "There were no blood clots in the anal area, though the faecal matter was present. It proved that water could not have washed away everything," he said.

Well, if that be true, the other doctors must be dismissed from service since two diametrically opposite findings cannot be correct simultaneously. The first set of doctors contested it strongly. A woman gynaecologist, who was part of the five-member team from Bhandara district hospital that conducted the post-mortem on the three minor girls came out in support of their findings about the vaginal and anal injuries to the two younger girls. Dr. C. S. Khobragade, the gynaecologist who has been in service for around two decades at the government hospital, emphatically said there were clear evidences of hymen ruptures in the two girls aged six and nine apart from the prominent injuries in the anus. "The bodies were in water for long enough for the traces of bleedings and other evidences to get washed off. The eldest sister did not have any anal injuries but her hymen too was found ruptured," said Khobragade who claims to have handled numerous cases of rape at the district hospital since 2003. Khobragade's colleague Dr. Aparna Rangari took a similar stand. "If we were so wrong, then how come we did not suggest anal injuries to the eldest sister which were not there," she said. Apart from Dr. Khobragade and Dr. Rangari, the team comprised Dr. Pradeep Anand, Dr. Prashant Padole and Dr. Bhagyesh Gulhane.

Since both teams could not be correct simultaneously, the heads of at least one team must roll. But that was not to be because the police leadership failed. What was done to clarify the situation? What did the police leadership do? Are they obliged to play only the role of mute spectators? If they accept one set of report, what is the basis of it? Either they must give their own scientific arguments for or against one report or admit that they merely go by the rank of the doctors. But is there any guarantee that senior doctors cannot be wrong ever? Does science go by ranks or positions?

And that's not the end of it. Police officers often share their suspicions regarding suspects with lab workers before forensic examinations are performed. This has been shown to prejudice lab personnel in areas as diverse as fingerprint examination and chemical testing for accelerants in arson investigations. Further, some lab examiners feel they are part of the prosecution team, helping the police and prosecutors convict suspects regardless of the results of forensic testing. In such cases, forensic experts and other lab personnel are found to lie about test results; misleading about the reliability of their methods; and/or cover up test outcomes when they are beneficial to the defendant.

8.2 The Truth is that the Whole Edifice is Built Upon a Shaky Foundation

8.2.1 *Some Long-Held Myths are Debunked on the Altar of Rigorous Scientific Scrutiny*

The so-called forensic science is actually 'junk science' or a 'pseudo science' at best. After a series of crime lab scandals and the FBI's erroneous identification of an American attorney as a terrorist suspect in the

2004 Madrid train bombings, in 2006, the US Congress instructed the National Academy of Sciences (NAS) to review the status of forensic techniques used in criminal prosecutions. It was found that misleading and erroneous forensic science has been a significant contributing factor in many of the known wrongful convictions. It is important to recognize that these concerns are not merely abstract or theoretical. In fact, a recent study of wrongful convictions found that flaws with forensic science—including interpretive errors, overstated testimony and inaccuracies—were present in a whopping 60 percent of the cases studied.

The findings of the NAS have been earth-shattering. They have shown that far from being infallible, the so-called expert comparisons of hair, handwriting, marks made by firearms on bullets, and patterns such as bite marks and shoe and tire prints are unscientific and subject to human bias. So is the case with other techniques, such as in bullet-lead analysis and arson investigation, which are also plagued by poorly regulated practices and a lack of scientific method. Even fingerprint identification is partly a subjective exercise that lacks research into the role of unconscious bias or even its error rate. Most of the existing forensic stuff is close to voodoo science. **The NAS thundered: "No forensic method has been rigorously shown to have the capacity to consistently, and with a high degree of certainty, demonstrate a connection between evidence and a specific individual or source."**

To understand the path-breaking research of the NAS, you must first understand what scientists understand by scientific methods. **The scientific method** is instrumental to our understanding of the physical world. To scientists, the process is sacrosanct: Research your topic, generate a hypothesis, test the hypothesis, analyze your data and then publish the results for peer review. Forensic science, in contrast, was not developed by scientists. It was mostly created by cops in the West, who were guided by little more than common sense —looking for easy-to-do ways to match patterns from clues with evidence tied to suspects. That there was little scientific research behind them became evident as hundreds of criminal cases were unravelled contrary to what the forensics had suggested—that's how the finger of suspicion turned towards the so-called established forensic practices. **It was found that much of the so-called "science" behind forensic science rests on surprisingly shaky foundations. In fact, the 'science' content is so meagre that instead of forensic science, it ought to be called forensic techniques**. It has now been shown that many well-established forms of evidence are the product of highly subjective analysis by people with minimal credentials. And even the most experienced and respected professionals can come to inaccurate conclusions, because the body of research behind the majority of the forensic sciences is incomplete, and the established methodologies are often inexact.

"There is no scientific foundation for it," says Arizona State University law professor Michael Saks. "As you begin to unpack it you find it's a lot of loosey-goosey stuff." Most of the forensic techniques are not based on the methods and approaches that we usually associate with validated research science. Their claims and the limits to their claims are not closely based on or constrained by the formal collection of data. Their empirical assertions are not grounded in careful research that has been subject to peer review and publication. There has been remarkably little formal validation of their methods. And there has been far too little study of how often forensic scientists might make mistakes, and when or why these possible errors are more likely to occur. The situation is so bad that currently, even in the USA, no national or widely accepted set of standards for forensic science written reports or testimony exists. No entity promulgates such standards or ensures that all analysts adhere to standards for permissible scientific conclusions regarding forensic evidence. Even wound certificates in medico-legal cases and post-mortem reports are prepared by doctors in a most arbitrary manner.

Forensic science has had, over the years, developed a culture of its own—a culture in which claims derived from experience have been accepted as a substitute for data; a culture in which interpretations have often been framed in absolute terms rather than in more limited or modest language; a culture in which potentially biasing information is not systematically kept away from the forensic examiner; and a culture in which institutionally cozy relationships between detectives, forensic analysts, and prosecutors has encouraged unconscious partisanship. Having been thrashed by the NAS, it is this culture that needs to change; new and improved forensic techniques will not, by themselves, provide an adequate solution.

Accordingly, to check the validity of the existing techniques, controlled studies were performed that included blind testing (where the answer is known to the evaluators but not to the persons performing the forensic analysis) and statistical testing (in which a large number of samples are compared to see how often a random "match" occurs). Further, issues of investigator bias, unknown error rates, lack of crime lab independence, underfunding, poor training, lack of lab personnel qualifications, low academic requirements, and lab personnel making exaggerated claims about the accuracy of forensic techniques were also repeatedly noted in the NAS report. The report also examined how the existing practices survived for so long. In the first place, nobody had undertaken an exhaustive study of this type to debunk the. Secondly, it was also helped by careful window-dressing. As an article "Criminal Law Forensics: Century of Acceptance May Be Over" in the January 8, 2009 issue of the New York Law Journal observed, *"The art of junk science is to brush away just enough detail to reach desired conclusions, while preserving enough to maintain an aura of authoritative science."*

Jennifer L. Mnookin, Professor of Law, UCLA School of Law, has shown in her paper 'The Courts, the NAS, and the Future of Forensic Science' that for many long-used types of forensic science, including fingerprint identification, firearms identification, handwriting identification, and tool-mark identification, experts' claims about their field, the authority of their methodologies, and their own abilities have dramatically outstripped what has actually been established by persuasive research and careful study. She has further shown that forensic scientists have regularly testified in court to matters that are, quite honestly, both less proven and less certain than they are claimed to be. They have overstated their degree of knowledge, underreported the chances of error, and suggested greater certainty than is warranted.

In 1993, the Supreme Court of the USA, in the now legendary case of **Daubert vs. Merrell Dow Pharmaceutical** [509 U.S. 579, 590 n.9 (1993)], had made clear that judges have a gate keeping responsibility with respect to expert evidence. Expert evidence now needs to be sufficiently reliable, that is, scientifically valid—in order to be legitimately admissible in court. Following the NAS report, as a matter of formal evidence doctrine, then, forensic science evidence should only be permitted if it meets Daubert's requirements. Specifically, Daubert invites courts to look at whether the evidence or technique in question has been tested adequately, whether it has a known error rate; whether it has been subject to peer review; and whether it is generally accepted by the relevant scientific community. Following the NAS report, numerous challenges invoking the requirements in terms of Daubert have been made in respect of many forensic results in the USA.

Conventional forensic disciplines were unable to identify a perpetrator with any great discrimination. For example, conventional serology analysis of blood group substances was widely used in sexual assault cases through the 1980s in the USA. While serology could exclude or place an individual within a percentage of the population with a given blood type, it could not distinguish particular individuals with any greater specificity. Starting with the case of Gary Dotson, by the end of January 2009, 232 innocent persons, who were convicted on the basis of 'invalid' forensic methods, have now been exonerated by post-conviction DNA testing in the USA. Stung by this, lest the dumb police leadership now repose all their faith in DNA testing, we must warn that DNA analysis itself is not immune from inaccurate presentation of results.

A study by Brandon L. Garrett and Peter J. Neufeld entitled *'Invalid Forensic Science Testimony and Wrongful Convictions'* raised a neglected question: Even assuming that a particular forensic technique has been validated and deemed reliable for casework, how do we ensure that the data will be interpreted, reported, and testified to within appropriate scientific parameters? They pointed out that traditionally, there has been almost no oversight of what the so-called 'experts' say in the courtroom once the court has deemed the method used as valid and reliable. Therein lies the catch—even if the method is valid, the man using the method can still commit serious errors and he is not subjected to any scrutiny! In other words, they also examined the validity of conclusions reached by the 'experts'—that is, whether what the analysts said in court was supported by empirical data—the analysis confirmed that the analysts had been bluffing all these years. Scientists typically distinguish between 'validity' (does the principle support what it purports to show?) and 'reliability' (does application of the principle produce consistent results?)."). Hitherto, in the joy ride of forensic techniques, both were given a go by. In fact, people have woken up only now to another prophetic observation in Daubert: "Expert evidence can be both powerful and quite misleading because of the difficulty in evaluating it...Expert testimony may be assigned talismanic significance in the eyes of lay jurors, and, therefore, the district courts must take care to weigh the value of such evidence against its potential to mislead or confuse".

Two very important questions should underlie the law's admission of and reliance upon forensic evidence in criminal trials: (1) the extent to which a particular forensic discipline is founded on a reliable scientific methodology that gives it the capacity to accurately analyze evidence and report findings and (2) the extent to which practitioners in a particular forensic discipline rely on human interpretation that could be tainted by error, the threat of bias, or the absence of sound operational procedures and robust performance standards.

Often in criminal prosecutions and civil litigation, forensic evidence is offered to support conclusions about "individualization" (sometimes referred to as "matching" a specimen to a particular individual or other source) or about classification of the source of the specimen into one of several categories. The NAS report found that with the exception of nuclear DNA analysis, however, no forensic method has been rigorously shown to have the capacity to consistently, and with a high degree of certainty, demonstrate a connection between evidence and a specific individual or source. The simple reality is that the interpretation of forensic evidence is not always based on scientific studies to determine its validity. This is a serious problem.

The NAS report warns: "Though the technology has changed over time, the sources of human error, misinterpretation, and misconduct have not...The scientific community can take the lead in reform efforts. Detailed scientific standards are needed to establish permissible parameters both for report writing and for trial testimony...If reforms are not implemented to regulate the practice of forensic science during criminal investigations long before the adversary process begins, the opportunity to avert miscarriages of justice may be lost.

8.2.2 *The National Academy of Sciences (NAS) Report*

The NAS is an extremely well-regarded, independent, and nonpartisan body. The committee established by the National Academy of Sciences had included reputed members of the forensic science community, prominent members of the legal community, and a diverse group of eminent scientists. The committee heard an exhaustive amount of expert testimonies and deliberated over the information it heard and received. Of course, they also reviewed numerous published materials, studies, and reports related to the forensic science disciplines, and engaged in independent research on the subject. ***Their 328-page report published in 2009 drives the last nail in the coffin of forensic techniques***.

After two years of studying fingerprints, handwriting, ballistics, and other common forensic techniques, the Academy concluded that "...forensic science disciplines are supported by little rigorous systematic research to validate the discipline's basic premises and techniques." The report found "a notable dearth of peer-reviewed, published studies establishing the scientific bases and validity of many forensic methods." There is no evident reason why such research cannot be conducted. The report also found that research on proficiency, performance, and the role of bias and observer effects is "sorely needed." In view of the lack of mandatory standardization, certification, and accreditation of the forensic science community, its facilities and practices, the NAS recommended for the creation of a new independent federal agency [christened the National Institute of Forensic Science (NIFS)] to regulate, supervise, develop best practices and oversee the forensic science infrastructure.

The NAS report identified a number of deficiencies not only in the forensic sciences but with crime lab personnel who use and testify about such evidentiary methods in court. "In a nutshell, these people aren't scientists," stated NAS member Jay A. Siegel. "They don't know what validation is. They don't know what it means to validate a test." *And mind it, this is the situation in the USA; you can easily imagine the rot we would have in India*! The report pointed out that lawyers and judges often have insufficient training and background in scientific methodology, and they often fail to fully comprehend the approaches employed by different forensic science disciplines and the reliability of forensic science evidence that is offered in trial.

Summing up the NAS report, the Honourable Harry T. Edwards, Senior Circuit Judge and Chief Judge Emeritus United States Court of Appeals for the D.C. Circuit and Co-Chair of the Committee, wrote in his paper 'The National Academy of Sciences Report on Forensic Sciences: What it Means for the Bench and Bar': "I started the NAS project with no scepticism regarding the forensic science community. Rather, I assumed, as I suspect many of my judicial colleagues do, that the forensic disciplines are well grounded in scientific methodology and that crime laboratories and forensic practitioners follow proven practices that ensure the validity and reliability of forensic evidence offered in court. I was surprisingly mistaken in what I assumed...Our committee found that the quality of practice in the forensic disciplines varies widely and the conclusions reached by forensic practitioners are not always reliable."

The Judge added that if a particular forensic methodology or practice, once thought to be scientifically valid, has been revealed to lack validation or reliability, no prosecutor would offer evidence derived from that discipline without taking the new information into account and no judge would continue to admit such evidence without considering the new information regarding the scientific validity and reliability of its source. **If courts blindly follow precedent that rests on unfounded scientific premises, this will lead to unjust results. Nothing in established law compels this course.** In the past, the admissibility of this kind of evidence was effectively presumed, largely because of its pedigree – the fact that it had been admitted for decades. As such, counsel rarely challenged it, and if it were challenged, it was rarely excluded or limited."

8.3 Debunking of the Pseudoscience of the So-called Forensic Techniques

This book intends to expose the ignorance of the police leadership. Unfortunately, it is not a book on forensic science. Although we would have loved to hammer it in but it is beyond the scope of this book to discuss in greater detail the research on forensic science that we have been talking about. We have made the point and cited authorities. Those who are interested in acquiring this great knowledge can read the references cited in the bibliography. However, for the sake of completeness, we are presenting a very brief account of the basic logic used by the NAS in debunking them.

8.3.1 *Fingerprints Can Very Well Lie: The Pseudoscience Exposed*

For more than a century, fingerprints, palm prints and sole prints have been used as identification tools by law enforcement. Collectively known as "friction ridge analysis," this forensic method involves examiners comparing the details of an unknown print with a set or a database of known prints. These details include ridges, loops, whorls and other points of similarities. The popular impression is that fingerprint identification was infallible and that it was possible for an examiner to determine that a print comes from a single unambiguous source. No longer true. The reliability of fingerprint forensic evidence has been questioned in view of the errors that are now being detected. **The most prominent case was that of Oregon lawyer Brandon Mayfield. After the March 2004 terrorist bombings in Madrid that killed almost 200 people, a partial print found on a bag of detonators was sent to the FBI. An examiner determined that the print belonged to Mayfield, who was later detained. In total, four fingerprint examiners—including one hired by Mayfield's defence team—declared that his print matched the partial from Spain. Except there was a problem: the print wasn't Mayfield's at all. Spanish officials matched the partial print to an Algerian man named Daoud Ouhnane. Mayfield later sued the government, which settled for $ 2 million. Get it?**

A 2006 study by the University of Southampton in England asked six veteran fingerprint examiners to study prints taken from actual criminal cases. The experts were not told that they had previously examined the same prints. In 67 percent of the instances, the results were inconsistent with their own previous results. Further, recent studies have also shown that fingerprint examiners can be influenced by contextual bias when comparing fingerprints—if they were told that the suspect had confessed, they necessarily gave a positive match.

In fact, the very basis of fingerprint identification is suspect. According to the National Academies of Sciences, no peer reviewed scientific studies have ever been done to prove the basic assumption that every person's fingerprint is unique. The basic approach taken by latent fingerprint experts involves what they call ACE-V (for analysis, comparison, evaluation and verification). At its root, ACE-V in its current incarnation amounts to no more and no less than a set of procedures to describe the careful comparison of a latent print with a potential source print by an initial examiner and a subsequent verifier. The devil is in the details—what constitutes analysis? How exactly does a competent comparison take place? When are apparent similarities misleading, and when might apparent differences be attributed to something other than the two prints deriving from different sources? ACE-V, as a methodology, does not help answer any of these critical methodological questions, because its categories are too general and insufficiently substantive.

Latent fingerprint examination as a field lacks any formalized specifications about what is required in order to declare a match. There is no required minimum number of points of resemblance or minimum number of total print features, or any required quantum of any specific kind of ridge detail. Instead, examiners decide for themselves, based on their training and experience, how much similarity is sufficient to declare a match. Two fingerprint analysts will often focus on different minutiae in their examination of the same print; indeed, sometimes the same examiner, when given the same print at a different time, will focus on different minutiae than he or she did the first time. The judgement is fundamentally a subjective one, not based on any formalized measures of either quantity or sufficiency. Moreover, the technique does not have or make use of robust statistically-based data about the frequency of different friction ridge characteristics. Analysts do not make regular or structured use in their comparisons of empirical studies showing how common or how rare different fingerprint details might be. They do not presently make use of any statistically-validated standards to justify how many identifying characteristics must be the same on two prints in order to warrant a finding that they match. Nor do they employ a probabilistic approach to determining the likelihood that a print selected at random would have that quantum of similarity, akin to the use of "random-match probability" in DNA identification. Obviously, this is not science.

8.3.2 *The Age-Old Fraud of the Lie Detector or Polygraph*

The polygraph was a massive fraud—as big as it could ever be imagined. Polygraphs became popular due to popular culture, fiction and films that became obsessed with it. The polygraph depends on an almost religious notion that man is inherently good—that the soul of even a criminal is good and it is only the mind that is perverted. Hence the soul or the inner self sides with the truth whereas the mind may be inclined towards the untruth. This tussle results in the physiological responses when the subject is lying. The polygraph measures emotion-based physiological signals such as heart rate, sweating, and blood pressure—respiration is measured through a pneumograph; electrodermal skin response through a galvanometer; and blood volume and pulse rate through a cardiospymograph. Needless to say, the very premise is hopelessly wrong and without any scientific basis at all. They have been summarily disproved in a number of instances in the USA when several notorious spies were learnt to have passed the test with flying colours. Interested readers can read more about it from our book '**Intelligence and Security Management**'.

Because there is no characteristic physiological response associated with lying, it is not possible to ask a person to answer a relevant question about an alleged misdeed (e.g., "Did you shoot so-and-so IPS officer because he was so dumb and irritating?"), record nervous system reactions, and make a determination of truthfulness. Polygraphy has therefore attempted to circumvent this problem by including in addition to a relevant question, a comparison question that is also used to elicit physiological reactions (typically electrodermal activity, blood pressure, and respiration). William G. Iacono, in his paper "Forensic 'Lie Detection': Procedures Without Scientific Basis," has undertaken a critical overview of the scientific status of the Control Question Test (CQT). Examples of control questions include "Have you ever hurt someone to get revenge?", or "Have you ever lied to a person in a position of authority?" The theory of the CQT assumes that it is highly likely that you have hurt someone or lied to an authority figure, so these questions will provide an example of what your physiological reactions to lies look like.

CQT theory further assumes that innocent people, because they are being truthful when they answer relevant questions "no," will be relatively un-aroused by these questions. For the CQT to be valid, two assumptions must hold. The first requires innocent individuals to be more responsive to control than relevant questions. The second requires guilty persons to respond more intensely to relevant than control questions. The plausibility of both of these assumptions is easily challenged. Iacono has shown that the CQT is based on an implausible set of assumptions that makes it biased against innocent individuals and easy for guilty persons to defeat using countermeasures.

8.3.3 *The Utter Irrationality and Illegality of the Finger Test for Rape*

This test is not mere stupidity; but an outright atrocity based on gross ignorance. And yet generations of police officers have been deriving perverse pleasure in getting this test conducted on living as well as dead women that have remained buried for four months under wet ground! In this atrocious practice, the examining doctor notes the presence or absence of the hymen and the size and the so-called laxity of the vagina of the rape survivor. The finger test is supposed to assess whether the woman is "virgin" or "habituated to sexual intercourse." Yet it does none of this. Contrary to common misconceptions, the hymen is a flexible membrane that partly covers the vaginal opening and does not seal it like a door. Hence the notion that there was no rape if there is no "broken" hymen is utterly false. Conversely, a hymen can have an "old tear" and its orifice may vary in size for many reasons unrelated to sex, so examining it provides no evidence for drawing conclusions about "habituation to sexual intercourse." Whether the vagina admits one finger or to fingers is pure bullshit. In the first place, this does not take into account the inherent elasticity of the vagina and which may be vastly different in different women. Secondly, when they say finger—what is the thickness they mean—fingers come in great variety.

Secondly, even for a woman who is admittedly used to thousands of intercourses, the extent to which the vagina would be stretched in intercourse depends on the girth of the penises used for intercourse. Now penises also come in a great variety. How much a vagina would be stretched would also depend on the girth of penis used therein. Obviously, there cannot be any quantitative standards. Hence the practice has rested upon pure nonsense. Now you can understand the comments that we had made in respect of the farcical post-mortem that was got conducted on the dead bodies of the two women in the Shopian case which had remained buried for four months under rainy ground and the team of doctors which exhumed the bodies for post-mortem went on to pronounce judgement on whether they were raped or not! This farce of the finger test needs to be demolished thoroughly because it has got both ethical and legal implications.

The ethical issue is that the doctors keep the victim in the dark about what they are to do. Since doctors tend to seek blanket consent for the forensic examination as a whole, and not to mention the finger test specifically, many survivors have little understanding of what the test entails; what information is collected for what ends; and the implications of refusing to undergo a forensic examination or any part of it—including the risk of appearing to hide information. A report that identifies an unmarried girl or woman as allegedly "habituated to sexual intercourse" attaches extreme stigma to her, compounding the considerable stigma unmarried women already face when reporting rape, and adding to a general stereotype about sexually active women. Furthermore, the question of whether a woman has had any previous sexual experience has no bearing on whether she consented to the sexual act under consideration.

The legal issue is that the whole thing is farcical ab initio. In **State of UP vs. Pappu @ Yunus and Anr.** [AIR 2005 SC 1248], the Court held that a prosecutrix complaining of having been a victim of an offence of rape is not an accomplice after the crime. There is no rule of law that her testimony cannot be acted upon without corroboration in material particulars, for the reason, that she stands on a much higher pedestal than an injured witness.

The Supreme Court while dealing with the issue in **State of Uttar Pradesh vs. Munshi** [AIR 2009 SC 370], had expressed its anguish and held that even if the victim of rape was previously accustomed to sexual intercourse, it cannot be the determinative question. Even if the victim had lost her virginity earlier, it can certainly not give a licence to any person to rape her. It is the accused who was on trial and not the victim. So as to whether the victim is of a promiscuous character is totally an irrelevant issue altogether in a case of rape. Even a woman of easy virtue has a right to refuse to submit herself to sexual intercourse to anyone and everyone, because she is not a vulnerable object or prey for being sexually assaulted by anyone and everyone.

In **Narender Kumar vs. State (NCT of Delhi)** [AIR 2012 SC 2281], the Supreme Court dealt with a case where the allegation was that the victim of rape herself was an unchaste woman, and a woman of easy virtue. The court held that so far as the prosecutrix is concerned, mere statement of prosecutrix herself is enough to record a conviction, when her evidence is read in its totality and found to be worth reliance.

In **Narayanamma (Kum) vs. State of Karnataka and Ors.** [(1994) 5 SCC 728], the Apex Court had held that fact of admission of two fingers and the hymen rupture does not give a clear indication that prosecutrix is habitual to sexual intercourse... The factum of admission of two fingers could not be held adverse to the prosecutrix, as it would also depend upon the size of the fingers inserted. In **State of Karnataka vs. Muniyappa and others** [(1994) 5 SCC 728, para. 4(iv)], the Supreme Court called it hypothetical.

The most common descriptions of findings from finger tests in medico-legal reports are: "two fingers admitted," "two fingers easily admitted," or "two fingers not easily admitted. In some reports these types of comments are combined with observations about whether the tear of the hymen is "old." Some doctors describe the vagina using different phrases such as "patulous vagina" or "distended vagina." These findings are then used to give opinions about whether the rape survivor was "habituated," "used to," or "accustomed to" sexual intercourse. The descriptions are so ridiculous that in some cases, the Courts had to point out that the gang rape itself could have caused the doctor to conclude that the girl or woman was "habituated" to sex. In **Uday Narayan Jana vs. State of West Bengal** [2007 (1) CHN 258], the Court noted that "habituation" to sex was evidence of "mass scale violation" against the survivor. In **Harpal Son of Om Prakash Yadav and Dr. Ram Niwas son of Bharat vs. State of Uttar Pradesh** [June 8, 2007], the defence had argued that the medical testimony indicated that there was an old tear and that two fingers had passed. The Court, however, reasoned that the "old tear" finding was probably because of a 10-day delay in conducting the forensic examination and that two fingers passed easily because the survivor was gang-raped.

In April 2013, a Division Bench of the Apex Court [in re **Lillu @ Rajesh and another Appellants vs. State of Haryana**, Criminal Appeal No(s). 1226 of 2011)] came down heavily on this atrocious practice and ruled that it "violates the privacy, physical and mental integrity and dignity" of rape victims. "This test, even if the report is affirmative, cannot ipso facto, give rise to presumption of consent," the bench of Justices B. S. Chauhan and F. M. I. Kalifulla ruled. "Medical procedures should not be carried out in a manner that constitutes cruel, inhuman or degrading treatment," the SC said.

What is most lamentable is that the police leadership is blissfully unaware of these orders of the Apex Court and has still been subjecting women to this degrading 'test'. Remember, doctors in India are just practising doctors—they are not medical scientists and their knowledge of forensic medicine often does not go beyond the archaic book of Modi. They are admittedly dumb.

We are personally aware that in most cases police officers ask doctors to conduct the finger test. In many cases, the protocol of the stupid hospital itself includes this. In their utter imbecility, police officers start with a presumption that if the accused is not known to the woman, then the charge of rape could be correct, but where the man is known to the woman, it is usually not rape, and it is a case of false charge. What we wish to emphasize is that the police leadership is so intellectually bankrupt that in spite of overwhelming scientific evidence to the contrary, they never applied any mind of their own and waited for the Supreme Court to take a position on it. The question is why should we need the leadership then?

8.3.4 *The Essential Inaccuracy of the Diatom Test for Drowning*

Yet another massive fraud—a classic example of ignorance that pervades the doctors who have not read anything beyond J. L. Modi and the police leadership which has not studied anything at all! Diatoms are microscopic, unicellular algae found in all sources of fresh and salt water. They have a silica body that is hard, acid-resistant and can be seen using a microscope. Diatoms can enter the bloodstream of a drowning person if the lungs fill with so much water that the alveoli break. This allows the water (and any diatoms contained in it) into the bloodstream. Diatoms have been used for diagnostic test for drowning based on the hypothesis that unless victim was alive in water (i.e., circulation is functional), diatoms will enter the systemic circulation and be deposited in organs like the bone marrow, kidney and the brain—a long shot for someone who would die within four minutes!

The point to be noted is that the presence of diatoms in lung tissue alone cannot distinguish between drowning and immersion in the water after death. Diatoms have been found in the organs of individuals who had not drowned. One can also obtain diatoms by inhaling or digesting them, or by aspiration of water containing them. Diatoms can also be present in the air and enter the lungs by being inhaled—found in the environment such as building industry and on dusting powder for rubber gloves. Way back in 1963 itself, W. V. Spitz, at the Third International Meeting in Forensic Medicine, in London had shown that diatoms were plentiful in the air of Berlin. This means that one should test for both kidneys as well as bone marrow. Another basic limitation of the test comes on account of the low numbers of diatoms in some waters and the very small number of diatoms recovered from the body.

It is critical that control samples be processed to check for contamination which could be caused, for example, from diatoms in the reagents and the water used in the laboratory. Diatom may also enter the body through the gastro-intestinal tract with contaminated foods like salads and shell fish. Moreover, the morons never realized that the species of the diatom found in the body must be matched with the species found from the alleged site—and there are 15,000 species!

Moreover, most cops and dumb doctors are not aware that 10-15 percent of all cases of drowning are actually what is known as "dry drowning." This takes place when a small amount of water enters the larynx or trachea and causes a spasm of the larynx. The larynx becomes clogged by mucous, foam, and froth, and water never even enters the lungs. Hence the question of diatom does not even arise. We have never seen any doctor making a reference to dry drowning in any post-mortem report—indicating that they are actually unaware of it—once again a consequence of having read only Modi's book.

8.3.5 *The Farce of Gunshot Residue (GSR) Analysis*

Gunshot residue tests were based on the presumption that as a gun is discharged, the burning of the primer mixture (the mixture that, when the firing pin strikes it, ignites the propellant that eventually propels the projectiles) as well as the propellant, the gaseous products escape from the gun in the form of a vapour or "plume" through any available openings in the weapon. It is not a pure gas—being more like smoke, it has very small particles also in it. Some of these particles may settle onto the hands, clothing, and surfaces in the immediate proximity of the discharged weapon. This is loosely called GSR—gunshot residue; or FDR—firearm discharge residue. GSR tests have sought to analyze the GSR. ***Gunshot residue tests based on a chemical analysis have been scientifically proved to be highly unreliable giving both, a large number of false positives as well as false negatives.*** International forensic experts have therefore abandoned them as inherently unreliable. ***The FBI stopped using them and announced so in March 2006 itself.*** In the case of **Owens vs. Russell** [November 7, 2006, California, 2006 WL3227755], firearms expert Don Dunbar testified that the Department of Justice no longer uses GSR testing because it is not reliable. The Court accepted it. ***The fact that the Indian FSLs are still using them only shows how miserably they have failed in updating their knowledge.***

A. J. Schwoeble and David L. Exline, in their celebrated work, 'Current Methods in Forensic Gunshot Residue Analysis' conclude that all chemical tests in this regard are inherently unreliable. The so-called dermal nitrate test or the paraffin test was discredited decades ago—the reason is that in addition to gunshot residue, nitrates are commonly found in many materials that could be found on the hands, including tobacco, cosmetics, fertilizers, bleaching agents, leguminous plants and urine. In connection with the assassination of J. F. Kennedy, the Warren Commission concluded that the test was 'completely unreliable'. The Interpol Conference in Paris in 1968 had officially concluded that the paraffin test should no longer be used. In their excellent review article 'Gunshot Residue Analysis: A Review, B. Caddy and H-h Meng categorically state that because of its unreliability, the paraffin test has been abandoned universally by forensic scientists. Does it not disgust you that the stupid Indians use it even now?

Another traditional test for finding gunshot residue, the modified Griess test, often fails because it lacks specificity. The so-called Harrison and Gilroy Method looks for the metallic elements lead (Pb), barium (Ba) and antimony (Sb). However, it was pointed out that they are used extensively in numerous applications in the commercial world—they are found in scores of innocuous things including storage batteries; solder; bearing metals; gasoline; paint; cable coverings, glass; matches; dyes; pyrotechnics; brake pads; inks; insecticides; and leather tanning.

The only tests with some degree of reliability are those based on Scanning Electron Microscopy/Energy Dispersive Spectroscopy; Flameless Atomic Absorption Spectrophotometry; Graphite Furnace Atomic Absorption Spectroscopy; Neutron Activation Analysis; High-Performance Liquid Chromatography; Gas Chromatography/Mass Spectrometry; Inductively Coupled Plasma-Mass Spectroscopy; and Capillary Electrophoresis. We must emphasize that even they are not foolproof. In **State vs. Glover** [2010-Ohio-4112], in the USA, a three-judge bench noted on the expert testimony of Dr. John Nordby that even Atomic Absorption Spectroscopy (AAS) gave dubious results and that AAS testing provides merely elemental composition results for gunshot residue, but is subject to false positive test results as they are obtained in numerous other products as well. C. A. Grove et al. have pointed out that even in respect of SEM, analysts "arbitrarily" choose a certain number of points of similarity for identification, because no consensus exists to dictate a number. In respect of Neutron Activation Analysis also, it was pointed out in a study for the US Department of Justice, that Neutron Activation Analysis also cannot detect lead (Pb). In a double-murder case, the Minnesota court in **State of Minnesota vs. Jason Moua** [K5-05-7335, July 7, 2006], threw out the gunshot residue evidence the police had produced. The court recorded that they lack scientific backing and had no place in a courtroom.

Moreover, since the particles do not adhere to the surfaces with any significant adhesive force, there is always a very strong possibility of cross-contamination. Most dumb police officers think that the doctor who takes the swab in the hospital does wear gloves and hence there is no question of contamination. This is both incorrect and a terrible mistake. The question is what happened to the subject before he appeared before the doctor. A study reported in 2000 by Debra Kowal and Steven Dowell at the Los Angeles county coroner's department showed that it was possible to be contaminated by being in the vicinity of a discharged firearm; touching various surfaces; and even from police vehicles. *In other words, at the very best also, all that positive GSR results can show is that GSR is present – not how those particles came to be there.*

8.3.6 *Bullet Matching and Ballistics Debunked Completely*

This is yet another fraud which has survived since long. Sydney Smith (we do not hope but presume that someone in the police leadership might have heard his name) was a well-meaning man but unfortunately, was no scientist—he was just a cop. You should not expect him to create a science! In this business, a lab technician examines two spent bullets under a microscope to compare striations caused by the grooves in the gun's barrel. If the bullets show similar striations, a "match" is declared. If one bullet came from a known gun, the other bullet is "matched" to that firearm and the technician will testify the bullet must have been fired by that gun. So is the case with ballistics.

A subsection of tool-mark analysis, ballistics matching is predicated on the theory that when a bullet is fired, unique marks are left on the slug by the barrel of the gun. Consequently, two bullets fired from the same gun should bear the identical marks. How simple! And how wrong! Marks or "striations" on bullets are not necessarily unique to a specific firearm in the sense that other guns could also have similar features, and visually matching them, even with costly Comparison Microscopes, does remain a subjective process. There are no accepted standards for what constitutes a match between bullets or between tool marks. An examiner may offer an opinion that a speciûc tool or ûrearm was the source of a speciûc mark when "sufficient agreement" exists in the pattern of two sets of marks, but there is no precise definition for that statement.

The fundamental issue is that "the validity of the fundamental assumptions of uniqueness and reproducibility of firearms-related tool marks has not yet been fully demonstrated." As the NAS observed, a great deal of research is still needed to scientiûcally determine the degree to which ûrearms-related tool marks are unique or even to quantitatively characterize the probability of uniqueness. The NAS also found there have been no scientific studies to answer questions regarding variability, reliability, repeatability, or the number of correlations needed to achieve a given degree of conûdence.

8.3.7 *The Hoax of Comparative Bullet Lead Analysis*

For nearly five decades, the so-called forensic experts testified about comparative bullet lead analysis (CBLA), a technique that was first used in the investigation into President Kennedy's assassination. CBLA compares trace chemicals found in bullets at crime scenes with ammunition found in the possession of a suspect. The analytical techniques included first, neutron activation analysis (NAA), and then inductively coupled plasma-atomic emission spectrometry (ICPAES) to determine the concentrations of seven selected elements—arsenic (As), antimony (Sb), tin (Sn), copper (Cu), bismuth (Bi), silver (Ag), and cadmium (Cd)—in the bullet lead alloy of both the crime scene and the suspect's bullets. The technique was not seriously challenged until a retired FBI examiner, William Tobin, began questioning the procedure in scientific and legal journals and in court testimony as well. As a result, the FBI asked the NAS to review the technique.

Neutron activation analysis etc. techniques per se were high-tech but the underlying premise that bullets with similar chemical make ups must have come from the same box of ammunition was found to be questionable. It was found that the tracing a bullet back to a specific box of ammunition is absolutely unreliable as there are great manufacturers' variations in packaging and frequency and range of distribution. The NAS report showed that millions of bullets have the same chemical composition, rendering CBLA useless as a forensic tool. **The 2004 NAS report led the FBI to completely abandon comparison (or comparative) bullet lead analysis, which had held sway for nearly 50 years.**

8.3.8 *The Joke of Handwriting Comparison*

Handwriting comparison is so unscientific that little needs to be said about it. Handwriting from the same individual can be naturally inconsistent depending on the position in which the hand is with respect to the paper (the writing is different if the paper is not at the usual height; also its angle and so on); the type of pen used (one produces dramatically different handwriting with a fountain pen the nib of which presents a directional writing surface against the omni-directional surface of a ballpoint pen); whether the man and the paper are on a moving platform (try writing in a car); and several such factors. Hence determining whether a comparison represents two different people is nothing but pure bullshit.

8.3.9 *Bite Marks, Ear Prints, and Lip Prints Do Not Tell Anything*

Yet another great fraud being perpetrated in the name of forensic science sans any scientific basis—for years people did not realize that bite marks are not so exact or precise that would lend itself to any meaningful comparison. Moreover, they change over time and are distorted due to factors like swelling and healing. In any case, as is the position with fingerprint analysis, the assumption behind bite mark comparisons that every person's dental characteristics are unique has not been adequately scientifically studied or scrutinized. ***In any case, the farce of forensic odontology was exposed when two men who were sent to death row on the basis of bite mark testimony were exonerated by DNA evidence***! One of those cases involved Ray Krone, who was convicted in 1991 of murdering a Phoenix, Arizona cocktail waitress and sentenced to death. The evidence against him included a bite mark on the victim's breast that supposedly matched Krone's teeth. Krone was exonerated by DNA a decade later and released in 2002. Krone's attorney, Christopher Plourd busted the farce further. He hired a private investigator who contacted Dr. West and sent him photos from the victim in Krone's case, telling him they were from an unsolved murder in a different case. The investigator also provided a dental mould of his own teeth, which he told Dr. West were from the prime suspect. Two months later West presented detailed results of his research—that the dental mould was a match to the bite marks in the photos! Ear prints and lip prints are even more hopeless.

8.3.10 *The Fraud of Forensic Speech Science*

Anders Eriksson and Francisco Lacerda have shown in their celebrated paper 'Charlatanry In Forensic Speech Science: A Problem To Be Taken Seriously' that while two types of 'deception' or 'stress detectors' (euphemisms to refer to what quite clearly are known since long as 'lie detectors'), are claimed to be based on voice analysis but they found no scientific evidence to support the manufacturers' claims. Such devices are also known as psychological stress evaluators (PSE) or 'emotion analyzer' etc. Not only that there is no scientific evidence of their claims, the companies are guilty of dishing out pseudo-scientific mumbo-jumbo. Their research found that these machines perform at nothing but chance level when tested for reliability. The morons among Indian police leadership often fall for such fancy things because they do not know a word more than what the vendors present before them.

8.3.11 *Functional Magnetic Resonance Imaging Busted*

The latest fraud in the lie detector business is functional magnetic resonance imaging (fMRI), which is being pushed by two private companies, No Lie MRI and Cephos Corp. The technique uses MRI scans and blood oxygen levels to display which parts of the brain are being used and to what degree they are used when people respond to questions. A strong critique of the pseudo-scientific nature of the technique can be found in an article titled "Playing Devil's Advocate: The Case Against fMRI Lie Detection," published in the February 2008 issue of Legal and Criminological Psychology and in a 2009 article in 'Perspectives on Psychological Science' by Ed Vul. In one amusing 2008 study, neuroscientist Craig Bennett took an Atlantic salmon to a lab at Dartmouth University and used fMRI to study it while it was shown a series of photographs. The fMRI data indicated activity in the area of the fish's brain, despite the fact that the salmon was "not alive at the time of scanning."

8.3.12 *Hair and Fibre Analysis had Always Been Wrong*

Popularized in fiction by Sherlock Holmes, hair comparison became popular in real life by the 1950s and carried almost a poetic value in courts. In reality, it is as much a hoax as other so-called forensic techniques. You see, you can identify whether the hair is animal or human; whether it is from the scalp, limbs or pubic area; whether it is from a discernible race (such as blond or black); whether it is dyed, bleached or otherwise treated; whether it is cut, forcibly removed or shed naturally; but there is no way you can tell that the hair is from Mr. A or Miss B. There is simply no scientific reason to even suspect that hair and fibre can be identified to one source. Hair comparisons can be confirmed only by mitochondrial DNA analysis. Fibre analysis has the same infirmities—in fact, even worse. You can identify the type of fibre, but how the hell can you ever say that this fibre came only from the shirt which you were wearing that day and not from any other source?

8.3.13 *Arson Investigation Found Unscientific*

There are not many pyromaniacs in India but the Western world has many of them—even Guy d'Maupassant wrote beautiful stories about them. That explains their fascination with arson investigation. With greater understanding of fire science, it stands busted now. For example, for many years arson investigators testified that the presence of glass with spider-web-like cracks at the scene of a fire indicated the presence of an accelerant, proving arson. It has now been proven that such "crazed glass" can be caused by water—e.g., from fire hoses—quickly cooling heated glass. Similarly, no accelerant is needed to melt aluminium or cause charring under an aluminium threshold, since wood fires alone can reach temperatures of more than one thousand degrees.

8.3.14 *Dog Scent Evidence has been Outright Deceit*

Aaah, the universally-loved *kutta,* so dear to cops whose intellectual capacities do not exceed those of the poor canines! We are also ardent dog-lovers but we love them as companions and not as devices that would solve our criminal cases! Nothing could be more primitive than this—the poor animal's process of picking up and matching scents is fraught with so many vulnerabilities that the whole thing is reduced to nothing but farce. We have ourselves tested scores of dogs that have won medals in Police Duty Meets. For one of the great explosive sniffers once we dug up seven holes in an area of the size of a badminton court and buried explosive in one of them, the rest being dummies. The poor dog went and sat at each one of them! Another champion once made one of us trek six miles through open country (where there was little possibility of scents getting mixed up) and yet led to an absolutely wrong place. *Lawrence J. Meyers, associate professor of animal behaviour at the Alburn University College of Veterinary Medicine, has disclosed that often when a dog is claimed to have identified a suspect, the poor animal is picking up a subtle signal from the handler or detectives – in many other cases, the swatch samples are contaminated.*

8.3.15 *The Great Farce of Narco-Analysis*

Narco-analysis is a farce that was debunked all over the world decades ago. It was debunked way back in 1951 itself during the experiments conducted at Yale University by J. M. MacDonald. Joost Meerloo of the Columbia University debunked it again in 1956, and then others followed. There is a vast body of scientific research that has conclusively proved that narco-analysis cannot ferret out the truth from the depths of the mind of a determined subject. Yet in this country, the police and the intelligence agencies still do it and the media regards it as the ultimate truth—simply because all of them are dumb.

For those ignoramuses in the police leadership who would not know, we must inform that on May 5, 2010, in the case of **Smt. Selvi and Ors. vs. State of Karnataka** [Criminal Appeal No. 1267 of 2004] dealing a major blow to the morons in the investigating agencies, a three-judge Bench of the Supreme Court declared as "illegal" the use of narco-analysis, brain-mapping and polygraph tests on suspects. Narco, polygraph or brain-mapping ('Brain Electrical Activation Profile') tests cannot be conducted on any person, whether an accused or a suspect, without their consent, the SC said. The impugned techniques cannot be read into the statutory provisions which enable medical examination during investigation in criminal cases, i.e. the Explanation to Sections 53, 53-A and 54 of the Code of Criminal

Procedure, 1973. The results obtained from each of the impugned tests bear a 'testimonial' character and they cannot be categorized as material evidence. "We are of the considered opinion that no individual can be forced and subjected to such techniques involuntarily, and by doing so it amounts to unwarranted intrusion of personal liberty," the bench headed by Chief Justice K. G. Balakrishnan and comprising Justices R. V. Raveendran and J. M. Panchal said. The Apex Court said that involuntarily subjecting an accused, a suspect or a witness to such techniques violates Article 20 (3) of the Constitution, which prohibits self-incrimination. Forcing an individual to such methods of investigation violates the scheme of legal process, it said, adding that even if such tests are taken voluntarily then also results cannot be used as evidence unless corroborated by other evidence because the subject does not exercise conscious control over the responses during the administration of the test. However, any information or material that is subsequently discovered with the help of voluntary administered test results can be admitted, in accordance with Section 27 of the Evidence Act, 1872.

This was a landmark judgement as the imbeciles in the police leadership have been abusing such tests basically with an eye on getting some cheap popularity in the media. No example of this nonsense could be better than the Aarushi murder case where it was conducted on three of the accused, namely, Krishna, Raj Kumar and Vijay Mandal (compounder/domestic helps). The stupid test proved to be CBI's undoing in the case against these three. Though they had reportedly admitted to have killed Aarushi and Hemraj in the narco test, the case was still thrown out of the court because the CBI was unable to find any corroborative evidence to back the test report. As we are all aware, the CBI finally charged none but the very parents of Aarushi and who, even to a fresh recruit police officer should have appeared to be the prime suspects. There is no need for us to conjecture on the motives of the cops in doing so. Intelligent readers can guess it very well themselves. Rank incompetence is one reason. The desire to get cheap publicity is another. Readers may recall that a leading news channel had even aired dramatized videos of the narco test conducted on one of the accused—the dumb public had just lapped it up—the baritone voice of the cop asking questions like *'haan to Krishna batao tab tumne kya kiya tha'*. From a professional point of view this raises serious suspicions that the questionnaire might have been dubiously framed to implicate the accused. That it debunks narco-analysis is obvious. This episode also exposes the class bias which the police officers harbour against the poorer people.

In 1943, J. Stephen Horsley had happened to observe that persons who were under the influence of narcotics were uninhibited, talkative, and answered all questions that were asked of them. He jumped to coin the term 'narco-analysis'. These days, narco-analysis involves the practice of administering barbiturates or certain other chemical substances, most often Pentothal Sodium, to lower a subject's inhibitions, in the fond hope that the subject will more freely share information and feelings. These are the substances that have been immortalized in popular fiction as the so-called 'Truth Serum'. The very term 'truth serum' is a misnomer because the drugs used are not serums and in any case, they do not bring out the truth.

Narco-analysis presumes that a man's brain is like the hard disk of a computer in which information is stored but the conscious mind or the 'will' of the man exercises 'access control' over the information. That is to say, the man will let out only what his conscious mind wishes. If his conscious control is somehow removed or weakened, such as under the influence of alcohol or a hypnotic drug, this access control will be removed or weakened and he will let out everything. This is an ages old belief and that's how we have had the Roman saying 'veritas in vino', that is, 'in wine lies the truth'. That is to say, the Romans believed that a man would speak the truth under the influence of wine. Needless to say, this is an utterly simplistic presumption without any scientific basis. Modern neurological research has proved that the human mind does not store information like the hard disk of a computer and neurons are not like sectors on a hard disk.

The human brain is actually an extremely complicated network of about a hundred billion neurons. Considered collectively, the network has electrical patterns meandering through it and individual signals are of little importance. Narco-analysis is based on an incorrect understanding of the subconscious mind. The subconscious is not merely what the conscious keep under access control. It comprises a million things, about which dear Dr. Freud had done considerable research. The subconscious contains, so to say, fantasies, imaginations, and permutations and combinations of the information stored. Everybody gets weird dreams at times—in fact sometimes so weird that one could be ashamed of having had such a dream when he wakes up. How do you get them? It is from this interplay of memories, suppressed desires, and images and so on—all in the so-called subconscious. When you dream, your subconscious is no longer under conscious control and that's how it gets complete freedom to indulge in the interplay. Precisely the same thing happens when you are drugged. As a result, what comes out is a similar product of an unimaginably complex interplay of all that is there. In fact the stronger the drugging, the more complex the interplay—that is, dreams of the weirdest kind. And these guys take it to be factual information!

8.3.16 *The Bigger Fraud of Brain-Fingerprinting and BEOS Profiling*

The so-called 'brain fingerprinting' is another farcical technique that hopes to determine whether specific information is stored in a subject's brain by measuring electrical brainwave responses to words, phrases, or pictures that are presented on a computer screen. The motivation behind brain finger-printing is one that has fascinated mankind since ages—the desire to 'read someone's mind'. This has been a tremendously popular motivation for the simple reason that it would yield terrific power in the hands of one who may accomplish it. Brain fingerprinting was sort of 'invented' by a scientist-turned-businessman Lawrence Farwell in the course of his doctoral work at the University of Illinois and he still remains its sole main proponent. No other scientist in the world supports him. There are numerous research publications in peer-reviewed journals in which the technique has been criticised. Some of them include the papers by Fox, Abdollah, and Rosenfeld. But the stupid idea has made a tremendous impact on the nincompoops in the media, the police and intelligence agencies who regard it as the ultimate discovery. In India this pseudo-science is being advocated by certain so-called 'forensic scientists', mainly from Bangalore, Gandhinagar and Bombay with the simple ulterior motive of garnering their seven seconds of publicity on the TV. We have a nexus of publicity-hungry pseudo-scientists, sensation-hungry media and dumb police officers who only want that they must have a single-shot magical solution to all their troubles of investigation.

The 'presumed' theory of brain fingerprinting is that the brain processes known and relevant information differently than it processes unknown or irrelevant information. The brain's processing of known information, such as the details of a crime stored in the brain, is supposed to be revealed by a specific pattern in the EEG (electroencephalograph). Farwell's brain fingerprinting originally used the well known P300 brain response to detect the brain's recognition of the known information. Later Farwell claims to have discovered the MERMER ("Memory And Encoding Related Multifaceted Electroencephalographic Response"), which includes the P300 and additional features and is reported to provide a higher level of accuracy than the P300 alone. It should be easy to see that it too, like narco-analysis, presumes a computer hard disk-like model of the brain in which information is neatly stored in different sectors and that the information is processed quite like a computer. Unfortunately, the brain does not function that simply and its functioning is infinitely more complex.

We may also mention that in India certain unscrupulous elements including a retired professor of clinical psychology and a company called Axxonet Solutions have taken the academic fraud further. They claim to have developed a computer programme called Neurosignature System or BEOS (Brain Electrical Oscillation Signature) Profiling. They say that it gives the signature in the brain of a specific activity. The work has not been peer-reviewed at all and hence does not deserve comments.

8.3.17 *Even DNA Fingerprinting is not Foolproof*

DNA fingerprinting is the only discipline among the forensic disciplines that faced rigorous scientific experimentation and validation prior to its use in forensic science. It is the only discipline which entailed the application of scientific methodology to determine whether or not the discipline was valid and reliable. In fact, DNA fingerprinting, in a way, called into question the reliability of other forensic sciences. And yet, scientists believe, it should not be taken as the ultimate in perfection. The Committee on DNA Technology in Forensic Science, Board on Biology, Commission on Life Sciences, National Academy of Sciences, USA, in its report 'DNA Technology in Forensic Science', admits that there is a lack of standardization of practices and a lack of uniformly accepted methods for quality assurance. Even for a country like the USA, it points out that the deficiencies are due largely to the rapid emergence of DNA typing and its introduction in the United States through the private sector.

As the technology developed in the United States, private laboratories using widely differing methods [single-locus RFLP (Restriction Fragment Length Polymorphism), multi-locus RFLP, and PCR (Polymerase Chain Reaction) began to offer their services to law-enforcement agencies. Each method has its own advantages and disadvantages, databanks, molecular-weight markers, match criteria, and reporting methods. DNA typing technology has developed without regulation of laboratories and their practices, public or private. A comprehensive quality-assurance programme, as they have recommended, must include elements that address education, training, and certification of personnel; specification and calibration of equipment and reagents; documentation and validation of analytical methods; use of appropriate standards and controls; sample handling procedures; proficiency testing; data interpretation and reporting; internal and external audits of all the above; and corrective actions to address deficiencies and weight their importance for laboratory competence. Nothing of this sort has been attempted in India simply because the people concerned including the police leadership are ignorant and the latter has no desire to apply any mind of their own.

Just for the knowledge of the ignoramuses, we must inform that errors can occur if DNA samples are damaged or contaminated from improper handling. Limited amounts or mixtures of DNA profiles can increase misinterpretation of results. In 2001, Kathryn Troyer, an Arizona crime lab analyst, was running a test on the state's DNA database when she happened across two entries that matched at 9 of the 13 locations on chromosomes (loci) that are commonly used to identify a person. Since the odds of a random 9-loci match between two unrelated people were estimated by the FBI as 1 in 113 billion, she assumed it was a duplicate entry. That belief was dispelled when she discovered that one person was black and the other white. Troyer then found dozens of similar 9-loci matches in Arizona's 65,493-profile DNA database.

Troyer's findings were a matter of significant concern. While labs in the US try to match 13 loci, DNA recovered from crime scenes may be degraded or damaged; thus, sometimes fewer than 13 loci are used for DNA matches. In the United Kingdom only 10 loci are required for a match. It surprised a lot of people because it had been common for experts to testify that a nine-locus match is tantamount to a unique identification. When word of Troyer's discovery got out, questions were raised about the accuracy of DNA match statistics. "Arizona searches" were performed in two other states pursuant to court orders. The searches of DNA databases in Illinois and Maryland turned up almost 1,000 additional matches with at least 9 loci. In the 220,000-profile Illinois DNA database, 903 nine-locus matches were found. In the case of **People vs. Wright** [2010 WL 1194903 (Ill.App. 1 Dist. 2010)], the court went on to reverse the conviction based on a 9-loci DNA match where the trial judge had refused to allow an Arizona-type search of the state's DNA database.

At the very least, the results of the "Arizona searches" have raised serious doubts about the statistical basis of DNA testing. Actually, this opened sort of floodgates. Dr. Itiel Dror of the University College London and a colleague at Boise State University in Idaho conducted an experiment in which they independently provided a mixed DNA sample from the victim, the defendant and other suspects in a real criminal case to 17 analysts. The result? One examiner said the defendant "could not be excluded" based on the DNA evidence. Four reported the results were inconclusive, while 12 said the defendant could be excluded. In the actual case, two prosecution experts had testified that the defendant, Kerry Robinson, charged in connection with a gang rape in Georgia, could not be excluded based on the DNA evidence. He was convicted. This shows how science must function—there are no ultimate truths—you must inculcate the habit of questioning everything, even if it enjoys the status of being sacred. If only the police leadership could understand this.

Ominously, in August 2009 it was reported that scientists in Israel were able to fabricate DNA evidence, including blood and saliva samples. Dr. Dan Frumkin, the lead author of an article on fabricating DNA evidence published in the February 2010 issue of Forensic Science International: Genetics claimed that if they could access a particular DNA profile in a database, they could make an artificial sample that would match it. In other words, you can just engineer a crime scene.

Chapter 9

The Absence of Integrity, Courage and Intellectual Honesty

9.1 Corruption, the Main Driving Force

At a conceptual level, corruption, though widely prevalent, is not a complicated matter. Millions of public servants in India could be corrupt. Police officers belong to the same milieu. Hence there is no surprise that they are also corrupt. Like everybody else, police officers are corrupt because they are greedy. It is simple cupidity. There is nothing called need-based corruption—that some civil servant in the past had happened to even mention this phrase was a terrible blunder—only dumb civil servants could commit that sort of blunder. ***The corruption of cops is, however, of greater importance because the police impact the lives of all of us, particularly the poor, in a very big way. It is a matter much more serious than corruption by other classes of public servants because the money which the cops make is often stained with blood and tears.***

It has been fashionable in academic circles to blame the corruption in the police on an organisational sub-culture. Often you would find expressions like 'police corruption in India is embedded in the culture and organisational norms that have encouraged and sustained venal practices'; mouthed at various forums. Beware of it. This is a very clever design of the police officers and their apologists to deflect blame. Even to speak of something called organisational sub-culture is a massive farce. The responsibility of any criminal act is that of the individual. If you live in an area where your neighbours often whistle at girls, does it mean that you should also whistle at them or does it give you any licence to do so? *All that can be said is that the system is tolerant of corruption in the sense that very few people are found punished for corruption, thereby engendering a notion that, at least in purely statistical terms, the chances of your getting caught are very poor and in all probability, you should sail through your three decades or so in the service.* But who is to be blamed for that? The system is an abstract entity—after all, it is the cops and the senior officers only who make up the system. *A tolerant system means that those who comprise the system are tolerant. They are tolerant by their own volition or design, not by any accident. They are corrupt because it suits them eminently; not because they fought any heroic battle against it and after having lost it, resigned themselves to their fate.* ***The police leadership has singularly failed in combating the menace of corruption because they do not have any will to do so—rather, they are actively involved in it.***

It pervades from the young entrants to the very top posts. Do not be under a fond impression that new entrants are impressionable kids of convent schools who get corrupted by the ambience of the police department. No, sir, by the time they enter service, their value system is already crystallized and hardened. *Most of them enter service with very clear objectives – that of making as much money as possible in the shortest amount of time. That's how you find even young ASPs and SPs getting occasionally caught by the Vigilance departments.* New entrants are as big crooks as their decrepit seniors. Just Google and you would get hundreds of stories about the hundreds of crores they have made. The DGP of a state was hassled on a TV show in which he had voluntarily agreed to participate. Referring to the enormous properties that he had created, they said, ***"Sir, you are not DG Police, you are DG Properties." Quite amusingly, he swallowed the insult.***

It needs no explanation that senior officers can never afford to claim that they were unaware of the corruption and other misdeeds of their subordinates. For if they do so, it would mean that they have been utterly blind. Hierarchy, in fact, is a convenient tool in the sense that it facilitates corruption. The SHO makes the money and passes on a percentage to his superiors. They do not have to shake their little fingers and get their share per police station. It suits them because all that they are obliged to do is to close their eyes to the misdeeds of the SHOs and his henchmen. They get their share by virtue of the posts they hold. *But this is not to mean that senior officers are happy being passively corrupt. There is another category of senior officers who are pro-actively corrupt.* They are more enterprising and do shake a leg or two to make some extra money.

These guys are on the lookout themselves and make money wherever they can. Wherever you find that the SP sahib, the DIG sahib or the IG sahib has a personal 'crime detection squad' (known by various names like 'intelligence cell' etc., and not always a declared affair), you can rest assured that he is an enterprising man. The squad members are trusted people who will extort money and get it to the man without the rest of the police force getting involved it—then the sahib grabs the entire booty instead of getting merely a share of it.

We would narrate an incident just to show how such enterprising officers work. There is a rural district with a large population of people of a certain community who work in the Gulf. Obviously, there is a thriving hawala racket because that's how they send money home. The money sent by them from the Gulf is delivered at the doorsteps of their people living in the villages in Indian currency. The hawala money is carried by couriers travelling in taxis or otherwise from a neighbouring district and it frequently runs to about Rs. 20-50 lakh at a time. Once an IG sahib's personal 'intelligence party' got information about such a movement. They, of course, never informed the DIG or the SP. The vehicle was intercepted by them alone. The IG sahib quietly pocketed some 24 lakhs out of the booty and splashed the recovery of the balance amount all over the local newspapers. The dumb journalists went gaga over the dashing IG sahib doing this daring job himself. The hawala operator could, of course, never claim that he had more money than what was shown. Even if he had claimed, who would have listened to him?

For any Indian who has not spent his life in a cocoon, we do not think that there is any need to describe the myriad ingenious ways in which the cops indulge in corruption. In fact, almost every single step of policing can be used for making money—ranging from investigation of cases, decision to arrest or not arrest a suspect, submit a chargesheet or close some pending investigation are all avenues of making money. Police have discretionary powers for almost everything they do and that is exploited to the fullest for making money. If we discuss that in greater detail, it might require a separate book. The mere fact of having been summoned to the police station is insulting for most middle class people. They would happily pay to avoid the insult. As you progress to other activities, the discretion; the stakes; and hence the money demanded increases. Getting the FIR registered is an uphill task. The SHO can very well argue that he would conduct some sort of preliminary inquiry before he registers the FIR. That inquiry may take an unknown length of time. This means that if he does not register the case, your immediate purpose is defeated. That's why people pay to get cases registered. Then the question of the sections being used arises. There is immense discretion here. Most people who give the complaints themselves are not knowledgeable in legal matters. This means that whatever they are saying would not fit *exactly* into the slots of various sections of the IPC or some other law—they are not expected to use a language which lifts the ingredients of the offence from the sections of law. This means that the SHO has discretionary powers. He has to decide what section would be, in his opinion, appropriate. That's where money comes in. Whether you are to be implicated in a 307 IPC (attempt to murder) case or a 326 IPC (grievous hurt) case, itself would yield a great deal of money. The cop is safe—he can always argue that it was his interpretation to use 326 instead of 307 and if the court disagreed, the court is very much empowered to try the accused under 307 IPC. The man who has paid the money to avoid 307 is happy with the temporary benefit—he would fight another battle in the court.

Having been given this much hint, now you can think of any part of the police work and it you would understand how it can be used to make money. The key is discretionary powers. If somebody has discretionary powers, rest assured that they will be abused. Whether it is checking of your driving licence, commercial vehicles, or whatever, they do make money in that. **Discretion is the font of corruption.** From this follows the corollary that if we have to reduce corruption, we must reduce the discretionary powers that are available with the police. All other measures would be merely cosmetic.

Police officers are known to demand money even for sanctioning casual leave and earned leave. When it comes to senior officers, they have discretion in transfers and postings and this has become an industry in itself whereat people make millions upon millions. Transfers and postings are known to have become an industry even in the armed forces where clever corrupt officers have gone to the length of asking the money to be paid to their relatives living in other states. In the normal course officers and men of the armed forces are likely to spend most of their lives in inconvenient 'hard' postings in Kashmir, the north-east or Naxal-affected areas. Hence, getting a 'convenient' posting often carries much money with it. A similar situation exists in large states also where life in certain districts in decidedly bad—even the avenues of corruption are limited in many backward places. Obviously, they detest such places. *That's why the police leadership starts seriously crying whenever such powers are sought to be 'usurped' (in their perception) by the political executive.*

And remember, when they lament the 'usurpation' of such powers, they always try to invoke the so-called 'independence' of police. The IPS officers do not have even the intellectual honesty to admit that what they are lamenting is really the loss of personal powers and income. ***Given the utterly unprofessional and in fact, even criminal record of the Indian police in the past 150 years and in which, we have very reason to believe that the senior leadership has had either actively colluded with the subordinates in all their misdeeds or was vicariously responsible for them. We do not think that the police leadership has any moral right to demand more independence.*** What moral right the senior officers have to complain that junior officers approach the politicians directly for transfers and postings? *They want the authority for transfers with them so that junior officers may kowtow before them instead of the politicians. There is nothing professional about the demand – no professional issue is involved.* They cannot claim that they know the professional mettle of the junior officers better and hence are more suited to decide on their postings.

Bullshit. Since when did they start bothering about professional matters and professional competence? In our 27 years of service in the IPS and several years before that in other departments, we have never had any occasion to find an ACR having been written objectively. ACRs are written in the most subjective manner and reflect only the personal likes, dislikes, idiosyncrasies, complexes and prejudices of the reporting officer. ACRs (or PARs) are now communicated and should push come to shove, we can produce several ACRs of several officers in support of the argument. Once there was an ADG level officer who wrote in the ACR of an IG that he has great professional knowledge but he thinks that he is the only font of knowledge! Poor fellow could not conceal his inferiority complex!

It has been complained that the politicians ring up the junior officers directly. But we are also aware of hundreds of instance where the DGPs ring up the SIs directly for outright illegal things without ever even informing the ADG, IG, DIG or the SP. In one instance in a state where a paramilitary force has had been deployed since decades and where once during a period of turmoil there were several police firings, the DGP of the state, in order to placate the politicians, rang up the SI directly and got a murder case registered against the paramilitary force with the entire hierarchy (including the DG Intelligence, IG Zone, DIG Range and the district SP) remaining blissfully unaware of it – they were in fact, sitting with the paramilitary officers all the while. ***Is there any single reason to suspect that the senior IPS officers would be just and professional in their decisions***

and the politicians would not be so? And should it be the case, why has the leadership not agitated against it all these 150 years? These guys are morally so bankrupt that they start cribbing only when it hurts their personal interests. They do not want the tyranny of the politicians to end; they want their own tyranny to continue instead. What the leadership across the country really laments on such occasions are the loss of their income in the transfer-posting industry and the power they could wield over their subordinates.

9.2 An Unholy Nexus that is Gang Raping the Country

Coming to the oft-discussed question of nexus, we maintain that anybody who still makes a reference to the Vohra Committee Report, is a kiddie. If he is still not able to see what has been right under his nose since so long, it can only mean that either he is telling a lie or he is blind. The Vohra Committee either suffered from lack of insight, or could not muster enough moral courage to speak out loud. To speak of a criminal-politician-police nexus is utterly simplistic and betrays a poor understanding of the dynamics of this country. ***The real nexus is that of politicians, bureaucrats (including police), criminals, businessmen, industrialists, and all those 'brokers' of power including the media houses and influential media persons. They have been systematically gang raping this country and its wealth. It is a win-win situation for all the parties concerned.***

Media people and the so-called academicians do not tire of talking of organised criminal gangs; criminalization of politics; politicization of criminals; corruption by politicians; criminals investing money in legitimate businesses; bureaucrats investing their ill-gotten wealth in legitimate businesses run by highly shady characters; industrialists; corporate lobbying, media manipulation; and businessmen tweaking the system at will for their personal gain and for the politicians. You have heard it all. All of them are true to some extent but not so important individually—they pale before what is happening now. The nexus mentioned above is one thing where the whole is much greater than the sum of its parts. There is only one loser in the game, the nation. Gone are the days when these guys generated wealth by some illegal methods. Now they have gone much higher. Now they are systematically looting the wealth of the nation. All these players help each other in ways so devious that volumes could be written on them. Earlier in the book, we have spoken of two things that make the police work, money and connection, recommendation or pressure. This nexus has both. That's how they have reduced the system to such a pathetic shape that it is extremely difficult to find an element of criminality in what they do. Readers may recall how the so-called

Radia tapes had exploded upon the national scene in 2010. The tapes seemed to expose them all; corporate houses, media personalities, media houses, politicians, and bureaucrats as integral parts of a nexus. In June 2013, according to a report in the *Times of India,* the CBI and the Income Tax department which jointly transcribed the tapes on the orders of the Supreme Court, eventually found no element of "criminality" in the transcripts of her 5851 conversations that were taped.

In July 2009, the **Supreme Court expressed deep concern** over the manner in which criminals were allowed to go scot-free by police. "What is happening in this country," exclaimed a Bench comprising Justices Dalveer Bhandari and A. K. Ganguly as it learned that Haryana police was yet to arrest a chartered accountant accused of defrauding more than a crore of rupees despite his anticipatory bail being rejected more than two months ago by the Punjab and Haryana High Court. Refusing to entertain chartered accountant Shubha Trimurthy's anticipatory bail plea, the Bench said, "You have evaded arrest for two months, you do not need protection from the court. You can manage without a court order." This sarcasm from the Bench explained its anguish over the manner in which such persons could manage to evade police for long periods. "Why have you approached the Supreme Court? Is it just to formalize a ritual," the Bench asked refusing to entertain arguments advanced by senior advocate K. T. S. Tulsi.

The police play their part in this nexus with great finesse and abject servility. When you think of the underworld, do not think merely of the stereotyped extortions, kidnappings, drug trafficking, human trafficking, and illegal arms. The police are very much involved in that but that still does not generate great money. The real big-money operations of the underworld, for example, are often a mix of legal and illegal activities, in which black money is converted into white and vice versa, and there are a number of players involved, including those whose responsibility it is to check such practices. It is for such activities that the collusion between the underworld and the police easily reaches the level of the two 'working together'. The nexus is not limited to bestowing mutual favours but extends to partnerships in carrying out all such activities for mutual financial gain which would, had the system been fair and impartial, not been permitted.

9.3 Kowtowing Before the Crimes of the Powerful

In 2004, in Bhawanipur village in Moradabad, Uttar Pradesh, 20-year-old Chetan eloped with Pinky, the daughter of an influential Yadav family. The boy belonged to the barber caste. The Tevatia Khap ordered that while the couple should be traced, Sia Dulari, Chetan's mother, should be raped turn-after-turn by the members of the Yadav family, since her son had dishonoured the Yadavs. Not only did they gang rape her, they burnt her alive.

In March 2009, Ved Pal, an Ayurvedic practitioner, married and eloped with Sonia, 22. When the Banawala Khap, under whose 'jurisdiction' Singhwala, Sonia's village is in heard about the marriage, they issued a decree stating that since the couple belonged to the same *gotra,* they were siblings and their marriage unholy. For the crime of "incest" and for dishonouring the community, the decree ordered that both be hunted down and killed. Ved Pal could not bear the injustice and put his hopes in the laws that are supposed to govern this land. He approached the Punjab and Haryana High Court and got a Court order for police protection. At 9 p.m. on July 23, Balwant Singh, the SHO of Narwana Sadar, and Suraj Bhan, a warrant officer of the High Court arrived along with a police party at Ved Pal's residence in Mataur village in Jind, Haryana. They promised to escort Ved Pal to Singhwala, where his wife Sonia was forcibly confined in her parents' house, in order to get her back.

As soon as he reached Singhwala, Ved Pal was attacked. He was dragged to the terrace in Sonia's house and stripped. His face and torso were beaten with sticks and his neck and shoulders were cut open with sickles and scythes. Suraj Bhan was pushed from the terrace, while, astonishingly, the 15 policemen fled. "Not a single bone in my son's body was left intact. They kept beating him long after he was dead," says Ved Pal's mother. Since then, Sonia has gone missing. Thankfully, Balwant Singh was suspended. On July 23, 2009, a man was lynched on the orders of the Sarv Khap Panchayat in Haryana's Jind district because his bride was from the same *gotra,* a lineage assigned to a Hindu at birth.

These are only a few of the scary stories. Khap panchayats are known to brazenly reject our Constitution and our laws. They are known to have ordered the assassination of couples who marry for love and snatched and sold the children of those who defied their rules. They have ordered the punitive gang rape and murder of mothers whose sons have eloped with another's daughter. A barbaric system that glorifies murder and lynching in the name of some self-proclaimed, self-defined 'honour' is ruling the roost and the police are behaving like Dhritarashtra. The question is what the police have done to stop this brazen mockery of law? Nothing, because they are scared! They cannot afford to claim that they did not act due to political pressures—they can't admit such things. They cannot claim that they were not aware of such things. They cannot claim that no complaint was lodged to them—even if no complaint is lodged, the law enjoins upon them to act suo motu too when they have credible information of a cognizable offence.

9.4 Cowards in Uniform

9.4.1 *Chronicles of Shame*

In March 2011, a police inspector Phool Mohammad was burnt alive by a mob after a man jumped to his death from an overhead water tank to protest alleged police inaction in a murder case in Sawai Madhopur district of Rajasthan. The mob torched his jeep with him inside. The remaining policemen had fled from the scene or, at least, did not do anything to save him from being lynched. The case was subsequently given to the CBI. Quite interestingly, the CBI arrested three persons for setting the SHO on fire, while a sub-inspector Sumer Singh, who had been placed under suspension after the incident, was charged with negligence in carrying out his duty and provoking the mob. The arrested sub inspector, Sumer Singh was deputed at Mantown police station and had allegedly produced false evidences after the SHO was burnt alive. When reports last came in July 2012, Circle Officer Mahendra Singh was absconding.

In July 2012 a married woman and her paramour were tied to a tree, stripped half-naked and severely beaten up for nearly three hours before a crowd of 1,000 people under orders of a caste panchayat at Sarada area in Udaipur district. The two were 'punished' for having illicit relations. The woman's husband himself stripped the woman and the youth. The police claimed that they came to know about the incident about 11.30 a.m. and a team was rushed there. But the fact is the police could not do anything. Acting fearlessly, the panchayat continued to discuss other penalties on the couple till late evening. Later the police rescued them and took them to Sarada police station. If they take the plea that the villagers surrounded them and started hurling stones, does it mean that in similar situations which may occur by the thousands in the country, the police would not do anything? Interestingly, the police said that 'they were trying to restore law and order.'

The **Special Court** which conducted the trial in the 26/11 case has criticised personnel of Azad Maidan police station, saying they acted in a "cowardly" manner and "ran away" instead of stopping the militants. Instead of coming to the aid of Additional Commissioner Sadanand Date, the officers from the police station possibly "ran away"—Judge M. L. Tahaliyani described it as "cowardliness and lack of devotion towards duty". The police station is at a stone's throw from Chhatrapati Shivaji Terminus and Cama Hospital where scores of people were killed. After firing indiscriminately on the passengers at CST, Kasab and Ismail had proceeded to Cama Hospital, and went up to the terrace. Date had rushed to the hospital after instructing Constable Suresh Kadam to go to the police station, collect some bulletproof jackets, weapons and ammunition, and come to the hospital. But, according to Kadam's testimony, he along with Senior Police Inspector Thorawade and four others went only up to the rear gate of the hospital in a Bolero jeep and did not venture further.

In August 2012 in Mumbai at Azad Maidan, a mob had gathered to protest against the atrocities on the Muslims in Assam and Myanmar. It turned violent and torched outdoor broadcasting vans, attacked media persons, molested women constables and tried to snatch arms from the police. Police were criticised for inaction when their comrades were being attacked and women police personnel were being molested. The excuse of the police was that any action on their part would have triggered more violence.

In the Assam riots of 2012, police were squarely blamed for being 'slow' in the first five days of riots. Readers may also recall the communal clash in Kosi Kalan town in Mathura district in 2012, where large scale vandalism, destruction and damage to properties to the tune of Rs. 50 crore crippled the town with no 'timely' strong measures from the police to control the same.

In Orissa, in September 2012, Congress workers clashed with police on M.G. Road while trying to picket the state Assembly building demanding resignation of the chief minister over the Coalgate row. One woman constable Pramila Padhi and inspector Anup Kanungo were seriously injured. The mob molested the woman cop. The cops had to hide behind police vehicles to shield themselves. A group of women constables was found hiding in a garage.

When Brahmeshwar Singh, founder of the dreaded upper caste militia Ranvir Sena, was shot dead by unidentified gunmen in Bhojpur district, Bihar in June 2012, his supporters went on a rampage. They set ablaze many vehicles, the circuit house building and the local block development officer's office and hurled stones at the Patna-New Delhi Rajdhani Express, shattering many of its window panes. When the SP, Arrah visited the spot, he was asked to leave and he did make a hasty retreat. Even the state's DGP was heckled by Brahmeshwar Singh's supporters. Over the next few days, the area witnessed a near total collapse of law and order and the abject surrender of the administration to the unruly mob. The breakdown of law and order affected Arrah, the road to Patna and Patna proper. A helpless administration was a mute witness to the wanton destruction of property and the police were criticised for merely making a video recording of the rioting. In May 2013, calling them "silent spectators", the trial court has severely criticized the role of Delhi Police during the 1984 anti-Sikh riots and blamed them for their "inaction" on the killings. The Court slammed the police for maintaining 'complete silence'.

9.4.2 *The Puerile Attempts to Justify Cowardice*

Cowardice is often sought to be passed off as exercising restraint. They say that it is their duty to show restraint and prevent the situation from worsening. We are personally aware of very senior IPS and IAS officers who have, in all seriousness, actually ordered that when faced with a violent mob that is attacking, hurting and murdering people as well as policemen, and burning public and private property, police should leave the place and retire to some safe place instead of opening fire on the people and may be killing them because it would not be politically expedient for the party in power. They said that even when the police stations were attacked, police vehicles burnt, or camps of paramilitary forces attacked, they should run away from the place—*gaadi ka kya hai, aur aa jaayegi*—that's what they argued. One chief minister expected the police to have a wrestling or kickboxing match with the rioters. He said that the police were at liberty to bash up the people, break their legs, but were not at liberty to open fire.

To say that firing became a taboo would be a gross under statement; it became the worst imaginable sin, a *mahapaatak*. Never mind that close to 2000 police personnel were injured (nearly one-third of them grievously); scores of vehicles damaged; and public property worth crores destroyed—you were not supposed to fire because somebody thought (albeit wrongly) that would have adverse ramifications for him (not for the state or the nation) politically. (*That the legal knowledge of a chief minister is poor can be understood. That he was fulminating or indulging in some public posturing is also understandable. In spite of all this, even he cannot be pardoned if he orders so in writing. But his loyal dogs in the IPS cannot be pardoned for actually ordering such unprofessional and illegal thing in writing. During a particular period when a border state was witnessing rioting on an unprecedented scale, the DGP of the state had gone to the extent of issuing another written order that the escort personnel of senior officers shall not carry weapons lest they open fire! Outrageous, but true. We obviously have evidence of all this and can give to anybody in person who dares doubt this.*) Apologists of the cowards argue that any action would have aggravated the situation. You also hear platitudes like: "Had the police used even mild force on protesters, it could have triggered a chain of violence with graver consequences. Maintaining restraint was the wisest thing to do for the police in a situation when people were high on emotion". *In effect, this means that if the people are high on emotion, they get a licence to commit mayhem. Some senior officers, in their infinite wisdom, advise that the police should take photographs and make videos of the rioters so that they may be prosecuted later. This led some newspapers to lampoon the Indian Police Service (IPS) as Indian Photographer Service.*

For the Azad Maidan violence, the cops tried to confuse the issue by claiming that there was not enough intelligence. Even if it is accepted that there was not adequate intelligence, should they have not acted on the spot? Do they act only when they have been forewarned? Does this mean that they cannot cope with the unexpected? We may also accept that the cops must remain calm under provocation. But does this mean that they should not react at all even as the law is being brazenly violated? If we have to have only calm people with Bhagwan Buddha-like countenance in the police, we might as well disband the police. Well, if they argue that backing down is not cowardice and it is 'tactical retreat' for the time being, we do not have any problem. But we do have a serious problem if they do it arbitrarily. ***Let the people of this country decide and let them make their elected representatives legislate on the subject—exactly defining the myriad situations when the police must use force and the situations when it must retreat temporarily or permanently. The point being made is that the cops are nobody to decide it on their own, and that too on a highly selective basis to please the powers-that-be.***

The impression which the people of this country have gained as a result of this sort of cowardly (or selectively cowardly) behaviour of the police across the country is that the mardanagi, the zulm of the police is for the poor and they start running away when face with really violent people. This has fostered a belief that you have only to muster sufficient numbers, a show of aggression or both and the police would skunk away in some corner—a sure recipe for promoting lawlessness in the country. The critical issue is not that at times the police act in a sissy-like fashion—well, if the people of this country want so, they are free to do so. The critical issue is when and how do the police decide that this time they have to behave like sissies and when they have to behave like goons—they cannot be allowed to decide it in a whimsical manner or in a manner which suits their vested interests or the vested interests of those with whom they are in an unholy nexus. ***The police leadership has never even dwelt on the issue.***

Referring to the deliberate inaction of the police over the rioting that had followed Brahmeshwar Singh's murder, we would like to quote from an article of a former IPS officer Sh. Manoje Nath 'What Law/Whose Order?': "His theory is rooted in the curtailment of the role of police merely to its detective functions of collecting evidence in the form of videographing the vandals and arsonists and prosecutes them later. Do not people have a stake in public property? Would the citizens be put to notice that they should mind their own lives and property? Will police now abjure their preventive responsibility in law to "interpose", in order to prevent the commission of a cognizable offence?...It is an open invitation for militarization of various groups in our fractious society...I would have used this occasion to make the honest confession that policing is about keeping the governments and other powerful groups happy; people are incidental to policing."

9.5 Police Reforms: A Covert Desire to Wield Power Without Accountability

9.5.1 *The Desire to Seek Simple Solutions to Complex Problems*

Indians have an extremely old habit of looking for a single-shot solution—one thing that would solve all the problems. Why? The reason is that traditionally, the Indians are utterly incapable of rational thought. In fact, complexity frightens them. They do not understand that there are no simple solutions to complex problems. Our overwhelming collective desire is to somehow latch on to a simple solution to complex problems. It reflects in every walk of life. That's how hundreds of thousands of Indians rooted for whatever they had understood of something called the Jan Lokpal—the desire was both simple and overwhelming: get the Jan Lokpal and India would be rid of all its problems. We want our leaders also that way. He must be like a prince with a flaming sword, riding a white charger and delivering justice left right and centre.

That's why even in 2013, politicians still hold '*janata durbars*', where the prince is supposed to deliver instant justice, solve all the problems of the *fariyaadi* with one word or one stroke of his pen—by God, if that were possible, we could dispense with the leviathan of the bureaucracy and save trillions. The *janata* also wants it that way only. It is actually a simple throwback to our deeply-rooted collective subconscious desire for a feudal system where the *maharaj, the jille ilaahi, the huzoor, the mai-baap or the maalik* was the single-window solution to all problems. Because the feudal lord was the problem-solver, the trouble-shooter, the care-giver, and the punisher all rolled into one, he acquired a larger than life status. Since whatever he did or was supposed to do was rather unusual and beyond the capacity of the *aam aadami,* it was natural for them to expect that he would have certain quirks in his personality—some idiosyncrasies; fierce anger; unusual eating habits; abnormal sexual appetite; strange hobbies; strange manner of speaking; the works. Now you can understand why Gabbar Singh was made to behave the eccentric way he did or why Marlon Brando, the Godfather spoke in that hoarse voice with slow raspiness. All such things became matters of fascination for the *aam aadami.* Many of them, in due course, came to associate the work and accomplishments of the 'master' with his queer personality traits. Eventually, it became a part of the collective Indian psyche.

A similar adulation was found for the top servants of the feudal lords also because the way to the lord was through them. Precisely for this reason the Indians even now appreciate those officers who do only those things which will generate some cheap publicity—in other words, some queer behaviour. A senior-IPS officer who was very keen on doing what should have been done by a traffic police havildar or sub-inspector in the matter of removing wrongly parked vehicles was raised to the status of a super cop by the dumb media persons. A young IPS officer who patrolled a university like the Banaras Hindu University on a horse along with some ADM (City) was highly admired by the media—what a smart officer! A district collector who did nothing else except diligently attending all the public functions in the district ranging from the inauguration of *paan* shops to paining competitions in primary schools for girls was highly popular. A chief medical officer who loved to crack adult jokes was regarded a great doctor.

That's why we, as a nation, are so obsessed with child prodigies. The moment the media spots one, the clarion call goes up: 'Yes, that's the Indian child prodigy and now with his help India would regain its lost glory.' You may recall how we 'created' a child prodigy and sent him to Germany to interact with Nobel laureates—we ended up making an ass of ourselves as the poor fellow was accused of mouthing jargon which he did not understand. For this guy, we even claimed that his father was some self-styled expert in eugenics who had fed a special raw vegetables-only diet and some special zinc supplements to programme his wife into producing a genius. Well, well. You may also recall how the entire nation had fallen for a fraud called Ramar Pillai when he had claimed that he could make petrol with plain water using some secret herbs. Sometimes we dig up those child prodigies also who have spent years in mental asylum after that and suddenly appoint them professor emeritus of mathematics in some university to 'rehabilitate' him. Some guy of Indian origin got Nobel Prize in economics. Fine, he deserved it but it did not mean that he would become your saviour. We jumped at it and gave him the highest award of the land—because, we genuinely believed that this Nobel laureate in economics would single-handedly bail us out—India would once again become the *'sone ki chidiya'* and poverty would be eradicated overnight. Some leader gave the call for a total revolution and millions believed that he was the long-awaited messiah.

In nutshell, the Indians simply need something to latch on to. They latch on to it with all their might and pin all their hopes on to it. **We need a messiah, a *'taaranhaar'*. This *'taaranhaar'* may be a charismatic person or may be an idea, but we need something. Police reforms is an idea in a similar situation—a *'taaranhaar'* idea—something that would salvage the bloody Indian police forever.** Police reform is the buzz word. Have police reforms and all your problems with the police would be solved. Just have them and tomorrow the neighbourhood crooked *thulla* would become the paragon of virtue. Of course, the Indians do not have time or intellectual capacity to reflect for ourselves. We do not want to hear that there are problems which are deep rooted and which would defy a 'misplaced' solution. But we have the *'taaranhaar'* idea. The Supreme Court of the land has spoken—*Roma locuta causa finita*. When the ultimate word has been given, it is for the multitudes to follow it, as simple as that. Why think?

9.5.2 *The Questionable Foundations of the Idea of Police Reforms*

The entire business of police reforms stems from an unstated presumption that the police officers are inherently good whereas the politicians are inherently bad. And hence the police officers must be given complete freedom so that he may do the good work. As we have comprehensively shown in an earlier chapter, this is simply illogical—there is no reason at all to even suspect that police officers are inherently good. On the contrary, they are often worse than the most notorious criminals. ***A criminal musters his own courage, uses his own force of arms, and risks his life and liberty to commit the sins; his victims too are free to resist them. Police officers, on the other hand, are cowards; they use the colour of their office and the power given to them by the system or the law to commit their sins; their victims are not free to resist them.*** The evils that beset the police are manifold, like the multi-headed Lernaean Hydra. We have exposed them comprehensively in this book. There are no simple solutions to them. One will have to grapple with complexity to devise solutions for it. But the police leadership has once again proven its intellectual bankruptcy by refusing to think. Like all other dumb Indians, they also want a quick and simple solution which is provided by somebody else. The current police reform campaign is trying to obfuscate the real complex issues and project that the evils that the police officers do are ordered by the politicians only. This is not only wrong, it is a white lie.

Is there any reason to believe that a State Security Commission comprising of however eminent persons would be able to ensure that the State Government does not exercise unwarranted influence or pressure on the police? For that matter, is there any reason to believe that the State Government necessarily exercises unwarranted influence or brings undue pressure on the police? If that be true, the solution is to change the very system of governance that this country has given to itself, and not bring cosmetic changes. How are we to believe that the persons in the Commission would not be corruptible—we have had a not-so-illustrious history of people occupying some of the highest offices in the country accused of all sorts of heinous things—corruption would pale before the videos of a very old man indulging in a sexual orgy with three women in the official residence of a very high dignitary that he was; molestation of women visitors in offices of ministers; and so on. *Intellectual corruption is actually more prevalent in the so-called eminent persons because they come with a lot of baggage.* In practice, the buck must stop somewhere. But if the place where it stops itself has its integrity compromised, the problem would not be solved. ***The track record of this country shows that institutions and individuals both at the highest level can be compromised and have suffered from numerous failings. It is both puerile and juvenile to hope that some Commission, CAG, CEC, or Lokpal would be infallible like God and would accomplish what hundreds of thousands of people could not accomplish in 65 years? The so-called police reforms seek to reform the system whereas the malady lies more with the men who work for the system.***

As for the fixed tenure to officers, there are numerous problems in it. We do know that frequent transfers of officers are one means to harass them—however; giving fixed tenure is not a solution of this problem. This is, at best, a knee-jerk reaction. This amounts to treating the fever with paracetamol; but not doing anything for the underlying infection. Given the sort of eccentric officers we have, it amounts to giving some fools a licence to indulge in their whims for two years. One who gives a loaded pistol to a monkey will end up getting shot. We have seen, in our long years of service, absolutely crazy, perverse guys in very high positions. One shudders at the very thought of their getting fixed tenures and tormenting people. Moreover, everybody has a legitimate right to aspire for the top post. Fixed tenure means that many would retire just like that. *And why do you require someone to be there for two years – what wonders are expected from fixed tenure? For that matter, what wonders have been delivered by those who had, by some contrivance, managed to hang on to their posts for as many as four years, even without the Supreme Court order?* Then consider the so-called field postings. The number of field postings like district SP may be very few but the aspirants many. Fixed tenure would mean that many of them would never get a chance for those posts and the exposure in their careers would remain incomplete. This is poor cadre management. And do they mean to say that a particularly obnoxious SHO would become inviolable with the fixed tenure? ***Unless elaborate conditions are meticulously prescribed for violations of which one would be liable to get transferred, such a carte blanche is highly dangerous.***

9.5.3 *What They Really Want is Something Else*

The entire reform business suffers from serious lack of analytical thought – an utterly simplistic approach to a complex problem. *It also suffers from intellectual dishonesty because it deliberately and completely ignores the real reasons of the evils that beset the police. The politician has been made out to be the only villain of the piece whereas the police system is teeming with dangerous villains of a myriad kind. The police reform campaign in this country, particularly the way it has been sold to the media, smacks strongly of trade unionism. Essentially, all they want is more power – unbridled power so that they may commit their misdeeds with more impunity. They want a licence to go berserk. They have cleverly exploited the popular (and actually misplaced) sentiments of the ignoramuses in the people and the media. The Indians, because of their limited intellect, never analyze a problem thoroughly. They need some place on the drawing board where to stick their pin. Political interference is one such place. The proponents of police reform found an object of hatred very much alive in popular perception and cleverly exploited it.* ***There is a serious danger in a reform agenda that seeks to free police from political control without making them more accountable to the public.***

There is no logical way in which anyone can permanently condemn the Government and the politicians as the epitome of evil. While it may theoretically be alright to have a strong system of checks and balances, how can you deny the elected people's representatives the right to administer those very checks and balances? ***To allow untrammelled jurisdiction and powers to the police in the name of independence or autonomy strikes at the very roots of the principles***

of responsible and accountable governance. Even if we assume, for the sake of argument, that the intentions of the reformwallahs are pure, this is not good for a democracy. If tomorrow the armed forces (who are also in uniform) were to similarly demand "autonomy" and "independence" on the grounds that an interfering and corrupt political/bureaucratic dispensation has undermined the all important security of the nation; we could be facing a very grim scenario indeed, isn't it?

Sometimes one happens to say something which exposes his subconscious. This is what happened recently. Readers may recall that in the Ishrat Jahan fake encounter case, the CBI proceeded to question a Special Director of the IB also. It was the first time that an officer of the IB (the likes of whom were hitherto considered inviolable) was faced with the prospect of being made an accused in the fake encounter case. Rediff.com reported that, incensed by this, a former Director of the IB went ballistic in June 2013. He told the Rediff.com that the CBI had implicated the Special Director. (*Well, sir, no one utters a word when thousands of other people of the country are made accused – should we say that they are also 'implicated? And by the way, how could you pre-judge the issue that he was 'implicated'? Are all people equal but the IB officers more equal than others?*) He made a reference to the IB, the RAW and the CBI being members of a security family of the country. (*Does he mean that there should be a different law for the family?*) The former DIB also said that the CBI ought to have displayed certain professional etiquette and finesse. (*Would he care to elaborate what he means by professional etiquette and finesse?*)

He added that it was possible for the Director, CBI to informally get in touch with his IB counterpart, discuss an IB officer's alleged involvement they suspected and deal with the case with adequate finesse, maturity and professionalism. (*Do you accord the same treatment to others? Does it mean to say that when government servants are involved, one must proceed only informally? Should the CrPC prescribe a different procedure for IB officers or those in the family? And what crime is committed if the matter got splashed in the media? So many other things also get splashed in the media. The IB officers, in the name of secrecy, do not enjoy any immunity from criminal law? Is there any law that an IB officer can commit a crime and yet there would be no talk about it in the media?*) He went on to say 'one wonders how the CBI, an agency working under and following the same security philosophy, proceeded to question the IB officer about Ishrat Jehan (with whom he nursed no prejudice or enmity). Who gave the dubious go ahead to the CBI to take this path?' (*Readers may please note that when the CBI acts against politicians and others, all IPS officers, in fact the entire police leadership screams at the top of its voice that the CBI must have complete autonomy, and there should be no interference from anybody. Their hypocrisy is exposed the very moment when one of their own got a taste of CBI investigation – then they start speaking of the necessity of finesse, maturity, and professionalism and want preferential or even a different treatment. By God, this is nepotism at its worst – these guys are so shamelessly claiming inequality before law.* ***Gentlemen, this is the truth of the demand of autonomy under the guise of reforms—these guys want selective autonomy!****)*

Chapter 10

Tyranny of the Intellectually Bankrupt

10.1 The Reasons of the Pathological Hatred of Knowledge

Like a demon possessing some poor soul in horror films, intellectual bankruptcy has come to possess the police leadership. Unfortunately, there is no exorcism for this demon and we, that is, the people of this country are doomed to suffer the tyranny of the ignorant. There are many reasons for it. For some it is pure ignorance; for some it is prejudice that has closed the mind to reason; and for some it is both. The consequences of ignorance are particularly torturous in respect of intelligence officers and officers of the security forces because the consequences of it are to be suffered by millions of people directly and the entire nation indirectly. There is no end to the stupidities that can be committed out of sheer ignorance. We agree that everyone is entitled to be stupid but some abuse the privilege—as we have shown comprehensively in this book, IAS and IPS officers are particularly guilty in this regard. *Since stupidity, like many other things in nature, flows from top to bottom; the higher the officer, the less he knows. That the senior police officers do not know anything is one thing; that they maintain that they need not know because they happen to wear the IPS uniform is quite another. Being ignorant is not so much a shame, as being unwilling to learn or closing one's mind to reason is.* Martin Luther King, Jr. had said: "Nothing in the world is more dangerous than sincere ignorance and conscientious stupidity." Ignorance is dangerous because it distorts perceptions. Distorted perceptions result in defective policy-making. Ignorance sends you on a wild-goose chase. Ignorance makes you spend billions on useless things which any intelligent terrorist can easily counter. Ignorance makes you see enemies where they are not. Ignorance makes you perceive threats which do not exist. At the same time, it keeps you oblivious of the real threats which may be far more serious.

One reason of the intellectual bankruptcy of the police leadership is their deep-rooted belief (sometimes stated, sometimes not stated) that police officers do not need brains – brawn alone would do. In other words, the image they have of a *Thulla* or street cop is transferred on to a senior officer also. These guys have actually started taking pleasure in being treated like a *Thulla* by others. Nobody resists this stereotyping. This internal belief of the police officers has become so widespread that even the public has come to believe that police officers need not possess any brains. Once, one of our friends (actually a batch mate of one of the authors of this book) happened to introduce him to his daughter studying in high school. Among other things, he narrated at length that he had written 26 books and several research papers and that he was a very knowledgeable man, and so on. The girl listened to it patiently and suddenly blurted out: "If he is so learned, what is he doing in the police?"

It can be argued by their apologists that they might have had possessed some intellectual capacity when they passed the UPSC exam. But, as we love to point out, even the best swords in the world need constant honing; otherwise they lose their edge rapidly. This is what happens to the IAS and IPS officers. *Reading of any kind becomes a more and more serious taboo as they progress in years.* Once, a senior officer almost forced us to present one of our books to him. Some months later we asked him how he liked the book. He confessed, "I have not read a single book in the past 33 years, how could I read this one"? Senior officers proudly proclaim that they cannot read anything more than a page. Some of them love to keep you in the dark. If you give them something in writing, they would ask to be spoken with instead; you go to speak with them, they would ask for a written report claiming they cannot think without something in print! Friedrich von Schiller, the famous German poet, philosopher and historian had very rightly observed: "Against stupidity the gods themselves struggle in vain!"

In fact, any effort to acquire knowledge of any kind, professional or otherwise becomes a no-no with the civil servants. The ignorance resulting from this is responsible for much travail of the common people. That the civil servants lack professional knowledge is well-known and convincingly proved throughout this book; we have, however, on hundreds of occasions, proved it to the amusement of our friends that even the general knowledge of most of them is terribly poor. Once we rang up 65 officers of approximately our seniority one-by-one and asked them the name of the then foreign minister of Pakistan (that was before Hina Rabbani Khar, whom many people remembered on account of her looks alone) – 62 of them did not know. Probing further, it was found that not one of them knew that what is known as the home ministry in India is called Ministry of Interior in Pakistan.

The service itself is to be blamed partially for this state of affairs. The system of promotions and rewards is such that the acquisition of knowledge is not on a premium at any stage. Your being knowledgeable would not get you anything extra, and not being knowledgeable would not make you lose anything. *A vicious circle, however, starts when they develop a serious complex with any process of acquisition of knowledge.* So much so that, by any chance, if they find some officer who still maintains a semblance of academic activity, it is pompously claimed that he must have been a failure on what they perceive as the 'real' professional front and has taken up the academic activity as a face-saving device. If he musters the courage to flaunt his academic activity or achievements, he is showered with condescending remarks like: "Acquiring knowledge and research findings are useless unless they are integrated with life and action. Knowledge which is not integrated with life and is not useful for action does not become wisdom and such knowledge is useless to the society. As we become seniors we understand the limitation of bookish theories and hence work from the plane of practicality. We are not empty in the brain; we are merely keeping it clean of useless stuff!" How profound, isn't it!

You would also frequently hear platitudes like: 'real' officers do not have time for all this – they deal with problems – not with conceptual issues. The 'real' field officer could be found playing golf for four hours a day; playing tennis in the afternoons; chatting with his *chamchaas* for hours in the name of holding meetings or discussions; or drinking through the evening – he needs to unwind after all the stresses of the day, you see. *First they start taking pride in not associating in any way with any intellectual activity. Eventually, they develop a clear hostility towards anything intellectual. Thus the de-intellectualization of the service becomes complete.* Hundreds of senior officers have confided in us – their reading of printed matter is limited to newspapers and magazines, and yes, they take care not to even touch 'heavier stuff' like the editorials of *The Hindu* in newspapers.

10.2 Because They Were SP or DM Once

They never try to learn anything in service because they presume that by virtue of having cleared the UPSC exam once upon a time by some fluke or the other, they are entitled to a mysterious process by which knowledge automatically descends upon them. In Indian mythology and in tantric practice we often hear of '*shaktipaat*' or the guru transferring the knowledge to the disciple by a mysterious process. Sage Vishwamitra, after his finally successful *tapasya* had also insisted from Bhagwan that '*Ved mera varan karen*'—that is, the knowledge of the Vedas must descend upon his soul and enlighten him. There is no such guru for the civil servants. But the mystical process does exist nonetheless. The mystical process perhaps lies in their having been SP or DM once upon a time. They are posts imbued with magical powers. *Having been a SP or DM is enough to enable them to know everything under the sun and at no point of time later in their lives they are obliged to learn anything more.* You must have heard of Draupadi's *Akshay Paatra* (a pot that got never emptied of its contents). The civil service believes to have something like this in it.

This obsession with the post of SP and DM has its roots in the typical stupid middle-class mentality of the civil service aspirants. When they are growing up; when they are college students; they see that in the local newspapers and TV channels most of the news items pertain to the activities of the SP and the DM. The papers cover all that they do in great loving detail, including the shoes they wear. If the SP/DM has attended a prize distribution function in some God forsaken *Kanya Pathshala* also, the papers still cover it in full, replete with the photo of the SP/DM and may be his dumb wife as well. This is a symbiotic existence. The SP and the DM get the publicity they crave for—the journalists get some trash to publish and more importantly, ingratiate themselves with the SP/DM.

By the same logic all the stupidities that they do—ranging from their tours (*Ilaqa haqim daure par hain*); the reprimand they administer to their subordinates (*Sahib ne jam kar lataad pilayi; jam kar class lee, etc.*); and the twists in their personality or behavioural pattern (*If the sahib wears sports shoes, it means that he has come prepared for some detailed field inspection; Sahib is very short-tempered; Sahib cannot tolerate any dust; Sahib does not take tea/coffee: Sahib takes only Black Label and that too neat on the rocks; Sahib takes ten pegs at least and does not take dinner before one-thirty in the night; Sahib loves to play tennis during afternoon office time: Sahib is a field officer and he does not like disposing files sitting on the desk, etc.*); to their freaky working style (*Sahib either does not work in the afternoons as army officers do, or starts working late in the evening and then works late into the night, compelling others also to work with him; Sahib loves to perform law and order duty on horseback, etc.)* – they cover everything in loving detail and with great adulation. For some people bird-watching or girl-watching could be a favourite pastime; for the journalists of a vast majority of districts, SP/DM watching is the favourite pastime. *All this creates a larger-than-life image of the SP/DM in the impressionable minds of the civil service aspirants. For them, the SP/DM becomes the pinnacle of achievement – there cannot be an officer greater than them. That's how they develop a fixation with these posts and eventually the unconscious (call it subconscious if you like) does not allow them to grow beyond that level.*

One of the manifestations of this fixation is a particularly irritating habit of the senior police officers; of recounting, 'when I was SP'! Their counterparts in the IAS recall, 'when I was DM'! ***It can mean only one thing that the poor bugger has not learnt a word after he ceased to be a SP or DM; that his maturity level; his perspective and level of knowledge all remain what they were those decades ago. He has not acquired three decades or more of experience; it is only one year's experience which he has repeated thirty times***. He is not ashamed of his utter ignorance because he genuinely believes that he does not need any knowledge – he has a far ponderous thing at hand – his experience. In his arrogant perception, experience beats knowledge any day. The weight of the experience is wielded like the mighty club of Bheema with some condescending looks thrown in – I have had seen this when you were still in school, you see. It is for such morons that the military genius Frederick the Great had famously stated: "I have two mules in my army and they have gone through forty campaigns, but they are still mules." Well, these mules have a natural tendency to become obstinate and, by God, they do become obstinate. One of the manifestations of their obstinacy is the 'pet theories' they develop. For every problem under the sun they have a pet theory which is simple, utterly absurd and wrong.

'Pet theories' and sweeping generalizations are claimed to originate from their valuable 'experience'. Every senior officer has some pet theory. Pet theories are found at both extremes, most regressive as well as highly futuristic. For example, some of them would blame all the ills plaguing the police to a 'lack of discipline'; police not performing the beat patrol duty religiously; or senior officers not checking the (nearly 100) archaic registers supposed to be maintained in the police stations. Some of them would blame everything on not having a CCTV behind the ass of every man in the country; people not submitting their income details to the SHO instead of the Income Tax department; and a GPS tracking device in every vehicle. Sweeping generalizations are sweeping indeed. They are reflected in strongly held beliefs like: police cannot conduct counterinsurgency operations, only the army can; the CRPF is a 'Tiffin Force' and all that they require is food; men of the Assam Rifles stand up and fight, the CRPF men don't; when the CO sahib of the Rashtriya Rifles picks up his VHF set, he is totally in command; police officers do not know how to give commands over wireless; and if you have a brigadier on deputation, he will solve all your problems.

In effect, it becomes a continuous downhill ride for the intellect after they join the service. Remember the aphorism, the higher a monkey climbs, the more you see of his ass. Even on the professional front, a downside of the professional ignorance of the seniors is that they can seldom afford to differ with their subordinates. The IAS/IPS have actually reduced themselves to a community of ostriches which keeps on pretending that just by being IAS/IPS officers, they are supposed to be intellectually equipped for all times to come. The delusions do not end there. They also believe that all of them are equally virtuous, equally competent and their thoughts and actions have equal merit. How many times we had to tell people: "*Kutta paalo, billi paalo, gadha paalo, magar ghalatfahami mat paalo*". But who listens? Even if their reading activity is limited to the glossy Femina/Stardust or to the Metro City supplement of the newspaper, they are all deemed to have equal intellectual capability. Moreover, in the context of the IPS, it automatically qualifies you to offer your comments on everything; counterinsurgency operations, jungle combat, urban operations, intelligence, forensic science, crime investigation, anything. Just as for a dumb SHO a B.Sc. graduate becomes a forensic expert whom he does not mind producing before the court, the very fact of having the IPS on their shoulders entitles them to know everything. *Clearing the civil services exam is the only activity of its kind in the entire human history where you make effort once and then you do not have to make any effort for the rest of your life – it's a job where you get paid for your entire life for having obtained the job in the first place!*

Some of them have gone to the extent of arguing that they may not be academic intellectuals but they are 'public intellectuals', whatever it might mean. In essence, they mean to say the same old thing, that is, the claim of possessing knowledge by virtue of having cleared the exam once. The so-called 'public intellectuals' are not under any obligation to prove their credentials by publishing their views on everything under the sun in peer-reviewed publications or placing it in the public domain by publishing a book. They expect that their credentials as so-called experts must be accepted because some sensation-seeking journalists are keen to print their views, or some TV channel is willing to place them along side some excitable anchor and some other equally ignorant people in a shouting match. *There exists a symbiotic relationship between such channels and such self-styled experts. The channels have to air something. These guys have to find some recognition.* You can say anything on the TV, make sweeping generalizations, make outrageous claims, anything—after all, they do not expect you to cite some authority or reference in support of your point. As long as you can keep on shouting, you are an expert. *Pandit vahi jo gaal bajawaa.* You have only to watch these people on various channels for a week and you will yourself realize how hollow they are. To be fair to the IAS and IPS we must mention that in our society at large, there is a huge disconnect between academic research and public policy. Academicians in this country have really no idea of the realities of public policy and how they are executed. Theirs is basically an ivory-tower view on most things. On the other hand, there is a general marginalization of and poor status accorded to academic research as a key input of public policy. In the West, it is common for top universities and their academicians playing an important role in policy planning and implementation.

10.3 The Fine Art of Keeping Up Appearances

Readers must be wondering as to how senior officers keep up appearances when they really do not know anything. What do they do to make the ordinary people think that these senior officers really know something? There is a secret to it but not difficult to understand. If you have ever carefully observed the girls who take part in beauty pageants and go on to become Miss Indias and Miss Worlds, you would know the secret. *The secret lies in attitude.* They may be the dumbest of the dumb girls but they have attitude. The winners exude confidence. Whatever they say in answer to questions, they say with great confidence and strength of conviction. Never mind that she would never touch a poor child, not to speak of a leper even with a barge pole 20 feet long, she would claim with great aplomb that she wants to be like Mother Teresa. She can claim that the mission of her life is to be the messenger of peace and happiness. She might even say that she wants to devote her life working with the starving children in Ethiopia. She knows that the stupid buggers, the judges, are not going to indulge in a debate with them. None of them knows a word more about Mother Teresa or Ethiopia except the names. No one is going to contradict her. The same thing happens in high-level meetings attended by top officials also. Everybody is equally dumb—nobody is going to contradict you. *You have merely to mumble the prevailing keywords; the buzzwords that are doing the rounds in the media; and the secret words that we disclose below.* Nobody is going to ask you the source of your information. You have only to sound like a man of experience—if some fool does get inquisitive, silence him with him a cold stare and mumble something about your 'sensitive assets' that need to be protected. If you are a woman, however, using the word 'assets' may be misconstrued; use the word 'agent' instead. It is at such moments that jargon and name dropping comes in extremely handy. *So here we go about the secret art of appearing knowledgeable when you are not so by any chance.*

We will illustrate the subject in reference to internal security because it is the in-thing these days. Internal security is a permanent bogey in reserve that can be raised anytime. Whenever or wherever you speak about it, you can appear both important and knowledgeable. ***You have just to memorize some jargon related to internal security like radicalization, counter-radicalization, alienation, trans-border funding, fundamentalist streak, manifold threats, 'the other dimension', and emerging challenges, etc.*** *A host of academicians are eking out a living by dropping jargon. If they can, why can't you?*

The other secret is to drop names – both of people and of places. Name-dropping does not mean that you have to tell that Bill Gates knows you. ***You have only to drop names of real or imaginary terrorists, maulanas, Naxal leaders and, if you want to be in the top league, some imaginary names of ISI handlers. You can also drop words like wahabism, salafism, comprador, and anti-Lin Biao faction etc. They are the ultimate.*** Do not bother about context—all that is required is that you must be able to recite names like Maulana Sufiyan Patangia, Maulana Tabarruq Hussain, Feroze Abdul Latif Ghaswala, Rahil Abdul Rehman Sheikh, Rasool Khan 'Party', Abdul Latif Sheikh, Mohammad Aslam Sardana and Zulfikar Fayyaz Kagzi and of course, Riyaz Bhatkal @ Shah Riyaz Ahmad Mohammed Ismail Shahbandri @ Riyaz Ismail Shahbandri and Iqbal Bhatkal @ Iqbal Shahbandri whenever someone is talking about anything remotely connected to terrorism in which Muslims are involved. Do not bother whether the names belong to real persons or are fictitious—the other guy is equally ignorant. And by any chance if you happen to drop an imaginary but Palestinian sounding name like some Abu Junaid Qasmi or Abu Khalid Maqsood, you will be on top. So is the case with names that sound like those of the Taliban—you can safely cook up any name but just take care to mumble about something like the Haqqani faction or the Northern Alliance in connection with that—that's enough to make you an expert on the subject. Just make sure that you mention them with complete authority. If you are mentioning the name of some stupid Major of the ISI, mention something like Major Ishtiyaq Qadiri so casually as if he had lunch with you yesterday or his wife calls you *bhaiyya*. Mentioning aliases makes you sound very knowledgeable—by God, this guy knows not only the names of terrorists but also their nicknames! You see, the police leadership is not expected to bother itself with details—that is for subordinate officers. You, as senior officer have only to mumble that the involvement of so-and-so was suspected in such-and-such incident. Do it twice in a meeting and you have a delivered a Lasith Malinga Yorker. That's all—rest assured, no one would ask you anything else. You can drop some imaginary female names like Mehrunnisa Bibi also and in rather hushed tones drop a hint with a wink that she is the girlfriend of so-and-so terrorist. They will be clean bowled, all three stumps flying.

If they are talking about Naxals, you can take any Telugu sounding difficult name—do you think any of those buggers remembers the names of the Polit Bureau members or the names of the zonal leaders of the Naxals? If by any chance, some Telugu guy is there and is puzzled by the name mentioned by you, mumble that this is an alias. You can take typical north-Indian first names also for Naxals but just make sure that they end with a respectful 'ji'. These Naxals love to be addressed as Sandeep ji, Arvind ji, etc.

When it comes to places, you must be able to recite names like Farkiyan gali, Damaar gali, Kralpora and Nallah Qazinaag etc. in the context of Kashmir. Remember the secret—you can concoct any name but make it end with a -pora, -iyan, -gali, -naag, -la or -gund. That will make it sound Kashmiri/Ladakhi enough. But don't ever bluff in front of a map. After you have dropped the name, you can safely claim that infiltration of such-and-such group was reported from such-and-such place. Who in the world can contradict you? In the context of Naxals, drop names of places like Sarkeguda, Bheji, Jagargunda, Basaguda and people will be zapped. The secret is to make the names end with -guda, -gunda, -pal or -pahar. It also helps greatly to use frightening acronyms like DKSZC (for Dandakaranya Special Zonal Committee), AOBSZC (for Andhra-Orissa Border Special Zonal Committee) and NTSZ (for North Telangana Special Zone), etc.

Sometimes, you can also drop some jargon like TCOC (for Tactical Counter Offensive Campaign). It would make them feel that you know the Naxal strategy intimately. If you could use some jargon plagiarized from the infantry like axis, sector, some God forsaken acronym like FZDL (for Forward Zone Defended Locality) and pincer movement etc., your place in the hall of fame of armchair generals will be reserved forever. Also, do not forget to drop some jargon doing the rounds with academicians and journalists like confidence-building measures, development deficit, trust deficit, and tactical in whatever you say. That would win you many admirers among journalists. You are guaranteed to have the stamp of authority on your shirt. Senior IPS officers, who might happen to read this, must be grateful to us for revealing these secrets.

You could also consider using the word 'we' for added effect when you talk of operations. The secret is to confuse the audience into thinking that the sahib is so brave that he was personally involved in everything. The bugger might have never left his office in a major city, would have never seen a jungle with his own eyes, *but he must talk of 'we went into Saranda'; 'we would clear Aboojhmaadh in two months'; 'we fired at them from 100 yards'; 'we were monitoring such-and-such imagery from the UAV'; 'we sent the helicopter for casualty evacuation'; and so on.*

We mentioned about armchair generals. Why do they want to become generals? The police leadership has a deep-rooted inferiority complex with respect to senior army officers. In the first place, the army officers are smarter-looking. Senior IPS officers, by and large, present a pathetic-looking sight in uniform, replete with huge paunches, *paan*-dribbling from the corners of the lips or chewing *paan-masala*, slouchy appearance, a *dabba* of paan-masala in hand, and eyes bloodshot with excessive drinking. The only characters who are more pathetic than IPS officers are IAS officers whom you would find utterly uncouth, poor build, often in hawai chappals—no better than their *chaparasis*. The extremely erudite Kautilya had said that the officers of the king must be men of pleasing personality *(sudarshan vyaktitva)* so that they do not create an instant feeling of revulsion in the minds of the public—the UPSC has obviously never heard of it. Secondly, the army officers are articulate. They may be duffers of the highest order but they are past masters of the art of window-dressing. Talk to any fool in the army and he would inundate you with jargon. Jargon is the secret of their sounding knowledgeable and, at the same time, confusing others. Thirdly, they take a little more care about their manners, particularly in dealing with women and in social interactions. *This inferiority complex leaves the IPS officers longing for at least projecting themselves like generals all the time.* This inferiority complex with the army officers has spread to the IAS also. They also want to become generals. ***Senior IAS officers even remotely involved with the business of internal security have been holding long meetings on things like combat tactics and intelligence generation. One of the very senior IAS officers has been so fascinated by the very word 'operation' that he is*** *prepared to recommend you for a gallantry medal if you happened to mention it to him that you just had a successful prostate operation.* They could be pardoned for some outright foolishness and simple abuse of their positions; the police leadership cannot be pardoned for allowing such stupidity to take place at all. *These guys would never tell the IAS officers that they are not professionally qualified to speak a word on such matters. Even operational decisions have been allowed to be taken by those who do not know from which end of a gun the bullet comes out and casualties have taken place as a result of such decisions.*

Some of the senior police officers have understood that the political leadership, the people and the media are often dumber than them. Time to exploit that. They start cooking up various innovative schemes—supposedly making inroads into the society by organizing meetings with resident welfare associations; starting all sorts of help-lines; 'winning hearts and minds' of the people; 'making a difference'; 'reaching out to the people'; 'bonding with the police'; 'citizens' groups'; Indian versions of neighbourhood watch; enrolling school kids to become some sort of unofficial junior policemen; counselling for the women suffering from domestic stress or violence; the list is indeed large.

There is one common factor to all of them. They are all bogus and have never had any measurable effect. The effect exists only in the reporting of some local newspapers, the reporters of which are obliged to suck up to them for a thousand well-known reasons. We must emphasize the word measurable. Any claim must be scientifically verifiable. This is where these guys run away and start growling from a distance. You ask them how did they measure the impact and they would say that a local journalist, a psychologist friend or teacher of statistics from the local degree college is the expert authority—and if they say so, there must have been some impact of the scheme. Dear dumbos, try to understand some research methodology—when a claim is made, there are well-established scientific methods of evaluating it. Why run way from it and take refuge in sweeping generalizations of half-baked journalists? The IPS leadership has fallen to such depths that they become happy at testimonials from local journalists also and flaunt it all over the country. Worse, they are not prepared to admit that such false and farcical claims do harm in the long run because they are simply not true—they distort perceptions and are potentially capable of leading to wrong decisions.

We distinctly remember, once some guy just happened to mention Cohen's Kappa (for the uninitiated, an index of inter-rater reliability that is commonly used to measure the level of agreement between two sets of dichotomous ratings or scores), while questioning the psychological impact of some such programme which sought to make the people more chummy with the police. The questions which he raised were rather simple. All he wanted to know as to what was the basis of the claim. First he wanted to know how the conclusion was drawn—through interviews, focus group or a questionnaire or some other way like thematic analysis, and what were the parameters on which the inferences were drawn?

Then he wanted to know whether the proponent of the scheme had compared a population not exposed to the initiative with a population exposed to the initiative while their demographic and economic characteristics remained more or less the same so that the samples were comparable if not identical; or, whether he had compared the same group with itself—once before the initiative and the later after the initiative. Obviously, none of characters amongst the police leadership had even heard the word Cohen's Kappa ever before. By God, all hell broke loose—the entire leadership pounced upon him for his flaunting his academic knowledge. A sampling of their reactions would be illuminating: academic arrogance; mere academics with all its rigor is sterile (*whatever it means*)—the focus must be on results; commonsense findings do not require any research methodology or sample survey (*well, well*); innovative policing strategies are required and there is no harm if they are taken up with pomp and show (*that is, without any proper evaluation*).

10.4 Take a Walk Through a Minefield of Monumental Stupidity

One of the basic jobs of the police leadership is maintenance of internal security. Now internal security is a mysterious thing. Everyone talks about it but no one knows for sure as to what actually is meant by internal security. However, every IPS officer, senior or junior, believes himself to be an expert in, and has some valuable advice on internal security. All sorts of advices are given freely and often they find echoes in official circles too—in fact, the more bizarre the idea, the more likely it is to find acceptance as a novel one. ***Now since they have a claim to be police officers as well as civil servants who had cleared the UPSC exam, this means that the solutions suggested by them are a curious mix of military exotica and the wisdom of the babus.*** Well, there are two major security challenges before the country. One is the Naxal problem and the other is Kashmir. It would be interesting to have a look at the solutions that are suggested by the police leadership in this regard—and mind it, we are absolutely serious. We swear to the God Almighty, not one word in the following is a product of our imagination—all of this comes from direct knowledge.

10.4.1 *Novel Solutions to the Naxal Problem*

The Dog Solution to Naxal Problem: Who will now save the country from the depredations of the Naxals? Well, it is your best friend, the dog! In order to appear genuinely involved in the business, you will have to abandon the old German Shepherds and Labradors; you have to take some exotic breeds like the Malinois or the Rottweiler. Well, these dogs would go in the jungles, tell you where the Naxals are and then you can shoot the jokers! Simple! Never mind the poor beast cannot tell a Naxal from some unfortunate adivasi in the jungle.

The UAV Solution to the Naxal Problem: The catchword is 'eye in the sky'. Give us UAVs (Unmanned Aerial Vehicle) and we will ferret those bastards out of their hiding holes. Don't you know what the Americans have been doing in Afghanistan? Never mind there is no jungle in Afghanistan, and the stupid thing cannot see anything under the cover of a tree canopy.

The Road-Building Solution to the Naxal Problem: The Naxal problem exists because there are not enough roads in the Naxal areas. Build 6000 km of roads and the problem would be over in a month.

The Khandav Van Solution to the Naxal Problem: For those of you who might remember a bit of the Mahabharat, Arjun had burnt the Khandav Van to propitiate Agni. The Khandav Van solution to the Naxal problem is that you must burn a mile of forest on both sides of the roads that you build—no jungle means that there cannot be any ambush.

The Basket of Oranges (or Sanitary Napkins) Solution to the Naxal Problem: You see the police has had committed terrible atrocities on the poor people for long and this has alienated them. You must win back their trust. For this, whenever you meet some villager or adivasi, do not address him as '*Oye, idhar aa be*'; rather, present him respectfully with a basket of oranges! You must also distribute useful items like T-shirts, torches, bicycles, solar lanterns, transistors, sanitary napkins, sports kits, vitamin supplements, *Shilajit* and the like amongst them—what was once the 'white man's burden', has now become the 'brown sahib's burden' and you, of the famed 'steel frame', must discharge the burden with great aplomb so as to civilize these guys and bring them in the mainstream. If you are in good mood, you can even drop currency notes from your car which those country children would run helter-skelter and pick up. You could even hum *'jaane wale zara hoshiyar, yahan ke hum hain rajkumar; aage peechhe hamari sarkar, yahan ke hum hain rajkumar'* as Shammi Kapoor did in the film Rajkumar (1964) – never mind he was riding an elephant – this is the 21st century and you are entitled to ride a car!

The *Paan-Ki-Dukaan* Solution to the Naxal Problem: Lack of actionable intelligence is the Achilles' Heel of the whole business of anti-Naxal operations. How will you get intelligence unless you have intelligence assets? This means you must have intelligence 'assets'. How do you go about creating 'human assets' on the ground? Here is the way shown by one of the highest-ranking officers in the country! You must pick up a good-for-nothing villager in the Naxal area and open a *paan-ki-dukaan* for him replete with faded posters of heroines of yesteryears. You see, your *paan-ki-dukaan* is in a remote area – the people there may not connect with the photos of Sherlyn Chopra, Sunny Leone or Sophie Chaudhary. Better to have photos of the hot stuff from the era when the founders of the Naxal movement used to be horny about them – late '60s and early '70s. And remember, that is the shop of your 'intelligence asset'; it is necessary that the heroines in the posters must be displaying their 'assets' generously, otherwise the poor fellow would forget that he is an 'asset' himself. Give your *paanwala* a sturdy mobile phone (preferably one with a torch in it – you may perhaps recall the ad of Nokia 1100 – *'raat mein bhi chalta hai'*) and tell him: *"Babu, ab koi Naxal aaye idhar to phone karke humein batana"*. *Bas,* you will see, the bugger is bound to tell you and you will have all the intelligence in the world. But for this brilliant idea, they have wasted 46 years!

The 'Bug' Solution to the Naxal Problem: A bug, as you know, in intelligence jargon, is a remote listening device – usually a very small wireless transmitter. You should have bugs planted in the hut of every stupid adivasi in the jungle. After all, the Naxals would come there and talk about their plans. Bingo, you get to hear everything and bust them before they hatch!

The 'Chakravyuha' Solutions to the Naxal Problem: This guy Prakash Jha came up with some brilliant ideas in his film *'Chakravyuha'*. They surgically planted a very small radio beacon in the body of a man who was 'infiltrated' amongst the Naxals. From scores of miles away, this beacon will tell you where the Naxals are going – just fly down there in a helicopter in a jiffy and shoot them down from the chopper. Jha also showed that the Intelligence had such gadgets that they could see every inch of the jungle with the help of the satellites sitting in their control room! *Wah, wah, Jha ji, tussi great ho; tussi toap ho – pahle bataya hota to Naxalwad ab tak khatm kar diye hote!*

The Long Crawl Solution to the Naxal Problem: You see the Naxal is a man of the jungle – he can crawl on his belly for 300 yards whereas your troops cannot. That's where they beat you in physical fitness and endurance. We must get our troops trained so that they are also able to crawl for 300 yards and then we will kill the Naxals easily.

The 'Stand Up and Fight' Solution to the Naxal Problem: The biggest problem with the troops is that they have a defensive mindset. The moment they come under fire, they hit the ground, crawl, and manoeuvre to take cover – '*leto, rengo, aad pakdo*'. These guys have no heart. In the well-considered opinion of a senior officer with several fake encounters to his credit, they must stand tall under fire with their chests puffed up and challenge the Naxals with '*nikal, teri bhain di...*' Brave soldiers do not take cover. If they had this courage, they would have wiped off Naxals decades ago.

The 'Better Coordination, Liaison and Synergy' Solution to the Naxal Problem: The biggest shortcoming of the system is that there is a lack of coordination and liaison amongst various agencies. If there was good coordination, liaison and synergy amongst the police, paramilitary forces, revenue department, forest department, health department, and the army, we would have got excellent results by now.

The Suspension Solution to the Naxal Problem: You must suspend the buggers freely. Anybody whom you suspect of not having good coordination, liaison or synergy, you must suspend immediately. He is like a virus. Anybody who does not stand tall and present his chest to be riddled with bullets must be ridiculed as a coward and suspended. If there is an IED blast, the SHO should have known that there was an IED planted in his area. The SHO, if he is really competent, must know everything that happens in his area – who does it missionary style; who does it reverse cowgirl style; he should know everything. Nobody should take more than 18 breaths per minute without his permission. If the bugger did not know that there would be an attack in his area, suspend him straightaway.

The 24-Hour Patrolling Solution to the Naxal Problem: You must be pro-active. You should be relentlessly patrolling your entire area of responsibility in the jungle You must eat, shit and sleep in the jungle. To beat a *junglee*, you must become a *junglee*. Never mind, the other guy could ambush you. If he ambushes, you must stand tall and fight.

Had you been pro-active and done this, probably incidents like the Jerum Ghati, Sukma massacre (May 25, 2013, in which the Naxals killed 29 people including senior politicians like Mahendra Karma and V. C. Shukla) could have been averted. You have to go out; you have to take risks—after all, that's what you are paid for. How does it matter if four-five of you get killed? Have you forgotten the 'Animal Farm'—all are equal but some are more equal than others! And remember, any bugger who mumbles about professionalism and combat tactics of the US Army, will be suspended immediately. If the senior officers have asked you to establish your camp in the jungle without even tents; get exposed to heat and rain; sleep in the mud; go hungry; get bitten by snakes, contract malaria; they know better than you—otherwise they would not have been IPS officers in the first place!

10.4.2 *Novel Solutions to the Kashmir Problem*

As some readers might recall, there were terrible riots in Kashmir in 2009-2010. Nearly two thousand police personnel were hurt in the rioting characterized by some absolutely fearsome pelting of stones; large-scale destruction of property worth millions; and 112 people or so losing their lives in police firing. The policemen were later rewarded handsomely for their devotion to duty in the face of such unprecedented ferocity. But the police leadership naturally blamed the subordinates for what they called a 'mess'. The leadership had the rich experience of handling far worse riots in some God forsaken district of Bihar, you see! ***Several novel solutions were suggested in that era—mostly from very senior intelligence officers belonging to the IPS—it requires specially putrefied brains to come up with such nuggets and they are found aplenty in the intelligence community. They have timeless value as Tahitian pearls of wisdom and hence must be preserved in this hall of fame.***

The Fifty Rupees Solution to the Kashmir Problem: A significant fraction of the rioters were young men, school kids, college students, and unemployed guys, all collectively described as 'misguided youth' by the police leadership. The police leadership clarified that they were to be treated like spoilt brats and not as law-breakers. They needed to be given incentives so as not to join the ranks of the rioters. A novel scheme suggested was to pay them Rs. 50 per day for every day they went to their schools or colleges. The day they absented themselves for pelting stones, the allowance would not be paid!

The 'Suffer Equal Casualties' Solution to the Kashmir Problem: It was argued that the anger of the people was boiling because while rioters were getting killed in police firing, the policemen were only getting injured. Now the top brass determined that this was absolutely unfair and not a *dharmayuddha*. The 'hurt feelings' of the people would be assuaged only if an equal number of policemen died every day. The problem was how to ensure that. Two brilliant suggestions were made for this, and they are described below.

The 'Disarm the Police' Solution to the Kashmir Problem: Policemen open fire because they have firearms. Disarm them. If they do not have firearms, how the hell will they fire? You won't have any casualties amongst the 'misguided youth'—and neither any problem for your masters to face. Moreover, unarmed policemen are more likely to get killed at the hands of the rioters and that would assuage their feelings.

The 'Employ the Unemployed Bihari Youth' Solution to the Kashmir Problem: The sheer ingenuity of the idea needs to be admired. As we have said elsewhere, the higher a monkey climbs, the more you see of his ass. This fart emanated from the ass from a monkey who had climbed a bit too high. The logic ran like this. Bihar has got a lot of unemployed youth. They are desperate and would do anything to get two meals a day—actually anything; *paapi pet ka sawaal hai.* Recruit them as Special Police Officers (SPOs), home guards or whatever and tell them that they have to work in Kashmir. They would not mind. After all, they work by the thousands in the freezing cold of Ladakh with the BRO (Border Roads Organization); Kashmir is heaven in comparison. Leave them unarmed to face the riotous mobs. The Biharis would not mind losing a couple of men a day amongst their ranks as long as the remaining can send the money order home, and the rioters would be happy.

The 'Run Away' Solution to the Kashmir Problem: Another deadly fart; in fact, of such a high class that it had to come from the very highest levels of wisdom and experience. The noble lord asked a fundamental question: "Why do policemen have to stand on the streets and engage the rioters?" He supplied the answer too: "If the rioters attack you, simply run away and retire to your camps. But do not open fire under any circumstance." After all, it is only public property that would be destroyed—the Government can afford to purchase more or build more. What is the problem if a thousand odd guys indulge in some violence on the streets? What is the problem if they demand to secede from India? What is the problem if they brandish some AK rifles? Admire it, gentlemen, this is the stuff that the UPSC has been selecting.

The 'Shoot the Feet' Solution to the Kashmir Problem: One of the old worthies had happened to visit the SAS (Special Air Service) commandos in England for a very short while some decades ago. In any case, we are enamoured of all things *gora,* a direct darshan of the *gora soldiers in action* meant that the worthy senior officer had seen the ultimate. He proclaimed that the SAS soldiers could shoot a cigarette pack at 500 yards—why can't the bloody Indian soldier shoot at the feet of the rioters from 100 yards? That would have ensured that nobody died in police firing!

The 'Gas from the Sky' Solution to the Kashmir Problem: Some officers tried to more innovative. The idea was that the police should not even stand on the ground. They should be flying up in a helicopter and lob tear gas grenades from the air—you don't get hurt; you don't have to shoot, and they don't die—everybody is happy.

The Shimla Solution to the Kashmir Problem: This valuable suggestion came from a retired officer. When he heard of the travails of Kashmir and those serving in Kashmir, his profound suggestion was to drop the whole thing. "Let us leave the place. We will develop Shimla instead as a tourist destination", he said.

10.4.3 *The Last Nail in the Coffin*

The examples of such legendary stupidity of the IPS officers are legion. However, a last nail in the coffin would be in order. The IPS Uniform Rules have many shortcomings, and glaring ones at that. It is just a clerical document and no scientific mind had ever been applied to it. The shortcomings of the Uniform Rules could be pardoned because they were made by clerks—what cannot pardoned is the ignorance of the IPS officers in not knowing the shortcomings in the first place and then not knowing the consequences of those shortcomings. What do you expect from a bunch of duffers who do not know even their own Uniform Rules? Have a look. We have checked with hundreds of IPS officers—not one of them was aware that the leather belt (single belt as some fools call it) that they wear everyday is not prescribed in the Uniform Rules.

The IPS Uniform Rules prescribe only three types of belts, namely, web belt, cloth belt, and the Sam Browne belt (called cross belt by very many fools). Even for these three types of belts, the Rules forgot to define the all-important buckles. We will list some other bloopers in the Uniform Rules. The very colour 'khaki' is neither defined in a scientific manner nor matched against a given standard kept like the standard 'metre' or 'kilogram' of the 19th and early 20th century. As a result, both policemen and officers are found wearing all sorts of colours ranging from near olive green to bright yellow. Is that tolerable? If yes, why should we bother to prescribe a colour at all? If not, what they have done about it? Obviously, nothing. Readers must have seen almost all IPS officers above the rank of DIG putting on braids on the visors of their peak caps. These braids on the visor of the peak cap are neither prescribed nor defined in the first place. Then great arbitrariness is to be found in the design of the braids. Some use silver; some use golden. Some DIGs use a single braid; some use double also—IGs and above use double braids. Using braids may be desirable as they are actually found in the uniforms of most armed forces (in the US Army, they are nicknamed as 'scrambled eggs') but the correct thing would have been to get them properly defined and prescribed in the Uniform Rules. For close to 60 years, the police leadership has failed in that. So is the case with the gorget patch.

The Uniform Rules prescribe the gorget patches of officers wearing the state emblem and two stars and DIGs as a central silver stripe. For all those above the rank of DIG, it is central oak-leaf pattern—and same for IG to DG. Now, as many careful readers must have noticed, the morons in the IPS have created an unauthorized caste system of their own in the gorget patches. IGs wear gorget patches with two leaves in the oak-leaf pattern; ADGs and DGs have made it three leaves for their gorget patches! Now, who prescribed it? Take the mundane beret. Have the Uniform Rules prescribed the manner of wearing it anywhere? Nowhere. We are raising this issue because in the Western world the crest is worn on the left side of the forehead; in the Soviet bloc countries, they wore it on the right side. Now can anybody find fault with someone who adopts the Soviet practice? There are many other shortcomings and irrationalities in the Uniform Rules. The intellectual bankruptcy of the IPS leadership can be gauged from the fact that, in spite of facing these issues almost every day; they have never taken them up.

We will mention a few of them. For example, name plates are not prescribed; no place is prescribed for keeping a pen *(perhaps they thought the IPS officers are so dumb, they are not obliged to use a pen ever—thumb impression would do)*; the baton is not prescribed; and the nature of the lanyard (single rope or double rope) is not defined. The design of the 'breeches' is not defined (who has defined what is Bedford type or Jodhpurs). The nature of the shoes/ankle boots/jungle boots is not defined. By God, there are thousands of types of shoes. Further, what brown is the brown they mean in the shoes—and who has defined what *exactly* is an Oxford type. The length of the hair on the head is not prescribed—how short is short? Under what Rule someone can be prevented from keeping the type of hair which Hindi film actors playing the role of inspectors are found to keep? The length of the sideburns is not prescribed. The nature of the moustache is not prescribed, leading to people keeping all sorts of weird moustaches to allay their anxieties regarding their masculinity. The nature of the police whistle is not defined nor it has been explained why an officer should be obliged to carry a whistle at all? The Rules say that the stars on the badges would be of 'Star of India' pattern, but where have they defined the 'Star of India' pattern? Whether there would be a black or dark blue velvet patch beneath the badges or not is not defined. The list is long. Without a clarification on them, one could wear the uniform in a most weird way.

A princely sum of Rs. 1,200 grant towards horse and saddler still continues *(ha, ha, you may not get even a mongrel at that cost!)* The point being made is that the Uniform Rules may be stupid; they may be the result of some clerk's lack of wisdom; they may reflect an utter lack of application of mind—there is, however, greater stupidity in not even knowing that there is such-and-such stupidity in the Rules in the first place. Generations of IPS officers have retired since 1954 (when the Uniform Rules were framed) but not one of them knew the things mentioned above. Because they did not know, the question of asking for any amendment to the archaic rules never arose. That's how the stupidity continues by the time of writing this book in 2013. Readers, please reflect upon it. When IPS officers do not know even something as elementary as their Uniform Rules, can you ever expect them to know more complex things like the law; the judgements of the honourable Supreme Court; and a large number of other professional matters? What service such imbeciles can render to the public and the nation?

Do not be surprised, dear readers. Einstein had said once: "Only two things are infinite, the Universe and human stupidity; and I'm not sure about the former!" Nothing could be truer than this, at least for the police leadership in India. You must end this tyranny of the ignorant if you ever want a better police.

Chapter 11

Do We See a Ray of Hope and How?

11.1 Redemption is Still Possible but There are No Quick Fixes

Police is one of the most important instruments of governance. When this instrument fails, people start losing faith in governance itself. A higher standard of morality and performance is therefore expected of the police. Unfortunately, the exact opposite took place over the decades. The police fell way below the standards of other departments of the government. As shown comprehensively in the previous chapters, the ills and evils that have consumed the police and the police leadership of this country are serious and multifarious. Moreover, most of these ills and evils have been there since a long time—almost since the inception of the police. They have therefore become like drug-resistant bacteria and the patient has landed up in ICU. But it is still curable. Quite like such complicated cases in medicine, this too will require an aggressive treatment and patience. No one should expect a magic wand, any quick fixes or single shot solutions. Miracles do not take place in real life. Let us stop the age-old Indian habit of placing all our trust and hopes in a single entity. No single institution like Jan Lokpal or whatever; no single Commission; no single judgement; no single individual; or no single legislative enactment would solve all the problems of the police. It would require a tremendous multi-dimensional effort. As we have shown earlier, the so-called police reforms which have caught the fancy of popular imagination would simply not help because they ignore the most critical part of the problem—the man. Yes, we do know, there is problem with the system as well and they have to be addressed, but there is a more serious problem with the man. Unless the problems with the man are addressed, all attempts at improvement on system alone would remain essentially cosmetic.

Let us therefore muster moral courage to do two things. First we must admit that there are such-and-such ills and evils that have consumed the police. Unless we admit this truth, a beginning cannot be made. Then we must perform some drastic surgery. We would like to emphasize the word drastic. Nothing short of drastic measures would be of any help. We are emphasizing this because Indians have an incorrigible habit of resisting change and changing any attempt at change—to such an extent that they succeed in changing the change itself!

In this chapter, we would present a brief outline of what, in our considered opinion, ought to be done to salvage the situation. Obviously, a comprehensive discussion would require a separate book on the subject and if we were to include that in this book, it would have become too bulky. This chapter is considered necessary so that it may not be alleged that we only discussed shortcomings but did not suggest any means of improvement. The purpose of the several previous chapters of the book has been to conclusively prove that the police leadership suffers from such-and-such malaise or deficiency. Work on them methodically and you would notice great improvement.

11.2 Tackling Intellectual Bankruptcy and General Ignorance

11.2.1 *Make Training Harder, Exams Tougher*

As we saw in the previous chapters, both the officers and the police service have got completely de-intellectualized. This process has to be reversed. The process of reversal of de-intellectualization must begin at the basic training stage itself. The basic training of the IPS officers has to be much harder than what it is at the moment and the standards have to be much tougher. The current regimen leaves much to be desired both amongst the trainees, and the trainers. After all, if we have to continue the archaic and colonial system of recruiting IPS officers directly at such high level, they must meet very high standards of both training and examination. Otherwise, we must dispense with the system. Much harm has been done to this country by what we call the 'CBSE syndrome'. As the readers are well aware, kids have been regularly scoring close to 100 percent in the CBSE examinations since decades. Does it indicate that they are absolute geniuses? By God, if they had been geniuses, Indian should have reached the skies by now. What did they do afterwards? Did they do anything innovative? What has been their contribution to world science or even literature in all these decades? Nothing! In real life, they have all turned out to be as much mediocre as anybody else. This means that the marks scored by them in a system characterized by easy question papers, liberal marking, and emphasis on giving structured responses have had really no connection with their total knowledge and creative intellectual ability.

The same thing has been happening with the training of IPS officers as well. Much of the business of training is show, with little substance. Have you ever heard of any IAS or IPS probationer having been failed in the Lal Bahadur Shastri National Academy of Administration or the Sardar Vallabhbhai Patel National Police Academy? Never. Why? Are they so brilliant that they pass all the examination without much effort? Well, if it is so, how come they are found to be so utterly intellectually bankrupt and professionally ignorant immediately after they enter the 'field'? Obviously, something is very wrong somewhere. Either, we are not teaching them the right things, our examinations are not tough enough, or both.

One of us has been an IPS officer himself for close to 28 years. We know it first-hand that the academy examinations are indeed not tough enough. Moreover, a subconscious effort is made to see to it that probationers do not fail in critical subjects—some guys could be made to fail occasionally in non-critical subjects like horse riding, swimming, the regional language or something like that just to show that the academy does maintain some standard. What most outsiders do not know that the probationers thus failed have the facility of appearing in those subjects in the states and there, with 'proper management' of the examiners (who are government officials anyway), they are made to pass. The unstated belief of the system is that these guys have cleared the UPSC examination—let us not be harsh to them. It is this platitude which has cost the nation so dearly. We are personally aware of not one but scores of officers who could not grasp one word of forensic science or cite even one judgement in criminal law for some section. We have known officers who never understood how even pistol functions, not to speak of other weapons? We have known hundreds of officers who never knew a word about explosives and yet are allowed to advise their subordinates about protection from IEDs. Senior officers are imbued with great powers regarding financial and disciplinary matters. And yet, almost as a matter of rule, they do not know anything about rules and regulations and that's how they can seldom afford to disagree with the noting of the lower division clerk!

The training must therefore be harder, much more comprehensive and the examinations tough. Anyone can check the extremely low pass rate (that is, a very high rate of failure) which the British SAS (Special Air Service), US Marines; US Navy SEALs; and Royal Marine Commandos have and understand what we mean. Nearly 80-85 percent of the candidates do not make it—that's how they get the best of the best.

11.2.2 *The Content of Training and the Standard of Trainers Both Need Drastic Improvement*

We will first consider the issue of the content of training. There is indeed a serious problem with the content of the training. The content is hopelessly deficient. The content is deficient because there is total intellectual bankruptcy in the training institutions. They must have knowledge themselves first before they can impart it to others. The training institution, or for that matter, the country as such, does not have an institutional knowledge bank of a very high order. You can understand the importance of this statement only if you have seen something to compare with. We implore the readers to have a look at the content of the Manuals, Field Manuals, Correspondence Course Materials, and Training Manuals of the US Military including the Army, Air Force, US Marine Corps, US Navy, and for the Joint Service. It's all in the public domain and anyone can download them and see for himself.

The first thing that will strike you is the sheer extensiveness both in terms of the sheer numbers as well as the topics covered. They have produced a whopping 779 manuals and other publications mentioned above. And do not think that they are small pamphlets—each one of them is hundreds of pages long. They have covered almost every topic that can be imagined under the sun to be of any use to the man in uniform at any rank. In fact, they are characterized by their lucid style of presentation and yet maintain a very high standard which does not compromise on technical rigor or accuracy anywhere. They are unique in the sense that while many of them provide how-tos for lower level functionaries, the others are comprehensive reference works for officers of the highest level. Any information that you need on a subject will be found in the manual on that subject. In fact, they are widely used by people outside the military for gaining complete knowledge of the subject in one cover.

Now let us carry out an honest introspection. Let us compare whatever we have in the police and the army, air force and the navy with this. Let the ARTRAC (Army Training Command) and the Sardar Vallabhbhai Patel National Police Academy come forward with all the stuff they have created in the past decades and compare the contents of at least the common subjects with those of the US Military. Even a lay man would be able to convince himself that the material with us is nothing but pure trash.

We, as a nation, must therefore gird our loins and prepare world-class resource material in all the fields—particularly so in the fields of deficiencies that we have pointed out throughout the book. The modalities of preparation can be worked out but, for God's sake, it should not be got prepared by some committee headed by some ignorant senior officer. Committees of all types have been largely responsible for the perpetuation of mediocrity in this country. As dear Boris Pasternak said in Doctor Zhivago, "It is always a sign of mediocrity when people herd together. Truth is always sought by individuals and they break up with those who do not love it enough." Our love for committees is a reflection of the fact that we do not have sufficient brilliant men.

The British could be accused of many bad things but they could not be accused of failing to spot talent, wherever it was. William Wilson Hunter (later to be knighted) was an ICS officer who had joined the service in 1852. When the mutiny broke out he had just five years of service. Yet, the then Viceroy could sense that the boy had extraordinary talents. Of all the senior administrators and generals of the Empire, this boy was asked to analyze the reasons of the mutiny—his inexperience notwithstanding! The result was the highly perceptive analysis 'The Indian Mussulman: Is He Bound In Conscience To Rebel Against The Queen?' that he got published in 1861 and which guided the British policy towards the Muslims for 90 years to come! And that was not the end of it. Having got it confirmed that here was a genius par excellence and an extremely hard-working man, he was charged with a task that was to serve as the ultimate resource and support system for generations of ICS officers. The problem was fundamental. Young men from England came to India in high positions and were posted in far flung corners of the empire with hardly any other Englishman for company, not to speak of guidance. For obvious reasons, they could not trust their Indian subordinates implicitly. How they were to know about the land, the people, the agricultural produce, the economic activities, the festivals, the flora and fauna, the communal problems, the criminal problems, the political problems and everything that the officers of the Empire might need to know in the course of their duties of maintaining the Empire. Where would they learn? Whom would they ask? What would happen if they were misled? All these problems were solved by William Wilson Hunter. In 1869, he was entrusted with the task of producing what became famous as the Imperial Gazetteer of India. In 12 years of backbreaking work, he produced nine volumes of the Imperial Gazetteer, a phenomenal encyclopaedic work. British officers had only to read it once and then they need not ask anything from anybody. A second edition, augmented to 14 volumes, was issued in the years 1885-87. An independent volume was published in 1893, under the title of The Indian Empire: Its Peoples, History, and Products. All of these were edited by Hunter. We must therefore learn to spot talent and make use of it.

Next comes the question of quality of trainers. The *guru* must know much more than the *shishya.* In fact, the *guru* must know even those things which are not found in the books. Then only he can impart real training—otherwise one could as well learn from the books. The training institutions instantly become defensive the moment you raise the question of the competence level of the faculty. Let us face it—what are their credentials? After all how do you assess someone's academic credentials? One way is degrees earned; the other is their independent publications. You will find that they do not have any extra proven qualifications to qualify as trainers for officers of such high post as IPS officers. The qualifications of the faculty members of the Sardar Vallabhbhai Patel National Police Academy or the Lal Bahadur Shastri National Academy of Administration are in public domain. Anyone can check and if he so desires, can do a Google search also. None of them have ever made any independent contribution of any consequence. They are just like those officers whom they train. We hope readers would agree that wisdom is not directly proportional to seniority and seniority cannot be counted as a qualification. Well, if the trainers were to be treated as just another posting on which anybody could be posted, then you can never expect any improvement.

11.2.3 *Fill in the Terrible Gaps in Knowledge*

The current syllabus of the training of the IPS officers leaves much to be desired. While they try to cover many subjects, none of them is covered in depth. The subjects covered include: Police in Modern India; Indian Evidence Act, 1872; Indian Penal Code, 1860; Code of Criminal Procedure, 1973; Special Laws; Crime Prevention and Criminology; Investigation; Forensic Medicine; Forensic Science; Maintenance of Public Peace and Order; Internal Security; Police

Leadership and Management; Ethics and Human Rights; and Information and Communication Technology.

In-depth knowledge is critical. We have very good reasons to believe that the training does not seek to impart in-depth knowledge. We will illustrate the point with a few examples. We have pointed it out earlier that as far as forensic science and medicine are concerned, they do not touch anything beyond the hopelessly archaic and low-level books of J. L. Modi and C. L. Parikh. So is the case with other subjects also. We have had occasions to interact with several hundreds of probationers over the years. On the subject of investigations, we invariably ask them if they have read V. S. Mitter's 'Police Diaries' (in two volumes). We never found anyone who has had studied these books in the Police Academy. Now this is the seminal work on police investigation replete with hundreds, if not thousands of judgements—perhaps no book better than this has been written in India. Unless they have studied this, no one can claim to have understood the nuances of police investigation. As far as law is concerned, most of them manage to pass the course with P. L. Malik's 'Criminal Court Handbook' which deals with all the three Major Acts in one volume. We never found any probationer who had bothered to study Sir Hari Singh Gour's 'Penal Law of India' (in four volumes) or Sohoni's 'The Code of Criminal Procedure' (in five volumes).

Then training must be intellectually honest. The probationers should not be presented merely a goody-goody view of the department. They are not kids of some ancient convent schools who are never exposed to the dirty side of life. One should never forget that they are recruited at a very high level. If they do not know the ugly truth, who else will? The IPS officers must know the police inside out. They must have a thorough knowledge of what the ills that beset the police are and what are the evils that the police do. They must know all the dirty tricks that their subordinates play. Unless they know these, they can never set out to correct them even if they develop a desire to do so. At present, they only get to hear about them in half jest, half vague terms. They should actually be presented with a very large number of case studies of decided cases in which the courts have exposed the deliberate wrongs committed by the police. At present, we find that there is no such compendium except this book. Moreover, they should also be given a complete grounding in the inadvertent mistakes which the subordinates commit.

More than one-and-a-half lakh policemen are deployed in anti-naxal operations and nearly the same number are deployed in Kashmir where the operations are in an urban terrain. Jungle combat and urban combat are extremely complex subjects. One must study hundreds of references just to get an elementary idea of jungle warfare and urban warfare. A perusal of our books '**Jungle Warfare: An Ultimate Handbook**' and '**The Ultimate Handbook of Urban Warfare**' would prove that. The very lives of so many lakhs of policemen depend on the leadership provided by the young IPS officers. How are they supposed to lead them into combat and conduct operations when they do not have the foggiest idea of these things themselves? It is a very serious shortcoming. It is utterly juvenile to expect that they can get any reasonable idea of the subject in a short attachment with the Greyhounds or some two weeks long course on tactics. Combat is a matter of life and death. In such courses and attachments, people learn to merely latch on to catch words like counter-ambush drill, but do not know anything more than the word—nobody knows what exactly must be done when you come under fire. So is the case with assault—there could be a defended enemy position in front of you; nobody knows how to take it without causing extensive collateral damage or getting killed oneself. Anything short of comprehensive knowledge and complete command of the subject is a sure recipe for the massacre of their subordinates.

Even in outdoor training, relevant things are not taught adequately. For example, what is taught in the name of UAC (unarmed combat) is utterly farcical. The basic throws of judo and basic punches and kicks of karate etc. that are taught have no relevance in real life street fighting which the officer might have to do at some point of time in his life to save himself or somebody else. The basic drawback is that the training is no-contact type. This is precisely what happens with those thousands of schools across the country also where they award black belts by the hundreds of thousands for punching and kicking in thin air without the black belt ever having received a single punch in his whole life. As a result, if any punch connects with his face by mistake even in *kumite* (sparring), the poor guy is knocked out flat. In real life street fights, black belts end up in hospital. Just to illustrate the point, we may mention that in September 2011, a 37 strong team of Taekwondo from Jharkhand was travelling in the Moori Express from Ranchi on their way to Yamuna Nagar in Haryana to take part in the National Open Championship. A fight broke out with some hoodlums in the train near the Mauwari Block Halt, Meja Road railway station over the issue of misbehaviour with women members of the team. Well, the Taekwondo players were severely beaten up and six of them were so badly injured that they had to be admitted in the SRN Hospital, Allahabad. Yes, we are aware that we do not expect the IPS officers to master filmi fights that defy the laws of nature (a la Dabangg 2, Vijayanthi IPS or Tejaswini) but the fact remains that unless one is used to getting a feel of the punch in the face (or elsewhere), a couple of slashes from a blade or hits from a heavy implement like a club, he cannot fight in real life. The training must be realistic—otherwise it is a waste of time.

As real life fighting is not stylized where the opponent leads with a pre-determined punch or kick which is countered with a pre-determined block or counter-attack, so is the case with riotous mob also. Probationers will not learn anything with the so-called 'riot drill, lathi drill, or tear smoke drill' because they are drills—that is, the pattern of response is set. Real mobs behave in an absolutely vicious and unpredictable way. In karate schools, a stick *(jo or bo)* fights with a stick; a *shinai* (a bamboo sword) fights with a *shinai*; and so on. They never teach you what would you do if you are barehanded and the guy in front of you has a bicycle chain; you have a stick and he has a GI pipe; you have a stick and he has a proper sword; you have a baton and he has a knife, and so on. Even Muhammad Ali was flummoxed when he was made to face a wrestler Antonio Inoki—he could connect only six punches in 15 rounds. So is the case with riotous mobs. In the riot drill taught in the Police Academy, you warn the rioters as per law, use tear gas on them or lathi-charge them and they disperse. It does not happen in real life. It real life, and we have photographic as well as video recording evidence for this claim, rioters brave tear gas for the whole day and engage you from 40-75 yards with a barrage of stones so powerful that policemen have been knocked out cold under their riot helmets! Rioters have frequently fired from the mob. Now probationers will not learn anything from the stories that the senior officers love to regale them with—how they controlled that riot when they were SPs—by God, officers must be given actual exposure.

If the total requirement of the revised syllabus cannot be met within the present period of training, the duration of training must be extended. God has not prescribed that the training must end in two years. In any case, the time spent in training is counted towards total service and the probationers get full salary from the first day. Thus there cannot be any cause for complaint.

11.2.4 *Inculcate Creative Intellect*

We need to understand one thing clearly. Creative intellect has little to do with marks scored in a structured examination. Hence, even when we make the exam tougher, it still cannot be guaranteed that the officers will acquire the ability to think for themselves. The only way to develop creative intellect is to exercise it.

The United States Army Command and General Staff College (CGSC) at Fort Leavenworth, Kansas is a graduate school for United States Army and sister service officers, interagency representatives, and international military officers. It educates and develops leaders for full spectrum joint, interagency and multinational operations; acts as lead agent for the Army's leader development program; and advances the art and science of the profession of arms in support of Army operational requirements. The students are normally mid-career field-grade officers preparing for battalion command or staff positions at the division, brigade, or battalion level. Many of them go on to earn a Master of Military Arts and Sciences (MMAS) degree. For this degree they have to write a thesis. One must see the standard of these theses. They are in the public domain. Anybody who desires can have a look at the quality of the creative work at the website of the Combined Arms Research Library Digital Library at http://cgsc.contentdm.oclc.org/cdm/landingpage/collection/p4013coll2. The MMAS theses provide in-depth research on military history and military science, military doctrine, strategic issues, tactical issues, operational issues, logistics, planning, technological aspects and organizations, both existing and proposed. Since the degree awarded is accredited, the theses, in their academic merit, are on a par with the theses at famous universities of the USA.

The point being emphasized is that they force their officers to think for themselves. They are not merely given training material, lecture notes, or course material which they would mug and regurgitate in the examination as we do. We need to do make our officers think for themselves. Writing a dissertation must be mandatory in the basic course. The topic must be selected in such a manner that they have to apply their own mind, logic and reasoning to give an opinion of their own. The standard Indian university/college practice of writing a dissertation essentially on the strength of a literature survey must not be allowed at all. Earlier in the book, we have discussed how generations of IPS officers have failed to address some of the fundamental issues of law that have been left ambiguous. The training must focus on them. As we have pointed out in connection with the fallacies of the so-called forensic techniques, police lust learn to apply their own minds and not accept the version of some so-called self-styled experts with dubious qualifications and even more dubious intentions.

11.2.5 *Introduce and Enforce In-Service Exams*

As we have mentioned earlier also, the Indian Civil Services operate on an unstated belief that one who has cleared the exam once, need never learn anything again in his entire life. Nothing could be more ridiculous than this. Actually, this is a famous Indian belief system. Take professionals from any field—the Indians regard the older as better—experience takes precedence over knowledge anytime. The old neighbourhood doctor sahib might have acquired his MBBS degree four decades ago and all these years would not have bothered to read even a single research paper or book. All that he knows about modern medicines is acquired courtesy the medical representatives of the pharmaceutical firms who give him samples of medicines. His knowledge is hopelessly dated—yet people value him. In several countries of the world, it is a legal requirement that doctors would write the year of their degree on their signboards so that the people may know how old his knowledge is. Senior engineers would have got their degrees decades ago and by themselves many of them may not be capable of calculating even the minimum thickness of a wall or column needed to support a given load. Yet they are assigned mighty responsibilities. In fact, even university professors stop reading as they become senior. Many of them cannot explain even those research papers in which they figure as senior authors but which are actually written by their Ph.D. students. But they are cleverer people and have mastered the art of keeping up appearances. What they acquire as they get older is the art of dropping names and snippets of jargon picked up mostly during conferences and interaction with others like them.

This nation has suffered since long at the hands of very senior but inept administrators, police officers, doctors, engineers and professors to name a few because we have not bothered to introduce and enforce a system of rigorous in-service examinations. This needs to be done pronto. This will force them to keep on updating their knowledge and re-learning what they might have forgotten.

11.3 Put the Fear of the Law in Their Minds

11.3.1 *Provide for Exemplary Punishments*

We are firm believers of the theory that stringent punishment is the best deterrent to wrongdoings. The punishment must be harsh and immediate. At this juncture, some people might cite the Service Rules of other departments and ask why the policemen must be handed out harsher punishment. Well, there are several reasons for it. In the first place, the police officers know it very well that they are charged with the responsibility of protecting the citizens. People go to police only when they are in acute stress. Protecting them is a vital job because in a civilized society, it is both the moral and legal responsibility of the nation-state to protect its citizens from the depredations of all those people who could use the force of 'connections', money, muscle or weapons to deprive them of their rights. The nation state must ensure that the society is not reduced to a jungle where the powerful devour the weak. If the nation-state fails in that responsibility, it loses all moral authority to govern. If the nation state fails in that because those public servants who are charged with discharging that responsibility have not been discharging it diligently, the nation state must address the problem by punishing them.

The police fail in their duty on account of several reasons including shirking *(kaamchori);* apathetic or even hostile attitude towards all forms of human suffering; lack of basic human sensitivities; unfair, partial, biased or partisan attitude; corruption; abuse of power, laws and the legal processes; collusion with the very predators from who they are supposed to protect the citizens for the sake of monetary gains or some other undue advantage; becoming predators themselves; and sheer professional incompetence, etc. The issue of professional incompetence can be handled to some extent by better training and in-service exams as discussed above. All other reasons pertain to his personality, attitude or something else in his mental makeup. All of those wrongs are committed knowingly. Precisely for this reason, all of them lend themselves to punishments. Corruption, for example, is thriving because it is extremely rare for the corrupt to get punished. People do calculate that the chances of getting punished are so low that it is worthwhile to take the risk. Have a system of proving guilt and prescribing stringent punishments, and the cops will gradually start behaving. The delinquent cop deserves a harsher punishment than other public servants because the intent behind the wrongs they commit is more deprave. As the saying goes, one could pardon a *ghalati* (mistake), but not a *gunaah* (sin)! The wrongs committed by the police fall in the category of *gunaah*!

All those who might find the suggestion very strict are requested to consider the following situations. Suppose your own son is killed in a fake encounter or your own daughter raped in the police station. Maybe your wife has been molested in the train and the cops refuse to even register a case. Maybe you have been robbed on the highway and the police turn a deaf ear. Maybe your neighbour has dispossessed you and captured your house and the cops tell you that it is a civil case. May be your brother is held on a false charge and is being tortured in the police station. Suppose your girlfriend has been subjected to gang rape and the policemen, instead of helping you, are casting aspersion on her character. Suppose your father has been murdered in a property dispute, and the murderers are roaming free because they have *pataoed* the police. Suppose the police refuse to register FIR for several days and the accused flee in the meantime. How would you feel? Gentlemen, these are not extreme or purely hypothetical situations. Should it come to that, we can cite real life instances for each one of them. Would you not demand harsh punishment to the cops? If something has not happened to you, it does not mean that it is not happening either. You must learn to empathize with those who have had the misfortune of actually suffering all these horrors not once but several times in their lives.

Providing for exemplary punishment to the cops for such delinquencies will require an amendment in the Service Rules and the Disciplinary Rules. The reasons are simple. The existing rules are simply inadequate. With the existing rules and procedures, punishments are more in the nature of exception. As the examples cited throughout the length of this book would amply illustrate, delinquent police officers have often been able to get away literally with murder.

11.3.2 *Respect the Observations of the Courts and Act Upon Them*

The courts have had innumerable occasions to pass adverse comments on the functioning of the police ranging from admonition, and strictures to recommend registration of cases against the police officers. Yes, the courts have done an admirable job but not everybody in this country can afford to slug it out in the courts. The percentage of cases in which the victims of police apathy or atrocities get justice from the courts is very small. The police leadership must therefore keep this in mind. Invariably, in all the cases where the courts find fault with the police, exemplary punishment must be awarded.

11.4 Improving the Quality of Service

11.4.1 *If the Desire to Serve the People is Not There, It Must be Forced*

The usual refrain of street cops and senior officers alike is that they are not able to render good quality service because they do not have enough resources. This is simple hogwash. The quality of service rendered also depends critically on the attitude of the cops and their professional competence. Good quality service can be rendered even with the present resources at their disposal if they have the desire to serve. As we have been discussing, police have fallen into the extremely despicable habit of identifying themselves with the ruling system. They think of themselves as a 'force' to be used by the rulers. It needs to be drilled into their minds, on the pain of punishment if necessary, that they have been created to serve the people, not to lord over them. This applies to all ranks—whether constables, sub-inspectors or senior IPS officers ranging from ASP to DGP. We know attitudinal changes are extremely hard to come by but if we have to have results, then stricter measures are absolutely essential.

When it comes to resources, the first lament is that of inadequate numbers. Senior officers in particular love to shout at the top of their voices that in this country we have, on an average, only 138 policemen for one lakh people and what they could do with that? For their benefit, we would like to quote from what had been argued in an editorial of *The Hindu* entitled "Rebuild India's Police Forces" (September 9, 2011): "Minutes after a bomb ripped through the Delhi High Court on Wednesday, India's politicians began sounding like an old broken record: the terrorists were "dastardly"; the attack was "cowardly"; the perpetrators would receive a "resolute response." Terrorists are unlikely to be cowed by this. The sad truth is that not one case of urban terrorism since 26/11 has been solved, and there's a mounting body of evidence that suggests the alleged perpetrators of attacks prior to that are being tried for crimes they did not commit. Post-26/11...the assumption seemed to be that technology and islands of excellence could substitute for the unglamorous business of building grassroots police capabilities and competence. The idea has failed...The battle won't be won by numbers alone: Bihar has a pathetic 74.29 police for every 1,00,000 residents, about a quarter of what it needs; Nagaland has a staggering 1,677.3 personnel per 1,00,000 population, almost seven times its requirement—but both are good examples of incompetent policing...

First, it must prepare a template for nationwide standards of police training and competence, compliance with which must be regularly assessed. Secondly, India desperately needs world-standard institutions for police tactics and investigation to produce the core of instructors who can develop the capacities of State police forces. States do run training programmes but their syllabi and training methods are, for the most part, unsuited to real-world policing. Few police forces have in-house forensic facilities, language specialists, or intelligence analysts. Thirdly, India's higher security management must be drawn through a process that tests aptitude for the job.

Professional competence must guide promotions and remuneration."

11.4.2 *Introduce a Robust System of Accountability*

As we have analyzed at length in the book, it has become fashionable to blame the politicians for all the ills and evils of the police. We have also shown that it is not only a false notion; it is utterly unfair too and is outright intellectual dishonesty. The politician, however bad he might be, is accountable to the people and can be booted out of his job after his term of five years if he does not come up to the expectations of the people. It is not so with government servants. The Service Rules can at best, unless drastically amended, provide for punishments—they do not provide for accountability. It is therefore dangerous to give unfettered, unbridled powers to the police without introducing a string system of ensuring accountability. We must be intellectually honest enough to admit this fact. Freedom of investigation does not mean the freedom to tweak or 'shape' the investigation. Yes, the courts could find fault with him later and even get him punished, but by the time great damage has already been done to the victim.

Precisely for this reason, the Sheriff, that is the top law enforcement office of a county in the USA, is an elected person. Sheriffs are elected for four-year terms in 41 states, two-year terms in three states, a three-year term in one state (New Jersey) and a six-year term in one state (Massachusetts). In all they have more than 3085 Sheriff's offices in the USA and the system is working excellently since ages. Even in the UK, the need of accountability was realized. In November 2012, elections for the post of Police and Crime Commissioner (PCC) were held in most police areas in England and Wales. The Government considers the elected Commissioners to have a stronger mandate than the "unelected and invisible police authorities that they replace". They maintain that PCCs will give local people more control over policing. An official statement said: "The police and crime commissioners are visible, they'll be accessible, they've been elected and crucially they will be accountable to people through the ballot box." Police and Crime Commissioner elections were for 41 of the 43 territorial police forces in England and Wales; only the City of London Police and Metropolitan Police were not involved (the elected Mayor of London is classed as the Police and Crime Commissioner for the Metropolitan Police Area, while the Court of Common Council serves the role for the City Police). Commissioners have a set four-year term of office and a maximum of two terms. They will have powers to hire and fire chief constables and set police strategy and budgets. And please do not be under a misconception that incompetent people could get elected. Quite interestingly, in the first elections in England, several former police officers contesting as independents did beat party candidates!

We are not saying that, with the given political system in India, we should blindly copy the Americans or the British. However, the point being made is that we must at least admit the need for accountability in the police leadership that others have realized. As the genius Prince Otto von Bismarck had said, "Fools learn from their own experience. I prefer to learn from other people's experiences." Once we admit the fact that government servants in general and the police in particular too need to be accountable, we can then work out how best this accountability can be incorporated in our Constitutional structure.

11.4.3 *Curb the Tendency Towards Corruption in Training Stage Itself*

Curbing the tendency towards corruption at the training stage itself is vital. If you think that it could be curbed in the field, you are already too late. It is a popular misconception that officers start as vestal virgins from the academies but are corrupted as they are exposed to the 'filth' of the field or the 'real world'. It is far from the truth. At least in respect of the IPS, candidates are now entering fairly late—well into their late '20s. Many of them enter the service with the experience of several other jobs. Gone are the days when boys in their early twenties straight out of university were selected into the IPS. The relative merits and demerits of early entry or late entry can be debated ad nauseam. However, the fact remains that those candidates who join service rather late, have already had considerable exposure of the 'real world', as against the 'cocooned world' of the universities and colleges. This exposure hardens their value system. The value system of a man depends on several things—his upbringing; his family; his social milieu; his experiences in life; the experiences of his family; his education; and so on. However, it can also not be denied that for quite some time in his life a man does remain impressionable to some extent. This is particularly true of university or college life or immediately thereafter. Hence, in the olden days when the entrants used to be younger, there was some chance of finding them impressionable or malleable. That's why the Royal Military Academy Sandhurst used to take boys straight from the public schools so that the military officers could be positively 'moulded' to conform to the value system of the Empire! Now the task is admittedly difficult. But we have to do it nevertheless.

In other words, the modern Indian trainee officer is not what Rousseau called '*tabula rasa*'—a blank slate on which you could write anything. He comes with a lot of emotional, psychological, and socio-cultural baggage. The academies cannot 'unburden' him completely. A 28-year-old man, for example, has had considerable exposure of life and his views about life are more or less fixed. If he comes from a family that swears by caste, chances are dim that training in police-related subjects would have any effect on his value systems related to caste. If he comes from a background where women have not been respected or are permanently relegated to a secondary status, the academies can only force him to rise when ladies enter a room—inwardly he would still be thinking the same things about them which he has always thought. Still, as we show in the next section, he can be persuaded to respect what the people, the society and the nation expect from his job.

Field or the 'real world' introduces a complication. The moment one enters the 'field', he is, for all practical purposes on his own and does not really look up to anybody for advice. The service, in any case, does not have an atmosphere where one could look up to his seniors for sane advice as elders. Such goody-goody days, if they ever existed, are long dead and gone. If the young officer goes wayward in the field, there is no stopping him. Hence whatever that needs to be done by the system, must be done in the training stage itself.

Inculcating values is not something that can be done by lectures or training notes. The CBSE has had ethics as a subject on its syllabi since long but that has not helped India becoming an ethical society by any stretch of imagination. Isn't it? Values can be imparted only by real examples. At least in the training academies, value systems can be spoken of only by those who can rightfully claim to be honest. This is important because in the modern era, everybody knows about everybody. If those officers who are known to have shady records, start lecturing on honesty, the trainees make fun of them behind their backs and dismiss the whole thing as yet another inanity imposed on them by the academy. It would not be easy finding such officers but this should well be a criterion for selection as trainers. Elsewhere in the world they pay great attention to the character of the trainers—it is not merely his qualifications that are taken into account.

11.4.4 *Professionalise the Police, Not Polarise It Politically*

Usually people speak of politicisation of the police. We would like to correct a semantic mistake here because loose, unguarded usage tends to reduce the issue to inanities. People speak of politicisation as if it is a dirty word. They forget that politics is the very lifeblood of any living democracy. We cannot stamp out politics from our lives. The very basis of democracy is that the people of the country will elect their representatives and they would govern the country for them. They are directly accountable to the people and that makes them earn the right to govern. It is the political leadership which has got the constitutional mandate to decide the policies of the nation on which the future of millions depends. If the people find that the policies of the representatives they elected are not doing them good, they can very well vote for another party in the next elections. That's how the system works. We cannot envisage a system where those, that is, government employees, who are not accountable to the people govern them. Politics would therefore necessarily pervade all aspects of life and you cannot take away the right of the political leader to frame policies as they deem fit.

The public is free to make its political choices. It is not under any obligation to even have a reason for its choices, not to speak of rationalizing them. They may like or dislike a political party for whatever reason. In a functioning democracy, you cannot have apolitical citizens. If the citizens become apolitical, democracy cannot survive. Like every citizen, the police and the army personnel also do vote in elections. This means that on a personal level they also have their preferences and they are also free to change their preferences on whatever considerations. Nobody expects them to cast their votes by tossing coins! Nothing comes in the way of their family members being political leaders also.

The question is what bearing their personal preferences could have on the discharge of their duties? The answer is simple. This is where the government servants are expected to walk a tight rope. While they are completely free to have their personal political preferences, this preference should not, in any way, affect the discharge of their duties. In the discharge of their duties, they must be guided by only one consideration—that they must uphold the Constitution of the country and the laws framed under it. This is not materially different from keeping your business life and personal life separate. Their personal political views must not colour their decisions as long as they are in service. Should they want, they can join politics after retirement or after resignation, but as long as they are in service, they must not be politically polarized.

Having a personal political belief is one thing; being politically polarized is quite another. We will elaborate on it. A police officer could be a voter of party X. Suppose there is a violent clash between workers of party X and party Y. When the police are rushed to control the situation, they must use their professional judgement to control the situation by a judicious use of force as mandated by the law. There should be no bias shown in the use of force against the rioters of one party over another. The matter does not end there. Cases and counter-cases are registered and investigation follows. If the police are politically not polarized, the investigation should be fair and no party should be favoured or victimized.

Is it a very difficult thing? Certainly not! The perceived difficulty arises on account of a wrong popular perception which has been engendered partly by the government servants themselves. The perception is that the government servants in general and the police in particular are not able to abide by the law of the land because the politicians prevent them from doing so. Let us do an honest introspection. Do we really believe that the politicians are hell bent upon doing only illegal things? Obviously, it cannot be true. It is nothing but popular cynicism. If it were to be true, why are we still persisting with democracy? The fact that we have willingly and wholeheartedly taken Indian democracy forward for 66 years because, in spite of all the scandals and scams, we, the people of India, believe in it.

Politics has its failings. But the politician is not above the law. The politician can make life difficult for the government servant but he cannot force him to forsake the law. The politician may desire illegal things to be done; but he cannot order it. What really happens is that they find someone eager to oblige them much more readily than they encounter officers who stand up to them. The government servants are not as helpless as they generally make out to be. *The number of government servants who are harassed or victimized is much less than the number of government servants who are ever ready to oblige the politician in his illegal demands so as to curry favours with him.* There is no reason to believe that a law-abiding police office cannot survive in the system. Those who start colluding with the politicians collude for comfort, not for survival. *Most of the so-called political interference takes place because the police officers themselves offer to be 'manoeuvred', 'manipulated' or 'used'.* Honestly, are we not aware of a very large number of police officers who take orders directly from the politicians and do not care two hoots for the departmental hierarchy?

We believe that the bogey of political interference has been created by those who want the best of both worlds. As long as their mutually beneficial relationship with the politicians keeps on bearing fruits, they do not utter a word. The moment they find that they are not getting the expected rewards, they start screaming of political interference. Quite often, when those officers who are regarded very 'close' to a given party and enjoy all the plum postings, find themselves relegated to some 'side' postings when the party in power changes or when they fall off with those who had been patronizing them so far, they go to town crying of political interference. How can they ever have a moral right to speak of political interference? There was no interference as long as the going was good for them; the moment they were denied the 'undue' benefits, they alleged political interference. Waiting for the political tide to turn in their favour, some of them go to the extent of proceeding on medical leave or apply for central deputation!

As we have been arguing, the police leadership is quick to blame the entire political class for their much-hyped, much-maligned interference; the IAS and other services for their jealousy and obstructionism; the people for being deprave and inherently unlawful; the media for not towing the police line all the time; and the judiciary for its lack of appreciation of 'practical constraints'. But there is no basis of such a claim. Such a claim could have been made by only a police force which had proven its professional integrity by its deeds over the decades. When did it do so? Never! There is no reason to believe that the bureaucrats in general and the police officers in particular are inherently 'good' whereas the politicians are inherently 'bad'—that, left to themselves, the bureaucrats would usher in the Utopia but the politicians make them do all the bad things. There cannot be any reason to believe that officers who are products of the same society are in any way morally superior to the politicians. It was never so, and it can never be so. The reality is that the 'business' of policing in India revolves around partisan behaviour, currying of political favours for plum postings, and wielding of power, entirely overshadowing the real duties of the police. They do not have a track record which could inspire a confidence that if they are somehow 'insulated' from the politicians, they would deliver professional policing to the people. The tragedy of the country is that the police have been functioning as the agents of those in power so as to get a share of the power—as simple as that—and they have never bothered to be professional, fair, and unbiased. Justice is not delivered according to the rights of the man demanding justice but according to what suits the collective interests of the nexus of all those who constitute 'power'.

It is precisely due to this legacy of the police that the common man has little faith in the police. Since he does not have faith, he often decides to take the law into his own hands. That explains why we have such lawlessness in our multi-cultural, multi-ethnic society. After every riot, the usual blame game starts and till the news becomes stale, we keep on hearing of how the politicians instigated the riots, and so on. Yes, they might have instigated the riots but the police could have still controlled it swiftly had they acted professionally. The police are not short of resources—we always deploy them in large numbers and supplement them with the paramilitary forces and the army. Now the situation is that rioters kill 50-100 people between them but nobody is found killed in police firing. Riots result in massive loss of lives and property because the rioters, in the back of their minds know that the police are neither professional nor effective. Worse, when they take action, they are often accused of highly biased action. Let the shortcomings of the men comprising the system be not transposed on to the system. When there was inaction on the part of the police in responding to the complaints of a girl who was stalked by a politician, the inaction was not due to any 'politicisation' of the police. For all you know, the policemen concerned would not even know the political ideology of the concerned politicians. It was not fear either for if you admit fear, you would be insulting the uniform; it was simple collusion. You collude with someone and hence you go out of the way to protect him.

The problem is not so much with the system as it is with the men manning the system. It has become fashionable to speak of changing the system. Our contention is that changing the system would not deliver results unless men in the system are changed. Thus, if the police officers remain as corrupt, as insensitive, as ignorant, as greedy as they are, 'insulating' the police would only result in a change of tormentors. Today if the politicians are being unfair to a section of the people, tomorrow the police officers would be unfair to that or some other section of the people. Politicians are much a product of the society as the police officers. It is unbridled power that corrupts them. There is no reason or even a historical example to believe that the same unbridled power would not corrupt the police officers.

Hence we must focus on the man. Even the existing system can deliver infinitely better results if the men of the system change for good. It all translates into inculcating a value system. Changing attitudes is indeed a tall order but a beginning has to be made somewhere. Professionalism lies in not merely being efficient; it lies in doing the right thing efficiently. One has to start respecting the profession and the onerous responsibility that goes with it. If the policeman of some other country is trusted by his people and they look up to him in times of need with full confidence, it is not because he is better equipped, it is because he respects his profession and considers it his '*dharma*' to discharge his duty without fear of favour. He is happy with what he is paid and does not bend himself or the law to reap millions. It is the man who makes all the difference; not the system.

A Select Bibliography

26/11 Court indicts some police officers for cowardice, *The Indian Express*, May 24, 2013, http://www.indianexpress.com/news/2611-court-indicts-some-police-officers-for-cowardice/622986/

26/11: 'Coward' Mumbai Cops To Face Action, *The Indian Express*, May 29, 2013, http://www.indianexpress.com/news/2611-coward-mumbai-cops-to-face-action/626394/

5 acquitted in Best Bakery Case, HC slams police, *Jai Maharashtra News*, July 10, 2012, http://www.jaimaharashtranews.com/en/politics-en/5-acquitted-in-best-bakery-case-hc-slams-police/

5,000 hardcore Maoists with armed militia in Chhattisgarh, Rediff.com, April 08, 2010, http://news.rediff.com/report/2010/apr/08/chhattisgarh-igp-on-the naxalites.htm

7 'terrorists' acquitted by Delhi High Court, *Times of India*, August 6, 2012, http://articles.timesofindia.indiatimes.com/2012-08-06/india/33064598_1_fake-encounter-delhi-high-court-gulam-moinuddin-dar

A. J. Peabody, Diatoms And Drowning – A Review, *Medicine, Science and the Law* 20 (1980) 254-61

A. J. Peabody, Diatoms In Forensic Science, *Journal of the Forensic Science Society* 17 (1977) 81-7

A. J. Schwoeble and David L. Exline, '*Current Methods in Forensic Gunshot Residue Analysis*' (CRC Press, Florida, 2000, ISBN 0-8493-0029-0

A. K. Jayasree, Searching for Justice for Body and Self in a Coercive Environment: Sex Work in Kerala, India Reproductive Health Matters 2004;12(23):58-67

A. Maehly, and L. Stromberg, *Chemical Criminalistics*, Springer-Verlag, New York, 1981, 189.

Abhinav Garg, HC Sets Free 2 Delhi Blast Accused on Death Row, *Times of India*, November 23, 2012, http://articles.timesofindia.indiatimes.com/2012-11-23/delhi/35318402_1_delhi-high-court-mohd-ali-bhatt-mirza-nissar-hussain

Abhinav Kumar, Rushdie row: Serving IPS officer calls Indian police cowards, ***DNA***, January 24, 2012, http://www.dnaindia.com/analysis/1641476/column-rushdie-row-serving-ips-officer-calls-indian-police-cowards

Abhinav Kumar, Showing The Way, February 10, 2011, Counterpoint, *Outlook*, http://www.outlookindia.com/article.aspx?270397

Abhinav kumar, showing the way, *Outlook*, Feb 10, 2011, http://www.outlookindia.com/article.aspx?270397

Abhinav Sharma, HC slams CBI, says it has lost credibility, *Times of India*, April 7, 2012, http://articles.timesofindia.indiatimes.com/2012-04-07/jaipur/31304414_1_cbi-court-bjp-mla-rajendra-rathore-fake-encounter

Abhishek Bhalla *and* G. Vishnu, The rapes will go on, *Tehelka*, Vol 9, Issue 15, Dated 14 April 2012, http://archive.tehelka.com/story_main52.asp?filename=Ne140412Coverstory.asp

Accused In Delhi Bomb Blast Case, Pakistani Acquitted, *The Hindu*, January 5, 2013, http://www.thehindu.com/news/national/accused-in-bombblast-pakistani-acquitted/article4273251.ece

ACHR Impact: Interventions for the victims, http://www.achrweb.org/ncpt.htm

Adarsh scam probe: Bombay HC slams CBI for inaction, Rediff.com, March 12, 2012 , http://www.rediff.com/news/report/adarsh-scam-probe-bombay-hc-slams-cbi-for-inaction/20120312.htm

Admit it, and Act, *The Indian Express*, May 1, 2013, http://www.indianexpress.com/news/admit-it-and-act/1109807/0

After High Court rap, CBI arrests 4, *Indian Express*, March 21 2012, http://www.indianexpress.com/news/after-high-court-rap-cbi-arrests-4/926314/

Ajai Sahni, India's Maoists And The Dreamscape Of 'Solutions', http://www.satp.org/satporgtp/ajaisahni/10AS-3Seminar.htm

Ajay Parmar, HC raps govt over missing persons, *Times of India*, September 25, 2012, http://articles.timesofindia.indiatimes.com/2012-09-25/jaipur/34081297_1_hc-raps-govt-justice-govind-mathur-chief-secretary

Ajit Sahi And Rana Ayyub, 'How Does A Poor Man Fight MCOCA?', CASE STUDY 6, *Tehelka Magazine*, Vol 7, Issue 02, Dated January 16, 2010, http://archive.tehelka.com/story_main43.asp?filename=Ne160110CS6.asp

Ajit Sahi And Rana Ayyub, Businessman, Squash Fan, MCOCA Survivor, CASE STUDY 2, *Tehelka Magazine,* Vol 7, Issue 02, Dated January 16, 2010, http://archive.tehelka.com/story_main43.asp?filename=Ne160110CS2.asp

Ajit Sahi And Rana Ayyub, Christmas Party, Finally, After 11 Years In Jail, CASE STUDY 9, *Tehelka Magazine,* Vol 7, Issue 03, Dated January 23, 2010, http://archive.tehelka.com/story_main43.asp?filename=Ne230110CS9.asp

Ajit Sahi And Rana Ayyub, Damned In The Name Of The Unholy Father, CASE STUDY 10, *Tehelka Magazine,* Vol 7, Issue 03, Dated January 23, 2010, http://archive.tehelka.com/story_main43.asp?filename=Ne230110CS10.asp

Ajit Sahi And Rana Ayyub, Deemed Guilty Until Proven Innocent, CASE STUDY 1, *Tehelka Magazine,* Vol 7, Issue 02, Dated January 16, 2010, http://archive.tehelka.com/story_main43.asp?filename=Ne160110CS1.asp

Ajit Sahi And Rana Ayyub, Done In By The Don Link, Saved By Bungling Cops, CASE STUDY 3, *Tehelka Magazine,* Vol 7, Issue 02, Dated January 16, 2010, http://archive.tehelka.com/story_main43.asp?filename=Ne160110CS3.asp

Ajit Sahi And Rana Ayyub, Have Law Will Jail, , *Tehelka Magazine,* Vol 7, Issue 04, Dated January 30, 2010

Ajit Sahi And Rana Ayyub, How The Law Is Made An Ass, *Tehelka Magazine,* Vol 7, Issue 03, Dated January 23, 2010

Ajit Sahi And Rana Ayyub, Married To The Mob And Paying The Price For It, CASE STUDY 8, *Tehelka Magazine,* Vol 7, Issue 02, Dated January 16, 2010, http://archive.tehelka.com/story_main43.asp?filename=Ne160110CS8.asp

Ajit Sahi And Rana Ayyub, One Flew Over The Cuckoo's Nest, *Tehelka Magazine,* Vol 7, Issue 02, Dated January 16, 2010

Ajit Sahi And Rana Ayyub, The Don's Brother Is Free. Long Live The Don In Dubai, CASE STUDY 12, *Tehelka Magazine,* Vol 7, Issue 03, Dated January 23, 2010, http://archive.tehelka.com/story_main43.asp?filename=Ne230110CS12.asp

Ajit Sahi And Rana Ayyub, The Grim Tale Of The Azmi Brothers, CASE STUDY 7, *Tehelka Magazine,* Vol 7, Issue 02, Dated January 16, 2010

Ajit Sahi And Rana Ayyub, The Grim Tale Of The Azmi Brothers, *Tehelka Magazine,* Vol 7, Issue 02, Dated January 16, 2010

Ajit Sahi And Rana Ayyub, The Man Who Was Jailed By His Beard, CASE STUDY 5, *Tehelka Magazine,* Vol 7, Issue 02, Dated January 16, 2010, http://archive.tehelka.com/story_main43.asp?filename=Ne160110CS5.asp

Ajit Sahi And Rana Ayyub, Top Cop At The Receiving End Of The Law, CASE STUDY 4, *Tehelka Magazine,* Vol 7, Issue 02, Dated January 16, 2010, http://archive.tehelka.com/story_main43.asp?filename=Ne160110CS4.asp

Ajit Sahi, Seema Azad, Vishwavijay step out of Allahabad Jail *Newzfirst*, July 8, 2012, kractivist, http://www.kractivist.org/2012/08/07/seema-azad-vishwavijay-step-out-of-allahabad-jail/

Amend dowry law to stop its misuse, SC tells govt, *Times of India*, August 17,n 2010, http://articles.timesofindia.indiatimes.com/2010-08-17/india/28308729_1_dowry-law-section-498a-complaints

Amit Jethava murder: HC slams probe, *Times of India*, September 26, 2012, http://articles.timesofindia.indiatimes.com/2012-09-26/ahmedabad/34101010_1_amit-jethava-murder-high-court-investigation-officer

Amnesty International, Torture, Rape And Deaths In Custody-India, AI INDEX: ASA 20/06/92, http://www.amnesty.org/ar/library/asset/ASA20/006/1992/en/da5ffdca-edaa-11dd-9ad7-350fb2522bdb/asa200061992en.pdf

Amnesty International: "India: Break the cycle of impunity and torture in Punjab." January 20, 2003

An Attack on Media Freedom, *The Hindu* (Editorial), November 2, 2012, http://www.thehindu.com/opinion/editorial/an-attack-on-media-freedom/article4055267.ece

An Interview by Harinder Baweja, September 27, 2008, *Tehelka*, Vol. 5, Issue 38, cited in Ajit Doval's Perspectives, http://ajitdoval.blogspot.in/2008/11/move-to-offensive-mode-doval.html

An Invisible Crime, People's Union for Democratic Rights, Delhi, August 2007

Anand Soondas, Inaction Of Assam Police Escalated Riots: Papers, Reluctance To Act Escalated Violence, Says Internal Report, *Times of India*, September 8, 2012, http://lite.epaper.timesofindia.com/08-2012&pubname=Times+of+India+-+Chennai+-+Times+Nation&title=Inaction+of+Assam+police+escalated+riots%3A+Papers&dname=&publabel=TOI

Anders Eriksson and Francisco Lacerda, Charlatanry In Forensic Speech Science: A Problem To Be Taken Seriously, *The International Journal of Speech, Language and the Law* IJSLL vol 14.2 2007 169–193

Andhra DGP V Dinesh Reddy stirs up salwar storm, *Indian Express*, December 31,2011, http://newindianexpress.com/states/andhra_pradesh/article313409.ece

Andhra Pradesh government to compensate youths affected in Mecca Masjid blast, ***NDTV***, December 7, 2011, http://www.ndtv.com/article/andhra-pradesh/andhra-pradesh-government-to-compensate-youths-affected-in-mecca-masjid-blast-156049

Andhra Pradesh Govt To Compensate 70 Wrongly Implicated Muslim Youth For Mecca Masjid Blast, ET Bureau & Agencies, December 9, 2011, http://articles.economictimes.indiatimes.com/2011-12-09/news/30498133_1_mecca-masjid-blast-muslim-youth-bomb-blast

Andrew E. Taslitz, Convicting the Guilty, Acquitting the Innocent: The ABA Takes a Stand, 19 *Crim. Just.* 18–19 (2005)

Anguished Gujarat high court raps cops for framing man, *Times of India*, March 11, 2012, http://articles.timesofindia.indiatimes.com/2012-03-11/ahmedabad/31144853_1_drug-peddling-case-traffic-cop-departmental-inquiry

Anil Kalhan, Gerald P. Conroy, Mamta Kaushal, Sam Scott Miller, and Jed S. Rakoff, Colonial Continuities: Human Rights, Terrorism, And Security Laws In India, *Columbia Journal Of Asian Law* [20:1], pp. 93-234], 2006

AP HC Asks Centre to Reconsider Awards to Top Cops, http://www.rediff.com/news/report/ap-hc-asks-centre-to-reconsider-awards-to-top cops/20100320.htm

Apex court fiat to States on registration of FIRs, *The Hindu*, July 27, 2007, http://www.hindu.com/2007/07/27/stories/2007072752740700.htm

Apurva, ACB detains Rajasthan IPS officer for bribery, *Indian Express* June 22, 2012, http://www.indianexpress.com/news/acb-detains-rajasthan-ips-officer-for bribery/965089/

Archna Shukla, One Of The Three Women With Tiwari Shot Video In Raj Bhavan, Says TV Channel,December 29, 2009, http://www.indianexpress.com/news/one-of-three-women-with-tiwari-shot-video-in-raj-bhavan-says-tv-channel/560930/

Arpit Parashar, "NHRC figures paint rosy picture of Kashmir and Northeast; UP and Bihar are worst offenders." *Tehelka*. August 30, 2011

Arrest last option in crime probe: SC, *Hindustan Times*, December 05, 2010, http://www.hindustantimes.com/India-news/NewDelhi/Arrest-last-option-in-crime-probe-SC/Article1-634842.aspx

Arun Sharma, Hindu-Muslim marriage: HC frees man, slams cops, *Indian Express*, November 12, 2010, http://m.indianexpress.com/news/hindumuslim-marriage-hc-frees-man-slams-cops/709907/

Arundhati Roy, "How Deep Shall We Dig?" *The Hindu*, April 25, 2004, http://www.hindu.com/2004/04/25/stories/2004042500041600.htm

Arundhati Roy, Walking With The Comrades, *Outlook*, March 29, 2010, http://www.outlookindia.com/article.aspx?264738-0

Arvind Verma, "Cultural roots of police corruption in India", *Policing: An International Journal of Police Strategies & Management*, Vol. 22 Iss: 3, pp.264 - 279, 1999

Arvind Verma, The New Khaki – The Evolving Nature of Policing in India: CRC Press, Florida

Ashish Khetan, An Angry Hall Of Fall Guys And Unfair Arrests, *Tehelka Magazine, Vol 8, Issue 2, January 15, 2011*

Ashish Khetan, Dazed & Confused. Again, *Tehelka Magazine, Vol 8, Issue 37, Dated 17 Sep 2011*

Ashish Khetan, **Sting Cam Exposé, Top Cop Caught, April 21, 2007, *Tehelka,*** http://archive.tehelka.com story_main29.asp? filename=Ne210407 Top_cop_CS.asp

Ashutosh Varshney, *Ethnic Conflict and Civic Life: Hindus and Muslims in India,* New Haven and London: Yale University Press, 2002

Asian Human Rights Commission, Hong Kong. Article 2: Torture Prevention & Police Law in India. Vol. 09 - No. 03-04. "India's Prevention of Torture Bill requires a thorough review." December 2010

Assault case: Court rap for CID over delay in arresting former MLA's son, *Indian Express,* August 22, 2012, http://www.indianexpress.com/news/assault-case-court-rap-for-cid-over-delay-in-arresting-former-mla-s-son/991436/

B. Caddy and H-h Meng, 'Gunshot Residue Analysis: A Review', *Journal of Forensic Sciences,* Vol. 42, Issue 4, July 1997

B. Schmitt and J. Swickard, Detroit Police Lab Shut Down After Probe Finds Errors, Detroit Free Press, September 25, 2008, http://www.freep.com/article/20080925/NEWS02/80925052/Detroit-Police-lab-shut-down-after-probe-finds-errors

Baba Umar, The Curious Case Of Liaquat Shah, *Tehelka,* 2013-04-06 , Issue 14, Volume 10, http://tehelka.com/the-curious-case-of-liaquat-shah/

Badly Fragmented Forensic Science System Needs Overhaul: Evidence To Support Reliability Of Many Techniques Is Lacking, February 18, 2009, News from the National Academies, http://www8.nationalacademies.org/onpinews/newsitem.aspx?recordid=12589

Bapu Deedwania and Sunil Baghel, Angry HC pulls up burking cops: Filing FIR is not a 'favour', *Mumbai Mirror,* January 19, 2012, http://www.mumbaimirror.com/mumbai/cover-story/Angry-HC-pulls-up-burking-cops-Filing-FIR-is-not-a-favour/articleshow/16198521.cms

Bapu Deedwania, High Court slams Kalwa police for criminal case against activist http://m.mumbaimirror.com/index.aspx? Page=article&sectname=News%20-%20City&sectid=2&contentid=20100303201003030200093761b766214

Bashaarat Masood, Shopian Dirt On This Dozen, *The Indian Express*, December 16, 2009, http://www.indianexpress.com/news/shopian-dirt-on-this-dozen/554708/

BBC, India Is World's 'Largest Importer' Of Arms, Says Study, March 14, 2011, http://www.bbc.co.uk/news/world-south-asia-12729363

Bhadra Sinha, Kapashera SHO transferred after court stricture, *Times of India*, March 16, 2003, http://articles.timesofindia.indiatimes.com/2003-03-16/delhi/27275159_1_delhi-police-police-commissioner-r-s-gupta

Bhajan Singh Bhinder and Patrick J. *Nevers, Demons Within: The Systematic Practice Of Torture By Indian Police*, A Report By Organization For Minorities In India, November 2011, Sovereign Star Publishing, Inc., 2011, CA, USA, ISBN 978-0-9814992-6-0; 0-9814992-6-0,

Bharti Jain and Deeptiman Tiwary, 2006 Malegaon Blasts: Aseemanand, Sadhvi Pragya's Names Missing From NIA Chargesheet, *Times of India* May 23, 2013, http://articles.timesofindia.indiatimes.com/2013-05-23/india/39474568_1_2006- malegaon-blasts-case-nia-official-nia-probe

Bhavna Vij-Aurora, Terra Crimson, *Outlook*, May 15, 2006, http://www.outlookindia.com/article.aspx?231235

Bill Pursell, The Not-So-Reliable Forensic Science, July 19, 2012, seeking justice for the innocent, http://www.seekingjusticefortheinnocent.com/index.php/featured-journalists/bill-pursell/560-bill-pursell-forensic-science

Brad Reagan, CSI Myths: The Shaky Science Behind Forensics, *Popular Mechanics*, December 18, 2009, http://www.popularmechanics.com/science/health/forensics/4325774

Brandon L. Garrett and Peter J. Neufeld, Invalid Forensic Science Testimony And Wrongful Convictions, *Virginia Law Review*, Volume 95 March 2009 Number 1

Brandon L. Garrett, *Judging Innocence*, 108 Colum. L. Rev. 55, 58–59 (2008)

Brass, The Production Of Hindu-Muslim Violence In Contemporary India

Broken System: Dysfunction, Abuse and Impunity in the Indian Police, *Human Rights Watch*, August 4, 2009

C.A. Grove, et al., Evaluation of SEM Potential in the Examination of Shotgun and Rifle Firing Pin Impressions, 19 *J. Forensic Sci.* 441, 442 (1974)

Carlo Torre, et al., Brake Lining: A Source of Non-GSR particles Containing Lead, Barium and Antimony, 47 *J. Forensic Sci.* 494, 494-504 (2002)

Cash-for-vote scam: SC slams Delhi Police for 'callous' probe, *Headlines Today*, July 15, 2011, http://indiatoday.intoday.in/story/cash-for-vote-scam-sc-slams-delhi-police-for-callous-probe/1/144941.html

Caste panchayat strips, thrashes woman, lover, *Times of India*, July 23, 2012, http://articles.timesofindia.indiatimes.com/2012-07-23/jaipur/32803514_1_caste-panchayat-villagers-thrashes-woman

Cathleen C. Webb and Marie Chapian, *Forgive Me*, 1985

CBI a caged parrot speaking in its master's voice: SC, *The Hindu*, May 9, 2013, http://www.thehindu.com/todays-paper/tp-in-school/cbi-a-caged-parrot-speaking-in-its-masters-voice-sc/article4697433.ece

CBI rapped over probe, *DNA*, July 10, 2012, http://www.dnaindia.com/mumbai/1712894/report-cbi-rapped-over-probe

CBI report uncovers the 'Shopian conspiracy', *Indian Express*, June 21, 2010, http://www.indianexpress.com/olympics/news/cbi-report-uncovers-the—shopian-conspiracy-/555547/0

Centre homes in on Sec 498A of IPC as men plead for cover against harassment law, *Indian Express*, August 20, 2011, http://www.indianexpress.com/news/centre-homes-in-on-sec-498a-of-ipc-as-men-plead-for-cover-against-harassment-law/834552/

Charles O'Hara and L. Gregory, *Fundamentals of Criminal Investigation* 5th Edition, p. 771

Charul Shah, 2006 Malegaon Blast Case Probe Full Of Errors: NIA, *Hindustan Times*, May 28, 2013, http://www.hindustantimes.com/India-news/Mumbai/2006- Malegaon-blast-case-probe-full-of-errors-NIA/Article1-1066953.aspx

Christin Mathew Philip, Police Revamp Funds Go Waste, *Times of India*, February 28, 2013, http://articles.timesofindia.indiatimes.com/2013-02-28/chennai/37350992_1_tami-l nadu-police-modernization-fund-police-forces

CID nails top cops for faking their way to prez medal, *Times of India*, July 13, 2005, http://articles.timesofindia.indiatimes.com/2005-07- 13/hyderabad/27852084_1_ips-officers-prez-medal-cid-probe

Close encounters of the troubling kind, *The Hindu*, February 25, 2012, http://www.thehindu.com/opinion/editorial/close-encounters-of-the-troubling-kind/article2929337.ece

Colin Gonsalves, Institutionalized communalism in the police force: The breakdown in the criminal justice system, *Combat Law: Human Rights Magazine*, vol. 1, no. 1, April-May 2002

Committee On Identifying The Needs Of The Forensic Science Community, National Research Council Of The National Academies, Strengthening Forensic Science In The United States: A Path Forward, 2009, http://www.nap.edu/catalog.php?record_id=12589

Cops always side with rapists: Karnataka HC, *Times of India*, November 8, 2012, http://articles.timesofindia.indiatimes.com/2012-11-08/india/34993590_1_justice-sen-vikramajit-sen-karnataka-high-court

Court frees man branded a gangster, slams police, ***NDTV***, December 28, 2011, http://www.ndtv.com/article/cities/court-frees-man-branded-a-gangster-slams-police-161278

Court rap on cops for filing false case, *Times of India*, May 29, 2012, http://articles.timesofindia.indiatimes.com/2012-05-29/delhi/31886990_1_court-rap-sessions-judge-trial-court

Court rap on police for not filing FIR, *Times of India*, June 8, 2012, http://articles.timesofindia.indiatimes.com/2012-06-08/delhi/32123600_1_fir-cognisable-offence-elderly-couple

Court raps cop for shoddy murder probe, orders action, *Times of India*, September 4, 2011, http://articles.timesofindia.indiatimes.com/2011-09-04/delhi/30112209_1_orders-action-murder-delhi-police

Court raps cops for altering case facts, *Asian Age*, Aug 07, 2012

Court raps cops for putting wrong man on trial, *Indian Express*, May 28 2012, http://www.indianexpress.com/news/court-raps-cops-for-putting-wrong-man-on-trial/954843/

Court raps cops for putting wrong man on trial, *Indian Express*, May 28 2012, http://www.indianexpress.com/news/court-raps-cops-for-putting-wrong-man-on-trial/954843/

Court Raps Cops for Trial of Wrong Man in Rape Case, *Outlook*, May 28, 2012, http://news.outlookindia.com/items.aspx?artid=763927

Court raps Delhi police in rape-cum-murder case, *The Statesman*, October 21, 2012

Court raps Delhi police in rape-cum-murder case, ***Zee News***, April 14, 2012, http://zeenews.india.com/news/delhi/court-raps-delhi-police-in-rape-cum-murder-case_770004.html

Court raps police for manipulating evidence in murder case, *Deccan Herald*, January 3 http://www.deccanherald.com/content/44634/content/218410/lessons-american-schools.html

Court raps police for saving accused, *Times of India*, October 16, 2011, http://articles.timesofindia.indiatimes.com/2011-10-16/delhi/30285658_1_court-raps-police-chargesheet-criminal-case

Court raps police, charges man with gang rape, murder, *Asian Age*, April 15, 2012

Court Slams Gujarat Police Over Naroda Patiya Riot Case, *Outlook*, September 3, 2012, http://news.outlookindia.com/items.aspx?artid=774087

Court slams police for lax probe into suicide, *Mid Day*, April 29, 2012, http://www.mid-day.com/news/2012/apr/300412-Court-slams-police-for-lax-probe-into-suicide.htm

Crime in India, Compendium 2012, NCRB

Custodial murder a rarest of rare crime: SC, ***Zee News***,, March 29, 2011, http://zeenews.india.com/news/nation/custodial-murder-rarest-of-rare-crime-sc_696450.html

Custodial Rape: A report on the aftermath, People's Union for Democratic Rights, Delhi, May 1994

Cynthia Keppley Mahmood, Fighting for Faith and Nation: Dialogues with Sikh Militants (Philadelphia: Univ. of Pennsylvania, 1996) pp. 223-224

D. G. Rushton, Drowning – A Review, *Med Leg J* 1961; 29: 90-7

Dan Vergano, Judges Growing Critical Of 'CSI' Evidence, *USA Today*, May 09, 2011, http://content.usatoday.com/communities/sciencefair/post/2011/05/judges-becoming-more-critical-of-csi-evidence/1#.UdP5s9hjEVI

Degrading 2-finger test must end: Supreme Court, ***DNA***, April 23, 2013, http://www.dnaindia.com/india/1825887/report-dna-exclusive-degrading-2-finger-test-must-end-supreme-court

Delhi court grants bail to suspected Hizb militant Liyaqat Shah, *Times of India*, May 17, 2013, http://articles.timesofindia.indiatimes.com/2013-05 17/india/39335539_1_liyaqat-shah-special-nia-court-delhi-court-grants-bail

Delhi gangrape: Jairam Ramesh slams politicos' shameful anti-women remarks, says I'll be glad to take Women and Child Development Ministry, *Mail Today*, January 11, 2013 , http://indiatoday.intoday.in/story/anti-woman-remark-misogyny-has-no-place-in-politics-says-jairam-ramesh/1/241692.html

Dennis McGuire, "The Controversy Concerning Gunshot Residue Examinations," *Forensic Magazine*, August/September 2008

Devika Mittal, An Open Letter to the Government of India: On Rape, and What Follows, *Youth Ki Awaaz: Mouthpiece for the Youth*, October 21st, 2012

Dhananjay Mahapatra, 191 Fake Encounters In Last Five Years, NHRC Tells Supreme Court, *Times of India*, December 5, 2012, http://articles.timesofindia.indiatimes.com/2012-12-05/india/35619403_1_fake-encounter-encounter-killings-sohrabuddin-and-tulsiram-prajapati

Dhananjay Mahapatra, Just being member of banned outfit not a crime: Supreme Court, *Times of India*, February 5, 2011, http://articles.timesofindia.indiatimes.com/2011-02-05/india/28356519_1_violence-or-incites-people-arup-bhuyan-confessions

Dhananjay Mahapatra, No Narcoanalysis Test Without Consent, Says SC, May 5, 2010, *Times of India*, http://articles.timesofindia.indiatimes.com/2010-05-05/india/28319716_1_arushi-murder-case-nithari-killings-apex-court

Dhananjay Mahapatra, Supreme Court Fumes At Facebook Arrest; Government Tries To Curb IT Act Abuse, *Times of India*, November 30, 2012, http://articles.timesofindia.indiatimes.com/2012-11-30/india/35483881_1_arrests-dhada-and-shrinivasan-mumbai

Dhananjay Mahapatra,SC worried about criminal-police nexus, *Times of India*, July 2, 2009, http://articles.timesofindia.indiatimes.com/2009-07-02/india/28212402_1_nexus-haryana-police-bench

Di Maio, J. Vincent J. and Dominick, *Forensic Pathology*, Second Edition, CRC Press, New York, 2001

Di Miao and J. M. Vincent, *Gunshot Wounds: Practical Aspects of Firearms, Ballistics, and Forensic Techniques*, Elsevier, New York, 1999, p. 327

Did Narco Tests Fail To Crack Aarushi Murder Case?, February 18, 2010, http://news.in.msn.com/national/article.aspx?cp-documentid=3636005

DNA Technology in Forensic Science Committee on DNA Technology in Forensic Science, National Research Council, ISBN: 0-309-58369-1, 1992, National Academy of Sciences

Document on Terrorism and Justice, All India Milli Council's National Convention on "Terrorism and Justice" at Khalsa College, Mall Road, Delhi on April 27, 2008, http://www.aimcnd.org/document.htm

Douglas MacGowan, William Burke & William Hare, http://www.trutv.com/library/crime/serial_killers/weird/burke/foursome_2.html

Edward Connors, Thomas Lundregan, Neal Miller & Tom McEwan, National Institute of Justice, Convicted by Juries, Exonerated by Science: Case Studies in the Use of DNA Evidence to Establish Innocence After Trial, 51–52 (1996)

Explanation on police brutalities an eyewash, says apex court, *The Hindu*, May 7, 2013, http://www.thehindu.com/todays-paper/tp-national/explanation-on-police-brutalities-an-eyewash-says-apex-court/article4690812.ece

Faizan Ahmad, Blind Rage And Anguish, 30 Yrs On, *Times of India*, April 16, 2010,http://articles.timesofindia.indiatimes.com/2010-04 16/patna/28125879_1_blinding-victim-police-station-monthly-pension

Flavia Agnes, *Violence Against Women: Review of Recent Enactments*

Framed, Damned, Acquitted: Dossiers of a 'Very' Special Cell, A report by Jamia Teachers' Solidarity Association, 2012, available at many places in the public domain including http://www.jamiajournal.com/wp-content/uploads/2012/09/JTSA-Report-Framed-Damned-and-Acquitted-Dossiers-of-a-Very-Special-Cell.pdf and http://kafila.org/2012/09/23/jtsa-responds-to-delhi-polices-comments-on-their-report-framed-damned-acquitted/

From CBI to the police, regaining credibility demands rejecting political interference, *Times of India*, May 2, 2013, http://timesofindia.indiatimes.com/home/opinion/edit-page/From-CBI-to-the-police-regaining-credibility-demands-rejecting-political-interference/articleshow/19823216.cms

Gaurav Vivek Bhatnagar, Delhi Police underbelly exposed, *The Hindu*, September 18, 2012, http://www.thehindu.com/news/cities/Delhi/delhi-police-underbelly-exposed/article3910004.ece

Gautam Navlakha, Maoists in India, *Economic and Political Weekly* June 3, 2006, http://www.internationalcentregoa.com/southasia/maoists%20 in%20india.pdf

Geetika Sharma Suicide: Gopal Kanda Charged With Rape, Unnatural Sex, May 10, 2013, http://www.dnaindia.com/india/1832959/report-geetika-sharma-suicide- gopal-kanda-charged-with-rape-unnatural-sex

Gender violence in India: A Pranjya Report, The Prajnya Trust 2009

Giridhar Jha, Ranvir Sena Founder Brahmeshwar Singh's Supporters Resort To Violence In Ara, *Mail Today*, June 2, 2012, http://indiatoday.intoday.in/story/brahmeshwar-singh-killing-violence-in-ara-ranvir-sena/1/198750.html

Gopal Krishna,Communal Violence in India: A Study of Communal Disturbance in Delhi, *Economic and Political Weekly* Vol XX No 3 January 19, 1985

Gudiya Rape Case: What Action Have You Taken Against Erring Cops, HC Asks Delhi Police, ***PTI***, NEW Delhi, May 14, 2013.

Guidelines of the SRE Scheme, Naxal Management Division, MHA, http://mha.nic.in/pdfs/NM-SRE-Scheme.pdf

Gujarat minister murder: All accused acquitted , ***IBN Live***, August 29, 2011, http://ibnlive.in.com/news/gujarat-minister-murder-all-accused-acquitted/179533-3.html

Haryana crime branch reconstructs accident scene, ***Day And Night News***, September 30, 2012,http://www.dayandnightnews.com/2011/10/haryana-crime-branch-reconstructs-accident-scene/

HC Asks Police Chief to Tender Apology for Harassing Man, *Outlook*, March 25, 2010, http://news.outlookindia.com/items.aspx?artid=677835

HC flays attitude of Dindigul cops, *Deccan Chronicle*, August 31, 2012, http://dindigul.tamil-nadu.news.in/news-20120831-8385-HC_flays_attitude_of_Dindigul_cops_Deccan_Chronicle.html

HC raps CID over sluggish probe against Kalani's son, *Business Standard*, September 12, 2012, http://www.business-standard.com/article/pti-stories/hc-raps-cid-over-sluggish-probe-against-kalani-s-son-112091200517_1.html

HC slams Allahabad police for hushing up kidnap case, *Indian Express*, February 11, 2009, http://www.indianexpress.com/news/hc-slams-allahabad-police-for-hushing-up-kidnap-case/421809/

HC slams CBI's UT branch, hands probe to Delhi unit, *Indian Express*, March 31 2012, http://www.indianexpress.com/news/hc-slams-cbi-s-ut-branch-hands-probe-to-delhi-unit/930785/

HC slams cops for pulling up man over traffic rule, ***DNA***, October 9, 2012, DNA, http://www.dnaindia.com/mumbai/1750428/report-hc-slams-cops-for-pulling-up-man-over-traffic-rule

HC slams Gujarat govt over torture, *Times of India*, June 17, 2012, http://articles.timesofindia.indiatimes.com/2012-06-17/ahmedabad/32281386_1_custodial-torture-gujarat-govt-prakash-jani

HC slams Mumbai Police for arresting cartoonist on 'frivolous' grounds, *Indian Express*, September 14 2012, http://www.indianexpress.com/news/hc-slams-mumbai-police-for-arresting-cartoonist-on-frivolous-grounds/1002543/

Henry F. Fradella, Lauren O'Neill, and Adam Fogarty The Impact of Daubert on Forensic Science, 31 *Pepperdine Law Review*. 2 (2004), http://digitalcommons.pepperdine.edu/plr/vol31/iss2/1

High Court adverse remarks against Police, Govt, *Outlook*, August 5, 2008

High time CBI was shut down: Rajasthan HC, ***DNA***, April 7, 2012, http://www.dnaindia.com/india/1672525/report-high-time-cbi-was-shut-down-rajasthan-hc

How accurate is forensic analysis? *Washington Post*, http://www.washingtonpost.com/wp-srv/special/local/forensic-analysis-methods/http://articles.baltimoresun.com/2006-05-26/news/0605260327_1_gunshot-residue-forensic-evidence-analysis,

http://globalwrong.files.wordpress.com/2012/03/the-current-status ofc2a0gsrc2a0examinations.pdf

http://profsegal.blogspot.in/2006/05/fbi-stops gun-residue-testing.html

http://sikhinformationcentre.org/files/Demons.pdf

http://truthinjustice.org/gsr-reject.htm

http://www.chron.com/news/nation-world/article/FBI-ends-analysis-of-gunshot residue-1655046.php

http://www.thehighroad.org/archive/index.php/t-210227.html

Human Rights in India: Police Killings And Rural Violence In Andhra Pradesh, Human Rights Watch/Asia (formerly Asia Watch) , September 1992, ISBN 1 56432-071-5

Human Rights Watch phone interview with Dr. Indrajit Khandekar, an assistant professor in the Department of Forensic Medicine, Mahatma Gandhi Institute of Medical Sciences, Wardha, May 7, 2010

Human Rights Watch, "Everyone Lives in Fear": Patterns of Impunity in Jammu and Kashmir, Volume 18, No.11(C), September 2006

Human Rights Watch, Dignity on Trial: India's Need for Sound Standards for Conducting and Interpreting Forensic Examinations of Rape Survivors, 1-56432 681-0, September 2010

Human Rights Watch, Protecting the Killers: A Policy of Impunity in Punjab, India, Volume 19, No. 14(C), October 2007

Hundreds die of torture in India every year, Reuters. June 25, 2008. http://in.reuters.com/article/2008/06/25/idINIndia-34225620080625

Hundreds of Muslims named in terror cases without proof: Paper, *DNA,* April 05, 2012, http://www.dnaindia.com/india/report_hundreds-of-muslims-named-in-terror-cases-without-proof-paper_1671728

In Radia Tapes, An Alarming Picture Of Media Manipulation, *The Hindu,* December 12, 2010, http://www.thehindu.com/news/national/in-radia-tapes-an alarming-picture-of-media-manipulation/article948425.ece

India Maoist Violence 'Grave Concern', Says Minister, February 2, 2010, http://news.bbc.co.uk/2/hi/8492605.stm

India: Torture, rape and deaths in custody, Amnesty International, AI INDEX: ASA 20/06/92

India's Prevention of Torture Bill requires a thorough review, Asian Human Rights Commission, Hong Kong

Indian Dowry Law (498A) : Myth Vs. Reality An Investigative Report, April 2006, 2005-2007 Asha-Kiran

Indranil Basu, Dubbed Terror Mastermind Without Any Proof, February 24, 2012, *Times of India,* http://articles.timesofindia.indiatimes.com/2012-02-24/delhi/31094441_1_blast-sites-serial-blasts-bomb-factory.

Inspector Burnt Alive By Mob In Rajasthan, *The Hindu,* March 18, 2011, http://www.hindu.com/2011/03/18/stories/2011031861600100.htm

International Security Assistance Force (ISAF): Key Facts and Figures, http://www.isaf.nato.int/images/stories/File/Placemats/20130624_130624-mb-isaf placemat.pdf

Investigation shows cops blame women in Delhi for 'provoking' rape, ***NDTV***, April 6, 2012, http://www.ndtv.com/video/player/news/investigation-shows-cops-blame-women-in-delhi-for-provoking-rape/228576

Is Nalin Prabhat a Gallant officer, *Times of India*, August 16, 2011, http://articles.timesofindia.indiatimes.com/2011-08-16/hyderabad/29892120_1_ips-officers-dig-dg

Ishrat Jahan case: Is the CBI succumbing to dirty politics?, Rediff.com, June 24, 2013, http://www.rediff.com/news/column/ishrat-jahan-case-is-the-cbi succumbing-to-dirty-politics/20130624.htm

Israel Seeks Major Arms Deals With India, *Business News* Feb. 4, 2013, UPI.com, http://www.upi.com/Business_News/Security-Industry/2013/02/04/Israel-seeks- major-arms-deals-with-India/UPI-62081359996041/

J. Balaji, Punjab extra-judicial killings: NHRC orders relief, *The Hindu*, April 3, 2012, http://www.thehindu.com/news/national/article3277636.ece

J. J. Koehler, Fingerprint Error Rates And Proficiency Tests: What They Are And Why They Matter, 59 *HASTINGS L.J.* 1077 (2008)

J. L. Mnookin, The Validity Of Latent Fingerprint Identification: Confessions Of A Fingerprinting Moderate: *Law, Probability and Risk* 7(2):127, 2008

J. McCullough and L. Niewoehner, "European Study on the Prevalence of GSR in Random Population and Selected Professional Groups" (lecture, SCANNING 2009)]

J. Venkatesan, Court raps CBI for "irresponsible" statement in Sohrabuddin case, *The Hindu*, November 29, 2011

J. Venkatesan, Dowry law is a shield, not an assassin's weapon: court, *The Hindu*, July 22, 2005, http://www.hindu.com/2005/07/22/stories/2005072202631500.htm

J. Venkatesan, Encounters: A.P. High Court order stayed, *The Hindu*, March 5, 2009, http://www.hindu.com/2009/03/05/stories/2009030560870900.htm

J. Venkatesan, Supreme Court recalls 'kicking daughter-in-law not cruelty', *The Hindu*, March 15, 2013, http://www.thehindu.com/news/national/supreme-court-recalls-kicking-daughterinlaw-not-cruelty-judgment/article4510382.ece

J. Venkatesan, Use of narco analysis, brain-mapping unconstitutional: Court, *The Hindu*, May 05, 2010, http://www.thehindu.com/news/national/use-of-narco-analysis-brainmapping-unconstitutional-court/article422149.ece

Jaipur serial blasts: 14 Alleged SIMI Activists Acquitted, *Times of India*, December 10, 2011, http://articles.timesofindia.indiatimes.com/2011-12-10/jaipur/30501516_1_jaipur-serial-blasts-sajid-mansoori-simi-activists

James Smyth Wallace, '*Chemical Analysis of Firearms, Ammunition, and Gunshot Residue*', International Forensic Science and Investigation Series, CRC Press, Florida, 2008

Jane Campbell Moriarty, "Misconvictions," Science, and the Ministers of Justice, *Neb. L. Rev.* 1 (2007)

Jayant Sriram, HC slams police for not acting against Kanda, *Indian Express*, August 18, 2012, http://www.indianexpress.com/news/hc-slams-police-for-not-acting-against-kanda/989796,

Jean Dreze and Amartya Sen, Putting Growth In Its Place: It Has To Be But A Means To Development, Not An End In Itself, *Outlook*, November 14, 2011, http://www.outlookindia.com/article.aspx?278843

Jennifer L. Mnookin, The Courts, the NAS, and the Future of Forensic Science, *Brooklyn Law Review*, Vol. 75:4, 2010

John O. Eylar and S. Siegel, A Photoluminescence Technique For The Detection Of Gunshot Residue, Report No. ATR-74(791S)-1 Law Enforcement Development Group, Law Enforcement Assistance Administration, US Department of Justice and Chemistry and Physics Laboratory, USA

John Stride, Forensic Sciences Under Scrutiny, *The Prosecutor*, January-February 2011, Volume 41, No. 1, cited in Texas District & County Attorneys' Association, http://www.tdcaa.com/node/7752

Jonathan Jones, Forensic Tools: What's Reliable and What's Not-So-Scientific *Frontline*, April 17, 2012, http://www.pbs.org/wgbh/pages/frontline/criminal-justice/real-csi/forensic-tools-whats-reliable-and-whats-not-so-scientific/

Jones Calloway, Nesbitt Loper, and M. Martinez Wolten, "*Occupation Study*", (Lecture, FBI GSR Symposium, 2005)

Joost Meerloo, *The Rape Of The Mind: The Psychology Of Thought Control, Menticide, And Brainwashing*', Department of Psychology, Columbia University, Netherlands Forces, World Publishing Company, 1956.

Judge Harry T. Edwards: How Reliable is Forensic Evidence in Court?, *Frontline*, April 17, 2012, http://www.pbs.org/wgbh/pages/frontline/criminal-justice/real-csi/judge-harry-t-edwards-how-reliable-is-forensic-evidence-in-court/judgment,

Julia Eckert, The Social Dynamics of Communal Violence in India, *International Journal of Conflict and Violence, IJCV*: Vol. 3 (2) 2009, pp. 172 – 187

Julie Bykowicz, In Priority Shift, FBI Halts Gunshot Residue Analysis, *Los Angeles Times*, May 28, 2006, http://articles.latimes.com/2006/may/28/nation/na fbi28

Julio Ribeiro, A police force of his own, *Indian Express*, May 4 201

Justice Katju condemns girl's arrest for Facebook post, fires strong second email to Prithviraj Chavan, *Times of India*, November 19, 2012, http://articles.timesofindia.indiatimes.com/2012-11-19/india/35204312_1_arrest-state-bandh-prithviraj-chavan

K. Kumar, Shodhganga, 2011, http://shodhganga.inflibnet.ac.in/bitstream/10603/2714/10/10_chapter%201.pdf

K. S. Dhillon, Fake Encounters And The Indian State, *The Hindu*, July 8, 2007, http://www.hindu.com/op/2007/07/08/stories/2007070853271400.htm

Kanu Sharda, Leaked Tapes: CBI Says It Has 5,851 Recordings November 23, 2010, http://www.dnaindia.com/india/1470650/report-leaked-tapes-cbi-says-it-has 5851-recordings

Ketki Angre, Noida rape victim speaks out, ***NDTV***, April 07, 2012, http://www.ndtv.com/article/cities/noida-rape-victim-speaks-out-194915

Kevin J. Mahoney P.C,, *Drowning*

Kingshuk Nag, 'Undeserving' Top Cop To Retire In Gallant Way, *Times of India*, July 30, 2012, http://articles.timesofindia.indiatimes.com/2012-07 30/hyderabad/32941262_1_gallantry-cid-report-ips

Kirpal Dhillon, *Identity and Survival: Sikh militancy in India, 1978-1993* (New Delhi: Penguin Books, 2006) 320

Know Your Rights, Committee for the Protection of Democratic Rights ,Bombay, C/o Super Book House, Sind Chambers, Colaba, Bombay 400 005

Kuldip Nayar, Stop Tormenting Innocent Muslims, *The Sunday Guardian*, April 18, 2012

L. Haber and R.N. Haber, Scientific Validation Of Fingerprint Evidence Under Daubert: *Law, Probability And Risk* 7(2):87

Lajpat Nagar Blast: Never A Case Against Duo, Say Lawyers, *Times of India*, November 23, 2012, http://articles.timesofindia.indiatimes.com/2012-11-23/delhi/35318216_1_mirza-nissar-hussain-lajpat-nagar-blast-market-blast-case

Lakshmi Chaudhry, The truth about 'archaic' laws: Why Dhoble supporters are wrong, June 28, 2012, Firstpost, India, http://www.firstpost.com/india/the-truth-about-archaic-laws-why-dhoble-supporters-are-wrong-360125.html

Law Commission Suggests Dilution of Anti-Dowry Law, *Outlook,* January 19, 2012, http://news.outlookindia.com/items.aspx?artid=748272

Left Wing Extremism Most Potent Threat To India: Chidambaram, http://www.firstpost.com/politics/left-wing-extremisim-most-potent-threat-to-india chidambaram-84428.html

Lisa Sweetingham, "Expert: Gunshot Residue Does Not Mean Robert Blake Killed His Wife," COURTTV.com, January 19, 2005, http:// www.cnn.com/2005/LAW/01/19/blake.trial/

M. Saleem Pandit, 1st Shopian Autopsy Doc Under Lens , *Times of India,* http://mobiletoi.timesofindia.com/mobile.aspx?article=yes&pageid=13&sectid=edid=&edlabel=TOIM&mydateHid=01-10-2009&pubname=Times+of+India+-+Mumbai&edname=&articleid=Ar01301&publabel=TOI

M. Saleem Pandit, Shopian 'Rape': Doc Tampered With Swab?, *Times of India,* December 17, 2009, http://articles.timesofindia.indiatimes.com/2009-12-17/india/28079622_1_vaginal-swabs-shopian-doc

Madness in Mumbai, *Times of India,* June 19, 2012, http://articles.timesofindia.indiatimes.com/2012-06-19/edit-page/32300404_1_archaic-laws-mumbai-police-birthday-party

Maloy Krishna Dhar, *Open Secrets: India's Intelligence Unveiled* (New Delhi: Manas Publications, 2005) p. 244

Maneesh Chhibber, 'Murdered' servant produced in High Court! CBI probe ordered; Batala police in the dock, *Tribune,* http://www.tribuneindia.com/2006/20060608/punjab1.htm

Manoje Nath, What Law? Whose Order? *PatnaDaily*.com, http://www.patnadaily.com/index.php/manoje-nath/7905-what-law-whose-order.html

Manu Joseph, *The Hilarious Case of Avatar Tulsi,* Open, July 24, 2010, http://www.openthemagazine.com/article/voices/the-hilarious-case-of-avatar-tulsi

Maoist Insurgents In India: More Bloody And Defiant, *The Economist,* July 22, 2010, http://www.economist.com/node/16650478

Margaret A. Berger, The Impact of DNA Exonerations on the Criminal Justice System, 34 *J.L. Med. & Ethics* 320, 321–22 (2006)

Masjid blast: Rs.3 lakh for acquitted, *The Hindu,* January 05, 2012, http://www.thehindu.com/news/cities/Hyderabad/masjid-blast-rs3-lakh-for-acquitted/article2777116.ece

Mateen Hafeez and Rebecca Samervel, 7 Accused In Malegaon Case Freed, *Times of India,* November 17, 2011, http://articles.timesofindia.

indiatimes.com/2011-11-17/india/30409703_1_shabbir-masiullah-maharashtra-anti-terrorism-squad=malegaon-serial-bomb-blasts

Matt Clarke, Crime Labs in Crisis: Shoddy Forensics Used to Secure Convictions, *Prison Legal News*, March 15, 2013, https://www.prisonlegalnews.org/displayArticle.aspx?articleid=22698&AspxAutDetectCookieSupport=1

Michael Trimpe, The Current Status of GSR Examinations, May, 2011, *FBI Law Enforcement Bulletin*, http://www.fbi.gov/stats-services/publications/law-enforcement bulletin/may_2011/The%20Current% 20Status%20of%20GSR%20Examinations,

Mine Proof Vehicle—Its Shortcomings, *Awam-e-Jung Military Magazine*, January- June 2005

Minimum Proof, Maximum Sentence, *The Hindu* (Editorial), November 24, 2012, http://www.thehindu.com/opinion/editorial/minimum-proof-maximum-sentence/article4127404.ece

Ministry Of Home Affair's Annual Report 2004-2005, http://mha.nic.in/pdfs/ar0405 Eng.pdf

Mob Kills India Police Inspector, March 18 2011, ***BBC News South Asia***, http://www.bbc.co.uk/news/world-south-asia-12781908

Modi Theory Fails, All Accused In Haren Pandya Case Acquitted By The High Court, August 30, 2011, *IndianMuslimObserver*.com, http://www.indianmuslimobserver.com/2011/08/modi-theory-failed-all-accused-in-haren.html

N. I. Hendrey, Diatoms And Drowning–A Review (Letter), *Medicine, Science and the Law* 20 (1980) 289

N. K. Singh, Bihar To The Bad: Nitish Kumar And The Politics Of Caste, *The Island*, July 1, 2012, http://www.island.lk/index.php?page_cat=article-details&page=article-details&code_title=55763

Naxalism Is A Bigger Challenge Than Terrorism: Chidambaram, http://articles.timesofindia.indiatimes.com/2011-09-14/india/30153889 1 naxalism bigger-challenge-home-minister

Nearly 8,500 Armed Naxals In Country, Govt Tells Rajya Sabha, *Daily News And Analysis*, August 11, 2010, http://www.dnaindia.com/india/report_nearly-8500 armed-naxals-in-country-govt-tells-rajya-sabha_1422067

Neeraj Chauhan, CBI, I-T Dept Find No Proof To Nail Niira Radia, *Times of India*, June 21, 2013, http://articles.timesofindia.indiatimes.com/2013-06 21/india/40118703_1_niira-radia-tapped-conversations-income-tax-department

Neha Dixit, A Taliban Of Our Very Own, *Tehelka, Magazine,* Vol 6, Issue 32, Dated August 15, 2009

NIA Files Charge Sheet In Malegaon Blast Case, May 22, 2013, *The Hindu,* http://www.thehindu.com/news/national/nia-files-charge-sheet-in-malegaon-blast- case/article4739573.ece

NIA Malegaon Blast Chargesheet Contradicts CBI, ATS Findings, May 24, 2013, ***Zee News***, http://zeenews.india.com/news/maharashtra/nia-malegaon-blast- chargesheet-contradicts-cbi-ats-findings_850487.html

No Rape Or Murder In Shopian: CBI, *The Economic Times,* December 15, 2009, http://articles.economictimes.indiatimes.com/2009-12-15/news/28382529_1_cbi-report-neelofar-cbi-investigation

Noida rape: Police face flak for revealing rape victim's identity, India Today, February 28, 2012, http://indiatoday.intoday.in/story/noida-cops-face-flak-for-revealing-identity-of-rape-victim/1/175657.html

Odisha Police Register Case Against Jagdish Tytler, Other Congress Leaders For Violence, *Times of India,* September 8, 2012, http://articles.timesofindia.indiatimes.com/2012-09-08/india/33696246_1_naveen-patnaik-congress-leaders-police-case

P. P. Rao, India: Connivance of Gujarat State Functionaries in Protecting Impresarios of Naroda Patiya Massacre, *Indian Express,* 7 September, 2012

P.C. Giannelli, Wrongful Convictions And Forensic Science: The Need To Regulate Crime Labs, 86 N.C. L. REV. 163 (2007)

P.V. Swati, Gurgaon Police: After 8 PM Women Would Be 'Inviting' Rape, *Youth Ki Awaaz: Mouthpiece for the Youth,* March 19, 2012, http://www.youthkiawaaz.com/2012/03/gurgaon-police-after-8-pm-women-would-be-inviting-rape/

Pallavi Shahi, Brutal police kill at least four a day in custody, *Sunday Guardian,* December 11, 2011, http://www.sunday-guardian.com/investigation/brutal-police-kill-at-least-four-a-day-in-custody

Paul C. Giannelli, Daubert And Forensic Science: The Pitfalls Of Law Enforcement Control Of Scientific Research, University Of Illinois *Law Review,* Vol. 2011

Paul C. Giannelli, Wrongful Convictions and Forensic Science: The Need to Regulate Crime Labs, 86 *N.C. L. Rev.* 163 (2007)

Pavan Dahat, Forensic Reports Rule Out Rape In Bhandara Case, *The Hindu,* March 13, 2013, http://www.thehindu.com/todays-paper/tp-national/forensic-reports-rule-out-rape-in-bhandara-case/article4503146.ece

Philip Bowring, Maoists Who Menace India, *International Herald Tribune*, April 18, 2006, http://www.iht.com/articles/2006/04/17/opinion/edbowring.php

PM's Speech At The Chief Minister's Meet On Naxalism, April 13, 2006, http://pmindia.nic.in/speech/content.asp?id=311

Police Brutality In Punjab And Bihar; Supreme Court Takes Suo Moto Cognizance; AG To Assist Court, Salve And UU Lalit As Amicus, *Bar & Bench News Network*, March 08, 2013, http://barandbench.com/content/police-brutality-punjab-and-bihar-supreme-court-takes-suo-moto-cognizance-ag-assist-court

Police can't refuse to register FIR, asserts Supreme Court, *The Hindu*, July 25, 2007, http://www.hindu.com/2007/07/25/stories/2007072557300100 .htm

Police Chief told to file FIRs against 4 Special Cell officers, *The Hindu*, September 14, 2011, http://www.thehindu.com/news/cities/Delhi/police-chief-told-to-file-firs-against-4-special-cell-officers/article2452428.ece

Police Medals: Court Expresses Dismay, *The Hindu*, March 20, 2010, http://www.hindu.com/2010/03/20/stories/2010032065050600.htm

Police Strength, Expenditure And Infrastructure, Chapter-17, http://ncrb.nic.in/CD CII2011/cii-2011/Chapter%2017.pdf

Policemen involved in fake encounters should be hanged: Supreme Court, *The Hindu*, August 8, 2011, http://www.thehindu.com/news/national/policemen-involved-in-fake-encounters-should-be-hanged-supreme-court/article2336677.ece

Prafulla Marapakwar, 'Mumbai needs normal, not moral, policing', *Times of India*, August 1, 2012, http://articles.timesofindia.indiatimes.com/2012-08-01/mumbai/32980175_1_mumbai-police-commissioner-senior-inspectors-officers

Prasoon S. Majumdar, Rioters' Advantage: State Police Has Failed Miserably In Controlling Riots , Common Sense Simplified, (an IIPM think tank blog), August 9, 2012, http://prasoonsmajumdar.blogspot.in/2012/08/rioters-advantage.html

Pratidnya Bhat, Mumbai ACP Vasant Dhoble goes berserk over city's nightlife, June 13, 2012 in World Comments, cited in http://digitaljournal.com/article/326573

Praveen Swami, Forensic Evidence In Shopian Case Fabricated, *The Hindu*, August 11, 2009, Delhi Compass, http://blogs.thehindu.com/delhi/?p=27702

Preventive Detention Only for Imminent Danger: SC, *Outlook*, August 17, 2011,

R. Arivanantham, 215 Sentenced To Jail In Vachathi Case, September 29, 2011, http://www.thehindu.com/news/national/tamil-nadu/215-sentenced-to-jail-in vachathi-case/article2497067.ece

R. Krishnakumar, ISRO Spy Case: A Battle Half Won, *Frontline*, Volume 29, Issue 21, Oct. 20-Nov. 02, 2012, http://www.flonnet.com/fl2921/stories/20121102292102801.htm and http://www.hindu.com/thehindu/thscrip/print.pl?file=20121102292102801.htm&d te=fl2921/&prd=fline&

Raghav Ohri, Finances of Administrator, son-in-law & ADC not probed, points out CBI Court, *Indian Express*, August 31, 2012, http://www.indianexpress.com/news/finances-of-administrator-soninlaw-- adc-not-probed-points-out-cbi-court/995584/

Rahul Tripathi, Delhi Police CCTV Footage Backing Liyaqat Arrest 'Damaged', New Delhi, *Indian Express* June 26, 2013, http://www.indianexpress.com/news/delhi-police-cctv- -backing-liyaqat-arrest-damaged/1133934/

Ram Narayan Kumar, Amrik Singh, Ashok Agrwaal, and Jaskaran Kaur, Reduced to Ashes: the Insurgency and Human Rights in Punjab: Final Report (Kathmandu, Nepal: South Asia Forum for Human Rights, 2003) p.9

Ramlila crackdown: Supreme Court slams Govt, Delhi Police; also pulls up Ramdev,***NDTV***, February 23, 2012, http://www.ndtv.com/article/india/ramlila-crackdown-supreme-court-slams-govt-delhi-police-also-pulls-up-ramdev-179184

Rapes By Police And Security Forces Rise: The Ugly Face Of Law Keepers, Human Rights and Conflict Monitor, February 12, 2007, Forum For Fact-Finding, Documentation And Advocacy (FFDA)

Rapist DIG On Run In Rajasthan For 13 Years, December 30, 2009, *Times of India*, December 30, 2009, http://articles.timesofindia.indiatimes.com/2009-12- 30/india/28095694_1_madhukar-tandon-ruchika-case-ips-officer

Rashme Sehgal, India: No Country For Women, *Deccan Chronicle*, July 22, 2012, http://indiantechnology.com/india-no-country-women-deccan-chronicle

Robert Bazell, DNA Acquittals Shaking Up Forensic Science, ***NBC News***, Feb. 12, 2008, http://www.msnbc.msn.com/id/23113417;

Robin Mejia 'Why We Cannot Rely On Firearm Forensics', *New Scientist*, November 23, 2005, http://www.newscientist.com/article/mg18825274.300 -why we-cannot-rely-on-firearm-forensics.html

Rosy Sequeira, HC raps cops for 'ganging up against woman', *Times of India*, April 5, 2012, http://articles.timesofindia.indiatimes.com/2012-04-05/mumbai/31293329_1_review-petition-police-officers-cbi-inquiry

Rosy Sequeira, HC slams cops over senior citizen attack, *Times of India*, February 24, 2012, http://articles.timesofindia.indiatimes.com/2012-02-24/mumbai/31095083_1_police-station-senior-citizens-crime-branch

Rosy Sequeira, HC slams top cop, civic chief, *Times of India*, September 15, 2012, http://articles.timesofindia.indiatimes.com/2012-09-15/mumbai/33862253_1_wecom-trust-shivaji-park-justice-dhananjay-chandrachud

Rosy Sequeira, Senior citizens held for playing cards, HC slams police, *Times of India*, June 26, 2012, http://articles.timesofindia.indiatimes.com/2012-06-26/mumbai/32424001_1_senior-citizens-andheri-police-station

S. S. Negi, SC: Do Not Misuse Preventive Detention, *Asian Age*, August 18, 2011, http://archive.asianage.com/india/sc-do-not-misuse-preventive-detention-190

Sam Greenhill and Stephen Wright, "Dando 'Killer' Barry George to Face Retrial After Winning Appeal," *Mail Online*, November 16, 2007, http://www.dailymail. co.uk/news/article-494180/Dandokiller- Barry-George-face-retrialwinningappeal. html

Samarth Moray, HC slams police for not granting bail for bailable offence, *Mid Day*, http://www.mid-day.com/news/2012/jun/140612-mumbai-HC-slams-police-for-not-granting-bail-for-bailable-offence.htm

SATP.Org, Fatalities in Left-wing Extremism : 2005-2013, http://www.satp.org/satporgtp/countries/india/maoist/data_sheets/fatalitiesnaxal05 11.htm

SATP.Org, Fatalities in Left-wing Extremism : 2006, http://www.satp.org/satporgtp/countries/india/maoist/data_sheets/fatalitiesnaxal06 htm

SATP.Org, Fatalities in Left-wing Extremism : 2007, http://www.satp.org/satporgtp/countries/india/maoist/data_sheets/fatalitiesnaxal07 htm

SATP.Org, Fatalities in Left-wing Extremism : 2008, http://www.satp.org/satporgtp/countries/india/maoist/data_sheets/fatalitiesnaxal08 htm

SATP.Org, Fatalities in Left-wing Extremism: 2009, http://www.satp.org/satporgtp/countries/india/maoist/data_sheets/fatalitiesnaxal09 htm

SATP.Org, Fatalities in Left-wing Extremism: 2010, http://www.satp.org/satporgtp/countries/india/maoist/data_sheets/fatalitiesnaxal10 htm

SATP.Org, Fatalities in Left-wing Extremism: 2011, http://www.satp.org/satporgtp/countries/india/maoist/data_sheets/fatalitiesnaxal11 htm

SATP.Org, Fatalities in Left-wing Extremism: 2012, http://www.satp.org/satporgtp/countries/india/maoist/data_sheets/fatalitiesnaxal12 htm

SATP.Org, Fatalities in Left-wing Extremism: 2013, http://www.satp.org/satporgtp/countries/india/maoist/data_sheets/fatalitiesnaxal.asp

Saurabh Sharma, CJ fumes at state govt apathy, slams police, *Times of India*, September 3, 2012, http://articles.timesofindia.indiatimes.com/2012-09-03/jaipur/33562700_1_state-government-rajasthan-high-court-state-machinery

SC On Fake Encounter: Is Rs 5L Grant A Licence To Kill?, *Times of India*, December 7, 2012, http://articles.timesofindia.indiatimes.com/2012-12-07/india/35670070_1_fake-encounter-magisterial-inquiry-ranjana-p-desai

SC Puts Dowry Spotlight On Vengeful Wife, Says Courts Must Not Target Family, *The Indian Express*, October 26, 2012, http://www.indianexpress.com/news/sc-puts-dowry-spotlight-on-vengeful-wife-says-courts-must-not-target-family/1022362/

SC Seeks Explanation From Punjab, Bihar On Police Brutality, *The Hindu*, March 6, 2013, http://www.thehindu.com/news/national/sc-seeks-explanation-from-punjab-bihar-on-police-brutality/article4481900.ece

SC slams Chhattisgarh cops for doc's torture, *Indian Express*, August 4, 2012, http://www.indianexpress.com/news/sc-slams-chhattisgarh-cops-for-doc-s-torture/983552/

SC slams cops for chopping of man's penis in PS, ***Zee News***, August 30, 2010, Zee News, http://zeenews.india.com/news/nation/sc-slams-cops-for-chopping-of-man-s-penis-in-ps_651806.html

Sedition Case Registered Against Arundhati, Geelani, Nov. 29, 2010, *India Today*, http://indiatoday.intoday.in/story/sedition-case-registered-against-arundhati geelani-/1/121606.html

Sedition Case: 'Probe Against Arundhati, Geelani Still Inconclusive', Feb. 26, 2011, Expressindia, http://www.expressindia.com/latest-news/Sedition-case-%5CProbe against-Arundhati-Geelani-still-inconclusive%5C/755169/

Shankhajit Kar and Abhirup Ghosh, *The Law, The Power, The Nexus: Politicians Police & Criminal Nexus*, http://ssrn.com/abstract=1824422

Shazia Shaikh, Malegaon Terror: Targeting Muslim Identity and Emergence of Hindutva Terrorism, *Beyond Headlines*, Feb. 14, 2012

Shibu Thomas, Don't act like recovery agents, HC tells cops, *Times of India*, September 28, 2012

Shibu Thomas, HC Fines State Rs 6L For Illegal Police Arrests And Excesses, December 22, 2012, *Times of India*, http://articles.timesofindia.indiatimes.com/2012-12-22/mumbai/35968771_1_illegal-police-police-action-police-officer

Shocking state of affairs: Court rap for police 'inaction', *Indian Express*, February 24, 2012, http://www.indianexpress.com/news/-shocking-state-of-affairs—court-rap-for-police—inaction-/915968/

Shoeb Khan, Minority Report: NCM To Push For Damages For Freed Muslims, *Times of India*, December 12, 2011, http://articles.timesofindia.indiatimes.com/2011-12-12/jaipur/30508284_1_lakh-compensation-ncm-jaipur-serial-blasts

Shopian Case: Doctor Submits Own Vaginal Swab, ***NDTV***, November 16, 2009, http://www.ndtv.com/article/india/shopian-case-doctor-submits-own-vaginal-swab-11589

Shyam Parekh, When insensitivity drives rape victims to brink of death, ***DNA***, February 3, 2011, http://www.dnaindia.com/india/1502583/analysis-when-insensitivity-drives-rape-victims-to-brink-of-death

SI Held In Phool Mohd Lynching Case, ***DNA***, November 9, 2011, http://dnasyndication.com/showarticlerss.aspx?nid=011pEAq7ykme6dJmULFoQ1fm4XaX27qAN08yR3dPulsxRrA=

Smruti Koppikar, Resting their case? Objection, my Lord, *Indian Express*, November 17, 2001

Sneha Mary Koshy, ISRO Espionage Case: Documents Reveal No Action Recommended Against Investigating Officers, ***NDTV***, October 17, 2012, http://www.ndtv.com/article/south/isro-espionage-case-documents-reveal-no-action-recommended-against-investigating-officers-280667

Soumittra S Bose, Injuries Suggest Anal Sex With Younger Sisters, *Times of India*, March 2, 2013, http://articles.timesofindia.indiatimes.com/2013-03-02/nagpur/37389313_1_major-injury-forensic-team-sisters

Soumittra S. Bose, Bhandara Doctors Contradict Forensic Panel's Report, *Times of India*, March 11, 2013, http://articles.timesofindia.indiatimes.com/2013-03-11/india/37622795_1_post-mortem-forensic-expert-viscera-report

Spencer S. Hsu, Forensic Science Is Not As Dependable As You Might Think, *The Washington Post*, April 22, 2012, cited in The Bulletin, July 3, 2013, http://www.bendbulletin.com/article/20120422/NEWS0107/204220388/

Spencer S. Hsu, Forensic Techniques Are Subject To Human Bias, Lack Standards, Panel Found, April 18, 2012, *Washington Post* http://www.washingtonpost.com/local/crime/forensic-techniques-are-subject-to-human-bias-lack-standards-panel-found/2012/04/17/gIQADCoMPT_story.html

States Must Spend Allocated Funds On Police Modernization, May 24, 2013, *Times of India*, http://articles.timesofindia.indiatimes.com/2013-05-24/edit-page/39476018_1_police-modernisation-internal-security-respective-police-forces

Statistics of Naxal violence (2008 to 2012), Naxal Management Division, MHA, http://mha.nic.in/pdfs/SWENV-2008-12.pdf

Stephen Kiehl, "Defender Spotlights Faulty Forensics," *Baltimore Sun*, November 5, 2007, http://articles.baltimoresun.com/2007-11- 05/news/0711050172_1_forensic-scienceforensic-evidence-forensic-methods

Still Probing Sedition Case Against Geelani, Roy: Police, *Greater Kashmir*, July 05, 2011, http://www.greaterkashmir.com/news/2011/Jul/5/still-probing-sedition-case against-geelani-roy-police-46.asp

Subhash Mishra, HC rap leaves CBI red-faced, *The New Indian Express*, August 31, 2012, http://newindianexpress.com/nation/article598363.ece

Sudhanshu Mishra, Prosecution's Slip-Up Acquits Jaipur Blast Accused, *India Today*, Dec. 11, 2011

Suhas Chakma (Ed), *ACHR's Actions Against Torture and other Forms of Human Rights Violations in India*, Asian Centre for Human Rights, June 2009

Suhas Chakma (Ed), *India Human Rights Report 2005*, Asian Centre for Human Rights, 2005

Suhas Chakma (Ed), *India Human Rights Report 2006*, Asian Centre for Human Rights, January 2007

Suhas Chakma (Ed), *India Human Rights Report 2008*, Asian Centre for Human Rights, December 2008

Suhas Chakma (Ed), *India Human Rights Report 2009*, Asian Centre for Human Rights, May 2009

Sumitra Deb Roy, No Rape In Bhandara: Govt Panel, *Times of India*, March 10, 2013,http://articles.timesofindia.indiatimes.com/2013-03-

10/india/37597446_1_sexual-assault-deaths-regional-forensic-science-laboratory

Sunil Baghel, Mumbai High Court- Not everyone who believes in Maoist ideology is a terrorist', *Mumbai Mirror*, October 10, 2012, http://www.mumbaimirror.com/mumbai/others/Not-everyone-who-believes-in-Maoist-ideology-is-a-terrorist/articleshow/16969195.cms

Supreme Court quashes detention order against 7 persons, J. Venkatesan, April 7, 2011, *The Hindu*, http://www.thehindu.com/todays-paper/tp-national/tp-tamilnadu/expired-drugs-case-supreme-court-quashes-detention-order-against-7-persons/article1607165.ece.

Supreme Court Seeks Explanation From Punjab, Bihar On Police Brutality, *The Indian Express*, March 7, 2013, http://www.indianexpress.com/news/supreme-court-seeks-explanation-from-punjab-bihar-on-police-brutality/1083921/

Swati Deshpande, Lawyers back criticism by ex-DGP, *Times of India*, August 1, 2012, http://articles.timesofindia.indiatimes.com/2012-08-01/mumbai/32979942_1_maharashtra-police-amit-desai-advocate-and-human-rights

Swati Deshpande, Police Curbing Freedom Of Speech: Legal Experts Condemn Arrest Of Girls For Posting Comment On Facebook, *Times of India*, http://mobilepaper.timesofindia.com/mobile.aspx?article=yes&pageid=15&sectid=edid=&edlabel=CAP&mydateHid=20-11-2012&pubname=Times+of+India+-+Delhi&edname=&articleid=Ar01500&publabel=TOI

Telangana: Judge slams AP Police, Bar&Bench News Network, February 19, 2010, https://mail.google.com/mail/u/0/?logout&hl=en&hlor

The cat is out of the bag, *The Hindu*, May 1, 2013, http://www.thehindu.com/opinion/editorial/the-cat-is-out-of-the-bag/article4670986.ece

The Innocence Project Home Page, http://www.innocenceproject.org

The National Academy of Sciences Report on Forensic Sciences: What it Means for the Bench and Bar, The Honorable Harry T. Edwards, Conference on The Role Of The Court In An Age Of Developing Science & Technology, Washington, D.C., May 6, 2010

They Want To Sue Praveen Swami, But Fear Harassment From Agencies, ***TCN News Desk***, Dec. 21, 2011, TwoCircles.net, http://twocircles.net/2011dec21/they_want_sue_praveen_swami_fear_harassment_agencies.html

Thomas Young, *Forensic Science And The Scientific Method*, The Forensic Inference Series, Heartland Forensic Pathology, LLC, http://www.heartlandforensic.com/writing/forensic-science-and-the-scientific-method

Torture In India 2008: A State of Denial, Asian Centre for Human Rights, June 2008

Torture In India 2009, Asian Centre for Human Rights, June 2009

Torture In India 2010, Asian Centre for Human Rights, April 2010

Torture In India 2011, Asian Centre for Human Rights, November 2011

Torture in India 2011: 14,231 custodial deaths from 2001 to 2010 , Asian Centre for Human Rights, November 2011, Delhi

Trauma of a rape victim: After men, society raped me, again and again, ***IBN Live***, September 13, 2012 http://ibnlive.in.com/news/trauma-of-a-rape-victim-after-men-society-raped-me-again-and-again/289709-3.html

Unfriend The Thought Police, *The Hindu*, November 21, 2012, http://www.thehindu.com/opinion/editorial/unfriend-the-thought-police/article4116231.ece

Utkarsh Anand, Court slams CBI on Q: 'bias, malafide, cart before horse', *Indian Express*, January 7, 2011, http://www.indianexpress.com/news/court-slams-cbi-on-q—bias-malafide-cart-before-horse-/734534/

Utkarsh Anand, SC recalls '09 verdict, to examine if kicking daughter-in-law is cruelty, *Indian Express*, March 15, 2013, http://www.indianexpress.com/news/sc-recalls—09-verdict-to-examine-if-kicking-daughterinlaw-is-cruelty/1088268/0

Utkarsh Anand, SC Raps Punjab, Bihar Over Police Brutality, *The Indian Express*, March 12, 2013, http://www.indianexpress.com/news/sc-raps-punjab-bihar-over-police-brutality/1086702/

Uttar Pradesh health scam: Court slams CBI for poor investigation, ***NDTV***, August 30, 2012, , http://www.ndtv.com/article/india/uttar-pradesh-health-scam-court-slams-cbi-for-poor-investigation-260770

Vernon J. Geberth, *Practical Homicide Investigation*, Third Edition, CRC Press, New York, 1996

Vidya Subrahmaniam, No Excuses For This Error Of Judgment, *The Hindu*, December 5, 2012, http://www.thehindu.com/opinion/lead/no-excuses-for-this-error-of-judgment/article4164637.ece

Vijay V. Singh, Dhoble's career marked by controversies, *Times of India*, June 13, 2012, http://articles.timesofindia.indiatimes.com/2012-06-13/mumbai/32214858_1_custodial-death-police-station-police-officers

Vineeta Pandey, Govt asks police to stop misuse of dowry law, ***DNA***, August 22, 2010, http://www.dnaindia.com/india/1426912/report-govt-asks-police-to-stop-misuse-of-dowry-law

Vishwa Mohan, Government Approves Additional Fund To Modernize Police Forces, February 13, 2013, *Times of India*, http://articles.timesofindia.indiatimes.com/2013-02-13/india/37078733_1_home ministry-police-forces-12th-five-year-plan

Vladimir Radyuhin, Siberian Court Throws Out Case Against Gita Commentary, December 28, 2011, *The Hindu*, http://www.thehindu.com/news/international/siberian-court-throws-out-case- against-gita-commentary/article2754870.ece

Voice Of India Features, Editorial: Maoist-Naxal Menace Haunts The Nation, http://voi.org/index2.php?option=com_content&do_pdf=1&id=368

W. Spitz, Diagnosis Of Death By Drowning By Means Of Demonstration Of Diatoms In Organs. *Deutsch Z Ges Gerichtl Med* 1963; 54: 42-5

What Action Have You Taken In 5-Year-Old Gudiya's Rape Case? Supreme Court Raps Delhi Police, http://indiatoday.intoday.in/story/delhi-child-rape-case-gudiya sc-raps-delhi-police/1/268332.html

William G. Iacono, "Forensic 'Lie Detection': Procedures Without Scientific Basis," *Journal of Forensic Psychology Practice*, Vol. 1 (2001), No. 1, pp. 75-86.

Woman constable assaulted by Congress supporters, *Orissa News, Surya*, September 8, 2012, http://incredibleorissa.com/en/woman-constable-assaulted-by-congress-supporters/

Yagnesh Mehta, Dhruti Patel death case: High court raps Navsari cops for destroying evidence, *Times of India*, August 19, 2012, http://articles.timesofindia.indiatimes.com/2012-08-19/surat/33272217_1_punchnama-high-court-investigation-officer

Yogita Thakre murder: Court slams Nagpur Police, Wednesday, June 10, 2009, ***Zee News***, http://zeenews.india.com/news/nation/yogita-thakre-murder-court-slams-nagpur-police_538215.html

Youths send legal notice to Katju over remark, *The Hindu*, December 11, 2012, http://www.thehindu.com/news/national/youths-send-legal-notice-to-katju-over-remark/article4185424.ece

Index

Some of our Learned Authors/Contributors

General S Padmanabhan; General VP Malik; Admiral Vishnu Bhagwat; Admiral Arun Prakash; Vice Admiral Vijay Shankar; Lt Gen Arjun Ray; Dr A Sivathanu Pillai DRDO; Parvez Dewan IAS; Dhirendra Singh IAS; Kalyan Ray IAS; Sangeeta Goel IAS; HN Das IAS; Dr Surender Ghonkrokta IAS; Falguni Rajkumar IAS; G Sundaram IAS; PS Bhatnagar IAS; N Vittal IAS; PK Agrawal IAS; Sudhir S Baloeria IAS; NS Sisodia IAS; Dhirendra Singh IAS; Dr Yogendra Narain IPS; JK Bagchi IAS; TSR Subramanian IAS; Prakash Singh IPS; DC Nath IPS; Ajit Doval IPS; AP Mukherjee IPS; SP Mathur IPS; MK Dhar IPS; SK Datta IPS; HS Swan IPS; BR Lall IPS; PC Dogra IPS; DC Pathak IPS; ML Kumawat IPS; Dr. S Subramanian IPS; RK Ohri IPS; RB Sreekumar IPS; Kalyan K Mitra IPS; RS Gupta IPS; K Koshy IPS; Kuldeep Khoda IPS; Ajay Kashyap IPS; Dr N Dilip Kumar IPS; Dr Nazrul Islam IPS; Dr DV Guruprasad IPS; AP Maheshwari IPS; Loknath Behera IPS; Dr NC Asthana IPS; PM Nair IPS; Dr Sundari Nanda IPS; Keshav Kumar IPS; Dr Prateep V Philip IPS; Muktesh Chander IPS; Dr PS Pasricha IPS; K Ragothaman - CBI; M Narayanan – CBI; VK Agarwal IRS; Virendra Gupta IFS; Lt Gen SK Sinha; Lt Gen Raj Kadyan; Lt Gen Mukesh Sabharwal; Lt Gen HB Kala; Lt Gen PC Katoch; Lt Gen Gautam Banerjee; Lt Gen Ashok Kapur; Vice Admiral Suresh Bangara; Lt Gen CK Kapur; Lt Gen NS Narahari; Lt Gen Chandra Shekhar; Lt Gen ML Chibber; Lt Gen Ashok Joshi; Lt Gen DB Shekatkar; Lt Gen SRR Aiyengar; Lt Gen Utpal Bhattacharyya; Lt Gen Kamal Davar; Lt Gen Amitav Mukherji; Maj Gen Nilendra Kumar; Maj Gen Vinod Saighal; Maj Gen VK Singh; Maj Gen Anjan Mukherjee; Maj Gen Raj Mehta; Maj Gen Samay Ram; Maj Gen Y Behl; Maj Gen GD Bakshi; Gen Deepak Kapoor; Air Marshal SR Deshpande; Air Marshal RC Bajpai; Air Chief Marshal PV Naik; Air Vice Marshal AK Tiwary; Air Cmde (Dr) CN Ghosh; Ambassador Kishan S Rana IFS; Cmde Ranjit B Rai; Capt (IN) Alok Bansal; VK Singal IRS; Sudha Raman; Brig Yash Mohan; Brig Trigunesh Mukherjee; Brig. MS Patial; Col PK Gautam; Col MS Jaswal; Col Anil Shorey; Col KS Rajamani; Lt Col Anil Bhatt; Lt Col SS Parihar; Lt Col Arun Jha; Dr Harsh Vardhan; Ratan Sharda, Sudhakar Raje; Dr RK Tiwari; Anuj Dhar, Journalist; Ranjit Kumar, Journalist; SK Vikram; RA Rodrigues; Gopal Chowdhuri; Dr Pramod Sharma; Swati Sharma, etc.